302. 2303 CUR

Liz Curtis

Ireland:
The propaganda war

The British media and the 'battle
for hearts and minds'

Sásta

Liz Curtis was born in England and has taken an active interest in events in Ireland since the 1970s. She has written extensively on Irish affairs. Her books include two acclaimed histories, *Nothing But The Same Old Story: The roots of anti-Irish racism*, and *The Cause of Ireland: From the United Irishmen to partition*. She now lives in Ireland, where she is learning Irish and improving her photography.

Ireland: The Propaganda War was first published in 1984
by Pluto Press Limited, London

This updated edition published in 1998 by Sásta,
The Ashton Centre, Churchill Street, Belfast BT15 2BP

British Library Cataloguing in Publication Data

Curtis, Liz
Ireland : the propaganda war : the British media and the battle
for hearts and minds'. - Updated ed.
1.Mass media - Political aspects - Great Britain 2.Mass media -
Great Britain - Censorship 3.Northern Ireland - Politics
and government - 1969-
I. Title
070.4'49'9416'0824

ISBN 1 901005 15 1

Trade Distribution: Turnaround Publisher Services Ltd, Unit 3,
Olympia Trading Estate, Coburg Road, London N22 6TZ.
Tel. 0181 829 3000. Fax 0181 881 5088. Email: turnuk@aol.com

Cover drawing by Steve Lee
Cover design by Michael Mayhew

Printed by ColourBooks Ltd, Dublin

Contents

4. Reporting the British army / 68

Ulsterisation / Routine lies / The killing of Majella O'Hare /
More lies / BBC complaints / Reflex lying / Pressure /
Minimal accounts / Sympathy for the squaddies / Coffee
pot girls / Dog of war

5. Reporting loyalist violence / 89

Selective amnesia / McGurk's Bar / Assassinations /
Following the official line / Religious labels / 'Random'
violence / The shooting of the McAliskeys / UDA
interviews / The UWC stoppage

6. Reporting republican violence / 107

Dominating the coverage / Blaming the IRA / Bombs in
Britain / Human interest / Lord Mountbatten / Captain
Nairac / Sefton / Fantasies / The Margaret McKearney
saga / Bald Eagle and the white Opel / Not the day of the
Jackal / 'Godfathers' / 'Terrorists' in TV drama / Political
vocabulary

7. Televising republicans / 138

The rarity of IRA interviews / Arguments for and against
republicans on TV / Bans 1970–71 / Bans in the mid-
seventies / The veto tactic / Inhibitions / Rows about IRA
appearances / The second battle of Culloden / *Tonight* on
the IRA / The INLA interview / The Carrickmore affair / A
wave of fury / Scotland Yard / The Havers judgement

8. The reference upwards system / 173

Development of the rules / The role of the Northern Ireland
Controller / The scope of the rules / Rules on republican
interviews / Balance / Hostile interviews / Censorship /
Self-censorship / Radio Telefis Eireann / Conor Cruise
O'Brien / The effects of Section 31

9. Reporting nationalist perspectives / 197

Bans / Creggan / 'Credible witnesses' / The peace people /
The 1981 hunger strike / Opinion in Britain / 'Red Ken in
IRA storm' / History / Michael Collins / *Curious Journey* /
The Green, the Orange and the Red, White and Blue / Two
major series / A limited backlash / *The Crime of Captain
Colthurst* / Anti-Irish racism / A long tradition / Cartoons
and jokes

10. Propaganda machines / 229

British army propaganda / 'Information Policy' / Adjusting
to the North / Propaganda on the ground / 'Black'
propaganda / Tara / The Niedermayer smear / The
Northern Ireland Office committee / Surveillance / Fake
press cards / Routine PR / Use of the law / Harassment /
The RUC press office / The Northern Ireland Office press
office / Methods / Interventions overseas / Republican
publicity / Development of the press centre / Raids on
Republican News / Veracity / Relations with journalists /
Improvements

Conclusion / 275

Appendix: Programmes on the North of Ireland banned, censored or delayed / 279

References and notes / 301

Index / 335

Introduction

Ulster is not just another country. It is another planet.

Jon Akass, *The Sun*, 31 May 1983

This book tells a story that is sad, infuriating, and sometimes, in a perverse way, even funny. It is about the propaganda war that has been fought, through the British media, for the hearts and minds of the British people on the question of Ireland.

The level of awareness in Britain about the situation in the North of Ireland is of major political significance. The Westminster government rules the North in the name of the British people and using their money. The British people have the ultimate veto on their government's presence in the North and its policies there. Successive administrations have demonstrated that they are well aware that one way of keeping the people acquiescent is to keep them in ignorance.

Media coverage of the conflict reaches the people of the North and the people of Britain very differently. The population of the North is daily inundated with news. Local papers, hourly radio bulletins, regular local TV news broadcasts supplemented by the early evening magazine programmes all put out a stream of information about bombings and shootings, arrests and trials, the manoeuvrings of political groups.

Further, in the North the national media do not have a monopoly on news or analysis of the conflict. The unionist and nationalist communities each have their own papers, and their own political, educational and cultural institutions, and in an area with a population of only one-and-a-half million – roughly 60 per cent unionist and 40 per cent nationalist – news travels fast by word of mouth. While people in the North consume a relatively large amount of news and current affairs coverage, they are also very critical. Using mutually exclusive standards, nationalists and unionists evaluate the output of the national media according to how it reflects their own experiences and the perceptions shared by their respective communities.

People in Britain, by contrast, receive only a dribble of news from the North, except when a crisis hijacks the headlines. They have no direct experience of the conflict, save for intermittent bombings in British cities, and Ireland is conspicuously absent from educational curricula. Groups trying to circulate alternative information about events in the North are small and impoverished. British people are, therefore, almost entirely dependent on the mass media for news and interpretations of events in Ireland. The quality of the coverage is of vital importance, for it influences the extent to which British people can participate in an informed discussion about their government's Irish policies.

This book aims to highlight certain major characteristics of the British media's Irish coverage, and to describe the activities of the various interested parties – politicians, broadcasting chiefs, newspaper editors, journalists, the army and police – which influence the shape the coverage takes. It is written primarily for the general reader, but there are plentiful references for those wishing to pursue the issues further.

The book begins in 1971, the year when the first crucial battles over Irish coverage were fought. It then moves back in time, to sketch in the 'silent years' from 1920 to 1968, when British people heard nothing of the North, and then the media's responses to the civil rights movement and the arrival of troops on the streets. The central section of the book looks at how the media have represented the armed participants in the conflict – the British army and Royal Ulster Constabulary, loyalist paramilitaries and republicans. It also describes the development of the internal controls in broadcasting – the 'reference upwards' system – and looks at the media's handling of the views and aspirations of the nationalist community. Finally, it outlines the development of the 'propaganda machines' operated by the British army, the RUC and the Northern Ireland Office on the one side and the republican movement on the other.

I would like to thank the many people who have helped with this book: the journalists and television workers who have shared their insights and experiences with me, and most of whom wished to remain anonymous; the sociologists who have done the spadework on which parts of the book rely, especially Philip Elliott, whose research on the subject is invaluable and who died this year after a long illness; the republicans who discussed the history of their publicity work; the librarians, especially those in my local library, who have patiently unearthed old newspapers.

Warm thanks are also due to the many people who have offered ideas, sent newspaper cuttings and videos, and suggested stories that needed investigating: Frances Mary Blake, Sharon McCormick, Mairéde Thomas, Paul Madden, Deborah Devenny, Danny Devenny, Gerry McDonnell, Duncan Smith, Margaret Henry, students at the evening class I ran on the subject in 1981, and many others.

I would like especially to thank Alastair Renwick, Philip Schlesinger, John Lloyd and Gill Biggs for their constant help and support, and comments on the manuscript. The completed text remains, of course, solely my responsibility.

Finally, comments and additional information from readers would be welcome, and can be sent to me via the publishers.

London, October 1983

Preface to the 1998 edition

It is hard now to recall the fear that surrounded the issue of Ireland when this book was written 15 years ago. To criticise the government or put the nationalist case was to risk being cast into outer darkness. The Birmingham Six, the Guildford Four and the Maguire Seven were still abandoned in jail, evidence of the song: 'Being Irish means we're guilty — so we're guilty one and all.'

Today the world seems topsy-turvy. The English have fallen in love with Riverdance and Irish writers; the Irish recoil at drunken Brit stag parties in Temple Bar. The 'Celtic Tiger' is rampant, Irish emigrants are flooding home, and house prices have gone ballistic. British chainstores are recolonising the South — happy to put up signs in Irish if it brings in the punts. And in the North? Well, there is very cautious optimism for a peace based on compromise.

In the wider world, we have seen the rise and fall of Thatcher and Reagan, and the collapse of the Soviet bloc. In Britain, 'new money' has seen off patricians and labour stalwarts alike, and idealists reside in trees rather than on picket-lines. The much-ridiculed 'broadcasting ban' on Irish organisations has come and gone, and many miscarriages of justice have been exposed, tearing to shreds the image of Britain as a haven of free speech and fair play.

After many years of monitoring British TV coverage of Ireland, it becomes hard to watch. The hectoring questions and the macho obsession with men in balaclavas are cosmically tiring. A delightful bonus of moving to Ireland and learning the language is discovering a different kind of media — the Irish-language radio and TV stations, and the hugely popular community radio station that goes on air in Belfast during the summer festivals. Drawing on the talents, traditions and experience of the communities they serve, these stations are full of life and meaning. They show that there are a wealth of possibilities.

For help in updating the appendix, thanks to Yvonne Murphy and Ciarán Crossey of the Linen Hall Library, and to David Miller and designer Joy Arden.

Slán go fóill.

Liz Curtis
October 1998

1. 1971: Year of crisis

Echoes of Vietnam

In a few stormy months after the introduction of internment without trial in 1971, media coverage of the conflict in the North of Ireland was hammered into the shape we know today.

Ireland was buzzing with stories of torture and troop brutality. Massive protest demonstrations were being organised. The long dormant IRA was once again on the offensive. Immediately, the British authorities manifested a deep concern to control the flow of information to the British public.

The supposed effects of television coverage of the war in Vietnam on the American public were fresh in establishment minds. A *Sunday Express* commentator, heavily critical of television for showing the British army in Ireland 'in a bad light', noted,

> It is only now that we in Britain are running up against this problem. It is one that has assailed the United States for nearly a decade.
>
> There can be little doubt that television coverage of the Vietnam War was largely responsible for sapping the moral fibre of the American people to continue the struggle.[1]

Again and again the fear was expressed that the television coverage of Ireland would make it impossible for the government to continue with what was openly called a guerrilla war. Politicians and newspaper editors agreed that negative coverage of the British army and Northern Ireland government, and sympathetic coverage of detainees' torture allegations and the views of nationalists such as Bernadette Devlin, would undermine 'political nerve', would sap the morale of the army and would lead to pressure in Britain for withdrawal of the troops. And the British public was proving fickle: a national opinion poll published in the *Daily Mail* on 24 September 1971 showed that 59 per cent wanted the troops brought home.

The broadcasters clamp down

Within days of the introduction of internment, a backbench Tory MP, Evelyn King, wrote to Defence Secretary Lord Carrington accusing the BBC of a host of crimes, including undermining British army morale by daily 'sniping' at it. 'No national army', he wrote later to *The Daily Telegraph*, 'can in the 1970s sustain its morale without the support of home television and radio.'[2]

Carrington took up the theme, launching a public attack on the BBC. In a letter to BBC Chairman Lord Hill, he demanded that 'everything possible should be done to prevent repetition' of reports 'which are unfairly loaded to suggest improper behaviour by British troops.'[3]

The BBC partially gave in. One of Carrington's complaints concerned a *World at One* radio report on the death of Catholic priest Father Hugh Mullan, who had been shot dead by British troops on 10 August while giving the last rites to an injured man. Interviewed on *World at One*, the injured man said that Father Mullan had been shot in the back. Carrington complained that the radio presenter had accepted this statement 'without question', and had summed up with the words, 'An eye-witness putting the blame fairly and squarely on the British army.' The BBC agreed that in this instance it had made 'an error of judgement'.[4]

The political pressure from the right served rather to re-inforce the broadcasters' timidity than to set them on a new course. The BBC had for some time been operating stringent and unprecedented guidelines to keep independent-minded journalists in check. Reporters had to seek permission from senior executives, including the Director-General, before interviewing members of the IRA. Another new rule required that every programme on Ireland be 'internally balanced'. This rule, which needless to say applied when dissident rather than establishment views were being aired, demanded that critics of the government be answered within the same programme by government supporters. Further, all items on the North of Ireland had to be checked in advance with the redoubtable Controller of BBC Northern Ireland, Waldo Maguire. This prospect was very inhibiting: one former programme editor said, 'I'd rather walk through the Bogside in the middle of a battle than face half an hour with Waldo.'[5] Maguire had already made his mark: in 1970 BBC Northern Ireland had opted out of a film showing interviews with relatives of six people killed in Belfast on the grounds that it was 'inflammatory', and at the start of 1971 it was at Maguire's insistence that the BBC suppressed a *24 Hours* report which showed the widespread disenchantment among unionists with the relatively moderate policies of Northern Ireland's Prime Minister James Chichester Clark.[6]

Following the introduction of internment in August, the instances of internal censorship flowed thick and fast. BBC radio and television reporters were forbidden to broadcast interviews with released internees who alleged brutality by the army and RUC.[7] In August, senior BBC executives prevented *24 Hours* from doing an 'in depth' programme about the IRA.[8] In September a senior BBC man, Roland Fox, prevented the radio programme *Today* from using an interview with People's Democracy leader Michael Farrell, who had just been released from detention.[9] In October the BBC suppressed a filmed report on the Alternative Parliament set up by the SDLP and the Nationalist Party.[10] Numerous items which put the British army's role in doubt never reached the air: these included an incident in which many Catholics heard on their radios an army voice saying on a walkie-talkie 'I hope we killed the cunt' immediately after a Belfast woman, Emma Groves, was shot at point blank range between the eyes with a rubber bullet.[11]

At the same time, the Independent Television Authority, which had barely figured as an object of the politicians' spleen, panicked autonomously. Its reaction to the attacks on the BBC – which was to become habitual as the years progressed – was to censor potentially controversial material in order to stay out of the firing line. In early November 1971 the ITA overrode the wishes of the entire board of Granada TV and banned a *World in Action* programme sight unseen. The programme, *South of the Border*, examined how the troubles in the North were building up pressures in the rest of Ireland. It included film of IRA Chief of Staff Sean MacStiofain and Sinn Fein President Ruairi O Bradaigh speaking at Provisional Sinn Fein's annual conference: their views were dutifully balanced by interviews with Dublin politicians hostile to the IRA. ITA Chairman Lord Aylestone objected to the programme 'on principle', claiming that it was 'aiding and abetting the enemy'. Ulster TV Managing Director Brum Henderson, whose role is similar to that of the BBC's Northern Ireland Controller, was said to have been instrumental in securing the ban: he had already ensured that only two out of five *World in Action* programmes on the North of Ireland had been shown by UTV. [12]

The establishment attacks

The escalating censorship and network of restrictions inside the TV companies did not satisfy the politicians, who wanted to ensure that not a single hint of criticism of British policy penetrated the airwaves. They were, as they still are, particularly concerned about television because it has huge audiences, because its visual images have greater impact than radio and print, and also because, since it is technically non-party-political, it has a greater reputation for objectivity than the press. Their attacks on the BBC were particularly venomous, because it was felt to be identified in the public mind as 'the voice of the nation'. [13] Indeed, a *Times* survey of a representative sample of people listed in *Who's Who* found that a majority thought that the BBC was more influential than Parliament, the press, trade unions, the civil service, the monarchy and the church. [14]

On 17 October *The Sunday Times* finally published allegations that internees had been tortured by British soldiers and the RUC Special Branch: allegations which had appeared in the Irish press as long before as the end of August. The controversy over the British army's conduct which had been raging for months in Ireland was now spilling over into Britain, and the politicians were determined that none of it should reach the nation's TV screens.

Tory MPs wrote indignant letters to *The Daily Telegraph* attacking the BBC. Mary Whitehouse and the leader writers of the right wing press joined the attack. All were agreed that since there was undeniably a war on, the BBC, being 'British', must line up fair and square on the nation's side, just as it had done in World War II. As it was, the BBC was giving too much emphasis to allegations of brutality by the security forces, was harassing the army and giving aid and comfort to the IRA.

An interview by *Panorama*'s Alan Hart on 8 November with Stormont Prime Minister Brian Faulkner raised a fierce little storm. Faulkner had blandly predicted that in years to come Catholics would thank him for introducing internment, whereupon Hart retorted angrily that he thought he knew more about Catholics in the North than Faulkner did. 'A lot of people thought it was unfair to Faulkner,' then Director-General Charles Curran later recalled.[15] Mary Whitehouse complained that the interview 'makes one bound to ask where the sympathies of the BBC lie.'[16] The newspapers attacked televisions deviations with gusto. The *Daily Express* warned,

> While British troops are involved in fighting a terrorist-anarchist organisation . . . there is no room for impartiality . . . There is no question here of political censorship . . . people who bomb, kill and maim in order to smash the fabric of society put themselves outside the normal conventions, which include freedom of speech . . . the soldier or the policeman who never knows where the next shot will come from deserves support in a hazardous and desperately difficult task. The snide remark which undermines his morale is almost as bad as the sniper's bullet.[17]

Jak of the *Evening Standard* contributed a cartoon which showed a television producer asking British troops, one of whom lay wounded, to expose themselves to fire again for the benefit of the cameras.[18] Cummings of the *Daily Express* drew a television presenter, looking remarkably like Robin Day, happily presiding over a friendly discussion between Adolf Hitler and his Gestapo chief Himmler, with the caption, 'If only we'd had showbiz TV during the *last* war!'[19]

The Tory backbenchers mustered their ranks, and on 15 November more than eighty of them gathered to complain bitterly to Home Secretary Maudling that the government was 'losing the propaganda war'.[20] If the media did not voluntarily restrain themselves, they said, 'patriotic censorship' should be imposed.[21] Among their number was Lieutenant-Colonel 'Mad Mitch' Mitchell, who next day accused the BBC of 'subsidised subversion' and 'contributing towards IRA objectives by undermining the will of the home population to fight in Ulster.'[22]

The BBC succumbs

The furore produced results: Maudling immediately issued a summons to the chairmen of the BBC and the Independent Television Authority to see him. Maudling saw BBC Chairman Lord Hill on 19 November. The next day, Christopher Chataway, who as Minister for Posts and Telecommunications was then responsible for broadcasting, made a key speech. Radio and television, he said, were not required to strike an equal balance between the IRA and the Ulster government, nor between the British army and 'terrorists'. While propaganda should not be substituted for truthful reporting, it would be just as obnoxious to have the soldier and the murderer treated as moral equals.[23]

In a letter to Maudling three days later, Lord Hill adopted these sentiments wholesale. He wrote:

> The BBC and its staff abhor the terrorism of the IRA and report their campaign of murder with revulsion . . . as between the Government and the Opposition, as between the two communities in Northern Ireland, the BBC has a duty to be impartial no less than in the rest of the United Kingdom. But, as between the British army and the gunmen, the BBC is not and cannot be impartial.[24]

It was not long before the ITA Chairman Lord Aylestone was echoing this view, though in a rather cruder way. 'As far as I'm concerned,' he was quoted as saying, 'Britain is at war with the IRA in Ulster and the IRA will get no more coverage than the Nazis would have done in the last war.'[25]

Lord Hill had publicly abandoned the BBC's cherished pretension to impartiality at a time when, in the wake of internment and the use of sensory deprivation torture techniques against internees, the nationalist community's antipathy to the British government and army was stronger than at any time since the troubles started. *The Observer* lamented, 'The IRA has already succeeded, to an alarming degree, in becoming the champion of a large part, perhaps a majority, of Ulster's Catholics.'[26] In this context, it was impossible for the BBC both to report the IRA 'with revulsion' and to remain impartial 'between the two communities'. Nor was it possible for the BBC to take the side of the British army against the 'gunmen' and at the same time to expose atrocities committed by the troops. The commitment to non-impartiality meant that only one side of the story could be told, and that the views and experiences of a large proportion of nationalists were now taboo.

To censor or not to censor?

The more sensible pundits, along with the senior broadcasters, realised that there were wiser options than state control of television output. Their arguments were based more on pragmatism than on principle. A *Times* leader argued in mid-November 1971 that

> censorship would be directly counter-productive. Nothing would be of greater assistance to the IRA in the propaganda and political contests that are part of the wider conflict in Northern Ireland. It would mean that no fact, no assessment offered by British television, radio or newspapers would be free of the taint that it had been presented under government supervision. The suspicion would soon develop that the truth was being hidden, or distorted, because it was too unsavoury to be presented fully and fairly to the British public. Nothing could do more to undermine confidence. For those who wish to see constitutional authority winning the propaganda and political contests in Northern Ireland censorship is not a weapon but a temptation.[27]

The Times put forward an alternative remedy. The BBC's 'failings', such as the 'hectoring tone' of Alan Hart's interview with Brian Faulkner, were 'essentially professional errors requiring professional improvement.'[28]

Writing in *The Sunday Telegraph*, right-wing journalist Peregrine Worsthorne opposed political censorship on the grounds that the media would only accept it when there was a consensus in the country, as there had been in World War II. Ireland was different: unionists felt the government was not being tough enough, while according to the polls a majority in Britain wanted the troops withdrawn. He summed up:

> Public opinion, in short, is deeply divided. There is no patriotic line to cling to, no national ethos governing what should be said or done.
>
> Against this confused background only one point stands out with absolute clarity; no form of political censorship, either overt or covert, is either desirable or even possible, since any attempt to apply pressure on the media will have exactly the opposite effect from that desired.[29]

Two types of censorship were being mooted at the time: state-operated censorship, and 'voluntary' censorship regulated by the broadcasting authorities themselves. The BBC chiefs rejected both notions, mainly on the grounds that formal censorship of any kind would undermine their credibility. BBC Director-General Charles Curran said in October 1971 that for the BBC to censor the reporting of Ireland 'would be subject to one fatal criticism.' He continued:

> It is an essential function of news to be believed. Unless people have a conviction that the agency from which they are receiving their news is honestly attempting to tell the whole truth they will cease to believe it and the most valuable quality which news can have – its credibility – will be undermined.[30]

Writing to Home Secretary Maudling the following month, BBC Chairman Lord Hill echoed this argument, and responded to the idea of 'voluntary' censorship by pointing out that the BBC was already vetting its Irish coverage:

> The BBC already undertakes a scrupulous editorial watch at all levels. We believe that if we went beyond that we would do nothing but harm and we would reject any such suggestion, from whatever quarter it might come. Its immediate effect would be to destroy the credibility of all our reporting.[31]

As Hill's letter indicated, the broadcasters' solution was a new form of censorship, hidden from the public eye: the 'professional improvements' advocated by *The Times*, realised through a 'scrupulous editorial watch' within the broadcasting organisations.

The military, too, had reservations about censorship, though retired army officers were in the forefront of the parliamentary campaign for it. The army's counter-insurgency handbook, *Land Operations: Volume III – Counter Revolutionary Operations*, issued in August 1969 and based on the experience of the 53 counter-revolutionary wars conducted since World War II, states, 'The government should permit a free press to exist as far as this is possible . . . Action to muzzle the press almost invariably rebounds on the government, and any proposed restrictions on press activities must be carefully considered.'[32] The handbook argues, in effect, that manipulating the press is more effective than censoring it: 'The press, properly handled, is potentially one of the government's strongest weapons.'[33]

In a book based on his experiences as an army commander in the North of Ireland in the early seventies, Colonel Robin Evelegh wrote:

> The trouble with any form of censorship is that, like most forms of dishonesty, its advantages are short-term while its disadvantages are long-term and soon completely overwhelm whatever good has been done. The key question concerns the credibility of Government spokesmen. It does not matter what somebody says to the press or shows on television if no one believes him.[34]

As the war in the North escalated, the army concentrated on overhauling and extending its propaganda operation, which was much more important there than it had been in wars conducted in less accessible parts of the world. Shortly after the start of internment, the army set up an 'Information Policy' unit, responsible for a range of psychological warfare activities, including poster campaigns by local units, the planting of stories in the media, and straightforward press relations.[35]

Top BBC man Desmond Taylor, who in 1971 was Editor of News and Current Affairs, later expressed his appreciation of the army's approach:

> One of the most serious challenges to our reporting arose when the Army . . . came into conflict with large sections of the population. Allegations were made of mistaken and even indiscriminate killing by soldiers . . . Reporting these allegations raised in acute form the argument as to whether journalism should in effect be censored to help the authorities . . . Our critics suggested forcibly that we were in what amounted to a state of war, it was our job to help the Army and not to stab them in the back . . . but our arguments carried force with the Army itself, and it initiated a policy of putting up spokesmen to give its side of the story which sustained public belief in our fairness and impartiality and did the Army a great deal of good in the process.[36]

A maze of restrictions

The Tories of the 'imperial right' had not achieved the 'patriotic censorship' they wanted, but they had helped to get results. The self-policing by BBC and ITV executives was to prove more effective, because more subtle and concealed, than any overt censorship would have been. As the Secretary of the Federation of Broadcasting Unions, Tom Rhys, put it in a letter of protest to Lord Hill in early 1972, the 'checks and balances' introduced by the BBC 'were becoming as effective as censorship, probably more effective because they were not much known outside the circles immediately involved, were superficially merely an intensification of normal safeguards, and were too vague and distant a target for public criticism.'[37] Frustrated staff, said Rhys, were beginning to avoid 'items on which they ought to work', or avoid Irish subjects altogether, and members believed that their careers were jeopardised by disagreements over items on Ireland.

The internal controls allowed the BBC to implement,

without appearing to concede its independence, many of the critics' demands. From now on, critical questioning of the army was out, detailed probing of Unionist politicians was out, sympathetic questioning of victims of army brutality was out, and interviews with the IRA were out except in the most exceptional circumstances.

Those reporters who believed their role was to ask questions, however inconvenient for the government, were effectively muzzled. As Jonathan Dimbleby wrote in an unsigned article in the *New Statesman* in December 1971,

> The censorship and restrictions now imposed on reporters and editors make it practically impossible for them to ask the question 'why?' Why do the Catholics now laugh openly when a British soldier is shot down and killed, when a year ago they would offer the army cups of tea? Why do the Catholics refuse to condemn the bombings and the shootings? Why do they still succour the IRA . . . ? What influence today does the Civil Rights Movement have? Or the SDLP? The answers to such questions are fundamental to understanding the problem, crucial to any judgement of British policy, yet they cannot be asked by BBC employees: quite simply the management of the BBC has decided that it does not want such questions raised. Its reporters and editors stand transfixed – censored – in a maze of insuperable restrictions.[38]

Dimbleby's concern was shared by many leading journalists and broadcasters, and in November 1971 some 200 of them gathered at the Institute of Contemporary Arts in London to protest against 'the intensification of censorship on TV, radio and the press coverage of events in Northern Ireland'. Among them was senior BBC reporter Keith Kyle, who said, 'There is no higher national interest than avoiding self-deception in Northern Ireland.'[39]

But their protest was hampered by their refusal to declare themselves publicly. Fearing for their careers, they asked that their names not be published, and only *The Irish Times*, barely read in Britain, broke ranks. A few went on trying to cover Ireland conscientiously, some resigned their posts, while others gave up. gave up. They drifted into a silence that would not be broken again until 1976, when Jonathan Dimbleby startled a somnolent television discussion into life by declaring that 'the political institutions, BBC, IBA, British government, British opposition . . . don't wish us to know too much too well about Northern Ireland.'[40]

The right wins round one

So by the end of 1971 a tiny minority of the population – back-bench Tory MPs, letter writers to *The Daily Telegraph* with names like Colonel the Lord Clifford of Chudleigh OBE DL, a couple of government ministers, the top figures in the TV hierarchy and Fleet Street editors – had succeeded in excising from television most vestiges of questioning of the government's Irish policy. There had been scarcely a word of dissent from the opposition benches in the House of Commons.

Once tried and proved effective, the same tactics were to be used again and again. Whenever the broadcasting organisations appeared to be wavering from the narrow path of patriotism, the same group of people would raise the same rallying cries of television's treason and support for the rebels. 'We are losing the propaganda war,' they would lament, as they re-enacted the stylised drama. And the TV chiefs, while paying lip service to their independence from the state, would re-assert their non-impartiality and tighten up their internal controls. The ritual was to be played out once more, with almost uncanny similarity, in the controversy over TV coverage of the war in the South Atlantic in May 1982.[41]

Focussing their anger on television coverage, the politicians neglected to examine whether it was in fact their policies that were the problem. Television provided, as it was to do so often in the future, a convenient scapegoat and diversion. Political scientist Jay G. Blumler suggested in *New Society* that perhaps the real similarity with Vietnam lay not in the influence of television, but in 'the peculiarities of the cause at stake', 'in the intrinsic difficulty for a democracy of fighting a war that arouses little genuine passion among ordinary people, and also seems potentially endless.'[42]

A lone right-winger, Tory MP Philip Goodhart, suggested that the solution to the problem of public opinion might not be censorship but a change in political strategy. In a prophetic article in *The Daily Telegraph*, he argued that, like the Americans in Vietnam, Britain had made the mistake of pushing her own troops into the main combat role. Now, following the American example, they should be pulled back from the front line and locally recruited forces should be given 'more responsible and vigorous roles'. The solution to the media's 'damaging effect on public opinion' lay in 'the path of partial Ulsterisation . . .

machine-guns and armoured cars for the RUC and an offensive role for the UDR.'[43] As things turned out, both partial censorship and partial Ulsterisation were to be the order of the day.

The establishment had won, almost unchallenged, this crucial first round in the battle to control the flow of information about the war in the North of Ireland. The British public, as intended, had lost: their morale, or at least passive acquiescence in the government's Irish policy was to be maintained at the price of ignorance. Indeed, since the debate had largely been confined to the editorials and letters columns in *The Times* and *The Daily Telegraph*, many people were unaware that a battle was in progress. Since knowledge of the mechanisms of censorship in broadcasting was confined to the people who worked in that field, the public at large had little idea of how their information was being manipulated.

The Question of Ulster

At the turn of the year 1971–72, there was a major row between the government and the BBC over a marathon TV debate called *The Question of Ulster*, but this did not affect the trend towards ever tighter restrictions on programme makers. *The Question of Ulster* featured several Irish politicians being questioned by two Lords and a judge who was also a Tory MP. Home Secretary Maudling reportedly 'blew his top' when he heard about the programme,[44] and, along with the Northern Ireland government, tried desperately to stop it. What they were afraid of, said the *TV Mail*, 'is that any point of view other than their own will be expressed' and that 'the viewing public might realise that there *is* another point of view at all.'[45]

The BBC, which had not in any case invited the IRA to participate, responded to the pressure by agreeing to restructure the programme to give more emphasis to the 'special position of the majority party in Ulster'[46], but this failed to placate the politicians. The British and Stormont governments said they would boycott the programme, hoping that by 'unbalancing' it they would prevent the BBC going ahead. The BBC, which had been thrown into 'much anguished dithering',[47] said it would indeed scrap the programme if no one could be found to represent the Stormont point of view; but in the nick of time Ulster Unionist MP John Maginnis broke ranks and agreed to appear.

The government could have banned the programme by

invoking clause 13(4) of the BBC's licence, which permits the minister responsible for broadcasting to order the BBC not to transmit specified material.[48] The government stopped short of doing this, perhaps because Lord Hill had said he would make any such ban public. But the day before the programme was due to go out, Maudling issued an unprecedented public rebuke to Lord Hill: 'I believe that this programme in the form in which it has been devised can do no good, and could do serious harm.'[49]

Maudling had overshot the mark. The pressure was so blatant that, as the *Financial Times* observed, the BBC 'had little option' but to go ahead with the programme, 'since as an independent corporation it could not be seen to give in to political pressures.'[50]

After all the uproar, British viewers found the programme on transmission so boring that half of them switched over to a football match on ITV.[51] Lord Caradon, one of the tribunal members on the show, summed up with the words, 'We have not done much damage tonight. We may have been dull but we have not been dangerous.'[52] The atmosphere of the talk-in, which lasted two hours fifty minutes, was, said the *Financial Times*, 'typical of the BBC at its most sober, and within the programme itself there was not a single example of controversy.'[53] One letter writer to *The Times* quoted Sir Thomas Browne: 'This is the dormitive I take to bedward; I need no other laudanum to make me sleep.'[54]

The response in Whitehall, however, was less languid. There, according to *The Guardian*, it was argued 'with the utmost vehemence that the impact of the programme threatened to create an attitude of despair and indifference among the British public, and to feed the view that British troops should be withdrawn'.[55]

2. From silence to civil rights

The silent years

In the ferment of 1970 and 1971, as the television companies tightened up their internal censorship procedures and the press adopted an uncritical pro-British army stance, they were continuing a 50-year-old tradition of tacit support for government policy on Ireland. Ever since Ireland was partitioned in 1920, and the North given its local Parliament at Stormont, there had been a convention in the House of Commons that the affairs of the province were never discussed there. The British media made themselves part of this conspiracy of silence, which lasted until the civil rights explosion of the late sixties made it impossible to turn a blind eye any longer.

Until ITV arrived in the North in 1959, the BBC monopolised broadcasting in the Six Counties, and from the start it was intimately linked with the Unionist hierarchy. Gerald Beadle, who became manager of the first Northern Ireland radio station in 1926 and later director of BBC television, recalled:

> mine was a task of consolidation, which meant building the BBC into the lives of the people of the province and making it one of their public institutions . . . I was invited to become a member of the Ulster Club; the Governor, the Duke of Abercorn, was immensely helpful and friendly, and Lord Craigavon, the Prime Minister, was a keen supporter of our work. In effect I was made a member of the Establishment.[1]

The Unionist regime chose to act as if neither the South of Ireland nor any minority tradition in the North actually existed. The new BBC radio station dutifully followed suit. A locally owned news agency supplied all the news, no political statements were permitted unless made by major local politicians, and even the results of matches organised by the Gaelic Athletic Association, which organises traditional Irish games such as Gaelic football, were not broadcast.

Any divergence from the orthodoxy was greeted with a storm of Unionist protest. Beadle's drama department was attacked for using southern accents in some of its plays, and his decision to celebrate St Patrick's Day provoked outrage. But on the whole Beadle's policy was to act, as former BBC programme editor Anthony Smith put it, 'as if the Border was an Atlantic coast.'[2]

A BBC document of 1930 made the position absolutely clear. The BBC Regional Service, it said, 'reflects the sentiments of the people who have always maintained unswerving loyalty to British ideals and to British culture. Northern Ireland relies on broadcasting to strengthen its common loyalties with Britain.'[3]

Under G.L. Marshall, who was Director of BBC Northern Ireland from the mid-thirties until well after the second world war, the policy was 'to keep an iron grip on local news and allow nothing to go out which suggested that anything in Northern Ireland could or would ever change.'[4] As well as ignoring the existence of the nationalist community, the BBC steered clear of provocative Unionist activities, and did not report the Orange Order's annual 12 July demonstrations.

Crucially for the British and international audiences, Marshall managed to get into a position where he effectively controlled *all* BBC material relating to the North of Ireland. Smith writes that

> Marshall demanded and was given the right to be consulted by all departments of the BBC on any matter relating to Ireland in any way. Thus, the chief in Belfast came to act as a kind of censor over the whole of the BBC's output from London both in its domestic and overseas services, and naturally this tended to give a Unionist tinge to everything that came out.[5]

The Controller of BBC Northern Ireland still holds this power.

After the war, the system became a little more flexible. The Catholic Church was represented on the religious advisory committee, and both Gaelic games and the Unionist 12 July marches were now reported. But on the fundamental political questions there was no movement. When the BBC Northern Ireland Advisory Council, a body made up of influential people from the community, was set up in 1947, at the very first meeting the chairperson ruled that the question of partition and the border was out of order. The Regional Director issued a directive that BBC policy was 'not to admit any attack on the constitutional position of Northern Ireland.'[6] The BBC continued to ignore events south of the border, and gave no hint of discontent or injustice in the north. The arrival of television in Belfast – just in time for the coronation – brought no changes.

The Whicker affair

On the couple of occasions in 1959 when British television allowed fleeting glimpses of another version of reality, Unionist wrath descended on it with a vengeance. On Ed Murrow's talk programme, *See It Now*, Southern Irish actress Siobhan McKenna described some IRA internees in the South sympathetically as 'young idealists'. There was an indignant reaction in the North of Ireland: Northern Ireland's Prime Minister Lord Brookeborough protested vehemently to the BBC, who responded by dropping a second programme in which McKenna appeared, despite the fact that in it she discussed only the innocuous topic of the Irish sense of humour.[7]

The second occasion was both bizarre and illuminating. In January 1959 the *Tonight* current affairs programme sent reporter Alan Whicker to film eight ten-minute reports in the Six Counties. 'Each was matter-of-fact and straight down the middle. None took more than a tangential look at religion or politics,' he recalled in his autobiography. But the opening programme – about, of all things, betting shops – was enough to bring the sky down on the BBC's head.

Whicker sinned, quite unwittingly, in the opening sequence. Along with general shots of the Stormont Parliament and the City Hall, he showed graffiti on the walls such as 'No Pope here' and 'Vote Sinn Fein'. Then, showing a close-up of a policeman's revolver, he 'mentioned that Northern Ireland, though intensely loyal and the birthplace of most of Britain's best generals, had armed police but no conscription.'[8] Then he went on to describe how betting shops operated; already legal in the North, they were about to be introduced in Britain.

He describes how he watched the programme in a Derry hotel:

When the report ended there was silence in our hotel lounge. The man I had been drinking with turned to me: 'You can't say that sort of thing.' I was baffled. During the previous year I had reported in exactly the same straightforward way from 17 different countries without being told I could not get away with it. 'Why ever not? Every word's true.' 'I know,' he said, 'but that doesn't matter. You just can't say that sort of thing.' As I was to find out later – he was absolutely right.[9]

Next morning the little *Tonight* report dominated the local news headlines. A bishop and a senator flew to London to complain. 'The chairman of the Tourist Board expressed outrage,' Whicker recorded, 'and a BBC *Sportsview* team filming a local football match was dragged down from its camera stand and attacked.'[10] Northern Ireland's Prime Minister Lord Brookeborough intervened personally[11] and Stormont threatened to remove broadcasting from the BBC. The BBC's Northern Ireland Controller replied with, in Whicker's words, 'a craven statement grovelling at their "distress and indignation".' Apologising for the aspects of life in the North shown in the film, he dissociated himself and his staff from this 'unbalanced picture of life in the Province'.[12]

The BBC never screened the following seven *Tonight* reports, and did not attempt another programme on the Six Counties until several years later.

Ulster TV arrives

The opening of Ulster TV in 1959 put pressure on the BBC to liberalise its coverage. The group which owned UTV was headed by the Earl of Antrim, whose extensive business interests included the rabidly loyalist paper, the *News Letter*; UTV's managing director was Brum Henderson, whose brother runs the *News Letter* as well as the Century Press, which printed the Stormont *Hansard* and other Northern Ireland government papers. At least initially, however, commercial interest dictated that UTV could not afford to alienate the nationalist third of its potential audience. It reportedly gained a reputation for fairness in its coverage, although it did 'have to be nagged and cajoled at times into venturing into public affairs coverage on any important scale.'[13] In fact UTV only originated six hours of material a week: the rest was supplied from Britain.

As UTV developed, it proved itself ultra-cautious, and, like the BBC, quailed before the major political issues in the Six Counties. Its sister station, Rediffusion, produced the only two reports on the political situation in the North that were transmitted on national television prior to 1968: but UTV refused to transmit these reports, made by the *This Week* programme, in its jurisdiction.[14] Well over a decade later, and still under Brum Henderson, UTV was still displaying the same timidity. In 1980, a critic opposing the renewal of UTV's franchise said, 'They've tried to be neutral and ended up being nothing.' He went on to point out that in ten years of war UTV had not made a single programme which tried to explain what the conflict was all about.[15]

The arrival of UTV, which rapidly gained 65 per cent of the audience, forced the BBC into a measure of liberalisation, but in a framework of trying to 'maintain a consensus and build up the middle ground'.[16] The appointment of Waldo Maguire as the BBC's Northern Ireland Controller reportedly accelerated this process: 'reporters from London were welcomed and helped to do their work . . . local talent, Protestant and Catholic alike was encouraged.'[17]

But Maguire kept the London-based reporters on a tight rein, and the emphasis was still on giving a positive picture of life in the Six Counties. Like his predecessors, he had the right to be consulted on every programme dealing with either part of Ireland. Indeed, his power of veto over programmes transmitted in Britain was now for all practical purposes absolute, because in the sixties the BBC adopted a 'Catch 22' approach: it had decreed that all programmes on Ireland should be suitable for transmission throughout the United Kingdom, and the Director General had also instructed producers to do nothing that would provoke Maguire into shutting off the BBC Northern Ireland transmitter, as he then had the power to do.[18]

The civil rights movement ignored

As the civil rights movement gathered momentum, the BBC both nationally and locally continued to ignore the issues it raised. In 1966 a *Tonight* reporter, who later became a producer of ITV's *This Week*, reportedly left the BBC because he was not allowed to make a film about gerrymandering,[19] the process by which the regime manipulated constituency boundaries so that local election results were grossly distorted in favour of the Unionists.

Then in June 1968 one of the key events in the history of the civil rights movement occurred. The Unionist-controlled local authorities allocated council houses on a sectarian basis, giving precedence to Protestants regardless of their circumstances. In protest, homeless Catholic families squatted newly built council houses in Caledon, Co. Tyrone. The local authority evicted them and gave one of the houses to a 19-year-old single Protestant woman who was the secretary of a Unionist parliamentary candidate. A Nationalist MP at Stormont, Austin Currie, then occupied the house and was himself evicted, and in the process successfully drew attention to discrimination in housing. The BBC's reaction was later described by senior reporter Keith Kyle:

> The coverage of that became an occasion of much controversy, and the Regional Controller of the BBC in Northern Ireland at the time thought that a feature programme should not be made of this event. That became a sort of *cause celebre* within the BBC.[20]

The identification of the broadcasting companies with the status quo in the Six Counties and their refusal to acknowledge the underlying political schisms had profound effects. In the North, the alienation of the nationalist community from the state was paralleled by their alienation from TV and radio, which they generally regarded with deep scepticism. Broadcasters have argued that by preventing nationalists from putting their case on the air, TV and radio contributed to the conflict by forcing them to pursue their 'legitimate aims' outside the 'democratic framework'.[21]

In Britain prior to 1968 the only television investigations had been the two *This Week* reports, and there had been almost no in-depth newspaper coverage: a *Sunday Times* report on discrimination printed in 1966 was a rare exception.[22] Coupled with the veto on parliamentary discussion and the absence of 'the Irish question' from school and university curricula, the media silence meant that British people were scarcely aware of the existence of the Six Counties, let alone of the perverse and abusive system that was being operated in their name.

Civil rights in the spotlight

It was the North's second civil rights march, on 5 October 1968 in Derry, that finally brought the bizarre regime to international attention. The first march, from Coalisland to Dungannon six weeks earlier, had been ignored, but the Derry demonstration was well covered by television, and viewers throughout Britain and Ireland saw the RUC baton-charge the demonstrators, leaving an MP, Gerry Fitt, among the injured.

After 5 October, journalists poured into the North. Irish journalist and then civil rights activist Eamonn McCann told how British reporters roamed the streets of Derry's Bogside seeking articulate, Catholic, unemployed slum-dwellers to interview.[23] British Prime Minister Harold Wilson began pressing openly for reforms, and the Unionist regime was condemned by all sections of the British media. 'If you want roses, fishing or beautiful scenery,' wrote Punch cartoonist Mahood in January 1969, parodying a holiday brochure, 'Ulster has the best. The same goes for religious maniacs, gerrymanderers and bigots.'[24]

Bernadette Devlin's election and arrival at Westminster in 1969 were greeted with a rapture which reflected the media's attitude to the civil rights cause as much as their eagerness to exploit her sex and youthfulness. 'She's Bernadette, she's 21, she's an MP, she's swinging', enthused the Daily Express.[25] 'Swinging – that's petite Bernadette Devlin,' trilled the Daily Mirror.[26] 'She is a bonny fighter,' proclaimed The Times in a front page article headlined, 'Miss Devlin enthrals packed House with straight-from-heart speech.'[27]

With the arrival of British troops on the streets of Derry and Belfast in August 1969, all that was to change. Britain was now openly, and physically, involved, and British observers could no longer regard the situation with detached distaste. The media's identification with the troops was instant and total. Reporting their arrival in Derry, John Chartres of The Times wrote:

> Whatever happens now, and whatever the political implications turn out to be, one thing is certain – the 'dreaded' British Army is no longer dreaded by anyone here except the utterly bigoted . . . It is only after 24 hours that one can appreciate the impact that the arrival of 350 cheerful (but highly professional) Yorkshiremen with soft brogues from the Dales and Moors, a fund of good stories from the Leeds and Huddersfield public houses, but a skill at arms stretching back through Aden, Cyprus, Malaya, and the Greek insurrection, made on a town that really was beginning to twitch with fear.[28]

Rhona Churchill of the *Daily Mail* described how the troops handled the locals: 'Over and over again they said patiently and politely "Would you mind very much moving on, please?" And people have moved on. This was the British Tommy in action here. You felt proud of him.'[29]

Later, explaining why despite himself he felt more strongly about the death of a British soldier than the death of an Irishman, Simon Winchester of *The Guardian* described the emotional tie between British journalists and soldiers:

> There was an indefinable feeling of being in a foreign country in Ireland, North or South – and, it must be admitted, there was some identification, some commonality between the ordinary British squaddie on the street and the ordinary British reporter or photographer or television man who followed him around . . . Often both would moan about the ills of Ireland; often he would understand you, and equally often you would understand and sympathise with him. Like us, he, the individual soldier was no real part of the trouble; like us, he had been sent out from England to do a job.[30]

As stability rather than reform became the British government's priority, attitudes to the nationalist community shifted and began to resemble the views long held by Unionists. The seeds of the change were there early on. As troops arrived in Derry, Christine Eade reported in *The Guardian* that,

> Certainly the British government is now taking seriously reports that both the Irish Republican Army and Catholic extremists within Northern Ireland are being influenced by anarchists, Trotskyists, and Communists. Paisleyite factions may also be influenced by outsiders.[31]

Bernadette Devlin, who had already blotted her copybook in the eyes of the British media by breaking up paving stones during the 'battle of the Bogside' that precipitated the army's arrival, was soon transformed by the *Daily Mail* into the leader of a 'sinister army' of 'revolutionary extremists', who were now said to be in complete control of the civil rights movement.[32]

Biggles in Belfast

By the middle of 1970, when the troops were in almost constant conflict in nationalist working class areas, the British press had jettisoned any lingering sympathy with the nationalist community. From now on, the British army could do no wrong and virtually every act of violence and major outburst of rioting was blamed on the IRA.

There were no limits to the journalistic imagination when it came to portraying the British side as good and the nationalist side as evil, with sometimes farcical results. 'Troops fear the croak of the frog', announced the *Daily Sketch* in June 1970, explaining:

> Behind the swirling haze of CS gas, the croak of the frog summons Londonderry to riot. It blares above the crash of the gas cannisters and rises over the screams of terror. It is a voice the troops in the Bogside would dearly love to identify.
>
> They call it the frog and every soldier now recognises it after 48 hours of almost continual fighting. It moves from street battle to street battle pouring out a continual stream of hate, vilification and obscenities. [33]

Reporters put the best possible construction on army behaviour, making allowances even for flagrant brutality. *Evening Standard* reporter Max Hastings, who became one of the best known war correspondents in the South Atlantic in 1982, described an incident in which a soldier beat a man with such force that his baton broke:

> As the riot squad moved up they banged their shields with their batons in rhythm with their marching time, then, at a yell from their officer they sprinted into the darkness among the crowd to return dragging a youthful rioter. The whole Company cheered spontaneously. 'Broke my baton, this one,' said a corporal cheerfully holding up the stump. [34]

As Eamonn McCann commented, Hastings made the incident sound 'like a jolly adventure, more Biggles than Belfast.'[35]

When British soldiers shot somebody dead, the press had no qualms in accepting the army's word that the victim was a 'petrol-bomber' or 'gunman'. One article, by John Chartres of *The Times*, became part of nationalist folklore. On 31 July 1970 soldiers shot dead Danny O'Hagan in the New Lodge Road in Belfast. The British army said he had been throwing petrol bombs, but local people denied this so vehemently that most papers hesitated to repeat it. John Chartres, however, came up with a most original compromise. A civilian had been killed, he wrote, when 'the army for the first time carried out its threat to shoot assistant petrol bombers.'[36]

Even journalists who believed themselves to be sceptical

tended unquestioningly to accept the army's version, unless they had personally witnessed the event in question. Simon Winchester told how, after the curfew imposed on the Lower Falls in Belfast in July 1970, the British army said they had fired only 15 shots – but the true figure turned out to be 1,454 rounds. 'Never, since then,' he wrote, 'have I found myself able to take the army's explanation about any single incident with any less a pinch of salt than I would take any other explanation.'[37] Yet the following February, in a case that was publicised when Bernadette Devlin raised it in Parliament, Winchester accepted the word of a paratroop officer that a man just shot by soldiers, Bernard Watt, was a 'petrol bomber'. Defending himself against Devlin's accusation that he had 'casually libelled a Belfast worker . . . the effect of the libel being to justify his killing,'[38] Winchester explained his reasoning: 'a soldier cannot legally shoot "a rioter" . . . He has to wait until a man has committed one of a number of specific offences, of which throwing petrol bombs is one. I accepted at the time that this is what Mr Watt must have done, and this I duly reported.'[39]

The newspapers' flattering portrayal of the army was not all the fault of journalists. Some did try to report honestly on the increasingly widespread army brutality, but again and again such accounts were dropped. Kevin Dowling, who reported from the North for the *Sunday Mirror* between 1970 and 1974, recalled, 'What I remember most about the period is the number of uncomfortable news stories I have covered which were not printed, but which turned out to be true.'[40] He cited a story he wrote on the eve of internment. On 7 August 1971 Harry Thornton, a building worker, was driving his van past Springfield Road barracks when it backfired. Soldiers opened fire and killed him. His friend Murphy was dragged from the van and taken into the barracks. Dowling explained:

> It was obvious that evening that Thornton was killed by mistake and it also became obvious that his friend had been taken in and beaten mercilessly by the Paras and the police.
> He was brought to hospital later with a fracture of the skull. I phoned over my story. Not only was it not used, but I was threatened with dismissal if I ever again suggested that our army was doing such nasty things in Northern Ireland.[41]

The papers not only played down army violence, but also mobilised their readers into active support for the troops. In late

1971, the *Daily Mirror* was running an airlift to give 'home comforts' to the soldiers; *The Daily Telegraph* and *The Sunday Telegraph* had set up a colour TV fund for them – a project that was repeated in later years; the *Daily Express* had launched a campaign urging its women readers to write to the 'Ulster hermits'; and the *Daily Mail* was sponsoring tours of the camps in the Six Counties by well-known entertainers.[42]

Yet by this time, as the *Sunday Times* Insight team wrote, the army's conduct had emerged as 'the most sensitive single issue raised by military involvement in Ulster.[43] The refusal of most of the media to acknowledge this meant that the British public had a completely erroneous view of what was happening. It also meant that the media were, in practice, giving the government and army permission to continue hammering the nationalist community.

John O'Callaghan, then a senior reporter in *The Guardian*'s London office, took three weeks leave in January 1972 and went to Derry, Belfast and Dublin to investigate the situation. 'I found the Catholic minority have had a far worse battering than ever appears in any English papers,' he said later. He considered that if even *The Guardian*, with its 'tradition of opposition towards any kind of state or institutional violence', was behind the army, then the army would 'feel that nobody is looking or going to question them at all.'[44] After Bloody Sunday, he resigned from *The Guardian* in protest at its Irish coverage.

3. Reporting British violence

Reporting torture: 1971

Since the start of the conflict, a central problem for the British authorities has been how to use sufficient force to subdue nationalist protest without, at the same time, alienating 'moderate' nationalists, shattering the British public's faith in their government's policy, and undermining Britain's democratic image internationally. Counter-insurgency expert Frank Kitson advocates a balancing act. He counsels against 'the ruthless application of naked force' because 'it is most unlikely that the British government, or indeed any Western government, would be politically able to operate on these lines even if it wanted to do so.' He goes on:

> Although with an eye to world opinion and to the need to retain the allegiance of the people, no more force than is necessary for containing the situation should be used, conditions can be made reasonably uncomfortable for the population as a whole, in order to provide an incentive for a return to normal life and to act as a deterrent towards a resumption of the campaign.[1]

This position is difficult to maintain. The actions involved in making conditions 'reasonably uncomfortable for the population' may well, if word spreads beyond those immediately affected, alienate both world opinion and the local populace. One solution, therefore, is to try to stop the news getting out.

Repeatedly – as with torture and troop brutality in the early seventies, Bloody Sunday, the use of torture to obtain confessions, plastic bullets, and the shooting of unarmed people – Britain has resorted to a level of force which clearly violates democratic standards. Consequently, in every such instance, the authorities have tried to minimise the damage to their image by using various cover-up devices: pretending the incident had not occurred, lying about what had happened, blaming it on someone else, usually republicans, saying it was a creation of enemy propaganda, or advancing justifications for the action.

Within the Six Counties, it is impossible for the authorities fully to conceal what is going on, because the people have direct experience of events. Such concealment is also, to some extent, undesirable from the government's point of view, since violence has its uses both in intimidating nationalists and placating loyalists. But beyond the borders of the North, and especially in Britain, the authorities are able to exert a big influence on how the public perceives events. The British media have, by and large, promoted the establishment's version, though a very few journalists have insisted on reporting events as they saw them.

Allegations ignored

On 19 August 1971, ten days after the first big internment swoop, a local nationalist paper, the *Tyrone Democrat*, carried a page one headline which read, 'Warning! Don't Read This If You Have A Weak Stomach . . .' The paper contained eight pages of statements from men who had been arrested, detailing maltreatment by the army, together with reports of local protests. A 25-year-old man from Belfast, Henry Bennett, told of his experiences in Girdwood Barracks, one of the 'holding centres':

> I was forced to run over broken glass and rough stones to a helicopter without shoes. I spent only fifteen seconds in the helicopter and I was then pushed out into the hands of military policemen. I was forced to crawl between these policemen back to the building. They kicked me on the hands, legs, ribs and kidney area . . . [2]

Such accounts were widely published in Ireland, but the first response of British papers was to ignore them. As the *Sunday Times* Insight team noted in their book, *Ulster*,

> Most British newspapers found the mounting allegations so incendiary that they ignored them, or confined their concern to the events over the forty-eight hours of 9–10 August 1971, following the introduction of internment. Even the most formal of those inquiries was . . . inadequate. [3]

The most sinister allegations concerned 11 internees, later known as 'the guineapigs', who became the victims of a bizarre and terrifying experiment in the application of sensory deprivation torture techniques. By 20 August, statements from the torture victims had been circulated to the press by the Association for Legal Justice. By the end of August these accounts had appeared in the Irish papers. Then in the first week of September the British-based Anti-Internment League circulated a 10-page dossier to all British papers.[4]

But the British public heard nothing till 17 October, when *The Sunday Times* published an article titled 'How Ulster internees are made to talk' by the Insight team with John Whale. Both the headline and the introduction implied that the army was obtaining a flow of useful information through its interrogation methods: this was not the case, and no such claims were made in the article. Although the piece was on the front page, it played second fiddle to a story titled, 'Arms plane held in Holland: Top IRA man sought'. At any rate, two months after the allegations had first been made, British people now learned of the 'disorientation' techniques that were being applied by specially trained military interrogators and RUC Special Branch men.

> They had been rounded up at various points in the province . . .
> All were blindfolded by having a hood, two layers of fabric thick, placed over their heads. These hoods remained on their heads for up to six days.
> Each man was then flown by helicopter to an unknown destination – in fact Palace Barracks. During the period of their interrogation, they were continuously hooded, barefoot, dressed only in an over-large boiler suit, and spreadeagled against a wall . . .
> The only sound that filled the room was a high-pitched throb . . . The noise literally drove them out of their minds.[5]

One of the victims, Patrick Shivers, explained what it felt like:

> I was taken into a room. In the room there was a consistent noise like the escaping of compressed air. It was loud and deafening. The noise was continuous. I then heard a voice moaning. It sounded like a person who wanted to die. My hands were put high above my head against the wall. My legs were spread apart. My head was pulled back by someone catching hold of the hood and at the same time my backside was pushed in so as to cause the maximum strain on my body. I was kept in this position for four, or perhaps six hours until I collapsed and fell to the ground. After I fell I was lifted up again and put against the wall in the same

position and the same routine was followed until I again collapsed. Again I was put up and this continued indefinitely. This treatment lasted for two or three days and during this time I got no sleep and no food. I lost consciousness several times.[6]

Patrick Shivers, never, incidentally, a member of the IRA, was awarded £15,000 damages against the British and Northern Ireland governments in 1974. In the years following his experience, he saw five psychiatrists and was still suffering from intermittent depression when interviewed by Andrew Stephen of *The Observer* in 1976.[7]

The broadcasting organisations were no more anxious to report the allegations than were the newspapers. A former reporter for BBC radio's *World at One* recalled that weeks before *The Sunday Times* printed the article, BBC reporters were doing the same research because they were getting the same leads.

They came up with interviews which seemed compelling evidence. They were never transmitted and there was immense frustration inside the BBC. Then *The Sunday Times* printed its allegations and in the *World This Weekend* office – we got the newspapers in on the Saturday night – we said, 'Now is the time to run those interviews.' And the editor, I presume under instruction, and in a very, very fierce row with me, that ended up with me threatening to resign and him white-faced, the editor forbade the use of those interviews. This was a crucial demonstration for the people in that office of the emergence of a problem which up to then they hadn't been very aware of.

Then we finally got around it by a compromise, by getting Brian Faulkner to talk quite separately about the police. Then we went on to ask him if he had seen the allegations in *The Sunday Times*. He responded to the allegations, and we carried that as the first interview in the *World This Weekend*. There had been before that as far as I know in the news bulletins no reference to the *Sunday Times* report.[8]

Inquiring TV reporters, too, were running into a wall of hostility from their superiors. The BBC's *Today* programme did a filmed interview with Michael Farrell, a leader of People's Democracy who had just been released from detention, and now a noted historian. It was due to go out at the start of September, but was banned. At a top level internal BBC meeting on 17 September, Roland Fox, assistant to the Editor of News and Current Affairs, explained why. The minutes record his view that:

After weighing up all the factors, taking into account the fact that it had not been possible to make the item's treatment defensible as a whole on the grounds of fairness, he had decided that the item was expendable. It had in any case been an item of marginal importance, being a description by an admitted extremist of conditions in the Crumlin Road prison.[9]

The BBC reporters had been instructed to present all interviews with ex-internees 'in as sceptical a manner as possible'; they had done this, and the interviews had nonetheless been banned. They had also been forbidden to seek corroboration from doctors and priests, which would have lent weight to the allegations. As Jonathan Dimbleby wrote, 'Quite clearly, until the Compton Report bore out much of what had been alleged, the BBC's intention was to discredit the allegations and those who made them.'[10]

Army propaganda

Following *The Sunday Times*' disclosures, politicians, the army and sections of the press did their best to discredit the stories of torture by putting them down to 'IRA propaganda' which had been swallowed by a gullible press. As Northern Ireland's Prime Minister Brian Faulkner put it, the IRA 'had poured out propaganda aimed at undermining public morale, confusing the issues and discrediting the Government and security . . . Lurid stories of torture and brutality were blazened throughout the world.'[11]

The army press department, using a device that was to become familiar with the re-emergence of systematic torture in 1977, planted the story that the IRA was beating up its own people in order to present them to the press as victims of army and police brutality. On 24 October, a week after its first report, *The Sunday Times* planned to publish further allegations of brutality. Part of the report concerned 36-year-old Gerard McAllister, an IRA member previously imprisoned for wearing military-style uniform at an IRA funeral. On release, he was immediately rearrested and interrogated for 26 hours before being set free. Two men then delivered him to a hospital in County Louth in the South of Ireland. The consultant psychiatrist at the hospital, Dr James J. Wilson, London-trained and fervently pro-British, was not pleased when McAllister was brought in. He almost refused him admission and only agreed when he observed his mental state. McAllister's condition so shocked Dr Wilson that he wrote to *The Sunday Times*, *The Observer* and *The Sunday Telegraph*. The latter two responded with standard printed forms thanking him for his letter, but *The Sunday Times* sent over a reporter who took statements both from him and from McAllister. Dr Wilson told them that on admission McAllister

> seemed literally frozen with terror . . . a severe, acute anxiety case – the kind of condition you sometimes find among men who have been in heavy combat, or who have miraculously escaped from a road disaster. It is a condition of almost total immobility, with all bodily responses severely repressed – being almost frozen with fear . . . the dominant reason for his condition seemed to be his treatment in the interrogation centre.[12]

RUC Special Branch men and soldiers had inflicted a range of indignities on McAllister, including squeezing his testicles when he failed to give satisfactory replies to questions.

   The Sunday Times went to the army and asked about McAllister, but got no response. Then, the day before they broke the story, the *Daily Express* splashed across its front page a quite different story about McAllister. A huge headline, 'BEHIND THE WIRE!', was accompanied by two smaller headlines: ' "Brutality" charges denied' and 'Army tells how IRA beat up their own man after he was freed'.[13] The story began, 'A dossier is being compiled by police and the army in Ulster of IRA terror – against its own men.' It went on to allege that McAllister had been beaten up by the IRA after his release, then presented at the hospital as a victim of injuries sustained during interrogation. *The Sunday Times* concluded that this version of the case 'was presumably based on British military sources, as neither Dr Wilson nor Mr McAllister were contacted by the *Daily Express*.' For his part, Dr Wilson said,

> The allegations in the *Daily Express* leave me breathless. They are quite fantastic. What makes them completely absurd is the suggestion that he was badly beaten up by the IRA before he was brought here. The damage was psychological not physical.[14]

Committees of inquiry

With the allegations out in the open, and with the Irish government's decision to take a case against Britain to the European Commission of Human Rights, the British government set in motion a cover-up routine that was to last for seven years. The first, headed by Sir Edmund Compton, interviewed 143 witnesses, all but three from the military, police or prison staff. It confirmed the use of sensory deprivation techniques, and said that physical ill-treatment had taken place. But through a remarkable piece of sophistry, Compton concluded that there had been no brutality, because the interrogators had not intended to inflict pain.[15] The suffering of the victims was, it seemed, irrelevant. Compton also made the astonishing claim that techniques such as hooding might help the internees by protecting them from possible IRA retribution.

The Guardian's response to Compton was illuminating, undermining the paper's pretensions to liberalism. 'Vigorous and tough interrogation must go on. Discomfort of the kind revealed in this report, leaving no physical damage, cannot be weighed against the number of human lives which will be lost if the security forces do not get a continuing flow of information.'[16] Some of the paper's journalists protested, but to no avail.

The subsequent Parker Committee's majority report concluded that the techniques of interrogation were entirely justifiable and, despite the evidence of four distinguished psychiatrists and neurologists, rejected the possibility of long-term mental effects. The minority report submitted by Lord Gardiner held that the techniques were 'illegal alike by the law of England and the law of Northern Ireland'.

Disregarding Gardiner's conclusions, the Attorney-General announced in May 1972 that no prosecution would be brought against anybody involved in the interrogations. The government took a further step to keep the issue out of the limelight by deciding not to contest the cases brought by the internees for the mental suffering they had been caused. Instead, the government paid out compensation to the tune of more than £200,000 for fourteen men by 1978.

The European Commission

Both Tory and then Labour ministers expressed their displeasure with the Irish government for proceeding with the Strasbourg case, and made repeated attempts to get them to call it off. British governments also did their best to hinder the course of the Strasbourg enquiry, repeatedly finding excuses for postponing hearings – after months of delay, one hearing was held at British insistence on a remote Norwegian airfield – and refusing to answer detailed questions.[17]

The British media took their cue from their government. Criticism of British interrogation methods was out; criticism of the Irish government was in. In general, the media preferred to forget the issue altogether, but when it was forced on their attention they minimised the effects of sensory deprivation, justified the use of the techniques and unleashed a flood of invective against the Irish government.

The BBC demonstrated its sensitivity in its treatment of *Article 5*, a play by Brian Phelan which attempted to unravel the moral implications of Britain's use of torture. The play's title referred to the section of the 1948 Universal Declaration of Human Rights which condemns torture. The half-hour play was commissioned by the BBC, and was recorded on 12 January 1975. But in May or June 1975 it was viewed by Aubrey Singer, Controller of BBC2, who said that it would not be allowed to be shown.[18] Singer's explanation, given in March 1976, was that 'The play would have caused such offence to viewers that its impact would have been dulled and its message negated.'[19] Later, in an attempt to stifle accusations of political censorship, it was put about at high levels in the BBC that the play was 'bad art'. But *Financial Times* TV correspondent Chris Dunkley wrote: 'It is certainly a horribly vivid and frighteningly thought-provoking play. But it is tightly written, well acted, and quite competent in all technical respects.'[20]

The media had no intention of asking awkward questions. When, in September 1976, the European Commission of Human Rights ruled that the sensory deprivation techniques constituted torture, the media turned their indignation not against the British government, but against the Irish government. The response to the Commission's ruling was carefully manipulated by the Northern Ireland Office. The day before the report was to be published, Northern Ireland Secretary Merlyn Rees and his officials called several newspaper and TV editors into his Whitehall offices for drinks and a chat about what was likely to come out in the report. As a result, virtually every newspaper carried almost identical headlines the following day, highlighting not the torture verdict but Rees's reaction to it, and suggesting that it was the Irish government that was in the wrong for raising the issue in the first place.[21] The *Daily Express* headlined the story, 'Rees lashes Dublin over torture report', *The Times*, 'Angry Rees attack as

Dublin charge of torture is upheld', *The Daily Telegraph*, 'Rees angry as Eire presses torture issue', and so on.[22]

This theme was carried over into the editorial columns. The *Daily Mail* headed its comment, 'The fatal flaw of the Irish', and began 'Mr Merlyn Rees has every right to feel exasperated with the Irish'. Some papers, including *The Times*, accused the Irish government of providing propaganda for the Provisionals. *The Guardian* contended that the Irish government's motives would be 'seriously suspect' if it took the case on to the European Court: 'Dublin will be guilty of torturing Northern Ireland if it goes on force-feeding the Provisionals with propaganda.'[23] The papers made it easy to forget just who had tortured whom.

Excusing torture

Since the early fifties hundreds of scientific papers had been published on the effects of sensory deprivation, and in 1971 there were numerous predictions that the hooding would produce serious after-effects. This was confirmed in a study, by Robert Daly, a professor of psychiatry, of 13 of the 14 men who had been subjected to sensory deprivation. Daly found that 'in all but one case there was clear evidence of long-lasting psychological disabilities and suffering, in many cases severe, and that major psychosomatic illness had also been frequent.'[24] The study was made public in May 1976, yet in their responses to the European Commission's verdict in September the papers ignored it. Instead they went to great lengths to point out that sensory deprivation was less serious than other, more old-fashioned, torture techniques. As neuropsychologist Dr Tim Shallice commented, the media 'ignored scientific evidence on the techniques and encouraged the common-sense but fallacious view that psychological stresses are necessarily less inhumane than physical ones.'[25]

Thus *The Times* made 'a distinction between degrees of evil,' claiming that there was no conclusive evidence that the techniques would do mental damage and that they were different in purpose from 'the rack, water torture, electric torture, beating and such brutalities' because the aim of the latter was to induce terrifying pain, while the former aimed only at 'mental disorientation'.[26] *The Daily Telegraph*, which headed its leader 'Torture Misnamed', said, 'Surely there is a clear, common-sensical and useful distinction between such techniques and ripping out fingernails, beating people with steel rods and applying electric shocks to their genitalia . . . Many people who are neither callous nor fascist might accept the use of the Compton methods, whereas very few would endorse outright brutality.'[27] The *Telegraph* had drawn exactly the conclusion intended by the designers of this most modern form of torture. Producing the maximum distress to the victim with the minimum direct mutilation, sensory deprivation was intended to produce less political repercussions than cruder methods, and to be more acceptable to the inhabitants of liberal democracies. A telling example of this exercise in self-delusion was provided by a BBC World Service programme, *Ulster Today*, which said, 'Not since the days of hanging, drawing and quartering and the rack, has the word "torture" tainted the Mother of Parliaments here in Britain'. As journalist John Shirley, who cited this quote in the *New Statesman*, pointed out, that was 'simply not true':

> Britain holds the unenviable distinction of being the only European country to be accused before the Human Rights Commission *twice* for torturing people (the last time was in Cyprus). The techniques of sensory deprivation were not applied to *only* 14 men in Belfast *as long ago* as 1971, as the papers were so keen to emphasise. They have been used in varying combinations by British Army interrogators in almost every colonial campaign the UK has fought since the end of World War II.[28]

The European Court

When Britain appeared before the European Court in April 1977, two of Britain's most popular daily papers, *The Sun* and the *Mirror*, managed to ignore the four days of the hearing altogether. The other papers continued the old theme of bashing the Irish government but with a new twist: the Irish were now accused of helping the 'reds'.

'Russian interest in hearing of torture case against Britain', ran *The Times* headline above the story that 'An intensive new wave of anti-Western propaganda is expected to arise from the current final round of the protracted case over allegations of torture made against Britain by the Irish Republic . . .'[29] *The Sunday Telegraph*, in a feature article titled 'Ireland's Gift to Russia', attacked the Irish Attorney General, whom it called a 'fanatical' and 'blinkered Irish zealot'. He had, said the *Telegraph*, supplied the 'Reds' with 'human rights missiles', which 'can be used not only against Britain, but by inference against the entire Western democratic structure.'[30] But who, after all, had constructed the 'human rights missiles' in the first place?

The *Daily Express* tried another line of attack. A massive front page headline announced 'THE *REAL* OBSCENITY' over a picture of the aftermath of a bomb explosion in a Belfast street.[31] A no-warning car bomb had exploded the previous day at a funeral in the nationalist Ardoyne district, blowing the head off 19-year-old Sean Campbell and causing several serious injuries. Inconveniently for the *Express*, it was, as *The Irish Times* pointed out, obviously a loyalist bomb.[32] This did not suit the thrust of the *Express*'s article, which was that the IRA, rather than Britain, should be in the dock. So the paper stated that 'IRA or Loyalist splinter groups could be guilty.' It was not until the very end of the article that readers were told that the funeral taking place when the bomb exploded was for a volunteer in the junior IRA – hardly an IRA target.[33]

In January 1978 the European Court concluded that the techniques Britain had employed had caused 'intense physical and mental suffering and . . . acute psychiatric disturbance during interrogation'. But, they said – though with four of the 17 judges dissenting – this constituted not torture, but inhuman and degrading treatment.

The ultra-right-wing papers crowed with delight. 'Strasbourg Triumph' announced *The Daily Telegraph*, saying that a primitive reaction to the court's findings might be briefly indulged: 'That reaction is a whoop of joy at the discomfort of the Irish government.' It went on to justify the use of the techniques, with the words, 'Can a State threatened by anarchy be properly and realistically expected not to employ such methods?'

The *Daily Express*, too, decided that Britain was now entirely in the clear. Under two headlines, 'No torture, judges reject Irish bid to brand Britain' and 'Euro Court hits out at IRA terrorists', the *Express* announced that Ireland's bid to 'humble' Britain before the world had failed.[34]

The cartoonists responded to the verdict with vindictive glee. Jak of the London *Evening Standard* depicted an Irish bar in London where Irish building workers of neanderthal appearance were gloomily reading Irish papers headlined 'Torture – British army not guilty', while three English businessmen roar with laughter at the quip, 'How do you torture an Irishman? – You make him take you to court!'[35]

Sun journalist Jon Akass, in an article titled, 'Now the Irish have lost, let's pretend it didn't happen', wrote that 'the whole needling saga has wound up in an untidy mess, and it would be best if we followed our usual technique when it comes to unholy messes between Britain and Ireland. We should look the other way and pretend it hasn't happened.'[36] The irony was that while the press gloated over the Irish government's discomfiture and proclaimed Britain's innocence, they were once again pretending it wasn't happening. For a year now allegations had been coming out of Castlereagh and other interrogation centres of suspects being brutally beaten. Apart from a couple of television journalists, the media didn't want to know.

Reporting Bloody Sunday

Like the events of August 1971, Bloody Sunday, 30 January 1972, was to burn deep into the Irish consciousness but leave little imprint in Britain. Then, too, the British media fudged the events, suppressed investigations and blazened forth the idea that the British army had been 'cleared' of guilt.

Some British journalists, who were on the spot, conveyed something of the panic and grief of that terrible day. Simon Winchester told in the next day's *Guardian* how, just as the meeting at Free Derry Corner was getting under way,

> four or five armoured cars appeared in William Street and raced into the Rossville Street square, and several thousand people began to run away . . . Paratroopers piled out of their vehicles, many ran forward to make arrests, but others rushed to the street corners. It was these men, perhaps 20 in all, who opened fire with their rifles. I saw three men fall to the ground. One was still obviously alive, with blood pumping from his leg. The others, both apparently in their teens, seemed dead.
>
> The meeting at Free Derry Corner broke up in hysteria as thousands of people either ran or dived for the ground.
>
> Army snipers could be seen firing continuously towards the central Bogside streets and at one stage a lone army sniper on a street corner fired two shots at me as I peered around a corner. One shot chipped a large chunk of masonry from a wall behind me.
>
> Then people could be seen moving forward in Fahan Street, their hands above their heads. One man was carrying a white handkerchief. Gunfire was directed even at them and they fled or fell to the ground . . .

> Weeping men and women in the Bogside spent the next half
> hour in Lecky Road, pushing bodies of dead and injured people
> into cars and driving them to hospital. I saw seven such cars drive
> away with some of the bleeding bodies on the back seats, inert and
> lifeless.[37]

A national newspaper photographer, who was directly
behind the paratroopers when they jumped down from their
armoured cars, told *The Times*, 'I was appalled. They opened up
into a dense crowd of people. As far as I could see, they did not
fire over people's heads at all. There appeared to be no warning.'[38]

Times reporter Brian Cashinella said that he heard Land
Forces Commander General Ford say, 'Go on the paras, go and
get them.' Cashinella also noted,

> I found the reaction of the paratroopers in this situation interest-
> ing. They seemed to relish their work, and their eagerness
> manifested itself, to me, mainly in their shouting, cursing, and
> ribald language. Most of them seemed to regard the Bogsiders and
> people who took part in the parade as legitimate targets.[39]

John Graham of the *Financial Times* reported that 'there was a
great deal of shooting by the army at the crowd while the streets
were indeed full of people.'[40]

British army lies

But these eyewitness accounts, like those from Derry people, did
not prompt the British media into an outcry against the paratroopers' actions. For, soon after the shootings, senior British
army officers began to put out a succession of lying statements,
and the media gave these as much or more prominence as those
of the eyewitnesses. General Ford told BBC TV that Sunday night,
'Paratroops did not go in there shooting. In fact, they did not fire
until they were fired upon and my information at the moment
. . . is that the 3rd Battalion fired three rounds altogether, after
they'd had something between 10 and 20 fired at them.' Ford
went on to say that the dead 'may well not have been killed by our
soldiers.'[41]

Later that night, after a meeting of senior army officers at
the Lisburn HQ, an official statement, approved by Lieutenant-
General Harry Tuzo, GOC Northern Ireland, was released. This
said that after the paratroopers were deployed against rioters

they came under nail bomb attack and a fusillade of 50 to 80 rounds from the area of Rossville Flats and Glenfada Flats.

Fire was returned at seen gunmen and nail-bombers. Subsequently, as troops deployed to get at the gunmen, the latter continued to fire. In all, a total of well over 200 rounds was fired indiscriminately in the general direction of the soldiers. Fire continued to be returned only at identified targets.[42]

Next day, the Ministry of Defence gave the press what was claimed to be a repeat performance of the 'operational briefing' given to service chiefs. The briefing, given by Colonel Harry Dalzell-Payne and also released internationally through the British Information Services, the government news agency, was a ludicrous catalogue of invented detail. Seeking to demonstrate that 'all the army shooting was at identified targets in return of fire under the terms of the Yellow Card, which lays down when fire may be returned',[43] the briefing listed a series of incidents purporting to show that, during the main 'battle', the paratroopers 'returned fire' at eight nail-bombers and one petrol-bomber, killing two and hitting seven, and also at nine gunmen, killing two and hitting four. The Defence Ministry also claimed that soldiers of the Royal Anglian Regiment had hit two gunmen, and that four of the dead were on the army's wanted list.[44]

The army's version conflicted almost totally with the statements of eyewitnesses, including reporters. Virtually all the journalists present testified to the indiscriminate nature of the shooting. None had heard a concerted attack on the army. John Graham of the *Financial Times* reported that 'nobody who was present heard any nail bombs or the 50 to 80 shots which, the Army claims, started the battle.'[45] As it happened, though the army claimed that 'well over 200 rounds' were fired at them, not one soldier suffered bullet wounds. And even Lord Widgery, whose subsequent inquiry went to great pains to accommodate the army's view, was unable to prove that any of the dead had been handling arms; nor were any of the wounded prosecuted.

In fact, as Simon Winchester reported, 'The Provisionals had been under strict orders to keep their guns at home.'[46] Derry writer Eamonn McCann later recounted that both the Official and Provisional IRA had taken almost all their weapons out of the Bogside and into the Creggan Estate, since they feared it would be attacked by the British army when deserted during the demonstration. McCann reported that altogether only six shots were fired by both IRAs in the area where people were killed: two while the British soldiers were shooting, and four later. All missed.[47]

Deceptive headlines

Yet despite the fact that the British army's statements were transparently fictional, they strongly influenced the media coverage. In the headlines on the Monday morning, there was little trace of the army's responsibility for the deaths. '13 civilians are killed as soldiers storm the Bogside', said *The Times*, following this with 'March ends in shooting'; the next headline to meet the eye read, 'IRA told: "Shoot as many troops as possible" ', a reference to an Official IRA threat of retaliation.[48]

The Guardian, too, put its headline in the passive voice and left ambiguous the question of responsibility: '13 killed as para-troops break riot', it said, noting in smaller type, 'Soldiers were returning Derry sniper fire, says Army'. These headlines contradicted the spirit of Winchester's report, which began by telling how 'soldiers, firing into a large crowd of civil rights demonstrators, shot and killed 13 civilians,' and went on to take issue with the army's version.[49]

The Daily Telegraph's headline on the Monday was '13 SHOT DEAD IN LONDONDERRY', accompanied by 'Banned march erupts into riot' and 'IRA fired first says Army'. Its report began with wording which, like that in virtually every paper save *The Guardian*, again omitted to mention that the killing had been done by British troops: 'Thirteen men and youths were shot dead yesterday in Londonderry as a banned civil rights march turned into a riot on the edge of the Roman Catholic Bogside.' Like most other papers, the rest of its report balanced the army's version against the statements of eyewitnesses and nationalist politicians.[50]

Marchers blamed

The editorial writers spoke almost with one voice, putting most of the blame on the marchers. *The Times*, having noted 'the usual flat contradiction' between the official and local accounts of events, contended:

> It must be presumed that those who are inciting the Catholics to take to the streets know very well the consequences of what they

are doing. Londonderry had a taste of those consequences last night. The dead are witness to them.[51]

The Guardian carried a very lengthy leader arguing for improved security 'to keep the two communities from each other's throats', for talks on political arrangements and for the extension of economic aid. The leader is believed to have been written by John Cole, a Northern Ireland-born journalist who later went to *The Observer* and then became the BBC's political editor. Taking a view very different from that of the paper's reporter, Simon Winchester, the leader began:

> The disaster in Londonderry last night dwarfs all that has gone before in Northern Ireland. The march was illegal. Warning had been given of the danger implicit in continuing with it. Even so, the deaths stun the mind and must fill all reasonable people with horror. As yet it is too soon to be sure of what happened. The army has an intolerably difficult task in Ireland. At times it is bound to act firmly, even severely. Whether individual soldiers misjudged their situation yesterday, or were themselves too directly threatened, cannot yet be known. The presence of snipers in the late stages of the march must have added a murderous dimension. It is a terrible warning to everyone involved.[52]

Next day, leader writer and reporter clashed again. The editorialist argued that 'Neither side can escape condemnation,' and later, 'Bitter words after Sunday are understandable. They should not be treated as irrevocable.' Winchester, on the facing page, asked whether the 'dreadful Bogside tragedy' would 'become a fulcrum, which historians will argue led to fundamental and irrevocable change in the future and status of Northern Ireland'. Below Winchester's was an article by Harold Jackson arguing with belligerent dogmatism that 'the simple truth can be stated right now: if there had been no march 13 people would have been alive this morning, and no amount of specious rationalisation can get round that'.[53]

But the paper's readers were no so easily gulled. For a week the letters columns were dominated by Ireland, with many writers dissenting from the editorial line. Some attacked the discrepancy between Monday's leader and Winchester's report, and one prophesied angrily, 'because Derry is nearer home than Sharpeville, Stormont, Westminster, and the British army will escape with little more than mild tut-tutting from liberal editorials'.[54]

The Daily Telegraph, in a leader titled 'DEATH MARCH', equated the civil rights movement with the IRA, and blamed both for the carnage:

> It [the civil rights movement] does not murder; it simply creates conditions favourable to the murders attempted by others and leaves the army in the last resort with no alternative but to fire. Its courage may be less than that of the IRA; its guilt is not. The IRA has promised to avenge the dead. Their blood is on its own hands.[55]

The *Daily Express* took the same line:

> Many members of this organisation are neither civil nor right. They simply promote the aims of the IRA. And even those civil righters who do not condone violence provoke it by defying the ban on processions . . . The bloody battle in Londonderry follows the familiar pattern of gunmen using street protests as cover. The toll is the price of mindless violence.[56]

Again, the *Daily Mail*, in a 'comment' on the front page titled, 'The *real* killers?', asked,

> Who is really responsible for the 13 deaths in Ulster yesterday?
> British bullets will be found in most of their bodies . . . but the blood is on the consciences of irresponsible political leaders and the fanatical IRA.

On an inside page the *Mail* fulminated, 'those who died were not martyrs to civil rights . . . Whether terrorists, hooligans or innocent civilians, they are all victims of the bloody lunacy that convulses Northern Ireland.'[57]

The *Daily Mirror*

The *Mirror*'s commentators, however, refrained from blaming the marchers. On the Monday, the paper proffered no opinion. On the Tuesday, it carried a lengthy piece by John Beavan asking, 'Was there a blunder?', which questioned the army's account in some detail.[58] This was, however, partly negated by the centre-page spread. Proof of the media's susceptibility to army statements, this did a classic balancing act. The headline right across the top asked, 'Was the Army to blame for Bloody Sunday?' The left-hand page announced 'GUILTY, Bogside accuses troops', while on the right the verdict was 'NOT GUILTY, "Four of the dead were wanted men" '. Between the two was a cartoon showing a grave with two wreaths on it: one wreath carried a label reading 'BLAME THE BRITISH', while the other was labelled 'BLAME THE IRA'.[59]

On the Thursday, the *Mirror* departed radically from the line taken by the other dailies. A massive editorial, covering pages one and two and titled 'HOW TO END THE KILLING IN IRELAND', put forward a 'five point plan'. First, 'Bring back the British troops': 'Like it or not, it is believed throughout Ireland (North and South) that the soldiers are there simply to bolster up the Stormont Protestant majority.' Bloody Sunday had 'irrevocably hardened that belief', making the army's task impossible. The paper then called for the introduction of UN troops, the ending of internment, talks on the constitutional future perhaps leading to a redrawing of the border, and the appointment of a special minister 'to start and maintain the impetus of political effort.'[60]

But the *Mirror*'s reportage was not consistent. Like other papers, it directed more venom at Bernadette Devlin for hitting the Home Secretary – 'Murder! she screams – then hits Maudling', was one headline[61] – and at the 'mobs' who burned the British embassy in Dublin, than it had directed at the troops who had killed 13 civilians. On the Wednesday its front page cried 'THE FLAMES OF HATRED'. The accompanying picture was captioned, 'WALL OF FIRE – a huge wall of flames engulfs the front of the British Embassy in Dublin after demonstrators hurled a vicious barrage of petrol bombs in a night of bitter mob fury'. Inside was a half-page leader headed 'The song of Bernadette'. Describing her as 'Miss Bernadette Devlin of the long, lank hair and nasty left hook', the editorial went on,

> Miss Devlin is entitled to protest about what she says happened in the Bogside in Londonderry . . .
> But Miss Devlin, who protests about violence, is not entitled to import violence into the House of Commons . . .
> Bernadette the Member of Parliament sings her own song of cruelty. Exults about vengeance. Is dry-eyed about coffins. Equates protest with death and destruction . . .
> Bernadette, MP, is not singing a song. Or a lament. Or a protest. She is singing a dirge.[62]

While on Thursday and Friday the front page was devoted to the plea for troop withdrawal, on the Saturday the *Mirror* fell for a blatant piece of British army propaganda. 'FAKE TROOPS PERIL

IN ULSTER' and 'Army warned of an "IRA murder plan" ' were the front page headlines. Reporter Chris Buckland told how

> Army chiefs were warned yesterday of an IRA plot to start fresh bloodshed in Ulster.
>
> They were told that terrorists disguised in stolen uniforms will be in Newry, County Down, for tomorrow's illegal Civil Rights march.
>
> They fear that the IRA men may try to start a new bloody battle by firing on the crowds of marchers.
>
> A tip-off about the fake soldiers was given by a woman who telephoned the Army commander in the province, General Sir Harry Tuzo.
>
> She said her son and son-in-law – both IRA members – had been issued with British uniforms and told to wear them in Newry tomorrow . . .
>
> Security chiefs took her warning seriously because of the theft of 157 Army combat suits from a Londonderry dry cleaner's a month ago.[63]

It was not till the end of the story that Buckland noted briefly, 'Civil rights leaders in Newry dismissed the story as "propaganda" to clear the Army of responsibility for last Sunday's thirteen killings in Londonderry.'[64] In the event, the Newry march passed off without incident.

The Widgery Tribunal

In Britain, at least, where the ideological ties between the media and the army were strong, the army's lies had helped to stave off condemnation of their actions on Bloody Sunday. The authorities' second diversionary thrust was the immediate setting up of a tribunal of inquiry under Lord Widgery. It was to prove a valuable means of hindering investigation and, finally, of getting the army off the hook.

Taking advantage of the vagueness of the contempt laws, the Press Office at 10 Downing Street was quick to seek a blanket ban on coverage of Bloody Sunday.[65] They claimed that anything which anticipated the Tribunal's findings could be in contempt. But in fact there had never been a prosecution over media investigations of issues that were the subject of tribunals of inquiry. Though technically the contempt laws do apply, legal opinion would consider that contempt in such cases would not involve journalists' investigations into what had occurred, but would involve attempts to influence directly the progress of a tribunal, such as intimidation or bribery of witnesses, or abusing members of a tribunal and trying to influence them improperly. Legal opinion would not support using the contempt laws to stop the media investigating a matter of public concern just because a tribunal had been set up.[66]

The Sunday Times and Thames TV nevertheless used the hypothetical possibility of prosecution as an excuse to suppress accounts of Bloody Sunday which would have been very damaging to the army's case. *The Sunday Times* suppressed an investigation by their Insight team, which according to one account would have revealed that the army had planned to draw out the IRA and shoot them down and then, when the IRA did not surface, shot down unarmed civilians instead.[67] *The Sunday Times* claimed: 'The law is that until the Lord Chief Justice completes his inquiry nobody may offer to the British public any consecutive account of the events in Derry last weekend.'[68] *The Observer*, too, suppressed a 'detailed reconstruction' of the day's events, maintaining that its publication was 'precluded by the law of contempt of court'.[69]

Thames TV were preparing a programme piecing together the events of Bloody Sunday. After the Downing Street warning, they consulted the IBA and their own lawyers, who felt the risk should not be taken despite the fact that there was no precedent for prosecution. The lawyers apparently thought that even editing the filmed interviews would be prejudicial, because it would mean selecting certain evidence for presentation. In the end Thames compromised by choosing two of the rolls of film they had shot, and transmitting them on 3 February unedited. One roll was the eyewitness account of a Welsh ex-warrant officer, who lived in the immediate area of the shootings. This was 'balanced' by the second roll, which consisted of interviews with paratroopers. The paras harmed their case by contradicting one another; but much more damaging material was left out in the 20 or so rolls of film that were not used, which included interviews with local Catholics. One of the paras, a lieutenant, said in the televised programme that he had seen a gunman: he later admitted to the Widgery Tribunal that this statement was a lie.[70]

Whitewash

Thus the media were effectively silenced until April, when the Widgery Report came out. The report was so self-evidently a whitewash that 'to widgery' became a new verb to describe the process. Widgery began with the spurious argument, already advanced by the press, that there would have been no deaths if there had been no march. Not only was this proved fallacious by the fact that the subsequent, equally illegal, Newry march passed off peacefully; but also, as some commentators noted, it could equally well be argued that there would have been no deaths if Northern Ireland had never been set up, if Catholics had been treated decently, if the army had not been sent in, and if there had been no internment policy.[71]

Widgery gave far more credence to army evidence than to evidence from other sources, resulting in conclusions based on wishful thinking rather than fact. He concluded, for example, that 'There is no reason to suppose that the soldiers would have opened fire if they had not been fired upon first,' and that 'The soldiers escaped injury by reason of their superior fieldcraft and training.' His conclusions were self-contradictory: 'Soldiers who identified armed gunmen fired upon them in accordance with the standing orders in the Yellow Card,' he wrote, and 'There was no general breakdown in discipline.' Yet he also concluded that 'None of the deceased or wounded is proved to have been shot while handling a firearm or bomb.' Further, in one incident, at Glenfada Park, where four civilians were killed, Widgery found that on the balance of probability 'when these four men were shot the group of civilians was not acting aggressively and that the shots were fired without justification'.[72] In this incident, Widgery found, 'Soldier H' had fired 19 shots which were wholly unaccounted for.

But Widgery's findings, bland as they were, were themselves whitewashed for presentation to the British public. The first front page reports scarcely referred to even the limited criticisms Widgery had made, let alone offered a serious probe of the report. Simon Winchester later explained,

> The report itself was to be issued on the afternoon of Wednesday, April 19. In fact, the astute press officers of the Ministry of Defence telephoned the Defence Correspondents of the national newspapers the night before – the Tuesday night – to 'leak', in highly selective terms, the Lord's conclusions to be published next

day . . . Those who read their front pages on Wednesday morning
would have had to be very short-sighted indeed to have missed the
results of the PR work.[73]

'Widgery clears paratroops for Bloody Sunday', announced
The Daily Telegraph.[74] 'Bloody Sunday Paras "clear" ', said the
Daily Mirror.[75] 'Widgery blames IRA and clears the Army', said
the *Daily Express*, with reporter Gordon Greig telling how

> The Army was not to blame for Londonderry's Bloody
> Sunday. This is the crucial finding of Lord Widgery . . .
>   The main guilt is fixed firmly on the IRA.
>   But the army is not completely cleared.[76]

But the Ministry of Defence had not finished. The day the
report was published, 19 April, they held a press conference. To
ensure a sympathetic hearing, the Ministry's PR people refused
to allow in any but 'accredited defence correspondents'.
Winchester, who had been in the thick of events on Bloody
Sunday, was refused admission. 'I was furious,' he wrote. 'None
of these accredited correspondents had been in Derry on the day
in question, save for the elderly Brigadier Thompson of the
Telegraph', who admitted in print next day 'that he missed the
entire story because he was parking his car.'[77]

The day after publication, *The Times* and *The Guardian*,
both of which had refrained from carrying the advance leak, did
at least include 'buts' in their headlines. 'Sniper started Derry
shootings but Army underestimated hazard', said *The Times*,
while *The Guardian* announced, 'Widgery clears the army but
blames individual soldiers'. The leader writers of both papers,
however, fully accepted Widgery's conclusions: *The Guardian*'s
editorialist once again clashing with Simon Winchester, who, in
an article on the facing page, bitterly condemned the report as 'a
profound disappointment'.[78]

Other papers were less equivocal, continuing in the same
vein as the previous day. 'SNIPER BLAMED FOR BLOODY SUNDAY',
said the *Mirror*.[79] 'Army did not fire first, says Widgery', was the
Telegraph's version,[80] while the *Daily Mail*, in a leader titled 'A
myth defused', bragged sanctimoniously,

> Against cynical propagandists the British Government replies with
> judicial truth.
>   It is like trying to exterminate a nest of vipers by the Queens-
> berry rules.
>   Even so, over the past 2½ years of mounting terrorism, the

record shows – and it is a record which now includes Lord Widgery's report – that our troops are doing an impossible job impossibly well.[81]

Self-delusion could scarcely go further. The British army had, in effect, been absolved and the British public could rest easy.

In the years that followed, the media continued to write British responsibility for Bloody Sunday out of history. It became the day 'when 13 men died in shootings during a demonstration', as Chris Ryder wrote in *The Sunday Times*,[82] or, as in *The Guardian*'s review of the decade, 'Bloody Sunday: 13 civilians killed during army dispersal of Bogside anti-internment marches, Londonderry.'[83] The Attorney-General declined to authorise prosecution of any of the soldiers involved, and the authorities quietly made out of court payments, to the tune of £95,000 by September 1976,[84] to the injured and relatives of the dead. The BBC asked writer David Wheeler to edit the transcripts of the Widgery inquiry for re-enactment: but, in Wheeler's words, 'enthusiasm for the project cooled and the script remains in the files.'[85] In 1978 the BBC made a film about Derry called *A City on the Border*. One scene showed a mother putting flowers on her son's grave, which bore the words, 'Murdered by British Paratroopers on Bloody Sunday'. The woman laying her bunch of flowers on the grave stayed in: but the shot of the tombstone was cut on the instructions of the Controller of BBC1. The British public was not to know the significance of her action.[86]

Reporting torture: 1977–79

By the beginning of 1976, the Labour government had given up trying to patch up the situation in the Six Counties through political initiatives. Instead, they brought in the Ulsterisation policy, cracking down hard on nationalist dissent while at the same time trying to make the Six Counties appear 'normal' to the outside world.

At the end of 1975, internment, an overtly political measure, was ended, and the 'special category' status given to convicted political offenders was phased out. From now on, suspected members of paramilitary organisations were to be jailed through the courts, and, once imprisoned, to be treated – in theory at least – as ordinary criminals.

The new system, delivering prisoners to the H Blocks of Long Kesh prison – renamed 'the Maze' by the authorities in an attempt to rid it of its concentration camp image – by way of interrogation centres and non-jury courts, quickly became known to nationalists as the 'conveyor belt'. Resting on emergency legislation, which itself defined 'terrorist' offenders as being politically motivated, the system was anything but normal. The legislation not only allowed cases to be heard by a judge sitting alone without a jury: it also, crucially, allowed confessions obtained by force to be used as evidence. Torture to obtain these confessions quickly became the key element in the new security policy. But if the fact that torture was being used were to leak beyond the boundaries of the North, it would undermine once more Britain's pretensions to being democratic and place a question mark over the nature of its role in Ireland. The authorities were determined that this would not happen.[87]

Kenneth Newman, later to be appointed head of London's Metropolitan Police, was in charge of the police end of the operation. He became Chief Constable of the RUC on 1 May 1976, and soon made Castlereagh police barracks into a full-time, specialist interrogation centre. Within weeks of Newman's appointment, the brutality allegations began. Between them, the politicians and the British media were to ensure that no government action was taken to moderate brutality in Castlereagh and other interrogation centres until nearly three years later.

Two television journalists, the BBC's Keith Kyle and Peter Taylor of Thames TV, tried to bring the issue to the attention of the British public. But, far from provoking any investigation, their programmes led to such a barrage of vilification from politicians and the press that television, too, was effectively silenced.

The Bernard O'Connor interview

Keith Kyle's interviews with Bernard O'Connor, a Fermanagh schoolteacher and pillar of the local community, and Michael Lavelle, production controller at a factory, were shown on BBC1's *Tonight* programme on 2 March 1977.

Both men made horrifying allegations about the way they had been treated by interrogators at Castlereagh. Bernard O'Connor told how for three to four hours 'I was made to stand on my toes with my knees in a bent position and my hands out in front of me'. If he moved, he was slapped. He was kicked, punched and hurled across the room. The interrogators made him run on the spot, and do press-ups and sit-ups, and then repeat these activities naked. They made him stand with his slightly soiled underpants over his head, and pick up cigarette butts from the floor with his mouth. They tied a tracksuit top over his head and blocked his nose and mouth so that he fainted. All the while they were trying to get him to sign a confession.[88]

Keith Kyle, a senior and very experienced reporter, and BBC producer Janine Thomason came across the story by chance. They were in Enniskillen making a film about local government when a local councillor approached them about Bernard O'Connor. The *Tonight* team were evidently shocked by O'Connor's allegations: as journalist Mary Holland wrote in the *New Statesman*,

> Their surprise indicated powerfully just how effective the blackout of any really uncomfortable news from Northern Ireland has become. Every journalist who writes from Belfast (at least those with any contacts beyond the army and the Northern Ireland Office) knows that for some time now there has been growing evidence of the use of interrogation methods which, if they do not exactly amount to the scientifically controlled torture techniques which Mr Silkin swore at Strasbourg we would never use again, feel very much the same to those on the receiving end.[89]

At the first meeting between Keith Kyle and Bernard O'Connor, no mention was made of television. Keith Kyle put the idea to him a week later, and had considerable difficulty in persuading both O'Connor and Lavelle to appear.[90] Having done so, Kyle approached the interview very cautiously. He held three discussions with O'Connor, one of these cross-examinations lasting seven hours.[91]

The BBC authorities were also very nervous about the project. The programme was checked and rechecked at the highest level before it was given the go-ahead, as the BBC chiefs were keen to emphasise later when defending themselves against accusations that they had helped the 'terrorists'. The Northern Ireland Controller, Richard Francis, saw the programme twice before it was broadcast.[92] After the first viewing by what Francis described as 'a quorum of senior broadcasters in Belfast',[93] the *Tonight* team were sent back to do more interviewing, with the result that transmission was a week later than scheduled. Director-General Charles Curran elaborated:

> we did go back and check eight character witnesses, one doctor
> who had examined him immediately after release from interroga-
> tion, and his solicitor, and some of those character witnesses were
> produced on the programme. In addition, we did actually show the
> certificates given by the doctor.[94]

From Belfast the programme was referred to the Director-
General, who in turn referred it to the Board of Governors.[95]
The newly formed Campaign for Free Speech on Ireland com-
mented drily that such 'exhaustive checks for accuracy . . . did
not apply to stories emanating from British Army or Northern
Ireland Office sources.'[96]

Fury from the right

Immediately after the programme was transmitted, on 2 March,
the storm broke. Unionist MP Robert Bradford said he had been
petitioning the BBC not to run the 'insensitively timed' programme.[97] Belfast Orange Order leader Thomas Passmore said
it was 'republican propaganda'.[98] Northern Ireland Secretary
Roy Mason was reportedly 'very annoyed indeed'.[99] He issued a
statement saying that 'the questioning of the two men is considered to be fully justified in the light of information available'
and that the programme was 'one-sided'.[100] This 'one-sidedness',
however, could hardly be blamed on the *Tonight* team, since the
RUC had declined their invitation to appear, offering the shaky
justification that, since a police inquiry was in progress, the
matter was *sub judice*. The RUC were furious and put forward a
line of argument that was to pay off handsomely later. 'RUC fear
"brutality" claim on TV will lead to IRA killings', ran the headline
over a *Daily Telegraph* article. Reporter James Allan quoted a
'senior officer' as saying, 'The fear here is that terrorists might
seize on this as provocation to kill more policemen.'[101] The
Northern Ireland Police Authority wrote a letter of complaint to
BBC Chairman Sir Michael Swann.[102]

A dozen Tory MPs, some of them 'extremely angry',
launched a heated attack at a private House of Commons meet-
ing on 7 March when they confronted BBC Northern Ireland
Controller Richard Francis. The meeting, chaired by Aldershot
MP Julian Critchley, had been organised by the Tory Northern
Ireland and media backbench committees.[103] Tory Northern
Ireland spokesman Airey Neave launched a sustained campaign
against the BBC, first protesting to Sir Michael Swann and then

making a speech in which he accused the BBC of undermining the propaganda war and helping 'terrorism':

> We are losing the propaganda war in Northern Ireland. The security forces may make arrests, but skilful propaganda is as lethal as a gun or a bomb. A review of present attitudes to media freedom is needed therefore, to take account of a desperate emergency. Some of the media deny that we are really at war with terrorism. Some of their actions actually stimulate the hardcore terrorist mentality. The BBC, in particular, pronounce on the security situation in Northern Ireland with studied grandiloquence and ignore the true dangers . . . This *Tonight* programme has had the most damaging effects on morale in the RUC. In justifying it on grounds of 'impartiality', the BBC have given the impression that they are not really on the side of the civil power in Northern Ireland.[104]

Neave, who was speaking with the approval of Tory leader Margaret Thatcher and her deputy William Whitelaw, went on to call not only for a review of media guidelines but also for tougher security measures, including the reinforcement of the SAS and the creation of a new anti-terrorist force, concluding, 'We surely have a solemn duty to combine all legal, security and publicity weapons available to us.'

The more liberal papers took issue with Neave. *The Guardian* called his speech an 'unhappy echo from Pretoria'.[105] *The Sunday Times* said with colonial superiority that 'The notorious problem is how a civilised country can overpower uncivilised people without becoming less civilised in the process.' The paper went on to say that since the forces of order were 'understandably slow at disclosing their own lapses', it sometimes became 'the business of the media to inquire into them instead'.[106] The discussion had drifted right away from the allegations against the RUC and into a debate on media freedom.

As Eamonn McCann pointed out in an article in the Irish magazine *Hibernia* listing a host of unreported brutality allegations, 'A debate about the role of the media in the North would properly concern not one isolated instance of brutalisation being reported, but why most instances are not.'[107]

Two days after Neave's speech, the RUC union, the Police Federation, combined with the press to deliver the *coup de grâce* to any further consideration of RUC interrogation methods. Eleven days after the *Tonight* programme, an 18-year-old constable was shot dead in Fermanagh by the Provisional IRA. Police

Federation Chairman Alan Wright immediately blamed this on the *Tonight* programme. 'BBC blamed for police killing', said *The Guardian*'s headline. 'TRIAL BY TV: BBC ACCUSED', proclaimed the *Mirror*. The *Daily Express* capped them all with a huge headline reading 'MURDER BY TV'.[108]

Over the next couple of weeks the row petered out, Bernard O'Connor's experiences long since forgotten. The BBC governors lumbered slowly and with evident trepidation to *Tonight*'s support. As Keith Kyle wrote, 'Before the governors decided . . . that *Tonight* was correct in transmitting the interview they had asked for and received a detailed memorandum in which I described every stage of the preparation and production of the interview and the motives that determined every important decision that I made.'[109] BBC Chairman Sir Michael Swann reiterated in a letter to *The Times* that 'we do not give equal time to right and wrong', proffering a lengthy defence of the decision to transmit the *Tonight* programme: soul-searching that was never required when programmes stuck closer to the authorities' point of view.[110] The BBC now lapsed into a silence on the torture issue that was to last more than a year.

Keith Kyle tried staunchly to bring the discussion back to where it belonged, pointing out in a letter to both *The Times* and *The Guardian* that if Bernard O'Connor's account was correct,

> Mr O'Connor's experience is in direct violation of the directive of 1972, cited in the British Government's pleadings before the European Commission of Human Rights at Strasbourg that 'under no circumstances must there be resort to physical violence, blindfolds or hoods, standing or other positions of stress for long periods to induce exhaustion . . . [Prisoners] must not be threatened, insulted or subjected to torture or cruel, inhuman and degrading treatment.'[111]

Kyle went on to point out that if such interrogations were being carried on at Castlereagh 'it means that practices declared in February 1977 by the Attorney-General to be five years out of date were in use in one of the main holding centres in Belfast in January 1977.'[112]

His pleas for action fell on deaf ears. In July that year the Director of Public Prosecutions decided that the detectives accused by O'Connor would not be prosecuted, and the police said no action would be taken on his complaint. RUC Chief Constable Kenneth Newman maintained that suspects were deliberately inflicting injuries on themselves to discredit the police.[113] It was not until June 1980 that O'Connor was finally vindicated, when he was awarded £5,000, with costs, 'in compensation as exemplary damages for maltreatment during interrogation by the Royal Ulster Constabulary.'[114] And two years later, in November 1982, the RUC was ordered to pay £1,000 damages to Michael Lavelle, the man interviewed alongside O'Connor in the *Tonight* programme.[115]

'Inhuman and Degrading Treatment'

When Thames TV's *This Week* team took up the issue of interrogation techniques in October 1977, they met an almost identical response. Peter Taylor was an experienced reporter, with some thirty programmes on the North of Ireland under his belt. The bulk of these were undeniably middle-of-the-road and, in politicians' eyes, uncontroversial. Indeed, in June 1977 *The Observer*'s then TV correspondent W. Stephen Gilbert had delivered a brief but stinging attack on Taylor over a film portrait of Ian Paisley: 'Taylor's wet line of questioning . . . gave the subject a triumphant ride.'[116]

In mid-1977 Peter Taylor and the *This Week* team began to take a more critical look at politics in the Six Counties. In August *This Week* made a film about the Queen's Jubilee visit which went right against the grain of the rest of the sycophantic media coverage by showing how 'more than anything, the Royal visit highlighted the political divisions in the province'.[117] The IBA insisted on alterations being made, then banned the programme two minutes before transmission, finally allowing it to be shown two weeks after the visit when it was no longer topical.[118] In September *This Week* made a programme about the life of 'special category' prisoners in the compounds of Long Kesh: the IBA had no objections, but it displeased the politicians. More than two weeks after the programme, 'Life Behind the Wire', went out, one of the interviewees, prison officer Desmond Irvine, was shot dead by the IRA. Although Irvine had written to Taylor praising the film, the authorities had no hesitation in blaming his death on *This Week*.[119] But this was mild in comparison with the storm that followed *This Week*'s Castlereagh investigation.

Peter Taylor wrote later that 'If Northern Ireland is the most sensitive issue in British broadcasting, interrogation techniques are its most sensitive spot.'[120] By October 1977, when *This Week* embarked on their programme 'Inhuman and Degrading Treatment', concern about the brutality allegations had spread to senior legal circles in Belfast. *This Week* decided to look at ten cases of alleged ill-treatment, each of which was backed by strong medical evidence. The RUC tried to get the programme banned and refused all co-operation with the programme-makers, and, since the IBA insisted that the RUC's views must be represented, it looked as if the programme was scuppered. The day before transmission, however, Chief Constable Newman offered to make a filmed statement: he refused an interview, which would have allowed Peter Taylor to challenge him. The inclusion of such an unchallenged statement of denial set a dangerous precedent,[121] but *This Week* accepted it. The IBA's stance had virtually blackmailed them into it: no RUC statement, no programme.

Newman strikes

Newman then launched a major pre-emptive propaganda strike against the programme. A few hours before it was due to go out on 27 October the 'very angry' Chief Constable issued a statement putting the RUC on special alert: 'It is feared that terrorists could use the occasion as an attempt to "justify" attacks against police officers and all members of the RUC have been advised to take every possible precaution as to their safety.'[122] Several papers took the hint. ' "Death sentence by TV" warning', proclaimed the *Daily Express*.[123] 'Ulster "murder risk" TV film screened', chorused the *Yorkshire Post*.[124] *The Daily Telegraph* headlined its leader 'LETHAL TELEVISION', demanding that 'If the IBA will not stop this homicidal irresponsibility, the Government must step in.'[125]

Again, press reaction to the programme concentrated overwhelmingly on the authorities' fury, and did not trouble to look at the torture allegations made by not only interrogation victims but also doctors in the programme.[126] Labour Northern Ireland Secretary Roy Mason, Tory spokesperson Airey Neave and Chief Constable Newman thundered into the attack, backed up by loyalist politicians such as Robert Bradford MP, who called the programme a 'disgusting spectacle'.[127] The Northern Ireland Office issued an unprecedented personal attack:

> It is significant that the producers and the reporter of this programme have produced three programmes in quick succession which have concentrated on presenting the

blackest possible picture of events in Northern Ireland.

After the last programme on prisons, a prison officer who appeared on the programme was murdered, and last night's programme may well place police officers, who deserve all support, at even further risk. That is not what one expects of responsible commentators.[128]

Roy Mason, reportedly 'very angry indeed', despatched a 'stern and strict' letter of complaint to the IBA.[129] Three weeks later in the House of Commons, when Labour backbencher Philip Whitehead called for an investigation into the RUC's interrogation procedures, Mason not only refused this, but went on to make a series of near-hysterical accusations against *This Week*. 'The programme was riddled with unsubstantiated accusations. I have said it was irresponsible and insensitive, and I still believe it.' He recalled *This Week*'s programmes on 'the black side of the Queen's visit' and on prisons, and with scant regard for accuracy claimed that a prison officer had been murdered 'within 48 hours' of the latter – in fact, Irvine was killed 15 days later. He went on to claim that 'there is a propaganda wave against the success of the RUC' and to make a statement that was bizarrely off the mark but was nevertheless used in a headline by *The Times*: 'We have to recognize that cheque book television is much more dramatic and dangerous than cheque book journalism. It can quickly frighten and more easily incite.'[130]

Chief Constable Newman, after first reportedly consulting police lawyers about the possibility of prosecuting Thames TV, entertained IBA Chairman (sic) Lady Plowden to lunch at his Belfast HQ and was apparently 'still furious' afterwards.[131] The IBA was clearly feeling the heat: it was, said *The Daily Telegraph*, 'privately alarmed and concerned by the genuine anguish and innumerable protests which the documentary provoked.' The *Telegraph* went on to say there was the possibility of 'a fence-mending documentary featuring the excellent work of the RUC'.[132]

Airey Neave made a virulent denunciation of Thames, accusing them of providing 'just the propaganda tonic needed to revive the flagging spirits of terrorism.'[133] He, too, protested personally to Lady Plowden, who for this meeting was accompanied by IBA Director-General Sir Brian Young.[134] The IBA buckled under the pressure: one of its officers told *This Week* producer David Elstein to 'lay off Northern Ireland' and to use another reporter.[135] *This Week* did not touch the torture issue again for eight months.

'Black' propaganda and diversions

A little 'black' propaganda was stirred into the brew for good measure. The assertions of Newman and Mason that the injuries suffered during interrogation were 'self-inflicted' surfaced in a highly imaginative article in *The Daily Telegraph*, which would have been comical were it not for the context. 'IRA AWARD PRIZES FOR FAKE CLAIMS OF "RUC BRUTALITY" ', announced the paper, and reporter Gerald Bartlett explained:

> Prizes are given according to the degree of self-inflicted injury, I understand.
>
> Investigations indicate that one hard-line Provisional was given large whiskeys and a box of king-size cigarettes for punching himself in both eyes while in the RUC's Castlereagh Interrogation Centre – and then filing a brutality complaint against police.
>
> Another, I understand, was given sweets and cigarettes after mysteriously 'acquiring' boot bruises on his legs and thighs while held for police questioning.

Bartlett quoted 'intelligence officers' as saying,

> It's now reached the level of a macabre prize draw for masochists.
>
> But it is also part of the deadly propaganda war being increasingly waged by terrorists in Ulster.[136]

Bartlett claimed that the story came from 'republican sources' and had been confirmed by mysterious 'intelligence officers'. A clue to the true source came towards the end of the piece, where Bartlett described some 'confidential documents' which 'sources close to Mr Mason said he was studying'. The alleged documents painted an extraordinary picture of life in Castlereagh:

> A prisoner was found slapping his boots against each other and slapping one of them against his thigh . . . a police officer saw a prisoner banging his head against the floor . . . After a prisoner was returned to his cell by two police officers, they claimed, they saw him stick his fingers in both eyes and also punch himself in both eyes . . . A man being interviewed took off a shoe and struck himself on the head.[137]

Needless to say, this dumbfounding report provoked some hilarity in the hard-pressed nationalist areas.[138] According to statistics provided by the *Telegraph* itself just two days before, in the previous year there had been 648 complaints laid against the RUC alleging assault during arrest or interview.

Meanwhile the *Telegraph* had also, in a clever diversionary move, started another investigation: not, needless to say, into the suffering of nationalists in Castlereagh but into 'the "squalid" conditions in which some British troops are forced to live in Ulster.' Troops were living 'in fetid, airless and overcrowded slums, which their officers admitted were worse than prison cells', said the paper, quoting Airey Neave as saying the conditions were 'worse than Colditz'.[139] Whether this 'investigation' had been prompted by the *Telegraph*, Airey Neave or the army was not clear. But *The Sun* lost no time in reproducing it, almost word for word, across its front page. 'SHAME OF OUR SOLDIERS IN ULSTER SLUMS: Barracks "worse than Colditz" ' declared the headlines incongruously placed alongside a near-naked woman. Inside, its leader was headed 'End this outrage!' – a demand the paper would never make about British-sanctioned interrogation methods.[140]

Once again, the media, following in the politicians' wake, had swiftly obliterated the point at issue. Once more, Mason got away with refusing to institute an inquiry. A few days after the programme went out, however, Amnesty International revealed that they were planning an investigation.[141] It was not until Amnesty reported on its findings in June 1978 that television touched the subject again. As Christmas approached, the leader writers complacently congratulated Roy Mason. In *The Observer*, John Cole opined that 'at last people well placed to judge are saying . . . that violence will probably peter out over the next year or two . . . Roy Mason has robbed the IRA of sustainable hope by his schoolmasterly precision.'[142] *The Times* declared that 'After too many misjudgements and vacillations security policy is moving along sensible lines.'[143] The *Express*, as usual, spoke with unconcealed jingoism:

WHAT DO WE WANT for Northern Ireland, that wretched, God-stricken back alley of Europe where they shoot people's kneecaps.

As a matter of fact, yes – there *are* prospects for Ulster. She has easily the best, toughest, least tractable and most effective Secretary of State ever in Roy Mason.[144]

The Amnesty Report

More than a year after Keith Kyle's interview with Bernard O'Connor, the publication of the Amnesty Report in June 1978 finally made it impossible for the politicians and the media to evade the issue of torture any longer. The Amnesty mission had looked at 78 cases, a tiny proportion of those who had alleged torture by the RUC. Amnesty listed a number of cases in which medical evidence corroborated the allegations, such as Case No. 3, who alleged 'psychologically exhausting procedure, threats, beatings, humiliation, attempts to suffocate him'.[145] The report concluded that 'Maltreatment has taken place with sufficient frequency to warrant a public enquiry to investigate it.'

The report was due to be published on Tuesday 13 June, but over a week earlier it was leaked to *The Guardian* and *The Sunday Times* and then to a group of politicians from the North of Ireland. The BBC's *Tonight* programme quoted extensively from it. But ITV was to be forbidden to touch it: the cumulative pressure from Mason, Airey Neave and the RUC had paid off.

Following in the steps of the national press and *Tonight*, Thames TV's *This Week* planned a programme to discuss the report. As described by David Wheeler in *The Listener*, the programme

> consisted of four or five minutes of edited film of interviews with Catholic doctors who had attended some prisoners, with the Rev. Ian Paisley and with a leading Protestant who spoke up for the police. This was to be followed by a studio discussion involving Enoch Powell, John Taylor and Patrick Duffy.[146]

Wheeler commented, 'Aficionados of the way the box covers Northern Ireland will recognise this as straight-down-the-middle stuff, balanced almost to the point of anaesthesia.'

The programme was due to go out on Thursday 8 June. The IBA met that morning and banned it without even seeing it. Disregarding the extensive leaks and the fact that all participants in the programme had full knowledge of the report, the IBA said that 'a discussion of the Report should be postponed until it is published, thereby giving those involved and the general public a chance to study it in detail.'[147] *This Week* reporter Peter Taylor described the ban as 'a disgraceful act of political censorship'.[148] Thames TV's management issued a statement expressing regret at the IBA's decision.[149] In an unprecedented gesture, Thames TV technicians, all members of the Association of Cinematograph and Television Technicians, refused to transmit the comedy show that, with utter tastelessness, Thames had put forward as a replacement. The only programme they would send out, they said, was *This Week*'s 'Inhuman and Degrading Treatment', made the previous year. As a result, screens in London and the North of Ireland – where UTV had been relying on Thames TV for a replacement – were blank for half-an-hour save for a caption regretting that the advertised programme had been postponed. The north of England did, however, see a comedy show, put out by Granada TV.[150]

Ironically, by acting this time in anticipation of political pressure, the IBA had made fools of themselves. For by the time they made the decision, Mason was already planning to offset the Amnesty leaks by making a statement in the House of Commons that afternoon, in time to catch the six o'clock news before *This Week* went on the air.

The IBA had also riled the politicians who had been lined up to take part in the programme, including Official Unionist John Taylor, who had been planning to defend the RUC against Amnesty. Their clumsy move provoked instant and united condemnation from the rest of the media, apparently anxious to score a few points for defending press freedom. The BBC's *Nationwide* show transmitted sections from the banned programme. *The Sunday Times* said that 'The Independent Broadcasting Authority is one of the biggest menaces to free communication now at work in this country.'[151] *The Economist* said the IBA needed a civics lesson,[152] and even *The Sunday Telegraph* said grudgingly that although *This Week*'s record in Northern Ireland was 'pretty deplorable', so was 'the IBA's recourse to banning the other night's edition'.[153] IBA Director-General Sir Brian Young responded to *The Sunday Times*'s criticisms with a feeble, if revealing, defence. Claiming that 'we are given teeth for biting, not gnashing', Sir Brian said that the IBA, 'which judges on behalf of the viewer', had to override journalistic imperatives where these conflicted 'with fairness, with an individual's rights . . . with truth and the public good.'[154] As Peter Taylor wrote later, 'What could have been more concerned with individual rights, the truth and the public good than the programme that *This Week* had planned?'[155]

Smearing Dr Irwin

Even after the Amnesty Report, the authorities were none too keen on probing the activities in Castlereagh. The government predictably rejected Amnesty's request for a public enquiry, claiming that it 'would not be the course most consistent with the public interest.'[156] They did, however, agree to set up an 'independent committee of inquiry . . . which will sit in private.'[157]

The Inquiry's terms of reference were restricted: it was not empowered to look into individual complaints of ill-treatment, nor into the cases investigated by Amnesty, but only to examine 'police procedures and practice' relating to interrogation, and the operation of complaints procedures.[158] Because of its limited brief, there was a widespread nationalist boycott.

The Inquiry team, under Judge Harry Bennett, produced their report early in 1979. Roy Mason was evidently not very keen to publish it, and reportedly sat on it for several weeks.[159] The events that preceded publication of the report were to reveal just how low the authorities were prepared to stoop in their efforts to deflect criticism.

On 11 March 1979, nine months after Thames TV's thwarted programme on the Amnesty Report, London Weekend Television's *Weekend World* presented a programme on the torture allegations. The reporter was Mary Holland, a widely respected journalist who had been made Journalist of the Year in 1970 for her coverage of Ireland for *The Observer* and who took a consistently sceptical approach towards British policy. Among those she interviewed was Dr Robert Irwin, a police surgeon who had done work for the RUC for ten years, three of them at Castlereagh, as well as running a general practice. He said on the *Weekend World* programme that he had seen between 150 and 160 people with injuries at Castlereagh. 'There are injuries which could not be self-inflicted', he said. 'Ruptured eardrums, I would say, being one of the most serious could not possibly be self-inflicted.'[160] His words carried particular weight not only because he had an authoritative inside view, but because he was known to have great respect for the RUC and had the reputation of being 'steady as a rock'.[161]

Next day all hell broke loose, as familiar voices raised familiar complaints. The Northern Ireland Office said the programme was one-sided and offered a thinly disguised attack on the RUC and the army.[162] They said Mason hadn't been invited to appear, but an LWT spokesperson said he had repeatedly been asked right up to the last minute, but had always refused. Airey Neave called the programme 'a calculated attack on the administration of justice and the security forces in Northern Ireland.'[163] Don Concannon, Minister of State for Northern Ireland, said it lacked basic content as well as fair judgement.[164] The Police Federation said the programme had 'certainly increased the risk of personal attacks on our members.'[165] *The Daily Telegraph* said it would put the lives of soldiers and policemen into still greater danger and would 'give comfort to the IRA'.[166] It was attacked by Official Unionist MP Robert Bradford and also Harold McCusker, who said on BBC Radio Ulster, 'If the police require occasionally to use strong-arm methods, as perhaps some people would describe them, in order to get confessions from them, you'll get no complaints from me.' Official Unionist Jeremy Burchill said, 'There are too many mischief-makers employed in certain organs of the media who glory in the denigration of the bulwarks upon which civilised society is based.'[167]

But worse was to follow, as the RUC tried desperately to discredit Dr Irwin. On 13 March, two days after the programme, Chief Constable Newman made a complex allegation against him, the substance of which was that Dr Irwin had got his figures wrong and had dealt with far fewer cases than he claimed. Newman said that this had been demonstrated by an 'exhaustive analysis' of the records, and an 'interview' with Dr Irwin conducted by an assistant chief constable. Dr Irwin then produced a long and detailed rebuttal, pointing out that Newman's figures were misleading. Further, the interview with 'my good friend Assistant Chief Constable Killen' had in fact been an informal chat over a cup of tea – Killen had not asked him to bring files with him so he had not been able to supply details accurately from memory. 'It is now obvious,' he said, 'that the Chief Constable had a taped recording of our private conversation.' Dr Irwin said he had the records of the 150 cases to whom he had referred on television, and accused Newman of attempting an 'injudicious hatchet job' in denying his allegations.[168]

Meanwhile the authorities were using even less savoury means to try to discredit Dr Irwin. The *Weekend World* programme was transmitted at mid-day on Sunday 11 March. That evening, RUC press officers began leaking a variety of smears against Dr Irwin to English and Irish journalists suggesting that he had personal reasons for discrediting the police. *The Irish Times* noted,

> First indications of press office willingness to supply background detail detrimental to Dr Irwin came on Sunday night when one reporter was told the doctor had 'got a bit of a demotion'.
> The press officer also mentioned: 'You know his wife was

raped a while ago' and suggested that Dr Irwin had seemed to hold a grudge against the police for failure to track down the rapist.[169]

An RUC press officer told George Brock of *The Observer* that Irwin's transfer from Castlereagh to a city centre police station had 'rankled', and that Irwin had 'domestic problems', which Brock took to be a reference to his wife's rape. One of *The Guardian*'s correspondents was told by a press officer over the phone that Irwin was 'a drunk', had lost his job in Castlereagh because he was 'foul-tempered' and that he was 'sour and bitter' at the RUC.[170] Initially no journalist touched this distasteful story. Peter Fearon of the Press Association went to interview Dr Irwin, who 'spoke frankly about the rape', saying it had been traced to a British soldier on undercover duty: but Dr Irwin, who was evidently distressed, asked for the conversation to be in confidence. Accordingly, Fearon did not release the story until it had been made public elsewhere.[171]

It was Gerald Bartlett, writing in *The Daily Telegraph* on 16 March, who made the smears public in a front page report titled 'Rape case bitterness denied by RUC critic'.[172] The report claimed that 12 hours after Dr Irwin had made his allegations on television, Whitehall officials had apparently sanctioned 'leakage' of the details of the rape of his wife. Bartlett went on to report Dr Irwin as alleging that his wife was in fact raped by an SAS NCO who was subsequently spirited out of the North of Ireland to avoid charge or inquiry.[173] Next day, the *Telegraph* defended itself against charges made in Parliament that the report was 'disgraceful' by claiming that Bartlett had 'checked and demolished this planted leak with exemplary care.'[174] This was a thin excuse: the fact remained that without Bartlett the rape of Mrs Irwin might never have been made public. The Irwins had kept this traumatic event to themselves, but now had to suffer the indignity of it becoming front page news, and of seeing the words 'MY RAPE NIGHTMARE' splashed across the front of the *Daily Mail* a couple of days later.[175]

The Bennett Report

Dr Irwin's allegations had led to widespread calls for the Bennett Report to be published. Although Mason kept refusing to be hurried, claiming he was studying it, the pressure brought publication rapidly forward. The report was published on 16 March, the same day that the 'rape smear' story appeared in the *Telegraph*. There was some irony in this timing since the Bennett Report, for all its praise of the RUC, confirmed Dr Irwin's allegations by concluding that there had been 'cases in which injuries, whatever their precise cause, were not self-inflicted and were sustained in police custody.'[176]

Now at last, nearly three years after the first torture allegations had been made about Castlereagh, two years after the first television exposé, steps were taken to lessen the brutal interrogation methods. This was no thanks to the press, who instead of promoting investigation had actually hindered it. Instead of demanding a public enquiry at the outset, the press had duplicated the authorities' fury, attacking the BBC and ITV instead of the government. The quality papers had been diverted into defending the need for press freedom in a democracy, instead of examining how that 'democracy' was infringing human rights. Some sections of the press had dutifully acted as a black propaganda outlet for the authorities. Both BBC and ITV had been intimidated into long periods of silence.

The Bennett Report confirmed the existence of the practices Bernard O'Connor had described to Keith Kyle in March 1977. Kyle wrote bitterly to *The Guardian*:

> Unfortunately it seems that, so far from the publicity surrounding my *Tonight* report having the intended effect of reducing the abuses and dangers to which it called attention, most of the incidents that are described in Bennett took place during the two years subsequent to the interview.
>
> I would suggest that the main reason for this was the success in most of the press (not *The Guardian*) of the authorities' reaction. The failure of the media as a whole to back up the BBC was most striking . . .
>
> Politicians thought it fit to make the BBC and not the situation at Castlereagh the target of vehement inquiry. The authorities got the impression that they could safely ride through the first exposure of what are now authoritatively revealed to have been among the methods permitted by their procedures.[177]

In short, with the exception of a very few journalists, the press had in effect given the authorities permission to continue with the brutal interrogation methods.

4. Reporting the British army

Ulsterisation

In the early years, the Six Counties had been inundated with journalists and was frequently a topic for front page news. By late 1974 this had all changed, and the coverage declined.

In March 1972 the British government dissolved the Unionist-dominated Parliament at Stormont, and began to rule the province directly. A search began for a formula which would allow a measure of self-government to be returned to the North, but which would also guarantee the nationalist community a share in power. The devolution process began with the election of a Northern Ireland assembly, on a proportional representation system, in June 1973. From this an eleven-member executive was set up, consisting of six Protestants and five Catholics. Headed by former Stormont Prime Minister Brian Faulkner, with then SDLP member Gerry Fitt as his deputy, the executive took office on 1 January 1974. It was also planned that the new assembly would be linked with the Southern Irish Parliament through a Council of Ireland: the details for this had been worked out at a London-Dublin-Belfast conference at Sunningdale in December 1973.

The power-sharing experiment collapsed in May 1974 in the face of a strike organised by the loyalist Ulster Workers Council, and direct rule returned. The demise of the executive spelt the end of British attempts to build links between North and South, and indicated that hopes of persuading loyalists to share power with nationalists were foredoomed.

The last months of 1975 saw the collapse of another British attempt to find a framework for devolved government – the Constitutional Convention – and also the breakdown of the truce arranged between the British government and the IRA. Soon the government abandoned attempts at tinkering with the political set-up. Increasingly, the problem was presented as being internal to the Six Counties, and as being caused by criminal elements, rather than as a political problem rooted in nationalist disaffection with the status quo.

The containment of the problem within the Six Counties was further emphasised by reducing the number of troops from Britain and lowering their profile. The troop level had shot up to a high of nearly 22,000 in July 1972 for the Operation Motorman offensive against republican no-go areas, then stabilised at around 16,000. By the end of 1976 there were 14,000 troops, and from then on the number was steadily reduced, to around 10,500 in 1982.

At the same time the Royal Ulster Constabulary and the Ulster Defence Regiment, both locally recruited, were strengthened both in equipment and numbers. By July 1982, the UDR had about 8,200 members, while the RUC had 7,500 along with a further 5,900 reservists.[1]

From being in the front line of the conflict, the troops sent from Britain were relegated to playing second fiddle to the RUC. Officially at least, they were no longer fighting a war but playing a back-up role to the police. Media interest declined. The soldiers stationed in the North became, as they protested during the South Atlantic war in 1982, a forgotten and uncelebrated army, with a role so ambiguous that their dead were not even recorded on war memorials.

Routine lies

Though there was less coverage of the British army, its tone continued much as before, with the media generally anxious to put the best possible gloss on soldiers' behaviour.

From the start, the reporting had been coloured by journalists' often unquestioning acceptance of army accounts of incidents. In his survey of newspaper coverage in 1974 and 1975, Philip Elliott found in the British papers a 'reliance on official sources to provide accounts of incidents, to identify victims and attribute violence . . . scepticism of the official account was rarely shown.' He contrasted the Irish papers, which 'often went further, not just printing alternatives but dropping versions, including official versions, they no longer believed and taking on themselves the responsibility of pointing the reader in the right direction.'[2]

Even where the media give a number of versions of an incident, the army's or RUC's account is almost invariably given first. 'I've always assumed the official line is we put the army's version first and then any other,' a BBC television sub-editor told sociologist Philip Schlesinger.[3] Inevitably, the version mentioned first carries the greatest credibility.

This acceptance of official versions would not be such a problem were it not that the army, in particular, is almost pathologically unreliable, especially where its own violence is concerned. When troops kill an innocent person, the army's routine response is to lie about the circumstances. The victim, they would claim, was a 'gunman' or 'rioter', or had been 'killed in crossfire' or had been shot not by troops but by the IRA or unknown assailants.

On 12 May 1972, for example, plain-clothes troops sprayed a group of unarmed men with sub-machine-gun fire in Andersonstown, West Belfast. Patrick Joseph McVeigh was killed and four others were wounded. The army first issued a statement saying the five men had been shot after a one-hour gun battle between troops and the IRA. They later put out a statement saying that the killings and woundings had been committed by unknown persons. Finally the army admitted that plain-clothes soldiers had been involved. Forensic tests carried out by the RUC to see if any of the victims had been carrying weapons proved negative.[4]

Another notorious case in which the army was caught lying – though not till some years after the event – concerned the killing of Brian Smyth in April 1973. *Times* reporter Robert Fisk recorded at the time:

> In Belfast . . . paratroopers shot a young man dead and wounded two others at a street corner in the Roman Catholic Ardoyne area. The Army said the three men were about to fire at soldiers, although the IRA, and some local people, say they were unarmed.[5]

Fisk, one of the best British journalists to report from Belfast, had taken care to give both sides of the story, although automatically giving the army's version first. As it turned out, three years later, the version given by the IRA and the locals was the true one.

After the shooting, the soldiers involved testified in court that the dead man and one of his companions, Eddie McClafferty, were holding an Armalite rifle and a pistol. The court accepted this and jailed McClafferty for eight years. But in 1976 one of the soldiers, Chris Hendley, revealed that he had been ordered to fire on a group of unarmed men and that the army's story had been concocted to justify the incident. McClafferty was then retried, acquitted and released.[6]

It was the same story when soldiers of the Black Watch regiment shot dead 17-year-old Leo Norney in Turf Lodge, West Belfast, in September 1975. The army claimed that a patrol had been fired on by two gunmen, and fire was returned. One gunman, they said, had been killed, while the other ran away, carrying the guns with him.[7] In April 1977, however, Leo Norney's mother was awarded £3,000 compensation, and the Ministry of Defence admitted he was a 'totally innocent party'.[8]

There have been many such instances. With the exception of a few sceptics, journalists were apparently unconcerned by the army's inability to tell the truth. Eventually, however, a series of blatant army falsehoods in 1976 prompted the media to question the army's veracity.

The killing of Majella O'Hare

When 12-year-old Majella O'Hare was shot dead as she walked to her local chapel in South Armagh on 14 August 1976, British papers uncritically repeated army accounts of her death. She had, as it later emerged, been killed by two bullets fired by a paratrooper. Her death was particularly awkward for the authorities as it happened the same day as the peace people were holding a major rally in Belfast.

The army immediately blamed her death on 'gunmen', claiming that at 11.15 a.m. two or three shots from an automatic weapon had been fired at a foot patrol, who had not returned fire, and that a young girl had been found injured.[9] After this first unequivocal statement, the army's explanation became more convoluted. They said they had returned fire, then that fire 'may have been returned'. They eventually settled for the claim that Majella had been 'killed in crossfire', and it was this that the Sunday papers duly repeated.

The Sunday Times reported her death at the bottom of an article about the peace march headlined '10,000 march for peace'. The last paragraph baldly stated, 'A few hours before yesterday's parade 12-year-old Majella O'Hare was killed in crossfire between a gunman and soldiers'.[10] There was no mention that this version had come from the army. The *Sunday Express*, which featured her death more prominently, said she 'was hit by a ricochet from a gunbattle between terrorists and paratroopers'. Again, the statement was unattributed, though the perceptive reader would have found further down the words, 'An Army spokesman said that a foot patrol of the Paratroop Regiment had come under automatic fire as they neared Whitecross church.'[11] Writing in *The Observer*, Andrew Stephen did at least name his source of information. After saying that a 12-year-old girl had been killed 'in another shooting incident involving troops', he wrote, 'The Army said later that the girl was caught in crossfire after gunmen had opened up on a foot patrol.'[12]

But none of the reports had given local people's views of the incident, which later proved to be correct. They unanimously said they had heard only one shot – two high velocity shots would sound like one to a layperson. Clearly there had been no 'gunbattle'. The police almost immediately decided that she was 'probably' killed by army bullets, and six weeks later *The Sunday Times* reported, 'The police . . . are now certain that Majella was hit by two bullets fired by a machinegun fired by a soldier of the Third Parachute Regiment. The police have no evidence that any other shots were fired.'[13] A soldier was later tried for unlawful killing, but escaped conviction apparently because of his 'belief' that he had fired at a gunman, even though none was present.[14]

As a result of the army's lies, nationalist politician Seamus Mallon, a leading member of the Social Democratic and Labour Party, found himself in an extremely embarrassing position. He had seized on the army's initial statement and publicly condemned the IRA for the child's death. When the true facts emerged, he contacted the press and accused the army of 'issuing false statements to the police, the media and to him.'[15] Mallon's outburst helped to stimulate an unusual amount of publicity both for the fact that the army hád lied and for their responsibility for Majella's death. 'Army gun slows tide of peace', said *The Guardian*'s headline on Monday 16 August, while the *Mirror* had 'Troops "killed my girl" ' and *The Sun*, 'Girl, 12, killed by army gun say police'.[16]

More lies

Two months after Majella O'Hare's death, on 4 October 1976, 13-year-old Brian Stewart was fatally injured by a plastic bullet fired by British soldiers in Turf Lodge. 'The first army statement,' reported Fionnuala O'Connor in *The Irish Times*, 'said two patrols had been attacked by stone-throwing youths, at first a few, then a crowd of about 400, and had fired "a number of baton rounds" to extricate themselves. "Unfortunately, one baton round hit a thirteen-year-old boy," said the spokesman.'[17]

This was duly reproduced in British papers. The *Daily Mail*, under the headline 'Boy, 13, hurt as mobbed troops fight to escape', said: 'Twenty soldiers had to fight for their lives in Belfast last night when they were surrounded by a 400-strong mob throwing stones.' The *Mail* also reported that 'Army chiefs believe the ambush was planned by the Provos, who gathered and instructed young tearaways for the attack.'[18] *The Daily Telegraph* headlined its brief item, 'Army patrol ambushed by 400 youths'.[19] By contrast, the *Belfast Telegraph* – an evening paper generally seen as having a liberal unionist stance – headlined its article, 'Injured boy was not in riot claim residents', and went on to give not only the army's account, but also the locals' view of the incident: 'local people say that the boy was not involved and the "riot" never took place.'[20]

The day after Brian Stewart was shot, the army issued another statement which increased the number of people involved in the alleged riot, raised the estimate of their age and implied that Brian Stewart had been deliberately targeted:

> Two Army patrols were being ambushed by a crowd of hooligans last evening . . . The initial crowd of about 50 built up over a period of half an hour to 500 extremely aggressive, well-organised people ranging in age from 10–30 years . . . When a number of baton rounds were being fired to disperse the crowd in order to protect the patrols, a 13-year-old boy seen to be one of the most active bottle-throwers among a particular group was struck on the head by a PVC round.[21]

As Fionnuala O'Connor commented, it was 'not an impressive change in story'. The allegation that Brian Stewart was a 'leading stone-thrower' was also made on television by a senior army officer. But in the court cases that followed his death, the army denied that he was deliberately targeted. The army also later admitted that there were, in fact, only a few children on the street corner, and, in an unsuccessful effort to dissuade Brian's mother, Kathleen Stewart, from further court action, they offered to provide a statement admitting that Brian was a totally innocent victim.

Brian Stewart died on 10 October 1976, and two days later the army was at it again. In the early hours of Tuesday 12 October, a social club run by the Gaelic Athletic Association in West Belfast was burned the ground. Local people blamed drunken soldiers, whom they had seen running away from the club. The army press desk initially denied that any patrols were in the area, and said the complaints were 'yet another example of the exploitation of recent incidents in West Belfast as part of a deliberate propaganda campaign to discredit the army.'[22] The statement claimed that soldiers had arrived on the scene only after having been called out by the police, who had been alerted to the fire by an anonymous telephone caller.[23] The statement was issued after the matter had been referred to the army commander in the North, Lieutenant-General Sir David House.[24]

The local witnesses then complained to the police that soldiers had started the fire. The army then issued a statement admitting that a number of soldiers had been involved. On the same day, eight soldiers were charged with arson.[25] All eight were subsequently convicted and received suspended sentences.[26]

BBC complaints

As far back as 1971, senior people in the media were privately expressing doubts about the truthfulness of the British army. The minutes of a top level BBC meeting, four days after the introduction of internment, reveal Derek Amoore, then Editor of Television News, commenting, 'Reporters in Northern Ireland were saying it was now difficult to take statements by army PR at their face value.'[27] But such complaints did not surface publicly until the start of 1977.

On 22 February 1977, the BBC's then Northern Ireland Controller, Richard Francis, made a lengthy speech at the Royal Institute of International Affairs. In the course of this he said:

> We work in an environment in which propaganda plays a large part, but propaganda doesn't stem only from paramilitaries and illegal organisations – neither are they always wrong. It stems too from government, political parties and the security forces, and it is up to all journalists to weigh propaganda as an inescapable ingredi-

ent of the situation which they have to describe. Of course, propaganda itself is not an evil; it's the cause for which it speaks which has to be evaluated. Sometimes, not often, as in the cases of Majella O'Hare and the burning of the GAA club, the Army's initial version of events turns out to be further away from the truth than that of the Provos.[28]

Francis was, however, less interested in seriously challenging the authorities' propaganda record than in using examples of army lies as part of a general counter-attack on the government. His speech was a response to Northern Ireland Secretary Roy Mason, who for months had been criticising the media, and television in particular, for aiding 'terrorist propaganda'.

Within days of Francis's speech, the government was claiming that army lies were a thing of the past. In a report headed ' "Black propaganda" blue-pencilled', *Guardian* journalist Anne McHardy wrote: 'All statements issued by the army press desk at Lisburn in Northern Ireland are being vetted by the Secretary for Ulster, Mr Roy Mason, to stop the use of "black propaganda" by soldiers.'[29] From now on, said the Northern Ireland Office, there was to be no more use of 'dirty tricks' – the deliberate planting of false stories – nor of 'any form of counter-propaganda not based strictly on the truth.'[30]

Reflex lying

Richard Francis's criticism of army propaganda had been carefully qualified: 'sometimes, not often' the army had proved less truthful than the 'Provos'. Even now, after the army had for years been issuing statements that were at best misleading and at worst downright lies, people like Francis were unwilling to admit that the army's lies were a systematic response to situations which were likely to generate hostile publicity. Indeed BBC trainee journalists were still being assured in 1983 that the army was a much more reliable source of information than republicans.[31]

The army's counter-insurgency handbook, *Land Operations Volume III*, in the chapter on public relations that was added in November 1971, instructs:

> Every local mention of the Army affects its image . . . every effort must be made to forestall or counteract accusations when through mishap, misdeed or misunderstanding a unit may find itself the subject of press interest which could lead to adverse publicity. This may be done by volunteering the true facts or, when adverse

publicity is likely, seeking the advice of the Public Relations Staff.[32]

As well as the need to protect its image, there are solid practical reasons why the army, like the police, should try to cover up its own unjustifiable acts of violence. Soldiers and policemen have repeatedly escaped being charge with, or convicted of, murder or manslaughter on the grounds that they 'believed' they were in danger. The courts have proved very susceptible to this excuse, even when the 'gunman' whom soldiers or police claimed to have fired at turned out to be non-existent, as in the case of Majella O'Hare, or to have been holding a paintbrush with his back to his assailant, as in the case of 16-year-old Michael McCartan, killed by the RUC in July 1980.[33]

Mason's reported clean-up of the army press desk notwithstanding, the military and police continued to respond in much the same way. In a notorious incident in July 1978, when an SAS squad shot dead 16-year-old John Boyle, the army thwarted the RUC, which in turn immediately exposed the army's lies.

On 10 July John Boyle had discovered an arms cache in a County Antrim cemetery near his home. He told his father about it, and his father – a Catholic – reported it to the RUC. The RUC in turn informed the army, who set up an SAS 'stake-out'. At about 10 a.m. next day, John, who was haymaking near the cemetery, returned to see if the arms were still there. The SAS – who were operating a 'kill don't question' policy which had claimed seven victims in the previous seven months – shot him dead.[34] John's father, Cornelius, was warned by the RUC about the stake-out and rushed to the graveyard to look for his son. An older son, haymaking in the next field, raced to the scene on his tractor. Soldiers arrested both of them.

The army press office issued a statement saying that 'at approximately 10.22 this morning near Dunloy a uniformed military patrol challenged three men. One man was shot; two men are assisting police enquiries. Weapons and explosives have been recovered.'[35]

By shooting dead John Boyle, the SAS had severely cramped the RUC's style. Information about arms from a Catholic family was a rare prize, and now the British army had shot the source of the information. The RUC swiftly issued a statement denying that the Boyle family were connected with 'terrorism'.[36]

Now the army press office somersaulted in an attempt to

find a new justification for the shooting. They put out a statement saying that 'two soldiers saw a man running into the graveyard. They saw the man reach under a gravestone and straighten
up, pointing an Armalite rifle in their direction . . . They fired
five rounds at him. The rifle was later found with its magazine
fitted and ready to fire.'[37] The army now also admitted that their
first statement, saying the soldiers had challenged three men,
had been inaccurate. A warning would have been 'impractical' in
the circumstances, they said.[38]

The authorities were reluctant to charge the soldiers involved. They eventually did so the following February, after
details of the pathologist's report, which journalists Peter Martin
and Peter Fearon had obtained from John Boyle's father, appeared in the press and caused an outcry. Two SAS men were
then tried for murder.

The trial revealed that, contrary to the army's statement,
the rifle had not been loaded. The judge was unable to decide
whether in fact John Boyle had picked it up. The judge concluded that the army had 'gravely mishandled' the operation and
that Sergeant Bohan – the only one of the two accused SAS men
to give evidence – was an 'untrustworthy witness' whose account
was 'vague and unsatisfactory'. He nevertheless found them not
guilty: their 'mistaken belief' that they were in danger was
enough to acquit them, he said.[39]

Even after the John Boyle fiasco, the lies continued. In
August 1982, for example, when soldiers shot dead an unarmed
IRA man, Eamonn Bradley, in Derry, the RUC issued four separate press statements within 24 hours of the killing. 'The first,'
reported Mary Holland in the *New Statesman*, 'claimed that
Bradley had been killed after an army patrol had been fired on.
During the day this was modified and the fourth statement
stressed that no shots had been fired at the army and that no
firearms had been found at the scene of the incident.'[40]

The RUC is generally regarded by journalists as a much
more reliable source of information than the British army. But
the RUC, too, dissembles when it comes to giving accounts of its
own violence. Thus from mid-1976 on, the RUC consistently
refused to admit that suspects were being treated with extreme
brutality during interrogation.

At the end of 1982, police shot dead six men in South
Armagh within six weeks. Two were members of the INLA and
three were IRA members: all were unarmed. The sixth victim,

17-year-old Michael Tighe, was unconnected with paramilitaries and was apparently examining an unloaded pre-1917 rifle when he was shot.[41] All six were killed by a special RUC anti-terrorist unit, whose operations were, according to *Irish Times* investigations, sanctioned at top level.[42] In each case, the RUC put out statements that were strongly disputed by local people.

The three IRA men, Jervais McKerr, Sean Burns and Eugene Toman, were killed on the night of 11 November 1982. The same night, the RUC released a statement saying the car had been chased by police after being driven at speed through a checkpoint. Next day, they altered their story, saying that the car had stopped at the checkpoint, then accelerated towards the policeman who had waved it down, striking him and then driving off. The statement continued: 'Other police opened fire on the vehicle which drove off in an attempt to escape. In doing so it careered off the road, down a bank. When police arrived at the scene it was found that the three occupants were dead.'[43] The RUC confirmed that all three had died of gunshot wounds and that there were no weapons in the car.

The car was later shown to journalists. There were between 25 and 30 bullet holes in and around the driver's door and a further 10 entry marks on the boot, reported *The Irish Times*. 'It was evident,' the paper went on, 'that several other bullets had passed through the windscreen and windows. Only the front passenger-side window was left intact.'[44] Local politicians, demanding an enquiry, pointed out that this contradicted the police statement that the car had been fired on from behind and suggested that it had been fired on after it had come to a halt.[45]

Despite the strong doubts expressed by nationalists of all political persuasions, the RUC version became British media orthodoxy. The BBC, for example, reporting a subsequent death at the hands of the RUC special unit, said, 'Two weeks ago three IRA men died in the same area after police opened fire on a car which failed to stop at a roadblock.'[46] In September 1983, three RUC men were charged with the murder of one of the IRA men, Eugene Toman, and an RUC man was charged with murdering one of the two INLA 'shoot-to-kill' victims, Seamus Grew.[47]

Pressure

Unflattering television portrayals of the army bring down the wrath of the establishment. Philip Donnellan's *Gone for a Soldier*, shown on BBC2 on 9 March 1980, gave a history of the army from Waterloo to the Six Counties through the songs, verse and letters of soldiers themselves. It also followed a young recruit who joined up and was sent to the North, but decided not to continue his army career. Donnellan, a highly respected documentary film-maker who had worked for the BBC for many years, later explained the thinking behind the film:

> Our imperial past surrounds us, encouraging fake images of military 'glory'. Three generations of my family have had the honour of killing Turks, Germans, Boers, Japanese and Irishmen: I'm sure we have always done this from the highest motives and with a due sense of comradeship and humour. But I don't want my son, or yours, to continue this tradition.[48]

The film provoked outrage among Tory MPs and peers and at the Ministry of Defence. Junior Defence Minister Barney Hayhoe told the Commons that the film was 'highly offensive'. Patrick Wall, a Tory MP and retired Royal Marine major, demanded government action over a 'disgraceful' film which, he said, portrayed the army as 'a strike-breaking, civilian-bashing mob commanded by incompetents.'[49] In the Lords, government defence spokesperson Viscount Lond threatened that in the future the Ministry would give assistance to the press 'more selectively'.[50] Tory MPs appealed to BBC Chairman Sir Michael Swann to ban sales of the film abroad.[51]

The BBC succumbed to the pressure straight away, without even a gesture of resistance. A week after the Tory MPs' approach to Swann, the BBC's Board of Management announced that there would be no further showings of the film in Britain, and that no overseas sales would be allowed.[52] The BBC's *War School* series two months earlier, which gave an uncritical picture of how the officer elite are trained at the Camberley staff college, had no such problems.

Feature film-makers, too, have run into trouble. John Mackenzie, director of *The Long Good Friday*, a thriller about London gangsters who cross the IRA, has described how the film's backers insisted on changes in one particular speech:

> Someone says to the gangster, 'You don't care about the IRA? When soldiers have been marching round Belfast for years with shit running down their legs from fear?'
>
> Now that was thought to be a very unpatriotic speech. I didn't think it was unpatriotic – I thought it showed the soldiers

were human beings, experiencing human fear. But I was asked to change the speech, so we did. We changed it to 'soldiers marching round Belfast with all the shit flying at them.'[53]

The Long Good Friday ran into further hitches. Lord Grade, head of the Associated Communications Corporation, whose subsidiary, Black Lion Films, had put up the money, apparently objected that the film was too flattering to the IRA. Eventually he sold it to George Harrison's company, Handmade Films, and it rapidly became a box office hit.

But *The Long Good Friday*, released in 1981, had better luck than another feature with an Irish theme, *Hennessy*. Released in 1975, *Hennessy* starred Rod Steiger as an Irishman trying to blow up the House of Commons after his wife and daughter had been killed by British troops. After EMI chiefs John Read and Bernard Delfont had viewed the film, the company decided against showing it in their chain of ABC cinemas. The Rank Organisation followed suit, refusing to show it on the Odeon circuit, Britain's second major cinema chain. Said EMI: 'Our decision is not a matter of commerce – it's a question of responsibility to the public and society in which we live.'[54]

Minimal accounts

The British media are generally very wary of reporting army or police violence. When brutality or killings by the army, RUC or UDR are reported, the accounts are often spare to the point of non-existence. For instance, when a drunk British soldier shot dead 26-year-old Angela D'Arcy in Enniskillen in November 1981 after she refused his demand for money, *The Guardian* managed just one column inch two days later saying the soldier had been charged with murder and concluding, 'Police said there were no political or religious motives.'[55] *The Guardian* gave four-and-a-half column inches to his trial and conviction for manslaughter, which compared with 21 inches in *The Irish Times*. The other daily papers did not report his conviction at all.[56]

One of the longest-running examples of how the media minimise army and RUC violence is the reporting of the deaths and injuries resulting from rubber and plastic bullets. When rubber bullets were introduced in 1970, the army presented them as not only harmless but humorous. This image went down well with journalists, as *Guardian* reporter Simon Winchester's account of the introductory press conference shows. He tells how the 'charming press officer' of the King's Own Scottish Borderers

> showed the soft and squidgy things to reporters that Saturday morning. Six inches long, one and a half in diameter, and rather obviously phallic ('the girls in Derry will love it' some soldiers used to say) it seemed a bizarre way for a modern army to be going to war. 'I just don't know what they're coming to,' mumbled one reporter from the *Observer* at the press show, 'firing bullets made of rubber. Soon they'll be lobbing grenades full of confetti, and guns that fire rose petals. You can't take this sort of thing seriously at all.'[57]

The reporters evidently did not handle the weapons which, far from being 'soft and squidgy', are harder than car tyres. Nor, it seems, did they probe for results of tests on the missiles: little, if any, testing had in fact been done.[58]

Within three years, rubber bullets had killed three people and caused countless injuries, including blinding. Their plastic successors had killed a further 11 people by early 1982. Yet there were hardly any investigative articles, even in the quality press. The first television report on the effects of the weapons was, it seems, an item on BBC2's *Newsnight* on 12 March 1982.

Most of the victims had died with only a passing mention in the British media. In 1981, when seven people were killed by them, plastic bullets became the subject of heated controversy in the Six Counties, but most British people remained unaware of this. When 11-year-old Stephen McConomy died on 19 April 1982, the media did little better, although his funeral, attended by around 1,000 people, provoked rather more coverage.

On the day Stephen died, BBC TV's *Nine O'Clock News* reported his death perfunctorily, but ITN's *News at Ten* did not mention it. Next day, *The Guardian* had six lines on its front page. *The Daily Telegraph*, the *Daily Mail* and *The Sun* had very brief reports which simply repeated the army's story that Stephen was injured, as *The Sun* put it, 'when troops tried to disperse a group of 30 to 40 youths who had been stoning them.' The *Daily Mirror* apparently decided that the event was of interest to its Irish readers but not to readers in Britain: its Irish edition carried a short item on his death on page seven, but the London edition made no mention of it. *The Times* did best with three column inches which pointed out that locals disputed the army's account, and mentioned that the weapons had caused 13 deaths in the past ten years. None of the accounts mentioned one particularly significant fact: that the child had been shot in the back of the head.[59]

When the European Parliament voted for a ban on plastic bullets on 13 May 1982, the two main television evening news bulletins adopted different but equally effective strategies for disposing of this awkward piece of information. The BBC's *Nine O'Clock News* dispensed with the item in a few seconds. ITN's *News at Ten*, however, gave it a minute but produced a small masterpiece of misinformation. It was nearly at the end of the news, after an item on how the Queen had just opened the world's largest greenhouse, that Alastair Burnet mentioned the European Parliament's decision, saying that it followed Stephen McConomy's death. He went on:

> The plastic bullet replaced the rubber bullet as what's called a minimum force weapon nearly seven years ago. Strict guidelines for its use were laid down by the government then, and last year over 16,000 rounds were fired by the police and army.[60]

The report used the military term 'minimum force' but failed to mention all the deaths and injuries. It referred to 'strict guidelines' but did not mention the many cases in which the guidelines have been broken or in which deaths have occurred even where they have been observed. It said that 16,000 rounds had been fired the previous year – in fact the figure was nearly 30,000 – but did not say that in the same period seven people, three of them children, had been killed. In short, the report gave a very reassuring impression, enhanced by Burnet's fatherly delivery, for which the kindest word is misleading. It totally failed to explain why the European Parliament had, as Burnet went on to remark, called the plastic bullet 'a murderous weapon'.

The last part of the report reinforced the impression that ITN was only interested in vindicating the British government. 'Many politicians in Northern Ireland are angry at the ban,' said Burnet, ignoring the fact that the entire nationalist community, 'moderates' included, was united against the weapon. He then gave a highly coloured quote, replete with 'Molotov cocktails' and 'gunmen', from Labour Northern Ireland spokesperson Don Concannon, justifying the use of plastic bullets. The fact that neither Molotov cocktails nor gunmen were in evidence when a British soldier killed Stephen McConomy was of course not raised.

Sympathy for the squaddies

While the media were minimising the violence of the British army, they were also actively enlisting sympathy and support for the soldiers. The media worked in tandem with the army's public relations staff. The army's counter-insurgency manual *Land Operations Volume III* advises,

> Every local mention of the army affects its image. There is no neutral publicity, and the scope for favourable unit publicity includes the fostering of good community relations by helping with the sick and aged, participation in local events, both sporting and civic, and the holding of displays where operational circumstances permit.[61]

The media were more than willing to assist. Former *Sunday Mirror* reporter Kevin Dowling, who worked in the North between 1970 and 1974, told how 'We had the happy story syndrome, with news editors saying find us a happy story.'[62] In his fictionalised account of his experiences, *Interface Ireland*, Dowling satirically describes a news editor trying to persuade a reporter to cover a story, set up by army PR, about soldiers manning a machine-gun nest in a shopping precinct growing geraniums out of the sandbags to make it feel like home:

> 'What we want to project,' the News Editor had said, 'is the impression that the lads can still live a normal life over there . . .'
>
> 'What's normal about a machine-gun nest in a shopping precinct, Lou?' . . .
>
> 'It's a question of morale back home. Growing a little garden in a gun emplacement is good for their families' morale. You get me?'[63]

Soldiers were photographed chatting up children, doing their bit in Santa Claus outfits, and, as in one picture published in London's *Evening News* in 1972, accepting a cup of tea in 'a friendly Protestant neighbourhood'.[64] Sociologist Philip Elliott, who examined press coverage in the autumn of 1974 and the spring of 1975, found that 'the army appeared as almost above the fray – brave, tormented, but largely inactive except as a rather superior kind of Boy Scout Troop.' There were 'several stories of soldiers coming to the aid of the local population on foot, in boats or in helicopters.'[65]

From the start, the army has boosted its image back home by the standard PR ploy of running free trips for reporters. These junkets enable reporters from local papers to visit their local regiment serving in the North and produce what are known as 'satisfied soldier' or 'local boy' stories. One such, in the *South London Press* in November 1978, showed a rather apprehensive-looking soldier with homely features holding a rifle in a lookout post. It was captioned:

> Looking out over Londonderry from the famous city walls is 23-year-old L/Cpl Paul Kempley, whose grandparents Charles and Rachel Kempley live in Catford. Married, Paul's wife Susan Anne also comes from Catford, where her father, Albert Thomas lives. Paul and Susan have three children – Paul junior, aged 6, Jason 4, and Donna 3.
>
> Paul joined the Army in February, 1973, and is just completing his fourth tour of duty in Northern Ireland. In Germany, where 2nd Battalion Royal Regiment of Fusiliers is normally stationed, he is an anti-tank gunner and in his spare time he enjoys writing poetry.[66]

This item gave local relevance to the accompanying story which explained that the army's 'softly softly approach' was paying off. The South London branch of the Troops Out Movement protested that 'softly softly' was hardly the way to describe an approach which, though it involved lowering the profile of uniformed soldiers, had brought an increased use of the under-cover SAS. They pointed out in a letter to the paper that 'In the past few months the British Army has admitted to the killing of three completely innocent people in such operations.'[67]

Coffee pot girls

The media are easily enticed by 'human interest' stories involving women or animals. 'THE FRONT LINE – Sunday Mirror salutes the Coffee Pot girls' announced a centre-page spread in 1979. The story, amply illustrated with photos, was about 'the girls of the 181 WRAC Provost Company', stationed in Belfast, whose crest includes a coffee pot and who 'DO regularly brew up for the lads.' The gist was that the feminine touch has its advantages in military work. An army spokesperson was quoted as saying that when searching people 'a girl will see something that a man misses like an overfull handbag.' The article explained, 'They must not even be seen holding a gun, because it might affect their peaceful image. But in private some girls do learn about fire-arms.'[68]

More common are stories about models or beauty queens visiting the troops. These give 'pop press' editors a chance both to display their patriotism and to titillate their readers. 'THE MAJOR ATTRACTION' was a *Daily Mirror* headline in 1976 over a picture of a model surrounded by laughing soldiers in 'Ulster'. Alongside was a much larger picture of the same woman clad only in pants. The text explained that the woman, Gillian Duxbury, was the 'official pin-up' of 4 Squadron of the Royal Corps of Transport: 'The link-up was arranged for Major Christopher Duxbury [no relation], the squadron's commanding officer . . . after a colleague saw her in the *Mirror*.' While the soldiers gave Gillian a plaque, 'she gave their morale a boost.'[69]

Dog of war

The army's biggest PR coup of the seventies was undoubtedly Rats, described by one pro-military author as 'the dog star of BBC television's *Nationwide*'.[70] Given the famous British predilection for animals, Rats was an army propagandist's dream. A Crossmaglen stray who had been adopted by the military, Rats first starred on *Nationwide* in 1979. It later emerged that he was not the only stray in the barracks. But the other one, 'a big and really dirty' black labrador called Fleabus, was evidently not thought suitable for the limelight.[71]

Unlike Fleabus, Rats had potential. He was speedily invested not only with the qualities of the ideal soldier, but with royal connections. Rats, *Nationwide* reporter Glyn Worsnip solemnly explained, 'as number D7/777 is the longest serving member of the British army in South Armagh. Of uncertain pedigree, Rats most resembles a corgi.' Rats was pictured accompanying soldiers on patrol, 'where they're most at risk', and providing 'another pair of friendly eyes'. A further bonus was that Rats was not an imported dog, but a deserter from the enemy camp, his qualities setting him apart from the universally hostile population as he comforted the beleaguered squaddies.

A ceremony to honour Rats was arranged for *Nationwide*'s cameras. As bagpipes wailed and Rats howled along with them, an NCO presented him with a medal with the words, 'we are gathered here this afternoon to pay homage and tribute to this small mighty dog, our one and only friend in the Crossmaglen area.' An officer gave the game away to the perspicacious by saying that among the soldiers 'you'll see a certain amount of friendship towards this animal, when there isn't that sort of friendship towards the local inhabitants of the town.'[72]

The Rats story ran and ran. The *Daily Express* featured him as 'DOG OF WAR', running gallantly alongside a foot patrol, with a text that began, 'EYES BRIGHT! Here comes Action Dog with a regulation shine to his nose after breakfasting in the officer's mess.' The *Express* told its readers that Rats, 'twice wounded in action', was soon to be awarded a gold medal by the canine charity Pro Dogs. The award ceremony provided an excuse for another appearance on *Nationwide*.[73]

That the publicity had struck a chord in the British psyche was demonstrated at Christmas 1979, when thousands of letters addressed to the dog, along with food parcels and toys, arrived at the Crossmaglen barracks: so many, that a special department was set up to deal with them.[74] Between them, *Nationwide* and army PR had created a bond between many British people and the soldiers in the South Armagh barracks, a place in which the colonial role of the troops is starkly obvious, since the population is uniformly antagonistic and the army cannot claim to be 'keeping the peace between rival factions'.

Rats' departure from Crossmaglen in 1980 was not the end of the story. His 'retirement' to the home of an ex-officer in Kent prompted more eulogies. 'AN OLD SOLDIER STANDS AT EASE', the Scottish *Daily Record* informed its readers, reminding them that 'he has patrolled the murderous streets of Crossmaglen with his army chums, and heard the crack of a sniper's rifle a thousand times.' The pictures showed the dog wearing a medal and reclining in a deck chair, and the piece concluded, 'if there's one thing he can't stand it is cocky young pups who think they know it all. What they need is a bit of National Service. AND LOOK AT THE LENGTH OF THEIR FUR THESE DAYS.'

Rats appeared on television yet again, this time as the Queen Mother was saluted during the Royal Tournament at Earls Court. And October 1981 saw the publication of a biography, illustrated with pictures provided by Express Newspapers, titled *Rats: The Story of a Dog Soldier*.[76] Interspersing his tale with pen-portraits of officers and soldiers who had served in Crossmaglen, author Max Halstock opined that Rats' 'lovability and loyalty' explained why he, of all the strays in the town, had 'emerged as "the soldiers' friend".' 'Rats took to the air like Biggles,' wrote Halstock, adding old imperial associations to the story of the 'corgi-like dog' ever ready 'to defend his comrades', yet with some weaknesses, like peeing on officers' beds, to endear him to the readers.

Through his portrayal of Rats, Halstock, like *Nationwide*, engaged the emotions of his audience on the side of the British army. The dog came out of it all infinitely more 'human' than the people of Crossmaglen, who remained an anonymous, threatening backcloth, a foil for the deeds of the troops like the Indians in a Western.

The publication of the biography prompted *Daily Mirror* journalist William Marshall to visit Rats on the Kent farm. He observed that behind the 'Grand Old Warrior' on the wall 'were his two favourite pin-ups, Prince Charles and Prince Philip, both of course in uniform.' The story ended on a sombre and patriotic note:

> The light was fading at the going down of the sun and I asked the owner where he intended to bury the Little Hero when he faded away.
>
> 'Oh I don't know – in some corner of a foreign field which is for ever England, I suppose.
>
> 'I know, I know, we *are* in England, but you know what I mean.'[77]

By the spring of 1983 Rats had still not faded away. In April he featured on ITN's *News at Ten*, which pictured him in his retirement home and recapped on his military exploits. In May, during the run-up to the general election, Rats appeared on *News at Ten* again, this time at the opening of an Imperial War Museum exhibition on 'Animals in War'. Here he was alongside Sefton, described by the newsreader as 'the army's most famous living horse', who had been wounded in an IRA attack which killed several soldiers in London the previous year. Said newsreader Alastair Burnet, 'If Sefton and Rats were standing for election, they'd be elected.'[78] Whether the media will celebrate Rats' military funeral remains to be seen. As a tool in the hands of the propagandists, if not as a soldier, he had certainly done his bit for England.

Rats, incidentally, was not the first canine colonial hero. British troops fighting guerrillas in Aden in the sixties adopted a local mongrel, said to resemble a labrador, named Oscar. His handler, Lance Corporal Barrie Dunn, was quoted as recalling, 'Down in Aden he accompanied us on Company cordons, but his main delight was in Crater when he was kept in the back of a three-tonner and was sent out if the golly prisoners got cheeky!'[79]

When Britain withdrew from Aden in 1967, the *Daily Mirror*, aided by an army public relations officer, launched a public appeal for money to pay for Oscar's fare and six months' kennelling fees. The *Mirror* said of Oscar, 'the dog that became a hero has won a place in the hearts of the Marines, and the Nation'.[80] David Young, chronicler of 45 Commando Royal Marines, recorded, 'The money soon poured in and on 17 September, 1967, Oscar, having been fortunate enough to travel by BOAC, duly arrived at Heathrow Airport to be met by a battery of press and TV cameras – a hero's welcome indeed.'[81]

5. Reporting loyalist violence

Selective amnesia

By May 1981, loyalists had been responsible for over 600 of the 2,000 deaths in the current round of troubles, and almost all of their victims had been civilians.[1] But few British people were likely to be aware of the extent of loyalist violence because of the way such incidents had been handled by the authorities and the media.

Loyalist attacks on Catholics began as far back as 1966. Objecting to moves by the Unionist establishment to modernise and liberalise the regime in the Six Counties, loyalists petrol-bombed Catholic schools and bars. The newly formed Ulster Volunteer Force, named after the private army organised by Carson in 1912 to oppose Irish Home Rule, also shot up the home of a Unionist MP in a mock-IRA attack. In May 1966, a petrol-bomb attack by the Shankill UVF on a Catholic-owned bar misfired, and an elderly Protestant, Mrs Martha Gould, was burned to death. Three weeks later the Shankill UVF murdered a Catholic, John Scullion, who was singing republican songs as he returned home from an evening's drinking. In late June, UVF leader Gusty Spence and his team attacked four barmen from the South of Ireland who were working in Belfast. They killed 18-year-old Peter Ward, and injured two of the others. But off-duty RUC men were in the bar in Malvern Street when the murder was planned, and Spence and his associates were jailed.[2]

Loyalist violence was next manifested in violent attacks on civil rights marchers in 1968 and peaked with the notorious incident at Burntollet Bridge at the start of 1969, where loyalists ambushed a group of marchers and, assisted by some of the marchers' police escort, attacked them with stones, bottles and clubs. The day ended with a police assault on Catholic houses in Derry's Bogside area in which, the Cameron report found, 'A number of policemen were guilty of misconduct which involved assault and battery, malicious damage to property . . . and the use of provocative, sectarian and political slogans.'[3]

In March and April 1969 loyalists were responsible for the first explosions of the troubles, wrecking electricity and water installations. Following another bombing in October, in which one of the bombers, a member of Paisley's Ulster Protestant Volunteers, was killed, a loyalist confessed to involvement in all eight bombings. But at the time, as intended, the bombings were blamed on the IRA. This successfully discredited the reformist policies of the Unionist government and forced Prime Minister O'Neill to resign.

Also in April, a minor riot in the centre of Derry culminated with police breaking into a house on the edge of the Bogside and beating the owner, Sam Devenny, unconscious. He died three months later. In August, a major RUC assault on the Bogside, successfully resisted by the inhabitants, precipitated the introduction of British troops. In Belfast crowds of loyalists, B Specials prominent among them, rampaged through Catholic streets burning down 150 homes in one night, 14–15 August. That night, five Catholics and a Protestant died. The burning of Catholic homes had started earlier. Altogether in July, August and September 1969 some 1,820 families, 82.7 per cent of them Catholic, fled their homes.[4]

The events of these early years have conveniently disappeared from the establishment mythology, as has the fact that in 1969 the IRA was conspicuous by its absence, as immortalised by the graffiti-artists in the slogan 'I Ran Away'. Soon forgotten, too, was the fact that the IRA did not go on the offensive until six months after the Conservative government's crackdown on the Lower Falls in July 1970. This amnesia set in rapidly. In November 1972, *Guardian* editorials were telling readers that 'the bloody struggle with the IRA' was 'now increasingly bringing in Protestant extremists also'[5] and that 'IRA violence' had been going on 'for the last three or four years.'[6] The books, in short, were being cooked in order to establish the IRA not as a product of the conflict, but as the cause.

McGurk's Bar

The authorities have, down the years, employed various means to discourage publicity for loyalist violence. Often they have gone further, seeking to maximise their propaganda advantage by blaming loyalist violence on the IRA, even where there were definite indications of loyalist involvement.

On Saturday 4 December 1971, 15 people were killed when a bomb wrecked McGurk's Bar, a Catholic pub in North Queen Street, Belfast. Two pieces of evidence pointed strongly to loyalist responsibility: a child selling papers said he had seen a car stop outside the pub, and a man getting out of it and planting the bomb, and the day after the explosion an anonymous phone-caller claimed that the 'Empire Loyalists' had done the bombing. Yet the army and police immediately blamed the IRA, cooking up a story, complete with 'evidence' manufactured to discredit the eyewitness account of the paper seller, that it was an IRA 'own goal'.

The effects of the army's efforts were immediately apparent in Monday's papers. John Chartres of *The Times* reproduced the army's account wholesale, in a front page article titled, 'Blast that killed 15 may have been IRA error'. He began:

> Police and Army intelligence officers believe that Ulster's worst outrage, the killing of 15 people, including two children and three women, in an explosion in a Belfast bar last night [sic] was caused by an IRA plan that went wrong . . .
>
> The theory assembled in the security forces intelligence circles is that a large IRA operation was planned for last night involving a bomb attack on a police station or an Army headquarters in the North Queen Street district of the city. An ambush of troops who would have had to move into the district would have followed.
>
> Word had been passed to several people in the Catholic community to 'keep out of North Queen Street' last night. This got back to security forces, who were alerted . . .
>
> The Army's theory is that the bomb in McGurk's Bar was 'in transit', that it had been left there, probably without the knowledge of any of the people who were killed or injured, by a 'carrier' for another person to pick up, and that the second person was unable to keep his rendezvous because of the security operation.[7]

Chartres went on to explain why neither of the other possible theories were felt to stand up. It wasn't a Protestant bomb because 'Royal Army Ordnance Corps explosives experts . . . think that the bomb was inside the building'. It wasn't a deliberate IRA attack, because this would not fit in with their strategy.

That Britain's leading quality paper, a 'paper of record' which historians turn to, had given over its columns to what can only be described as rubbish was not to be demonstrated till nearly seven years later. In 1978 a loyalist, 42-year-old Robert James Campbell from Ligoniel, was convicted of the 15 murders at McGurk's Bar. He was given 15 life sentences, with a recommended minimum sentence of 25 years. This event passed unremarked by the British media.

The McGurk's Bar bombing had caused more casualties than any single previous incident. Loyalists were responsible, but never stood publicly condemned for it beyond the nationalist areas. The army and police had, with the assistance of much of the press, successfully diverted attention from the evidence of loyalist involvement and gone on to use the atrocity to discredit their principal enemy, the IRA. In using this tactic, time was on their side. The probability of the culprits being caught was low, especially if the police had already made up their minds not to look in the loyalist community. Further when those responsible for such incidents are caught, it is usually after a considerable time, and the British media rarely give much publicity to it. The British media could be relied on not to take the army and police to task for lying several years previously, especially when the papers had themselves reproduced those lies.[8]

Assassinations

The introduction of internment on 9 August 1971 had made the North literally ungovernable. To the heavy physical repression by the British army, the Stormont government added punitive legislation against those who had joined the widespread protests against internment. In some local councils, a majority of councillors were refusing to attend: these councils were suspended. People on rent and rates strike were penalised by a new law allowing their debts to be recovered directly from their wages or social security benefits. The IRA campaign, involving attacks on soldiers and police, and bombings of commercial targets, rapidly escalated. British politicians urgently discussed alternatives. By the end of October, it was rumoured that the Tory government intended to suspend Stormont and introduce direct rule. And on

25 November former Prime Minister Harold Wilson put forward a plan proposing a united Ireland within the Commonwealth within 15 years.

The McGurk's Bar bombing came nine days after Wilson's speech. Loyalists saw their state collapsing around them. Then Bloody Sunday, 30 January 1972, brought nationalist disaffection to an unprecedented level and made a new political initiative inevitable. As they saw their previous total control over the province disintegrating, the loyalists became desperate. Former Stormont Home Affairs Minister William Craig organised a series of rallies reminiscent of the Third Reich and hinted ever more strongly that Catholics would be killed. 'We are determined, ladies and gentlemen,' he said on 12 February, 'to preserve our British traditions and way of life. And God help those who get in our way.'[9] And on 18 March he told 60,000 people in Belfast's Ormeau Park,

> We must build up dossiers on those men and women in this country who are a menace to this country because one of these days, if and when the politicians fail us, it may be our job to liquidate the enemy.[10]

At the start of March, loyalists began an organised campaign of sectarian assassinations of Catholics. When the British government dissolved the Stormont Parliament and introduced direct rule from Westminster on 24 March, the killing escalated. The truce between the British government and the IRA on 26 June brought an even more drastic increase, with almost forty killings inside five weeks.[11]

Altogether, between the start of 1972 and mid-1973, some 200 people were assassinated. That loyalists were responsible for most of the assassinations is now generally accepted, but at the time it was not.[12] For although Catholics were the main victims, the RUC described the killings as 'motiveless murders' and blamed a number of them directly on the IRA. Two journalists, Martin Dillon and Denis Lehane, did detailed research into the murders and in March 1973 presented four articles, showing that the bulk of the assassinations were carried out by Protestant groups, to their paper, the *Belfast Telegraph*. The *Telegraph* rejected the articles because, in the words of the journalists, 'these conclusions were so unpopular'. By the time their book, *Political Murder in Northern Ireland*,[13] came out five months later, their assessment seemed less incredible. For in June 1973 the Ulster Defence Association, using its cover name 'Ulster Freedom Fighters', issued a statement saying that 'We were responsible for most of the assassinations carried out last summer.'[14] Up till then, wrote Dillon and Lehane, 'There were many in the Protestant community, and also, it must be said, in the RUC, who believed that the Provisional IRA was responsible for almost all the dead.'[15]

Dillon and Lehane documented a number of killings which were immediately blamed on the IRA although the circumstances of the deaths made this very unlikely. On 4 July 1972, for example, the bodies of two young Protestant brothers called Orr were found on the outskirts of Belfast. 'This killing led to an immediate outcry, and it was at once assumed that the Provisional IRA were responsible,' wrote Dillon and Lehane. They pointed out that the Orrs had Catholic friends and had been threatened by the UDA: further, their bodies were found deep within Protestant territory, where the IRA were unlikely to venture. They concluded that 'the balance of probability' would place the responsibility for their killings on the UDA men who had previously threatened them.[16]

In other cases, the RUC's use of the term 'motiveless murders' served to cloud the question of who was responsible, hiding the fact that organised loyalist killer squads were operating. As a result, the media professed themselves perplexed, as in this item from London's *Evening News* in October 1972:

Man shot dead by Belfast terror squad by Ivan McMichael
POLICE in Belfast were handed yet another murder file today after mystery assassins walked into a crowded club and shot a man dead.

Lorry driver Edward Bonner, a 50-year-old Catholic, was about to leave the club when three masked gunmen burst in and ordered people inside to line up against a wall.

One of the gunmen then shot Mr Bonner through the head and they escaped . . .

There have now been over 70 mystery killings in Ulster in the past six months.[17]

Following the official line

In 1974 there were over a hundred assassinations in the North, and a further 31 people died when loyalists bombed Dublin and Monaghan in the South. A second truce between the British government and the IRA in 1975 saw assassinations rise to around

150. Republicans were now increasingly responding in kind, and continued to be blamed for killings they had not committed, as well as those that they had.

Summarising his survey of newspaper coverage in 1974 and 1975, Philip Elliott wrote, 'Evidence has accumulated of journalists being deliberately and repeatedly misled, mainly to implicate the IRA in violence carried out by loyalist extremists.'[18] In the six weeks covered by his survey, the death toll was fifteen Catholics, six Protestants, one member of the armed forces and one other. Yet despite the fact that Catholics were the main victims, the media blamed most of the violence on the Provisional IRA or some other republican group.[19] In this, they had taken their line from the army and police:

> In each of the periods covered in our content analysis, a new loyalist organisation declared its hand and claimed responsibility for a series of murders carried out in the previous few days. Most of these had been wrongly or ambiguously attributed in the reports which appeared immediately after each incident, apparently in line with the account put out by the army or the Royal Ulster Constabulary.[20]

One example given by Elliott concerned the killing of three Catholics in the spring of 1975 by a bomb planted in a farmhouse which they were renovating near Dungannon. Two theories were put forward to explain the incident: one that it was an IRA booby-trap bomb intended for troops searching empty property, the other that it was planted by loyalists as part of a continuing campaign against Catholics in the area, which had become known as the 'murder triangle'. While all the British papers reported it as a probable sectarian attack, both national television bulletins described it as an intended attack on soldiers. Nine days later a loyalist paramilitary group, the Protestant Action Force, claimed responsibility for this and other incidents. Elliott wrote that both local television bulletins reported the PAF's claim, 'but neither pointed out to their viewers that this was somewhat at odds with the story they had been told on both channels when the murders themselves had been reported.'[21]

Loyalist assassinations continued to be blamed on the IRA even in instances when such an explanation was far-fetched in the extreme. When Sinn Fein leader Maire Drumm was murdered in her hospital bed on 28 October 1976, attempts were made to attribute her killing to the Provisional IRA. But the following day two white hospital-type coats, of the kind worn by the killers, were found in the strongly loyalist Shankill area. Eventually, in August 1983, a loyalist – already serving a life sentence for killing a Catholic – was charged with her murder.[22]

In February 1978 the same black propaganda tactic was used after the attempted assassination of Belfast republican Kevin Hannaway. On 1 February a gunman burst into the Hannaway home and fired several shots at Kevin Hannaway who was standing in the kitchen holding his 21-month-old baby son. The child was hit three times, once in the face, and Hannaway was hit twice in a hand and arm. The next day *The Sun* printed an article by Trevor Hanna, titled 'BABY SHOT BY TERROR GANG', which told its readers that

> Officially Belfast police said they had an 'open mind' about who was responsible for the attack.
> But detectives working on the case were known to believe that it was connected with an internal Provisional IRA feud, elaborately planned to point the finger of blame at either the British Army or a Loyalist paramilitary group.[23]

The Sun followed this up next day with an even more emotive presentation. 'THE LITTLE VICTIM OF TERROR' was the headline, next to a picture of a charming chubby baby lying bandaged in a hospital cot. The item was unequivocal:

> This is the tiny victim of Ulster's latest terror outrage . . .
> He is just 21 months old. But that did not stop ruthless gunmen shooting him three times on Wednesday night . . .
> The real target of the Provisional IRA attack was his father Mr Kevin Hannaway.[24]

The story was self-evidently ludicrous. Kevin Hannaway was a member of a well-known republican family, the son of a prominent republican, Liam Hannaway. Kevin Hannaway was also one of the 14 men subjected to sensory deprivation torture in 1971. Further, the car used by the would-be assassins was taken from a loyalist district, and was abandoned after the shooting on the 'peace-line' where barricades divide nationalist and republican areas, after which the gunmen fled into a loyalist street which runs into the Shankill.

The same tactic was used again in May 1981, perhaps the most highly charged month since the troubles began. Bobby Sands, Member of Parliament for Fermanagh-South Tyrone, had died on hunger strike on 5 May. A week later Francis Hughes became the second hunger striker to die. Francis Hughes was buried on Friday 15 May, and the following morning a Catholic butcher, Joseph Patrick Martin, part-owner of two shops in West Belfast, was found dead in his bedroom. He had been shot in the head five times at close range.

Next morning *The Observer* proclaimed unequivocally, 'IRA kill Catholic butcher',[25] while the *News of the World* had 'Shopkeeper who defied IRA is killed'.[26] *The Sunday Times* hedged its bets, saying:

> In Belfast, police investigating the murder of a 38-year-old Catholic butcher are trying to determine whether it was a sectarian killing by Protestants or an IRA reprisal for his refusal to close his shops in sympathy with the H-Block hunger strikers.[27]

On the Monday, *Guardian* journalist Paul Keel reported that 'fellow traders on the Crumlin Road and at the Divis flats area said at the weekend that he had closed his premises on Friday,' and that the IRA's Belfast Brigade had 'issued a statement furiously denying any involvement in the murder and alleging that the incident bore the hallmarks of a sectarian killing "carried out by Loyalist assassins and designed to intimidate the Catholic community." '

The IRA was right. It was later established that the dead man had indeed closed his shops in mourning, and the Ulster Freedom Fighters – the alias used by the UDA – claimed responsibility for the killing.[29] The 'mystery' had been deliberately contrived, probably by the police, at a time when the authorities were thoroughly alarmed by the massive support generated in the nationalist community for the hunger strikers, and by international press coverage that was sceptical of British policy.

Religious labels

The authorities have also encouraged the media to underplay loyalist violence in other ways. Merlyn Rees was Labour's Northern Ireland Secretary from 1974 to September 1976. During his tenure, which coincided with a renewal of the loyalist campaign of sectarian assassinations, Belfast TV, radio and press representatives were invited to a meeting at Stormont Castle, headquarters of the Northern Ireland Office. There John Leahy, a Foreign Office official seconded to the Northern Ireland Office, asked them not to state in news reports the religious affiliations of the assassination victims.[30] The press representatives rejected the request.

The ostensible reason given for suppressing details of religion is that the reporting of them would exacerbate tension by provoking the other side into retaliating. In the context of the Six Counties, this argument was very thin, and senior BBC men have publicly demolished it. The religion of the victim, as Sir Charles Curran, Richard Francis and a later Northern Ireland Controller, James Hawthorne, have pointed out, is what above all their audience in the North want to know. As Francis said, 'a sectarian label is a piece of shorthand, it's no different in essence from the description of a person's background, his [sic] name, where he went to school, the street where he lived and, inevitably, where he is to be buried, all facts which in Northern Ireland are liable to indicate a person's religion.' He went on to note that 'Broadcasting is not indispensable to convey this sort of information in small communities.' People would immediately guess a person's religion from where they lived – and might draw the wrong conclusion. 'The possibilities and anxieties are endless if no details are given,' said Francis.[31]

From the security point of view, then, there was no justification for suppressing information about religion, since people in the Six Counties would rapidly guess it, and a wrong guess could worsen the situation. The authorities, however, were undeterred by either this argument or by the media representatives' refusal to co-operate. They played a different card: the police and army, on whom the media depend heavily for information about such incidents, simply refrained from giving details about the religion of victims.[32] Since Catholics were the main victims of sectarian assassinations, the effect of this policy could only be to minimise the extent of organised loyalist violence and give the impression, to those outside the nationalist areas, that the killings were 'mindless' and random.

Despite the case put up by Richard Francis that assassinations are often inexplicable unless the religion of the victim is given, the BBC does not always act accordingly. On 12 May 1982, for example, three Catholics were shot on the Antrim Road, a mixed area, and one, Frank Toner, died. The information that they were Catholics was obviously available that evening, since the commercial service, Independent Radio News, reported it. The BBC's television news bulletins, however, gave no indication of their religion.

'Random' violence

In their presentation of stories the media tend to play down all but IRA responsibility for violence. Philip Elliott's survey showed that the press tended to emphasise the IRA in their headlines where the IRA were being blamed for violence, and they stressed the army and police where they were the victims. But other stories involving violence were dealt with in 'human interest' terms, with the headline writers concentrating on aspects such as

> the particular misfortune of the individuals involved, for example that they were pregnant, about to leave the province or shouldn't have been there at the time; the ordinariness of the occasion – that it happened at work, on the way to work or as the family relaxed at home; the particular bravery of someone involved or the particular horror of the act itself . . .[33]

As a result, the media gave the impression 'that violence related to Northern Ireland was carried out by the IRA against members of the security forces and that many other people were suffering apparently at random.'[34] Yet at the time of the survey most of the victims were Catholic and loyalist assassination squads had claimed some of the killings.

Philip Elliott found that while IRA violence was treated in the media as a planned campaign, and was denounced as senseless and horrid, loyalist violence was handled in a 'guarded and ambiguous' way. Where loyalists were involved, the media tended to use the indeterminate label 'sectarian'. They also often implicitly justified loyalist violence, coupling reports of murders 'with explanations in terms of loyalist anger, reprisals or a protestant backlash.'[35]

When Maire Drumm, who had recently resigned her post as Vice-President of Provisional Sinn Fein, was assassinated in Belfast's Mater Hospital in October 1976, the popular papers could scarcely conceal their glee. They had already dubbed her 'Grandmother of Hate' on account of her fiery anti-British speeches. Now the *Daily Mirror* announced her death in huge front-page letters; 'HATE GRANNY SHOT DEAD'. The article, which began, 'The IRA's Grandmother of Hate was shot dead last night as she lay in a hospital bed', contained no hint of condemnation of the assassins, who were described as an 'execution squad' and 'cool killers'.[36] This theme was not restricted to the tabloids. *Sunday Times* journalists Anthony Holden and Chris

Ryder ascribed to her 'a household nickname: Grandma Venom.' They concluded their piece with what Eamonn McCann has described as 'one of the cheapest and certainly the most grotesque journalistic shots yet used in the North.'[37] They wrote: 'Her friends and enemies are already offering many an epitaph, but there is none more chilling than removing the final "m" of her surname and spelling Maire Drumm backwards: MURDER I AM.'[38]

Maire Drumm's funeral presented a further opportunity for the same theme to be pursued. The *Mirror*'s front page carried a large picture of mourners carrying her coffin as a uniformed firing party raise their pistols, framed with the words 'GUN SALUTE FOR GRANNY OF HATE'. The *Mail*, too, described her as 'Grandmother of Hate', while *The Sun* wrote, below a picture of her weeping daughters, 'The bitter harvest of hate that was sown by Maire Drumm is reaped by her two grieving daughters'. Analysing the papers' visual presentation of the funeral, sociologist Frank Webster concluded that 'A major theme of the press treatment of Maire Drumm's funeral was a concern to portray the occasion as an example of the "wages of extremism".'[39]

In this context it is perhaps instructive to note that when Unionist MP Robert Bradford was killed by the IRA in November 1981, the reaction was quite different. 'Ulster was plunged into fury yesterday by the terrorist killing of preacher MP Robert Bradford,' wrote Trevor Hanna in a front-page *News of the World* article titled 'IRA ASSASSINS GUN DOWN MP'.[40] Condemnations of the IRA flowed thick and fast from politicians and the media. Yet Bradford not only consorted with loyalist paramilitaries – he was a regular attender at meetings of their umbrella body, the Ulster Loyalist Co-ordinating Committee (ULCC)[41] – but he also repeatedly incited hatred against Catholics in general and republicans in particular, and issued thinly disguised appeals to loyalist hit squads, as when in 1978, using parliamentary privilege, he named several staff at Belfast's Royal Victoria Hospital, alleging that they were IRA sympathisers. During the 'no wash' protest in the H Blocks, he urged people to pray for typhoid to break out there which, he said, would solve the issue. Yet neither before, nor after, his death was Bradford dubbed 'Daddy of Hate', and the coverage focussed on the iniquity of the killers rather than of the victim. Bradford's death, unlike Maire Drumm's, was not portrayed as the 'wages of extremism'.

The shooting of the McAliskeys

When loyalists shot and seriously injured Bernadette McAliskey and her husband Michael at their remote country cottage on 16 January 1981, the coverage exhibited many familiar features. The southern Irish papers gave the story considerably more prominence than British ones: *The Irish Times*, for example, had nearly three times more coverage next day than *The Guardian*, which itself had more coverage than any other British paper. The British papers focussed their attention on Bernadette McAliskey, with headlines on the theme of 'Devlin is "very ill" after shooting'.[42] *The Irish Times*, by contrast, headlined its main story 'McAliskey weakens after UDA attack', and then Northern Editor David McKittrick explained that, 'The Ulster Defence Association was responsible for yesterday's attempt on the lives of the former MP, Mrs Bernadette McAliskey, and her husband Michael, according to reliable souces.' Another article in the same edition, headed 'Shooting fits pattern of UDA attacks', described in some detail the parallels between this attack and the killings the previous year of John Turnly, a Protestant politician who strongly favoured Irish independence, and republican activists Miriam Daly, Ronnie Bunting and Noel Little.[43]

The British papers showed relatively little concern about who the attackers were, and were more interested in Bernadette McAliskey's character and in portraying the British troops who arrived on the scene in a heroic light. The popular papers' description of Bernadette McAliskey betrayed traces of the 'wages of extremism' approach. She was several times called a 'firebrand' and a 'fighter' – becoming a 'warrior' in *The Guardian* – and the *Mail* told how she was 'indubitably' born 'to a life in which peace is merely a lull between bullets.'[44] One of the odder accounts appeared in the *Daily Mirror*, which told its readers:

> Just a few hours before her condition worsened, fiery Republican Bernadette had vowed to 'fight on'.
> She said as she lay in her hospital bed: 'I am not dead yet and I will never give up the struggle.
> 'I have been expecting this for a long time. I knew that I and my family have been at risk. Now they think they have got me.'[45]

The entire quote was a fantasy. Bernadette McAliskey was in fact unable to speak for some two weeks after the incident.

What most delighted the British papers was the presence of

British troops at the scene. 'How Paras saved Bernadette from death', was the *Mail*'s front page headline, and reporter Noreen Erskine began her story,

> BY A supreme irony, the British soldiers whom Bernadette Devlin has fought so hard to remove from Ulster saved her from bleeding to death after she and her husband were attacked yesterday.[46]

This angle appears in part to have been suggested by an RUC press statement: in *The Irish Times* the RUC were reported as saying that 'quick action by soldiers in summoning medical help undoubtedly had saved the McAliskeys' lives.' In the *Mail* this appeared, rather differently, as 'The prompt action of the soldiers in giving medical aid undoubtedly prevented the McAliskeys from bleeding to death.'[47]

But the emphasis on the life-saving role of the paratroopers was firstly inaccurate – the McAliskeys had to wait for a second group of soldiers, from the locally based Argyll and Sutherland Highlanders, to arrive before being given medical aid;[48] secondly, it diverted attention from the more important question of what the paratroops were doing near the cottage in the first place. That there was something odd about this was immediately apparent from the Press Association's reports on the day of the shooting. Soon after 2 p.m. the PA said that 'Three men were detained at the scene by an SAS patrol who had been operating nearby.' But later this was amended to read 'an army patrol'. By the next day the soldiers were being unanimously described as belonging to the Third Parachute Battalion.

Irish journalists were soon asking a number of questions about the incident. Why was a squad of paras operating in County Tyrone, so far from its normal area of work around Crossmaglen? If they were near enough to the cottage to catch the killers in the lane, why were they unable to prevent the attack? Why was the paras' commanding officer, Colonel Hew Pike, on the scene giving interviews before the police arrived? If the army knew an attack was likely, why had they not told the McAliskeys? The mainstream British media were not interested in pursuing these lines of enquiry.[49]

A year later, in January 1982, the three members of the Ulster Defence Association who were caught at the scene were given long jail sentences for attempted murder. The BBC's *Nine O'Clock News* report on their conviction, repeated later in *Newsnight*, managed to minimise the role of the loyalist would-be assassins and transform the event into a tale of army heroism. After a rudimentary account of the shooting incident, reporter Nicholas Witchell went on: 'The leader of the gang was Andrew Watson. Six years ago his wife's uncle was murdered by the IRA. According to counsel, he became hardened. He felt Mrs McAliskey was the type of person he was prepared to try to kill.'[50]

By failing to mention that the three were members of the Ulster Defence Association, by singling out Watson and by dealing with the event in terms of his personal motivation, Witchell had obscured a key feature of the affair: that it was the result of organised activity by a legal loyalist organisation. As *The Irish Times* revealed the following morning, the murder had been planned at a meeting of the South Belfast UDA, and was Watson's second UDA-sponsored attempt to kill Bernadette McAliskey. Nor was it a one-off event, but the latest in a series of attacks on prominent activists. Further, by highlighting Watson's supposed feelings, Witchell was in effect inviting the audience to understand his action. But the excuse – that his wife's uncle had been murdered by the IRA – was disingenuous, for by the time that happened, Watson had already been in the UDA for three years. Witchell also omitted to say that Watson had at one time been a member of the British army's locally recruited regiment, the UDR.

Witchell then embraced the theme so dear to the tabloids. He repeated the distortion that the McAliskeys had been saved by 'the immediate application of first aid by the military patrol outside their home.' He went on:

> Mrs McAliskey says her views about the British army haven't changed. Though, after she recovered, she presented a crystal decanter to the soldier who saved her life. That soldier was Colonel Campbell McFarlane . . .

Confusingly, Witchell failed to say that McFarlane was a surgeon, thus giving the erroneous impression that he had been in the patrol. More important, Witchell was implying that the soldiers' actions had proved Bernadette McAliskey's views on the army to be wrong. But this suggestion was higher on propaganda value than on logic. For it could equally well be argued that if there were no British presence in the north of Ireland, she would not have needed to oppose it, and consequently would never have been shot in the first place. Unlike ITN, the BBC asked no questions about what the troops were doing near her cottage, and devoted nearly half its report to the army's life-saving role, successfully obscuring the issue of assassination squads operating under the auspices of a legal loyalist body.

UDA interviews

The media's ambiguity towards loyalist violence reflects the attitude of the authorities: an attitude inadvertently revealed by Northern Ireland Secretary Humphrey Atkins in 1980 when he accused loyalist assassins of playing into the hands of 'the terrorists'. Nationalists were outraged by this remark, which implied that loyalists who killed Catholics were not terrorists, but the IRA were. The ambiguity is made plain by the legislation, which outlaws the IRA and the loyalist UVF, but leaves the UDA legal. Yet UDA leader Andy Tyrie admitted in 1981 that in the early days the organisation killed Catholics indiscriminately and now engaged in selective political assassinations against active republicans.[51] In 1981 on its own admission the UDA had over 320 members in prison for offences ranging from murder to possession of arms.[52]

Television reporters can interview members of the UDA without encountering the constraints that accompany interviews with IRA or INLA representatives. A clear example of the different standards that are applied occurred in 1976, when BBC Scotland made a film called *The Scottish Connection* which traced the cultural and political connections between the people of Scotland and the Six Counties. The film included interviews with UDA members, including Roddy MacDonald, the UDA's Supreme Commander in Scotland. Claiming there were 6,000 Scotsmen in the UDA, MacDonald said, 'we're training them to fight, but I can't say where'.

But the film-makers were forced to drop an interview with a Provisional IRA representative. The BBC's Northern Ireland Controller insisted on the ban, and Director-General Charles Curran, after viewing the film, confirmed the exclusion of the interview. The makers then planned to insert in the film a statement reading, 'We cannot show an interview with a spokesman from the Provisional IRA. The BBC's policy is not to interview them. Members of the UDA are, however, not subject to this restriction.' But when the film was shown on 23 October, the statement had been dropped. It seems the BBC did not want the public's attention drawn either to the act of censorship or to the double standards being applied.[53]

Interviews with representatives of the IRA or INLA have been so rare that each one has been a major event, provoking massive political recriminations. Interviews with the UDA have been more frequent. Because the UDA is a legal organisation, the television companies apply no restrictions. Nor do UDA interviews generate protests from politicians.

The UDA do not bulk large in the coverage, but when they do appear, they are not given the 'hostile witness' treatment which is mandatory when IRA or even Sinn Fein members are featured. An item on the BBC's *Nationwide* about a loyalist social club illustrated the latitude which reporters have when portraying the UDA. As a country band gave a rendering of 'Here comes the night' and the camera roamed over the faces of happy drinkers, the reporter remarked reassuringly that the club, in Belfast's Newtownards Road, was 'reminiscent of any social club in the northeast of England.' He continued, in the bedtime story tone beloved of *Nationwide*,

> An evening spent here is a release from the pressures of the troubles. Although it would be wrong to suggest that a majority of Protestants in East Belfast are members of the Ulster Defence Association, the UDA, the movement here is strong, and it's comforting to know that when there's sectarian trouble, the UDA is never far away.

The camera then cut to a man saying, 'We had no protection when it was formed. And it was just ordinary blokes . . .' To which the interviewer responded, 'But do you find it a comfort to know that the UDA is always there?' Predictably, the answer was 'Yes'.[54]

The portrayal of the situation of Protestants in the Newtownards Road as threatened by 'sectarian trouble' was misleading: the area is solidly Protestant for miles around, and the only Catholics are on the edge of it, in the tiny Short Strand enclave. More important, it is inconceivable that a television report would treat the IRA in the same way. Given that the 'sectarian' threat is primarily aimed by loyalists at isolated Catholic areas, it would be much more reasonable for a reporter to stand in a club in the Short Strand or Ardoyne and say, 'It's comforting to know that when there's sectarian trouble, the IRA is never far away.' Reasonable, perhaps, but unimaginable.

The UWC stoppage

Sympathetic media coverage of loyalists has almost always passed unremarked by politicians. The one major exception was BBC Northern Ireland's radio coverage of the Ulster Workers' Council stoppage in May 1974. This two-week strike directly, and in the event successfully, challenged the central planks of British government policy at the time, the power-sharing executive and plans for a Council of Ireland.

In his book, *The Point of No Return*,[55] journalist Robert Fisk described the BBC's indulgent treatment of the strike. Speaking on radio – the TV transmitters were put out of action after a week by power cuts – UWC leaders were allowed to publicise the strike and to get away unchallenged with ludicrous claims that there was no intimidation, that strike leaders were democratically elected and that the UDA were uninvolved. The BBC quoted the UWC's statements at great length: 'It was as if the BBC hung upon the UWC's every word, as to some extent it did,' wrote Fisk. The BBC also repeatedly broadcast doom-laden and often inaccurate reports predicting imminent chaos, implying, in Fisk's words, 'the inevitability of catastrophe if the executive remained in office.' The obsession with instant news meant that there was no attempt to explore the political issues behind the strike.

The British government and members of the executive bitterly criticised the BBC for assisting the strikers' cause. But since their own handling of the strike had been weak and indecisive, their complaints rang somewhat hollow. There was, nevertheless, considerable truth in them. Strike leader Harry Murray later said, 'The BBC were marvellous – they were prepared to be fed any information. They fell into their own trap that "the public must get the news". Sometimes they were just a news service for us; we found that if the media was on our side we didn't need a gun.'[56]

There is some irony in the fact that the BBC so markedly departed from its usually unsympathetic attitude to strikers in the case of a stoppage organised by a right-wing, self-elected body, assisted by loyalist paramilitaries and using overt intimidation to promote the restoration of loyalist supremacy.

6. Reporting republican violence

Dominating the coverage

Violence dominates British media coverage of the Six Counties. In his survey, Philip Elliott found that most stories were about 'acts of violence or the enforcement of the law' and that only a third of stories dealt with politics and other subjects.[1] The Irish media had a different perspective: they carried about five times more stories on the North than the British media, and they were much more concerned about the political dimension.[2]

The British media not only concentrate on violence to the exclusion of politics, but they also, as critics have long pointed out, report violent incidents without giving any context or explanation for them. As far back as 1971, critics were observing that television news bulletins were not attempting to explain what was happening in the North: comment was rigorously excluded from the news, and was treated as the preserve of current affairs programmes.[3]

As Elliott noted, the British media's emphasis on 'factual' reporting of incidents, concentrating on the 'who, what, where, when' and leaving out the background and significance, appears to be objective and straightforward but in fact is very misleading. This type of reporting provides the audience with details of 'age, sex, occupation, type of incident, injuries, location and time of day.' But such information says nothing about the causes of the incident, making violence appear as random as a natural disaster or accident.[4]

Not only does violence, reported in a non-explanatory manner, dominate the coverage: it is also presented as if it were the almost exclusive preserve of republicans. Elliott contrasted the approaches of the British and Irish media:

The overall tendency of the British press was to simplify by writing the IRA into the headlines . . . Reports in the Irish papers were more complex. More attention was paid to the way in which any particular incident fitted in with current trends. More emphasis was placed on assessing responsibility, not simply in the sense of reciting alternative versions but in the sense of deciding which was more likely to be correct. The Irish papers were less likely to quote official sources unless they contributed to this process of validating a version of the event . . . On occasions the Irish papers also provided a longer historical dimension.[5]

Blaming the IRA

The IRA has been blamed for numerous acts of violence per-petrated by the British army or loyalists. This process culminated during the 1981 hunger strike with the IRA being blamed for all the deaths in the troubles to date. Tory and Unionist MPs and Christopher Thomas of *The Times* asserted that the IRA had killed 2,000 people, while *Express* cartoonist Cummings marked the death of Bobby Sands MP with a drawing of a huge memorial inscribed '1969–1981 THEY HAD NO CHOICE 2094 MURDERED BY THE IRA'.[6]

Christopher Thomas began his front page *Times* report on the funeral of Bobby Sands thus: 'The Roman Catholics buried Robert Sands yesterday as Protestants lamented their 2,000 dead from 12 years of terrorism.'[7] He went on to refer to the '2,000 victims' of Bobby Sands' 'collaborators'. The implication was clear: that the IRA had killed 2,000 Protestants. Indeed, since the official figure for the number killed in the troubles since 1969 was just over 2,000, Thomas was in effect blaming the IRA for every single death.

London-based Irishman Donal Kennedy wrote to *The Times* to complain, pointing out that among the North's 2,100 dead were hundreds of Catholics killed in sectarian murders by loyalist paramilitaries, as well as hundreds of people, including IRA members, killed by the army and RUC.[8] He received a brief reply, saying that following the receipt of his letter 'our Northern Ireland correspondent has checked the figure and confirms it from several sources.'[9] Kennedy then made a complaint to the Press Council, which prompted *The Times* to publish a letter drawing attention to the inaccuracy. Some nine months later the Press Council finally reprimanded *The Times*:

> It was six weeks after publishing the inaccurate statement that 2,000 Protestants had been killed by terrorism that the newspaper printed a reader's letter correcting its error. The Press Council regards this as a most serious error of fact on a highly sensitive matter which should have been corrected by the newspaper at once and in a more forthright manner.[10]

The Press Council has no teeth: its only sanction is the convention that all newspapers report its findings. Among those that in this case did not were *The Observer*, *The Guardian* and *The Sunday Times*.

The fact that Thomas could confidently make such a grossly inaccurate statement without fear of rebuke from his editor testifies to the extent of the fact-rigging process that had gone on over the years. By May 1981, the army and police had been responsible for over 200 deaths, and loyalists for over 600. Further, loyalists had killed more civilians than nationalists had, and indeed virtually all of the victims of loyalists were civilians.[11]

The IRA have not only been blamed for loyalist and army violence, but also for a ragbag of other incidents, some real, some half-imagined, that they had nothing to do with. In June 1977, for example, television news bulletins announced that a 17-year-old soldier, Peter Wright, was feared to have been kidnapped and murdered by the IRA. He later turned up in Dorset, in Scotland Yard's words 'alive and well'.[12] Then on 1 January 1978, under the front page headline 'DEATH BOMB BLAST ROCKS MAYFAIR', *Sunday Express* journalist William Massie proclaimed, 'A Provisional IRA car bomb exploded in the centre of London last night killing the vehicle's occupant and another person.' In *The Sunday Times*, however, David Blundy established that the two dead men were Arabs and believed to be members of the Syrian embassy staff.[13] The police later concluded that the men had in fact been transporting the bomb themselves. Philip Elliott records how in 1974 the *Daily Express* immediately concluded that an army colonel, shot and injured at his home in Wiltshire by a single gunman, was an IRA victim. Yet other papers simply reported that police were looking for a motive, and *The Sun* said unequivocally that detectives and army chiefs 'do not believe the IRA were involved'.[14]

Similarly, when in February 1979 bombs exploded in the shopping centre of Yeovil in Somerset, the papers immediately headlined the news that the IRA was responsible, even though the police said it was too early to say who had planted the bombs.[15]

The police rapidly established that a man from Gloucestershire, who had been injured in one of the explosions, was responsible: he was able to tell them where to find six unexploded devices, and they found bomb-making ingredients at his home where an explosion had wrecked an outhouse two weeks before.[16]

Again, an arms raid on a barracks in Cambridgeshire in January 1982 led *The Sun* to announce on its front page 'TRAITOR IN ARMY CAMP' with the sub-headline 'Soldier stole guns for IRA'. Reporter Ian Hepburn told with complete conviction how 'A British soldier turned traitor to mastermind a daring arms snatch from an Army barracks. Then he handed the haul to the IRA.' *The Guardian* of the same day, however, put a different gloss on the story, quoting the policeman in charge of the inquiry as saying, 'It could be someone wishing to embarrass the Army, or a criminal hoping to use the weapons or sell them. Of course, we cannot totally rule out the IRA.'[18]

The habit of writing the IRA into the headlines on the slightest excuse sometimes has ludicrous consequences. When former Northern Ireland Prime Minister Brian Faulkner died in March 1977, the *Daily Express* headlined the story 'Faulkner, target of IRA dies in fall from horse'.[19]

Bombs in Britain

The amount of attention paid to acts of violence that really were committed by the IRA depends on the circumstances. Attacks taking place in Britain, killings of prominent people – especially if they are British, and bombings that result in civilian deaths, generate the most publicity. A journalist reporting from Belfast for a British paper said:

> The daily violence has got to be fairly exceptional to be a big news story . . . You're fairly limited in what you can write about incidents of violence – bombs going off and assassinations – because you weren't at the scene at the time. If you jump into the car and rush down, you're held up – you can be held even with a press card – almost out of sight of the scene, so you're not going to see much of it. So my approach is to try and deal with it as quickly and efficiently as possible, to make use of the radio, the *Belfast Telegraph*, television, and then try and save time to do the more in-depth pieces.[20]

Philip Elliott found in his study that the bombing of two pubs in Guildford 'received nearly twice as much space in the

British media as all the incidents which occurred in Northern Ireland taken together.'[21] Yet during that three-week period, nearly twice as many people were killed in the North of Ireland as at Guildford, and there were also numerous other violent incidents.[22]

Elliott also noted that the Guildford bombings were the only incident to become a running story in the British media. While killings in the Six Counties were generally reported once and then forgotten, the Guildford bombs were followed by numerous related news stories: messages of horror and sympathy from personages such as the Queen, the Prime Minister and the Leader of the Opposition; the setting up of a relief fund for the victims; debates on whether capital punishment should be re-introduced and on whether the Price sisters should be transferred from Britain to jails in the North of Ireland; and the police hunt for the bombers.

The prolonged attention given to the Guildford bombs did not, Elliott suggested, 'simply reflect the importance which British news editors attached to events on the mainland as against events in the province.'[23] It was rather as if British society, united against an external threat, was daily applying a new dressing to the wound it had received.

Trials of people charged with bombings and similar offences were treated in a similar way.[24] Elliott found that the British media gave far more attention to cases before the English and Scottish courts than to cases in the North of Ireland, and indeed the national television news bulletins only covered the cases being heard in Britain.

In stark contrast to the dramatic coverage given to such trials has been the way the mainstream media have almost totally ignored a crucial feature of many such cases, one which in other contexts provides fertile ground for investigative journalists. There is substantial evidence indicating that at least seventeen of those people convicted of bombing or explosives offences in Britain, some of them sentenced to imprisonment for the rest of their natural lives, are in fact innocent. These are Patrick Armstrong, Gerry Conlon, Paul Hill and Carole Richardson, sentenced in 1975 for the Guildford and Woolwich pub bombings; Anne Maguire, Paddy Maguire, Vincent Maguire (released in 1979), Patrick Maguire (also released in 1979), Sean Smyth (released in 1983), Pat O'Neill (also released) and Guiseppe Conlon (who died of tuberculosis in 1980 while still serving his sentence), all of whom were convicted in 1976 of explosives offences; and William Power, Gerard Hunter, Patrick Hill, John Walker, Noel McIlkenny and Hugh Callaghan, all convicted of the 1974 Birmingham pub bombings. The only British publications which have carried articles probing these cases are the *New Statesman* and *Tribune*, neither of which has a large circulation. Attempts to interest television programmes have not, at the time of writing, borne fruit.[25]

Human interest

The media usually report violent incidents in terms of 'human interest', concentrating on the experience of individuals rather than of groups or classes, and dramatising the single event rather than looking at the background. This is part of the normal approach of the media, especially the popular press and television, and journalists are expected to report in this way. A textbook used on journalism training courses puts the patronising view that

> The bulk of readers of the bulk of newspapers are people who left school at 14 or 15. Their primary interest is in people or the doings of people; they are not so much interested in abstract concepts . . . Readers are interested in how the news affects them and their children, and how it affects other people. They readily identify themselves with people in trouble, with people engaged in controversy, with people at the centre of great events.[26]

These sentiments are echoed in the BBC's *News Guide*, a handbook issued to all staff working in radio news, which writes of its audience that

> Whatever their circumstances and background, they are interested in news primarily when it affects them personally – for instance through their pockets (a tax increase) or their emotions (a badly treated child). They are concerned with facts rather than with argument. They are mainly concerned with 'what' but increasingly we have to explain 'why'.[27]

But the media are highly selective about whose lives they take an interest in. When it comes to the reporting of violence in the North of Ireland, 'our' lives are portrayed as more important than 'their' lives. Whereas victims of British or loyalist violence usually feature as little more than ciphers, nameless, ageless, without occupations or mourning relatives, victims of republican violence are fleshed out and given a human identity. The commentary on a BBC *Tonight* film neatly illustrates the contrasting treatment: over shots of Bloody Sunday, the audience was told that

> In January 1972 British paratroopers shot dead 13 unarmed civilians during a civil rights march in Londonderry. In retaliation the Official IRA bombed the paras' Aldershot headquarters. The explosion killed five women canteen workers, a gardener and a Catholic padre.[28]

Although fewer people were killed at Aldershot than on Bloody Sunday, their deaths, as presented here, have greater impact because their sex and occupations are specified.

The establishment and the media almost never ask us to feel compassion for the people they call 'terrorists'. Rather, we are asked to feel compassion for the victims of 'terrorists'. As sociologists Philip Elliott, Graham Murdock and Philip Schlesinger have pointed out, the suffering of these victims is reported in a way that carries a strong political message: 'that it is terrorism which is responsible for injury, death and increasing the sum of human misery'.[29]

The victims of 'terrorism' do not all, however, receive the same treatment. As Philip Elliott noted, 'The death of an ambassador, a judge, a magistrate, is worth more space than that of a 14-year-old mental defective, however heart-rending his story may be from a personal human interest.'[30] When a prominent person is killed, powerful sections of society respond with eulogies of the victim and condemnations of the killers: when an ordinary soldier or policeman is killed, they have little to say.

Lord Mountbatten

The assassination of Lord Mountbatten on 27 August 1979 provides a dramatic example. Within hours of Mountbatten's death, an IRA ambush near Warrenpoint in County Down killed 14 soldiers, with four more dying later. While the death of Mountbatten, whose grandson and boatman died with him, was given enormous coverage, the soldiers' deaths received much less prominence. *The Guardian*, for instance, on 28 August gave over the greater part of its front page to Mountbatten's assassination, and relegated the soldiers to a short column at one side.[31] The *Daily Mirror* devoted nearly eight full pages to Mountbatten:

a note at the bottom of page two read '14 soldiers massacred – see back page'. Even then, the greater part of the back page featured an editorial on Mountbatten, alongside an item on his dead grandson, while the piece on the soldiers' deaths was in the bottom right hand corner. While all the *Mirror*'s articles on Mountbatten were surrounded with the black lines of mourning, the item on the soldiers was not.[32] A few days later, the *Mirror* gave ten black-lined pages to Mountbatten's funeral.[33]

The coverage had strong ritual overtones, with Mountbatten symbolising goodness, civilisation and the British nation at its mythic best, while the IRA were portrayed as the irrational forces of evil: the *Daily Mirror* headlined its leader, 'LORD LOUIS and the enemies of man'.[34] As Philip Schlesinger wrote,

> The tone of the coverage was highly reverential, almost sacral, given his kinship to the Queen. Mountbatten was presented as the epitome of the finest British qualities: soldier, hero, noble, statesman, family man *par excellence*. The newspapers and television programs ran stockpiled obituaries, interviews with acquaintances and friends, and tributes from across the globe. The act of killing was widely interpreted as irrational, as that of 'evil men' (*Daily Mail*), 'wicked assassins' (*The Sun*), 'psychopathic thugs' (*Daily Express*), 'murdering bastards' (*Daily Star*), as 'cowardly and senseless' (*Financial Times*) and as the product of 'diseased minds rather than political calculation' (*Daily Telegraph*).[35]

The image of both the man and the nation had more to do with myth than reality. The *Daily Express*, for example, in a front page piece headlined 'THESE EVIL BASTARDS', contrasted the 'cowardly psychopaths' of the IRA with 'the British' who 'have never yielded to terror' and Lord Mountbatten, whom 'everyone loved'.[36] As journalist Geoff Bell commented,

> Obviously 'everyone' didn't 'love' Mountbatten, and obviously Britain has 'yielded to terror' on numerous occasions. Indeed, probably no other ruling class in the world has negotiated with more of what it defines as 'terrorists'.[37]

The major controversies of his career were submerged in the tide of eulogies or transformed into great achievements. A *Daily Mirror* obituary, titled 'PROFILE OF A HERO', revealed in the small print that 'even today, in Canada, Mountbatten's name is reviled', on account of the 1942 Dieppe raid, which he planned, and in which 3,363 out of 5,000 Canadians lost their lives. The same piece noted that 'the biggest question mark in his life hovers over India . . . He led it to freedom – but 200,000 people were killed in the riots that followed.' Reporter Terence Lancaster went on to comment, 'I believe Mountbatten was right.'[38] In *The Guardian*, Mountbatten's supervision of Indian independence and its partition became 'his greatest service'.[39] His vanity and arrogance went unremarked or were excused: an *Observer* 'appreciation' concluded that 'the touch of hubris in his nature was combined with so many glorious qualities that even the gods should forgive him.'[40]

Captain Nairac

Another person whose death became a conduit for patriotic sentiment was Captain Robert Nairac. Nairac received more coverage in death than probably any other soldier killed in the Six Counties since 1971. A Grenadier Guards captain, he was working undercover with the SAS in South Armagh when he was kidnapped and killed by the IRA in May 1977. The media immediately profiled him as a 'classic hero'.[41] Whereas most soldiers killed while on duty are described as having been 'murdered', Nairac was 'executed'. The notion that Nairac was executed rather than murdered was central to the portrait of a war hero, bravely sacrificing his life for his country: the *Mirror*'s front page featured a large picture of Nairac in uniform with the headline 'Missing while on active service, believed EXECUTED'.[42]

The media evidently reproduced without question the profile they had been supplied with by the military. ITN's *News at Ten* accorded his life and death a full five minutes, which, as journalist Steve Gilbert noted, was 'as substantial a report as would record the death of a major statesman.'[43] Gilbert described how

> Norman Rees, accompanied by two stills of Nairac as an adolescent, read a fulsome tribute: 'Captain Nairac was one of those people who, from an early age, combined academic brilliance with a love for tough and demanding physical sport. His big love was boxing. At Ampleforth, Britain's top Roman Catholic public school, he captained the boxing team while managing nine 'O' levels, three 'A' levels and a place at Lincoln College, Oxford. At university, he continued boxing and won a blue while studying history. Then it was off to Sandhurst and a commission in the Grenadier Guards, a commission that soon saw him on active duty in Northern Ireland'.[44]

The *Daily Mail* took up the same theme, titling its two page spread 'The boy who was good at everything'. The story opened, 'Robert Nairac was a genuine hero straight from the pages of the Boys' Own Paper . . . tough, intelligent, always anxious to be at the centre of the action.'[45]

Sociologist Frank Webster has pointed out that there was nothing 'natural' about the way Nairac's death was reported: instead, it stemmed from the British media's particular perspective, 'which interprets the British army presence and fighting in Northern Ireland as unquestionably legitimate.'[46] He writes,

> A different culture, one that perhaps defined the army's role in Northern Ireland as a classically colonial one of holding down an unwilling populace, would see the disappearance of Robert Nairac rather differently to the British press . . . Here what could well have been emphasised may have been Nairac's membership of the SAS (Special Air Service), his role as a 'spy' in Armagh . . . Or a theme of the success of republican 'partisans' against a well-trained and equipped army could have been developed. Other media could have stressed Nairac's background . . . as indicative of the British Army's class prejudices, which leads to the sort of amateurism that results in such loss of highly placed personnel . . .[47]

Several of these angles were indeed featured in the Belfast weekly *Republican News*, which carried a comic strip profiling 'Captain Nervewreck', an incompetent ex-public schoolboy with a taste for adventure.

Sefton

Perhaps the most potent 'human interest' stories in the British media are those which do not feature people at all, but animals. British soldiers in Crossmaglen reportedly became somewhat disconsolate when the much-publicised dog, Rats, received a much greater volume of fan mail than they did themselves.[48] In the aftermath of the IRA's London bombings in July 1982, in which 12 soldiers died and numerous soldiers and civilians were injured, the image that was most strongly imprinted on the national consciousness was that of a horse, Sefton, who was soon being described as 'the most famous horse in Britain'.[49]

The day after the bombings, practically every British paper carried a photograph of Sefton. While he did not bulk large in the qualities, the popular press spotted the potential of the story immediately. The *Mail*, *The Sun*, the *Express* and the *Mirror* each devoted half a page or more to pictures of the horse and detailed accounts of its wounds, hammering out the theme of the bombers' wanton cruelty. The *Mail* headlined its story 'The victim of savagery',[50] echoing the coverage of Mountbatten's death with its emphasis on civilisation versus the forces of evil. *The Sun* opted for another angle: 'SEFTON – THE HORSE THEY COULDN'T KILL'.[51]

The Sefton story ran and ran, on television as in the press. Sefton's wounds, his mountains of gifts and get-well cards, his convalescence, his return to barracks, were all recorded. The military arranged photo-calls and briefings on his condition, and the media responded. The horse rapidly attained symbolic status. A few days after the bombings, the *Daily Mirror* devoted its front page to 'The wonder horse that wouldn't die'. Concentrating on Sefton and how 'he battled back' and 'showed his spirit by tucking into a bunch of carrots', reporter John Jackson mentioned the death of a fourth cavalryman only in passing.[52] Next day *The Sunday Times* carried a front page feature headlined 'Sefton: symbol of suffering'. Racing correspondent Brough Scott told how 'Old Sefton stood bravely in his box, battered but unbowed, a superb dumb symbol of suffering.'[53] It was as if the horse had become a symbol of the British body politic, grievously injured through no fault of its own by savage outsiders, but battling through to survival despite the odds.

On the face of it, the avalanche of sympathy for Sefton might appear to be an innocuous expression of human compassion, unrelated to politics. In practice, however, it contained a political message that was all the more powerful for being concealed. As educationalist Albert Hunt put it, when discussing a BBC interview with two white Rhodesians whose relatives had died in a 'terrorist' attack, 'We're invited to identify with the characters, to share their suffering. But in sharing their suffering, we're also being invited to identify with their view of the world . . . But because it's presented in such a personalised way, it becomes hard to recognise as a political view at all.'[54] From Sefton's point of view, as interpreted by the British media, the IRA appeared as mindlessly cruel, while the British were innocent sufferers.[55]

The London bombings came shortly after the war in the South Atlantic, and some letter-writers to *The Guardian* protested at the way the media had handled each event so differently. One correspondent observed that ITN's *News at Ten* and *The Sun* had devoted much of their reports on the IRA bombings 'to a detailed account, with pictures, of the injuries suffered by the horses in Hyde Park,' but 'The very same media organs cheered the sinking of Argentine ships, downing of planes and bombing of the Falklands.' The writer concluded,

> What confuses me is the logic that is being used to praise one action and condemn the other. What concerns me is the way the British are being manipulated into accepting the contorted logic by suppressing pictures of dead and dying Argentine soldiers and publishing pictures of dead and dying horses.[56]

Fantasies

Coverage of the IRA has produced a remarkable crop of stories with no foundation in reality. These fantasies both satisfy the popular papers' need for drama, and serve the propaganda purposes of the authorities.

Manufactured atrocity stories, often featuring women, children or animals, were common in the early years when the British army's 'Information Policy' unit was in its heyday. A spate of stories in 1971 alleged that IRA leaders were ordering children to riot and even training them to kill, though none of the reporters responsible said how they had come by this information. In a particularly garish piece in *The Sun*, titled 'FRONT LINE KIDS', Roger Scott claimed that

> IRA terror leaders here are now sending their shock troops to war – their own children. Bomb-throwing eight-year-olds are in the front line. They steal out at dusk to play games with death, trained to hate and kill. And the children at war chant obscenities to nursery rhyme tunes as the bullets fly.[57]

Of course, as anyone familiar with the nationalist areas knows, the children need no encouragement to riot: the problem is to dissuade them. As Eamonn McCann pointed out, 'No one who knows the areas or the people who live there could accept these reports.' But most British readers had no such background knowledge.[58]

The media can get away with such concocted stories not only because of their audience's lack of local knowledge but also because when they are caught out they are under no obligation to publicise the fact. On 23 August 1972 ITN carried as its second item a story about three tiny eight-year-old girls who had been used by the 'unscrupulous IRA' to push a pram containing a huge bomb towards a military post at the back of the Royal Victoria Hospital in Belfast. The *Daily Mirror* also headlined the story. Some days later the British army press office admitted that the entire story was untrue. But the media made no denials.[59]

1972 was a fruitful year for manufactured atrocity stories. John McGuffin recorded how, in the same week as ITN carried the story of the children's bombing expedition, London's *Evening News* and *The Sun* both carried lead stories about IRA men raping young girls at gunpoint in the Markets area of Belfast, and alleging that four of the girls had become pregnant. Subsequently, however, the RUC issued a statement admitting that the story was completely false.[60] Also in 1972, popular papers seized on a story that IRA members had been using dogs as target practice. Again, the story was false: as *Time Out* reported, dogs had been killed, but it was British soldiers who had shot them. They had done so while on night patrol in the nationalist Ballymurphy district of Belfast because they were afraid the dogs' barking would betray their presence.[61] *Time Out* attributed this and other horror stories of the period to army press officers Colonel Maurice Tugwell and Colin Wallace.

Another bogus story painting the IRA as cruel to dogs, and thus certain to arouse the revulsion of the animal-loving British, was promoted in 1974 through then Northern Ireland Secretary Merlyn Rees. *Sunday Times* journalist David Blundy has told how soon after prisoners burned down Long Kesh camp in October 1974,

> Rees made a powerful speech in which he condemned the 'sadistic' burning to death of four guard dogs by internees. However, an army officer has told the *Sunday Times* that Rees had been misled. No guard dogs had been killed. When a local paper called Army HQ and asked to photograph the dogs' burial there was, apparently, 'quite a laugh'. The army joked about burying sandbags instead.[62]

Other fantasy stories have linked the IRA with an international 'red' conspiracy. On 23 October 1971, a few days after *The Sunday Times* had published details of the torture of internees, the *Daily Mirror* printed what must rank as one of the most bizarre stories of the decade. Huge letters on the front page announced, 'IRA HIRE RED KILLERS', with the sub-headline 'Czech assassin is shot by troops'. The 'Mirror Exclusive', by Joe Gorrod and Denzil Sullivan, began: 'IRA terrorists have hired assassins from behind the Iron Curtain to gun down British troops in Northern Ireland.' They continued:

> The disclosure came last night after it was learned that a paid assassin from Czechoslovakia had been killed by troops in County Londonderry.
> The gunman had ambushed an infantry patrol. The troops stalked him and cornered him in a graveyard.[63]

The source for the story was an anonymous 'Army officer in Northern Ireland' who was quoted as saying that the gunman ' "was dressed all in black and was a hired killer. He had been firing at the troops with a Czechoslovak rifle." ' The gun was 'a Russian-designed Kalashnikov AK 47 rifle, made in Czechoslovakia'. The sniper 'was killed by a soldier from the 1st Battalion the Royal Green Jackets'. Conveniently, the Czech's body had been taken away and there was no inquest. The troops 'were ordered not to talk about the incident,' and 'official Army sources refused to discuss the incident.' Indeed, at the end of the story an army spokesperson was quoted as saying, ' "We have no knowledge of this particular incident." '

In fact, as the army later admitted in the Belfast paper, the *Sunday News*, the entire story was 'a bit of fantasy' which 'had been going round for the past year.'[64] But the *Mirror* hadn't finished there. A later edition offered further proof of Red infiltration, telling its readers that

> On 3rd July, 1970, security forces shot dead 21-year-old Ulik Zbigniew [sic], a naturalised Pole from London. He was killed climbing over the rooftops dressed in a black sweater, with his face blackened and carrying a rifle.

Zbigniew Ulik (sic) was in fact a postman from West London, a British subject by birth. He supplemented his income from freelance photography, and in July 1970 went to Belfast where he was caught up in the Falls Road curfew. After spending some time in the house of a friendly local person, he decided to go back to his hotel to fetch another camera. Because the streets were still patrolled, he slipped out of the back over a shed. Some time that night British soldiers shot him dead. At the time, the army never said that he had been carrying a rifle, nor that his face was blackened, and a *Sunday Times* reporter who was present at the morgue when Ulik's body was brought in confirmed that his face was not blackened.[65]

Another 'red scare' theme concerns the alleged training of IRA members in countries such as South Yemen[66] or Libya. In September 1983, *The Mail on Sunday* carried a story dramatically headlined 'GADAFFI CAMP THAT TRAINS THE IRA KILLERS'.[67] The story, by Gloria Stewart, alleged that Libya had been secretly training 'hundreds' of IRA members at two camps near Tripoli. Freelance journalist Alan George investigated the story and found there was 'not a shred of evidence' to support Stewart's claims. The Foreign Office told him that it had 'no reason to believe that members of the IRA are being trained in Libya', and this was confirmed by the RUC and by 'security sources'. Further, the multinational company Massey-Ferguson was operating in the town where one of the 'camps' was allegedly sited: its business operations manager responsible for the area said he had 'never seen or heard any indication of any such IRA operation' anywhere in the town.

The only source that *The Mail on Sunday* gave for the story was a British businessman called Alexander Robertson, who said he had met two IRA men in Libya. Robertson's real name turned out to be Alexander Taylor – his middle name was Robertson. His company had played a key role in two Libyan contracts that had gone badly wrong, and was now in liquidation. Taylor refused to contact Alan George to clarify the 'IRA' story. Gloria Stewart, too, refused to discuss the story with George.[68]

In a variant on this theme, stories have been concocted which linked the IRA with British left groups. Because the IRA's media image was so bad, such stories had the effect of discrediting the British groups. Thus in 1977 the *Daily Mirror* produced a piece titled 'Trots hire IRA to bomb English cities'. Reporter Joe Gorrod told how

> IRA-linked Left-wing militants are planning a bomb war on English cities.
> And it could lead to a winter of havoc and bloodshed if the scheme works.
> British Trotskyists and Marxists have spent two months forging links with wildcat IRA bombers. They are believed to have offered help to the bombers in organising a blitz of shopping centres, railway stations and other government offices.[69]

Gorrod offered no evidence for this tale, and did not even claim to have got it from the army or police. Instead he proffered a 'quote' from a 'republican source', who, he claimed, said that

'These people have hired experienced IRA bombers as mercenaries.' Such 'quotes' are impossible to verify.

The same year, shortly after the major confrontation between police and anti-fascists at Lewisham, the *Mirror* carried an article headed 'THE MEN BEHIND THE MOB'. In this, reporter Alastair McQueen recounted how an 'Intelligence man' had told him that 'Maoists and Trotskyites' were studying the 'confrontation techniques' of the IRA and were using these 'to inflame Britain's latest series of race riots.' They had travelled to Ireland, he said, where 'They were billeted with families in the hardest-line areas of West Belfast and in Creggan and Bogside, Londonderry, to watch the IRA at work and learn.'[70]

In fact, the previous year the Troops Out Movement had taken a delegation of trades unionists to Ireland in order to give them first hand evidence of the need for British withdrawal. And, shortly before the article appeared, a small British delegation, which included pacifist Pat Arrowsmith, had travelled to the North to investigate allegations of army brutality. Both groups were put up in republican areas – but their purpose was to learn about Britain's activities, not the IRA's.

The same smear tactic has been used against the Irish community in Britain. In October 1976 the *Daily Express* published a front-page article alleging that Irish people were to the fore in a £200 million social security swindle: they were skimming off money to keep them and their often-bogus families, and millions of pounds were going to the IRA. Reporter Alan Cochrane cited as evidence a recent 'top-secret survey' done by the Department of Health and Social Security. Confronted by irate representatives of the Irish community, minister Stanley Orme stated categorically that the survey quoted by the *Express* was a myth. In August 1977, the Press Council upheld a complaint from the Federation of Irish Societies about the article.[71]

The Margaret McKearney saga

IRA activity in Britain has produced some spectacular tall stories. Steve Chibnall in his book *Law-and-Order News* tells how, after the trial in Winchester of those responsible for the Old Bailey bombings in 1973, a number of journalists collaborated to spin a yarn, that was carried in several papers, about an IRA plot to kidnap ten English villagers as hostages against the release of the convicted prisoners. According to Chibnall, the story was first floated by an Irish journalist.

A journalist who had covered the trial for a quality paper told Chibnall that a number of reporters thought it was a good story, 'but it was also a dodgy story so it needed more than one person to run it to give it credibility.' The reporters then put the idea to the police, who didn't discount it as a possibility: indeed they couldn't afford to dismiss the idea just in case it actually happened, in which case they would be in trouble. The journalist who spoke to Chibnall refused to write the story because it was ridiculous, and warned his news desk that there was likely to be 'a big flap on the night desk because we haven't got it'. His office agreed that they wouldn't carry the story whatever other papers did, but said 'If you prove to be wrong you'll have to answer for it'.[72]

Other dramatic scare stories, more dangerous because they targeted individuals, have been directly inspired by the police. At the end of August 1975 several bombs exploded in London and soon afterwards, on 4 September, Scotland Yard issued a press statement, accompanied by a photograph, identifying Margaret McKearney, a young woman from County Tyrone, as 'the most dangerous and active women terrorist operating here'.[73] This dominated the front pages the following day, as the press unanimously convicted Margaret McKearney in their headlines.

'SHE IS BRITAIN'S MOST WANTED WOMAN TERRORIST', cried the *Daily Mail*. The *Mirror* described her as 'TERROR GIRL', as did the *Telegraph*, which sub-headlined the story 'Murder hunt for "most dangerous" IRA blonde'. *The Sun* called her not only 'DANGER WOMAN' but 'DEATH COURIER'. The *Express*, in a highly evocative piece titled 'THE MOST EVIL GIRL IN BRITAIN', told its readers, 'Her Irish eyes may be smiling but her trade is fear and death . . . Consider this female of the species. . . But keep well clear. For Margaret McKearney is certainly more deadly than the male.' *The Times* and *The Guardian* also carried the story and picture on their front pages, but unlike the other papers they attributed it to the police in their headlines.[74]

The media had, overnight, invested Margaret McKearney with notoriety. Within days the McKearney family were given police and army protection after a threat from the loyalist UVF 'to get your family – each and every one of you.'[75] It was no empty threat. On 23 October a woman and a man were found shot dead in a lonely roadside bungalow near Moy, County Tyrone. They were also called McKearney, and had evidently been mistaken for Margaret's family, who lived in the same area.

The evidence for Scotland Yard's allegations was shaky. As the Dublin-based *Irish Press* noted, some of the statements given by Scotland Yard in their list of reasons for wanting to interview Margaret McKearney were 'so unfounded that our Special Branch were able, through their own surveillance, to dismiss them as utter rubbish because she was in Ireland at times when the "Yard" alleged she was committing crimes in England.'[76]

Scotland Yard's intention in releasing the McKearney story may simply have been to create a diversion in the wake of the IRA bombings and to suggest that the police were on the track of the culprits. It is also possible that the Yard intended to provoke a row about the Irish government's refusal to extradite people suspected of committing political offences, and thus to put pressure on the Dail to pass the Criminal Law Jurisdiction Bill, which had failed to go through that summer. The Bill, which was passed the following year, provided for people to be tried in the South for offences committed in the North.[77]

The Guardian suggested another possible motive. Northern Ireland Secretary Merlyn Rees had for some weeks been under heavy pressure from Unionist and Tory MPs and the military to bring in a tougher security policy. The McKearney saga effectively overshadowed the major policy statement that Rees made on 5 October, in which he refused to change direction. A few days later *The Guardian* reported that,

> Sources close to the Government . . . believe that the decision of Scotland Yard to make allegations against Margaret McKearney and publish her photograph, was approved at the highest political level in Whitehall. They point out that the British Government was probably desperate to take the pressure off the Northern Ireland Office, which has been under increasing criticism in the past few weeks over Government security policy.[78]

Bald Eagle and the white Opel

Another story sponsored by Scotland Yard turned into a wild goose chase of surreal dimensions. At around 2 a.m. on Sunday 17 December 1978, bombs exploded almost simultaneously in five English cities: Bristol, Southampton, Coventry, Manchester and Liverpool. The police went into overdrive, apparently desperate to demonstrate that they were doing something to counter the renewed IRA threat. First they arrested some 22 people, all of whom were later released, as they boarded the ferry for Belfast at the Scottish port of Stranraer. Then they cancelled all police leave in London and saturated the centre of the capital in a move dramatically titled 'Operation Santa'. In a masterstroke, the Yard also informed the media that they were looking for an Irishman called 'Bald Eagle'. The press seized on this with delight. 'FIND BALD EAGLE!' cried *The Sun*'s front page on 19 December, and reporter Trevor Hanna told that 'A huge hunt was on last night for a fanatical Irishman believed to be masterminding the Christmas terror bomb blitz on English cities.' The *Daily Mail* explained, 'Bald Eagle is a Provo bomb expert who has vanished from Belfast . . . He gained his nickname from his bald head which he invariably disguises with different wigs.'[79] Next day the *Mail* went a step further, naming Bald Eagle as Cornelius McHugh.

There was indeed a bald Belfast man of that name who answered to the nickname Bald Eagle. But on the day the *Mail* identified him as 'one of the most wanted men in Britain' he was in fact signing on the dole as usual in Belfast. That afternoon he gave interviews to Ulster Television and to journalists, explaining that he had never set foot in England and didn't intend to, and expressing himself mystified as to why, if half the policemen in England were looking for him, no policeman or soldier had come to his house. 'If they had,' he said, 'they would have found me at home with my wife and seven children.' He was also worried sick, said *The Guardian*, that all the publicity might lead to a 'trigger happy' soldier taking a shot at him.[80] The Belfast paper *Republican News* later reported him as saying that 'there is nothing more sinister about his bald head than the obvious dislike his hair has for staying with him; and he certainly never wears a wig.'[81]

Meanwhile back in England a new twist had been added to the plot. The Yard had issued another nationwide alert, this time for a white Opel Kadett, registration APU 827S. Over succeeding days there were a hundred or more reported sightings of this car, the most exciting of which was by Detective-Constable Ted Morley of Farnham in Surrey. ' "I faced Bald Eagle" ', was the London *Evening Standard*'s dramatic headline. Kenneth Tew's report began, 'The detective who chased the IRA terrorist "Bald Eagle" today told how he found himself looking down two barrels of a sawn-off shotgun.' He went on to tell how Morley, 32 years old and father of two, had chased the white Opel for two miles until it stopped. Morley said, 'I had it in mind to ram their car. The passenger took a shotgun and leaned out of the window. When I looked down those two barrels I swerved, hit the brakes and then I hit the deck . . . I was only on the deck for seconds but it had gone when I looked up.'[82] Morley then took an ITN camera crew in his car and re-enacted the drama for the benefit of the television audience.

Morley's Chief Superintendent stood staunchly by his account, and when asked why he thought the IRA were still driving the most wanted car in England said, 'Think of the worst Irish joke you know and draw your own conclusion.'[83] The joke was, however, to be on him. In mid-January the white Opel turned up in Ireland. It had been taken there via Holyhead on 24 November, nearly four weeks before Scotland Yard started looking for it in Britain.[84] The unfortunate Morley was then suspended from duty.[85]

The story had a serious postscript. Over several days in January, 23 people were arrested in Braintree, Essex. The press widely described the arrests as being in connection with the IRA's bombing campaign. Most of those thus stigmatised were in fact members of the Braintree Irish Society, a body that organised social functions for the Irish community in the area. One ITN bulletin even said some were to be charged with bombings at Greenwich and Canvey Island: the item was dropped from later bulletins. As it soon transpired, none of those arrested had any connections with the bombings.[86]

Not the day of the Jackal

Scotland Yard started another wild goose chase during the British general election campaign in 1983. On Friday 27 May the front pages of several papers were dominated by a story, released by the Yard the previous evening, about how two IRA men were planning to assassinate a leading British politician. Either or both of the men – depending on which paper you read – had 'slipped into Britain', and consequently top politicians of the three main parties were being given police guards.

The Yard had given the story first to the *Daily Mirror*, at about 6 p.m. on the Thursday, and later, at about 10.30 p.m. to the rest of the media.[87] Since the *Mirror* was the only national paper supporting Labour in the election, it is possible that the Yard's intention was to create a 'law and order' scare which would benefit the Tories.

The *Mirror* was the only paper to have the story in its first edition and billed it as an 'exclusive'. The front page headlines announced, 'IRA man's "Day of the Jackal" mission – "Kill a top politician" '. Reporter Sylvia Jones elaborated:

> The alert was sounded after a leading Provisional IRA terrorist slipped into Britain, apparently on a mission to kill.
>
> Police believe the aim is to bring chaos to the election with a real-life enactment of the Day of the Jackal assassination plot . . .
>
> . . . police have launched a nationwide hunt for 30-year-old Provo boss Sean O'Callaghan . . .
>
> O'Callaghan, from County Kerry in the Irish Republic, arrived in England several weeks ago. He is thought most likely to be in London.
>
> Police warned that he is armed and dangerous and should not be approached.[88]

The other dailies carried the story on the front pages of their later editions. 'IRA "JACKAL" IN THREAT TO MAGGIE', cried *The Sun*. The *Mail* proclaimed 'ELECTION TERROR WARNING', while the *Daily Star* said, 'Yard alert as IRA squad slips in'.[89] That evening, television news bulletins carried a photofit picture of a second wanted man, John Downey. Scotland Yard said they wanted to question Downey about the previous year's Hyde Park bombings, and believed he might still be in Britain.[90]

Next day the *Mirror* carried another front page piece by Sylvia Jones headlined 'SAS alert in Jackal hunt': 'Special Air Service troops are on 24-hour alert in the hunt for the IRA "Jackal" believed to be stalking top politicians in Britain.' Alongside was a picture of Sean O'Callaghan, named by the Yard as 'the hit man'.[91]

The following day, the Sunday papers exhibited some confusion over who the IRA's intended victim was. 'TARZAN IS IRA TARGET', cried the *News of the World*, referring to Defence Secretary Michael Heseltine,[92] but *The Mail on Sunday* proclaimed, 'Jenkins target of IRA Jackal'. That day Scotland Yard's story began to fall apart. The first wanted man, Sean O'Callaghan, turned out to be in his home town, Tralee in County Kerry, where he was photographed holding a copy of *The Mail on Sunday*. A spokesman for the gardai, the Irish police, said that O'Callaghan was not under surveillance and that, to the best of his knowledge, no request had been received from the British police to bring him in for questioning. The Irish police also said they were satisfied that he had not been out of Tralee for a month.[93] Then on the Monday the second named man, John Downey, telephoned journalists from Ballyshannon in County Donegal and said he had never been to England in his life.[94] The Irish police said that the previous Thursday, the day Scotland Yard had named him, Downey had been seen collecting his dole in Ballyshannon.[95]

'Godfathers'

The media have always endeavoured to depict the IRA as external to, and unrepresentative of, the nationalist community. In the early years, nationalist riots against the British army were often ascribed to IRA 'agitators' or 'infiltrators',[96] and newspaper stories linked the IRA to a Soviet-led communist conspiracy. Later the IRA were widely described as 'a small band of gangsters and thugs', while during the 1981 hunger strike they metamorphosed into masters of psychological manipulation, the possessors of a powerful 'propaganda machine'.

The word 'godfathers' entered the lexicon of reporters describing the IRA in the mid-seventies. This mafia metaphor gained currency during the term of office of Labour Northern Ireland Secretary Roy Mason, whose strategy was to deal with the IRA revolt as if it were purely a criminal matter.

Stories about IRA 'gangsterism' reach journalists through the RUC and army. One distinguishing feature of such stories is that they are generally impossible either to prove or to disprove – for which reason some journalists steer clear of them. A second is that the activities cited as 'evidence' are often open to contrary interpretation. For example, the black taxi service run by ex-internees in West Belfast has been portrayed by the army and RUC as a means by which the IRA brings an unwilling community under their control, but is seen by many locals as a welcome alternative to the expensive and frequently disrupted bus service. Similarly, social clubs where people go for an evening out were described by a police officer quoted in *The Sunday Times* as places where 'witch doctor' techniques are used to 'hypnotise' the young with republican songs: 'Then the next day the godfathers put a gun or bomb in their hands and send them out to kill somebody.'[97] As well as being unsubstantiated, this account excludes the possibility that republican culture has developed as the product of a community, and that young people might wish to join the IRA of their own volition.

Two articles on the 'gangster' theme written in 1975 and 1976 by Chris Ryder, a Belfast-born journalist, resulted in a partially successful libel action against his paper, *The Sunday Times*. The first, a full-page piece headlined 'When a city falls to gang rule' carried an introduction telling how 'plain gangsterism' was taking over from 'traditional sectarian terror' in Belfast: 'Chris Ryder reports on the armed robberies, murders and protection rackets which hold a city in bondage.' He began by describing two UDA killings and a series of armed robberies, almost all, again, done by the UDA. Then, to illustrate alleged IRA 'rackets', he turned to the Falls Road taxi service, social clubs – which he described as 'drinking clubs' – and the Andersonstown Co-operative Society, which runs various shops. The Co-op, said Ryder, was 'a key front organisation for the Provos'.[98]

The second article, titled 'Belfast's new godfathers', continued the gangland theme. This highly coloured 'exclusive report', written as the peace people's campaign was getting under way, told how

> Knowing they will never persuade the Catholics to vote for them at the ballot box, the Provos have resorted to controlling essential community needs, legally where possible, illegally where necessary, and in the process have created a new dimension to urban terrorism.
>
> Military intelligence analysts believe that the Provisionals could one day use their power over the supply of vital necessities, like food, to force the Catholic community to support them.[99]

The Andersonstown Co-op and its former Secretary, Seamus Loughran, and former Chairperson, Gerry Maguire, sued for libel. The case was heard in the Belfast High Court in October 1979, and the jury found that *The Sunday Times* had libelled the Co-op by describing it as a Provisional IRA front, and awarded it £200 damages against the paper. At the same time, however, the jury found that the article did not 'materially damage' the reputations of Loughran and Maguire by associating them with the IRA, and they were ordered to pay the newspaper's costs and their own.[100]

In March 1977 Ryder produced another sensational story, titled 'How IRA siphoned off £1m government cash in housing swindle'.[101] The article held that in 1975 'the Provisional IRA, and, to a lesser extent, the Official IRA' had diverted money from building firms, and that the government took no action because it was trying to preserve the truce. While there was some substance in the allegations, the sums involved appear to have been much exaggerated, and Ryder had misjudged who was receiving most. A police investigation later concluded that little or no money had gone to the Provisional IRA, but that a building firm had paid £5,000 to the Official IRA. A Commission of Inquiry did not recommend any prosecutions and its report said, 'We accept that paramilitary influence dictated who could work on the sites, but the loss of money was due mainly to the weak contract . . . rather than to organised fraud.'[102]

Ryder continued to write on these lines. In October 1981, for example, in the wake of the hunger strike, he revamped the stories he had written about republican clubs and the West Belfast taxis in an 'investigation' titled 'IRA racketeers tighten grip on Ulster'.[103] Adding a new ingredient – the allegation that the IRA was making money from video games – the article portrayed the IRA as a mafia-style oganisation with 'tentacles', which was now exercising 'an increasing measure of control over the Catholic community'.

The problem with such an approach is not only that it involves unprovable assertions and a contentious interpretation of the IRA's relationship to the nationalist community, but that, by reducing analysis of the IRA to the concept of gangsterism, the political issues are obscured.

'Terrorists' in TV drama

The picture of the IRA as gangsters and thugs carries over into television drama. *Eighteen Months to Balcombe Street* was a London Weekend Television drama-documentary, shown on ITV on 21 February 1977, about the IRA active service unit whose career ended when they gave themselves up after being besieged by police in a house in Marylebone, in central London. The tenor of the film was summed up by *Daily Telegraph* reviewer Richard Last, who wrote that *Eighteen Months to Balcombe Street*

> presented the London bombers as archetypal thick Micks, leading lives in which violence provided the only relief from stupefying boredom . . . The programme could only inspire loathing and

contempt, not merely for the actions and motives of the nauseous Balcombe mob, but their constant inefficiency.[104]

Philip Purser, writing in *The Sunday Telegraph*, shared that reaction:

> The first impression, I suppose, was of the sheer incompetence of the four terrorists, worthy contenders all, for starring roles in Thick Irish Jokes . . The lasting impression was of fanatics caught up in violence for its own sake.[105]

But this interpretation of the 'Balcombe Street Four' had not been the only one open to London Weekend Television's production team. Shane Connaughton, who co-scripted the play, had hoped it would explain, in the context of Irish history, why the bombers came to England. When he saw that the finished product presented them as psychopaths and omitted the reasons for their actions, he asked for his name to be withdrawn from the play's credits.[106] He later explained the background:

> When first brought into the project by the director, he assured me it wasn't going to be a thriller about four psychopaths going round bombing and shooting for kicks. There would be, he assured me, explanations for their behaviour – political explanations.
>
> We set about trying to build up the world of four men doing what they did out of political conviction. It soon became apparent that the executive producer and the producer were not interested in explanations. They were interested only in a straightforward documentary using the evidence that was available – the facts and figures of the bombings . . . culled from various newspapers and police files.
>
> Every five minutes someone mentioned the Mary Holland interview with David O'Connell and the trouble LWT got into over that interview, the mere mention of which and we were all supposed to pray fervently that we would never be tempted to say anything controversial . . .
>
> Not one of them had the slightest clue about contemporary Irish history or why the Provos act as they do.[107]

The film's description of the four as incompetents 'caught up in violence for its own sake' also involved a questionable interpretation of the facts of the case. The four had been one of the most tenacious IRA units to operate in Britain, and at their trial they made their political motivation clear. The four had refused to plead because they had not been charged with the Guildford and Woolwich bombings for which innocent people had been convicted. On behalf of the four, Joe O'Connell made a speech from the dock highlighting the evident Guildford and Woolwich frame-up, and repeatedly stressing the political rationale for the group's actions:

> We say that no representative of British imperialism is fit to pass judgement on us, for this government has been guilty of the very things for which we now stand accused. This government carried out acts of terrorism in order to defend British imperialism and continues to do so in Ireland. We have struggled to free our country from British rule. We are patriots.[108]

In theory television drama is freer in relation to Ireland than news or current affairs, since it is not constrained by the requirement of 'balance', and there are no blocks on portraying 'terrorists' in plays. But in practice television plays have generally reproduced stereotypes based on the conventional British view. *The Squad*, for example, was a short BBC play about four 'terrorists' discussing a sectarian shooting they had carried out a few days earlier. Whether they were republicans or loyalists was not made clear, but since loyalist violence gets little coverage in Britain, most British people would probably have assumed they were republicans. Their characters were summed up by Richard Hoggart: 'One of them is plainly psychopathic, another a near-idiot, a third nostalgic for the licensed slaughter of the last war, and the fourth is full of doubts.'[109]

Typically, 'terrorists' in television drama are not shown as having a reasonable case. They are abstracted from the community from which they spring and whose disaffection they express, and their actions are explained in terms of their individual psychology: they are half-mad, or stupid or addicted to violence. Politics generally gets a look in only through very unflattering portraits of middle-aged men intoning the words of dead republican heroes, with the effect that republican issues are denied contemporary relevance and are seen only as a way the old send the young out to die unnecessary deaths in an extinct cause.[110] The lived experience of the nationalist working class community, with continuing discrimination, endemic unemployment and poverty, and harassment by the army and RUC, is rarely, if ever, portrayed.

Like the 'terrorists' of the popular press, and the 'mindless thugs' execrated by politicians, the fictional characters bear little resemblance to their real-life counterparts. A secret British army intelligence document produced in 1978 that fell into the hands of the Republican Movement profiled the Provisional IRA's membership thus:

> PIRA is essentially a working class organisation based in the ghetto areas of the cities and in the poorer rural areas . . . there is a strata of intelligent, astute and experienced terrorists who provide the backbone of the organisation . . . Our evidence of the calibre of rank and file terrorists does not support the view that they are merely mindless hooligans drawn from the ranks of the unemployed and unemployable. PIRA now trains and uses its members with some care. The mature terrorists . . . are continually learning from mistakes and developing their expertise.[111]

The army intelligence expert recognised too that the fortunes of the IRA and its level of support in the community were intimately bound up with political life in the Six Counties, noting, 'We see no prospect in the next 5 years of any political change which would remove PIRA's raison d'etre.'[112] Clearly, what the establishment says in private about its number one enemy, and what it says in public, are two very different things.

Political vocabulary

The words journalists use when covering Ireland are chosen with care and are scrutinised by their superiors and by politicians. The approved vocabulary conveys an insistent message, contrasting the IRA with the forces of the state and asserting that the republicans are 'wrong' and 'bad', while the British side is 'right' and 'good'.

Ireland is a terminological minefield. 'Even before you begin to mention political violence,' said television reporter Peter Taylor, 'the words you use may betray the political path you seem to be treading.' He went on:

> At the most basic level, where is the conflict taking place? Is it in Ulster? Northern Ireland? The province? The North of Ireland? Or the Six Counties? . . .
>
> And once you've sorted out the names, what's actually going on there? Is it a conflict? Is it a war? A rebellion? A revolution? A criminal conspiracy? Or a liberation struggle? . . .
>
> Lastly, and probably most important, how do we describe those involved? Are they terrorists? Criminals? The mafia? Murderers? Guerrillas? Or freedom fighters? It depends on your perception of the conflict, and who you happen to be working for

at the time . . . Such semantic subtleties apply to scarcely any other conflict we report, be it El Salvador or Africa.[113]

Place-names are an immediate give-away. Northern Ireland was the name bestowed by Britain on the unit created by partition in 1920, when the border was drawn around six northeastern counties of Ireland. Republicans call it the Six Counties, while other nationalists often call it the North of Ireland: like the term Northern Ireland, this is geographically incorrect, since part of Donegal is further north than any of the British-ruled counties.

The term Ulster, the name of one of the four ancient provinces of Ireland, is frequently used by the British media and loyalist politicians to refer to the Six Counties. This usage is inaccurate, since three counties of Ulster lie in the Southern government's jurisdiction. The term is favoured by loyalists presumably because it suggests, albeit spuriously, that their present territory has a historic homogeneity.

Names used for the Southern state are also problematic. It is officially called Ireland, or Eire, or the Republic of Ireland. Republicans dispute these terms on the grounds that they cannot apply till Ireland is reunified. Instead, they talk of the 26 Counties, or the Free State, a term which has derogatory overtones: Irish Free State was the name given to the South, then a British dominion, in the Anglo-Irish treaty of 1922, and was later dropped by the Dublin government.

Again, some journalists refer to 'mainland Britain' when contrasting Britain with the North of Ireland. This usage is technically incorrect, since the North is not part of Britain, but part of the United Kingdom.

As it did in other colonial territories, Britain put its stamp on Ireland by altering indigenous place-names. Thus Derry – Doire in Irish – was renamed Londonderry several hundred years ago after the London companies which controlled it. The British usage has never been universally accepted, and nationalists still call it Derry. British journalists generally use Londonderry, although on occasions they use both terms within the same article or programme. Northern Ireland Secretary James Prior, asked by his wife which name she should use when visiting the city, advised, 'My dear, you just say how delighted you are to be in "this wonderful city of yours".'[114]

While the use of place-names indicates the speaker's view of whether or not the British presence in the North is legitimate, a host of other terms reveal attitudes to the armed protagonists. Thus for British politicians and the media, the British army, UDR and RUC are the 'security forces' – a reassuring term that is anathema to many nationalists – while the IRA and INLA are 'terrorists'. The army 'says' something happened while the IRA 'claims' or 'alleges' it.[115] Victims of the army or police are 'shot dead' while those of the IRA are 'murdered' or 'gunned down'.

Broadcasters are highly sensitive to such distinctions. In 1978, for example, an Ulster TV newsreader said in a news bulletin that a man, Paul Duffy, had been 'murdered by the SAS'. Thirty minutes later the bulletin had been rewritten: now Duffy had merely been 'shot dead', and the newsreader apologised for the earlier 'inadvertent phraseology'.[116]

The most potent words are undoubtedly 'terrorist' and 'terrorism'. Noam Chomsky and Edward Herman have written that these words 'have become semantic tools of the powerful in the Western world,' and observe that they 'have generally been confined to the use of violence by individuals and marginal groups,' while 'official violence which is far more extensive in scale and destructiveness is placed in a different category altogether.'[117]

In the Irish context, 'terrorist' and 'terrorism' are used frequently in relation to the IRA and INLA, occasionally in relation to loyalist paramilitaries – who are more usually called 'extremists' – and never in relation to the British army or RUC. The power of the words lies in the fact that they imply that the violence they describe is worse than violence from other sources. A BBC internal memo to television newsroom staff in January 1974, headed 'Guerrillas and terrorists', instructed:

> 'Terrorist' is the appropriate description for people who engage in acts of terrorism, and in particular, in acts of violence against civilians, that is operations not directed at military targets or military personnel.
> 'Guerrilla' is acceptable for leaders and members of the various Palestine organisations of this kind, but they too become 'terrorists' when they engage in terrorist acts (unless 'raiders', 'hi-jackers', 'gunmen' is more accurate).[118]

And in the BBC's *News Guide*, reporters are bluntly told:

> Don't use *'commando'* for terrorist or guerrilla. In the 1939–45 war, the word had heroic connotations, and it is still the name of units of the Royal Marines.

> Even so we still have problems with 'terrorist' or 'guerrilla'. The best general rule is to refer to 'guerrillas' when they have been in action against official security forces, and to use 'terrorist' when they have attacked civilians. Thus we should say 'Guerrillas have attacked an army patrol in the Rhodesian bush . . .', but 'Terrorists have killed six missionaries in Rhodesia . . .'.[119]

But in practice, the criterion that 'terrorist' should be applied to those who attack civilians is not used. If it were, the British army and RUC would on occasion be described as 'terrorist', while the IRA and INLA – the majority of whose victims have been soldiers or policemen – would be described as guerrillas. The fact that the term 'terrorist' is attached limpet-like to the IRA and is never used of the state forces indicates that a different logic is being applied.

As Conor Cruise O'Brien has written, the use of terms like 'force' and 'violence', 'terrorist' and 'freedom-fighter', depends not on the degree of force or violence used in a given act, 'but on a view of its justification.'[120] The terms used depend on whether the cause of the organisation in question is approved of or not. Thus Mrs Thatcher objected to the anti-government forces in Afghanistan being described as 'rebels', insisting that they should be called 'resistance fighters'.[121]

The terms 'terrorist' and 'terrorism' are, then, used to slur organisations which are perceived as illegitimate by implying that the violence they use is particularly unpleasant. The use of these terms immediately prejudges the issue, making an open-minded evaluation of the organisation in question impossible. The makers of Thames TV's major history series, *The Troubles*, recognised this. Co-producer Ian Stuttard explained, 'We never ever called anybody a terrorist; other people did in the film who were filmed at the time, Faulkner and so on, but we in contrary scrupulously avoided emotive terms like that.'[122]

As circumstances alter, and the British government's relationships to liberation movements shift, so the terminology changes: Britain's departure from its colonies has been punctuated by many a transformation of 'terrorists' into 'statesmen'. And as the authorities' attitudes alter, the media follow suit. Brian Wenham, Controller of BBC2, has argued that it is right for broadcasters to take their cue from the authorities:

> If . . . I am operating in a parliamentary democracy, where it is a primary assumption that broadcast journalism will take its cue

from the working of the parliamentary democracy, then I for one am not surprised to find the political language settling somewhere around the broad middle of that democracy. How could it do otherwise, without taking unto itself agenda-setting roles which are not its province?[123]

But if the broadcasters allow the 'broad middle of the democracy' to dictate the agenda, and adopt its definitions without question, the possibility of genuine freedom of discussion, and of assessing whether the consensus view is right or wrong, is severely limited.

7. Televising republicans

The rarity of IRA interviews

While the IRA is vilified as public enemy number one, and is often made to appear as the alpha and omega of the problem in the Six Counties, the organisation itself remains almost unheard and unseen. Representatives of the IRA and INLA are virtually excluded from the airwaves and rarely profiled in the press, so that the British consensus view of their rationale – or lack of it – and of the personalities of their members goes unchallenged.

Television interviews with spokespeople for republican military organisations are extremely rare and inevitably provoke an uproar from politicians and the press, who apparently see them as the thin end of the republican wedge. The resulting rows are as furious as the rows about exposures of British atrocities. The establishment's ground rule is evidently that Britain's activities must only be shown in a good light and the IRA's only in a bad light.

Politicians, anxious to keep 'the enemy' off the screen altogether, have grossly exaggerated the number of such appearances in order to pillory the broadcasting organisations as 'traitors'. Labour's Northern Ireland Secretary Roy Mason wanted a total blackout on reporting 'terrorist' activities: soon after taking office he accused the BBC of providing a 'daily platform' for the Provisional IRA. His remarks were enthusiastically seconded by General Young, then Commander of Land Forces in the North.[1] Former Tory Prime Minister Edward Heath complained in early 1977 that 'Television takes the view that if it can get a secret interview with the IRA in the backstreets of Belfast, it will do that.'[2]

In their defence, senior broadcasters have been quick to stress the scarcity of such interviews. At the start of 1971, the BBC showed two IRA interviews, one in January and the next in February, both on *24 Hours*. Then the BBC brought in its rule that all such interviews had to be sanctioned by the Director-General, and the IRA appeared only once again that year, when Joe Cahill gave a press conference on 13 August.[3]

In 1974 BBC Director-General Sir Charles Curran noted that he had given 'prior permission for two such interviews': these were in 1972 and in June 1974, and both were with David O'Connell, then an IRA leader.[4] In 1977 Richard Francis, then the BBC's Northern Ireland Controller, stressed that there had been no IRA interviews since O'Connell's appearance in 1974.[5] The IRA's political wing, Sinn Fein, had not fared much better. Francis told his audience at the Royal Institute of International Affairs that

> In the 12-month period from October 1975 to 1976 there were six interviews on BBC Northern Ireland Television with Provisional Sinn Fein and 12 with spokesmen for the Loyalist paramilitaries, six of them being elected representatives. These figures compare with a total of 307 interviews with elected representatives of all other parties, including 56 with UK ministers. In the same period there were 41 interviews with official Trades Union leaders and four with UWC spokesmen . . . So, over the year, the proportion of paramilitary interviews (18 out of 325) was extremely low, and incidentally contrasts with 18 interviews for the leaders of the Peace Movement in the first three months of its existence.[6]

Francis was referring to interviews carried out on BBC Northern Ireland, so it can safely be assumed that the number carried in Britain was considerably lower.

From 1977, the BBC transmitted just two further interviews with spokesmen for republican paramilitaries. Both were with the INLA. The first, in February 1977, was shown only in the North of Ireland, on the *Spotlight* programme. The second, in July 1979, was shown nationwide on *Tonight*. Thus between 1972 and the time of writing, BBC television had carried just four interviews with people speaking on behalf of the IRA or INLA.

ITV's record is similar, though the channel has carried no interviews with INLA representatives. ITV companies have issued no figures on the subject, but it appears that there have been very few IRA interviews. Mary Holland interviewed David O'Connell, who at that time was publicly acknowledged to be an IRA leader, for London Weekend Television programmes shown on 21 January 1973 and on 17 November 1974.

Also in 1974, Thames TV's *This Week* team produced a major retrospective documentary, titled 'Five Long Years', which had a remarkable cast. The interviewees in this 'special', which lasted an hour and a half, included not only several politicians from Britain and both parts of Ireland, and two loyalist paramilitary leaders, but also three British generals – Sir Ian Freeland, Sir Frank King and Sir Harry Tuzo – plus three acting or former IRA Chiefs of Staff. These were Sean MacStiofain and David O'Connell of the Provisionals, and Cathal Goulding of the Officials.[7] This mix of interviewees was never to be repeated. It is believed that, following this film, British army chiefs decided never to agree to appear again in the same programme as the IRA. That the film went out without provoking protests about the IRA presence was almost certainly because virtually all the political currents that might have objected were represented in it. All the interviewees were told beforehand that the IRA Chiefs of Staff were to be included, but the only person who refused to participate on this account was Ian Paisley.

Mary Holland's interview with David O'Connell in November 1974 was to be the last appearance of an IRA representative on commercial television until March 1983, when Channel 4 transmitted a documentary called *Ireland: The Silent Voices*, about media coverage of the North.[8] This included IRA interviews done by Italian, Finnish and American film-makers, which prompted *The Mail on Sunday* to carry a front-page article, replete with outraged remarks from Tory MPs, headed 'Storm over IRA film on Channel 4'.[9] But the makers of *Ireland: The Silent Voices* did not themselves interview members of either Sinn Fein or the IRA, though they did interview two spokespeople for the loyalist paramilitary UDA.

Arguments for and against republicans on TV

In the debates about coverage of Ireland, there have been basically three points of view about republican television appearances. The 'imperial right' believes republicans should not be seen or heard at all: *any* publicity will 'help the enemy'. Secondly, the media authorities, torn between their loyalty to the establishment and their need to preserve the credibility of broadcasting, argue that republican views should be given a very occasional airing, but only in strictly controlled circumstances. Thirdly, some journalists, mostly at the 'quality' end of the trade, contend that there should be unrestricted access to republicans, because without them the situation cannot properly be understood.

(1) The right

Perhaps the most drastic proposal on how to deal with IRA interviews was put forward in the early seventies by Lieutenant-Colonel 'Mad Mitch' Mitchell. His plan was to mount machine-guns in TV cameras and then mow down the IRA men being interviewed.[10] This suggestion was doubtless made more for dramatic effect than with any serious intent. As *Guardian* journalist Simon Hoggart commented, 'one feels that in the end the IRA might catch on.'[11] At the same time, it was a literal version of a view widely held on the right: that the media should take the side of the authorities and should help them to obliterate republicanism.

In the early seventies the main accusation levelled against republican interviews was that they were 'an affront'. *The Daily Telegraph* commented on ITV's January 1973 interview with David O'Connell that,

> Apart from the political damage which it must have done by building up the IRA's prestige, this programme was an intolerable affront to the relatives and friends of those who still serve there.[12]

Condemning O'Connell's second ITV appearance, in November 1974, Unionist politician Ian Paisley said it had led to 'a sense of outrage felt by all right-thinking members of the community'.[13] A few days later, after the Birmingham bombings, the chorus swelled. Tory MP Edward du Cann drew cries of 'Hear, hear' when he told the Commons, 'It is a gross affront to us to have a known terrorist allowed to flaunt his views on TV or any other way.'[14]

The attraction of this line of attack, where ITV was the target, lay in the legislation that controls commercial broadcasting. The Independent Broadcasting Authority Act states that the Authority must ensure 'that nothing is included in the programmes which offends against good taste or decency or is likely to encourage crime or to lead to disorder or to be offensive to public feeling'.[15] This stricture was repeatedly invoked by politicians. By transmitting the 1973 O'Connell interview, said Tory MP John Biggs-Davison, the IBA had failed to discharge its duty because 'the programme was offensive to public feelings, particularly among those who had served and suffered in Northern Ireland.'[16]

As the decade continued, a different accusation, apparently inspired by the military, came to the fore. 'All terrorist organisations,' said General King, GOC Northern Ireland, in the early seventies, 'thrive on propaganda and without the exaggerated attention of the media the IRA would probably have languished and died'.[17]

This line of thought was increasingly heard when two men who were both close to the military, former Defence Minister Roy Mason and former army officer Airey Neave, became Northern Ireland Secretary and Shadow spokesperson respectively. Mason reportedly told an audience of BBC chiefs at the Culloden Hotel in Belfast that the IRA would have been defeated years ago had the Northern Ireland Office been allowed to direct BBC policy.[18] Later, attacking the BBC over a *Tonight* report on the IRA, Mason said, as reported in *The Irish Press*, that

> propaganda was one of the major weapons for any terrorist
> organisation. IRA strength and support was lower than for many
> years and they were desperately looking for ways to regain that
> support. Any programme which increased the idea that the IRA
> was a movement to be reckoned with in political or military terms
> would help to recruit more people.[19]

Neave, who held that 'all terrorist movements rely for their recruiting on publicity',[20] said that the *Tonight* programme 'may well permit the Provisional IRA to renew their campaign of murder by glorifying violence and fostering a new generation of killers.'[21] He was echoed by John Biggs-Davison, another Tory spokesperson on the North, who claimed that 'access to the screen' was the 'life blood' of 'the terrorist', and said, 'Counter-insurgency is in measure a propaganda war; without publicity terrorism withers.'[22]

The corollary of this argument was that the broadcasters' duty, instead of being to inform the public, was to deny information to the public. Tory Home Secretary William Whitelaw said,

> Terrorists and terrorist organisations seek and depend on
> publicity. A principal object of their acts of violence is to draw

attention to themselves and gain notoriety . . . they bomb and murder their way into the headlines.

In doing so they make war on society and outlaw themselves from its privileges. The broadcasting authorities owe them no duty whatever, and can owe society itself no duty whatever, gratuitously to provide them with opportunities for the publicity they want.[23]

In sum, it was in society's interest not to be told what was going on.

Alan Wright, Chairman of the Police Federation for Northern Ireland, invoked the 'need to know' principle beloved of the intelligence services:

Without publicity terrorist acts would lose much of their effectiveness and very reason for being . . .

Surely it is time for journalists to think long and hard about the relationship that must exist between the public's right to know and the public's need to know. As regards terrorism, the crucial question is, does the public need to know everything immediately?[24]

Clearly, there is no tangible threat to national security involved in reporting the words or deeds of 'terrorists'. So why does the public not 'need to know'? The missing, unspoken link in Wright's argument, as in Whitelaw's, is the authoritarian conception that the public itself presents a problem. The public's response to information about 'terrorists' will not necessarily suit the authorities. Publicity alone will get the 'terrorists' nowhere: it is the public reaction that matters. So 'society' has to be protected from itself.

Ultimately, the force of such statements lies in the act of making them rather than in what is actually said. They are full of sound and fury, but signify very little. The argument never gets beyond the simple reiteration of the point that 'terrorism depends upon publicity'. This highly contentious assertion is rarely challenged. Instead, it is taken up and magnified by the press, and the bluster achieves the desired effect of intimidating the television authorities and inhibiting reporters. As journalist Mary Holland has written, what then sets in is 'a process of self-censorship which needs no *diktat* from authority to enforce it':

If an article or a programme or an interview is going to provoke rage from Airey Neave, cries of IRA-lover from Mr Mason and 'flak' from the press, then everyone involved, no matter how courageous, from the researcher to the Controller instinctively reacts by thinking 'Oh God, can we face it?'. And as each person in the hierarchy has this reaction separately when the problem arrives on his desk the disincentives to reporting on how and why a young man jumps out of a police-station window are formidable.[25]

The growing band of 'experts on terrorism' have generally kept in the background, confining their discussions to conferences and specialist journals though occasionally publishing populist tracts.[26] An international conference held in London in May 1982, for example, titled 'Terrorism and the News Media', brought together 'terrorism' experts such as Professor Paul Wilkinson of Aberdeen University and Professor Yonah Alexander of the State University of New York, politicians including Merlyn Rees and Lord Chalfont, and assorted journalists. The admission charge was £85, effectively excluding the general public.[27] One of the more populist counter-insurgency experts, former major-general Richard Clutterbuck, was for six years a member of the BBC General Advisory Council, a body made up of some sixty influential people chosen by the BBC that meets quarterly.

It is in these circles that theoretical justifications, such as they are, for the non-reporting of 'terrorism' are aired. The key phrase, supplied by the Rand Corporation's expert on 'international terrorism', Brian Jenkins, is 'Terrorism is theatre'. It is 'aimed at the people watching, not at the actual victims.'[28] American professor Walter Laqueur contends that

> Terrorists have learned that the media are of paramount importance in their campaigns, that the terrorist act by itself is next to nothing, whereas publicity is all . . . They are, in some respects, the superentertainers of our time.[29]

In this scenario the media are crucial: the channel through which the 'entertainment' or 'propaganda' is transmitted to the public. Consequently, the argument runs, if the media refuse to cover 'terrorism', the problem will go away.

Discourses on this theme rest on very dubious assumptions about 'terrorists' themselves, the validity of their cause, and their relationship with the community within which they operate. The social and political causes for the unrest are played down. Instead, the 'terrorists' are portrayed as the cause: they are seen as confidence tricksters, purveying lies and organising spectacular events to con both their own community and more distant audiences. The problem is located not in reality but in the mind: the 'terrorists' are said to manipulate or condition people into believing lies.

Frank Burton, a sociologist who spent several months in a nationalist enclave in Belfast, wrote that the 'many-sided reality' of the community he studied,

> exposes the counter-insurgency theorists' writings on Ireland for what they are: bad sociology and political theory, thinly veiling the right-wing sympathies of military men. The theory . . . portrays the civilian population as manipulable. Communities . . . are held to be malleable to the hands of Machiavellian guerrillas . . . There is no suggestion that the guerrilla is part of his [sic] community or that his causes can be intellectually grasped and rationally embraced by that community. The matter is simply one of propaganda and coercion.[30]

(2) The broadcasting authorities

In the early years of the troubles, the question of whether or not to interview the IRA led to intense self-questioning within the higher echelons of broadcasting. The minutes of an early BBC editorial meeting record how the two sides of the argument were posed:

> On the one side it was argued that a sensibly conducted face to face interview, with tough probing questions and a context which made the BBC's journalistic purpose absolutely clear, would be of positive value to the audience as an exposé of the anarchic bloodymindedness of the IRA bombers and gunmen. On the other side it was argued that nothing the BBC said in introducing the interview or questioning the IRA man would destroy the public impression that the BBC was giving comfort and a propaganda platform to murderers and enemies of the society of which it was a part.[31]

Soon the BBC arrived at the position on IRA interviews described by Director-General Sir Charles Curran shortly after David O'Connell was interviewed in 1974:

> in the case of the IRA, I have reserved such decisions to myself, as Director-General, since 1971. Since that date, I have given prior permission for two such interviews . . . On each occasion, the question I have to consider is whether the undeniable wish of the IRA to make propaganda through such interviews will be outbalanced by the value of the information which will be brought to the attention of the British public. The rarity of the permissions given indicates the way in which I have judged these questions.[32]

Later the same year, London Weekend Television used similar terms to justify their interview with O'Connell:

> On the one hand the material provided was of sufficient public importance to make publication . . . a matter of professional duty. On the other hand there is something profoundly repugnant in giving unnecessary exposure to terrorists . . . it was decided after careful thought that the obligation to transmit it outweighed any disadvantages.[33]

What the broadcasting authorities and the pro-censorship lobby have in common is that both start from the assumption that the IRA and INLA are a bad thing: they are the 'enemy'. Conversely, Britain is perceived as being on the side of the angels, a benign, democratic force, while 'the central problem of Northern Ireland' is located in 'the inability of the two communities to reach rational settlement of their difficulties' as BBC Director-General Ian Trethowan put it.[34]

The broadcasters are adamant that they are not neutral in this scenario. 'It must be stressed that we are not impartial as between democratic and undemocratic means. We do not give equal time to right and wrong', said Richard Francis, then the BBC's Northern Ireland Controller, in 1977. This restatement of the position formulated by BBC Chairman Lord Hill in 1971 has been echoed time and again by BBC chiefs.[35]

But the broadcasters disagree that helping the 'national interest' necessarily means obeying the wishes of a particular government or institution, such as the army, and insist on their social duty to provide information to the public. 'Surely,' said Richard Francis, 'the national interest must lie in solving the problem, and the public's interest in being given reliable information about the problem in their midst?'[36]

Although they accept the idea that 'terrorists' are intent on disseminating 'propaganda', senior broadcasters have on occasion implicitly recognised that the problem is rooted in social reality: it must be understood rather than dismissed out of hand. But reporting the enemy, they stress, does not mean supporting the enemy. Sir Charles Curran said,

> The reason we have never placed an absolute ban on talking to representatives of illegal organisations is that there can be occasions when it is necessary for the public to understand what their case is. That does not mean that we or the public are required to sympathise with the case. If you have an enemy – and the organisa-

tions are illegal precisely because they are the enemies of democracy – it seems to me necessary that you should understand the enemy. But that doesn't mean you have to hand over your medium to them, so that they can use you for propaganda.[37]

Richard Francis said, 'A thorough and reliable knowledge of society's ills and of the other man's unpalatable views are essential for any realistic evaluation.' He went on to argue against the notion that without media coverage 'terrorism' would vanish:

If the violent activities of terrorists go unreported, there must be a danger that they may escalate their actions to make their point. And, if we don't seek, with suitable safeguards, to report and to expose the words of terrorist front organisations, we may well be encouraging them to speak more and more with violence.[38]

Defending their refusal to accede to the wishes of the pro-censorship lobby and ban such interviews altogether, the BBC chiefs have repeatedly emphasised that the way they control and handle such interviews shows that they are on the authorities' side. They stress that permission for such interviews is very rarely given. Following the 1979 INLA interview Richard Francis said, 'As on all such occasions, we gave the matter the most careful thought, right up to the Director-General level, before proceeding to seek out the interview.' The BBC believed, he said, that 'from time to time it was right to show the public by way of a reminder who and what the extremists were, but such interviews must only be very occasional.'[39]

He was echoed by Director-General Ian Trethowan, who wrote to *The Daily Telegraph* that 'we believe that, on very rare occasions, the public can be reminded directly of the nature of the terrorists by the normal methods of television reporting.' The decision to show the INLA interview had, he said, been taken 'in the belief that on balance the public interest would be served by people here in Britain being reminded of the murderous and intransigent nature of the problem.'[40] The question of such interviews was 'a devilish difficult task,' said BBC Chairman George Howard in 1981, continuing, 'I believe that from time to time, on very rare occasions, the public has a right to know what terrorists are thinking and doing.'[41]

The BBC chiefs emphasise, too, that their abhorrence of 'terrorism' is made clear by the behaviour of their interviewers. 'Invariably,' said Richard Francis, 'paramilitary interviewees are treated as hostile witnesses.'[42] Defending the 1979 INLA interview he said, 'The manner in which David Lomax [the reporter] conducted himself and rebutted the most heinous accusations against Airey Neave made our moral stance quite plain.'[43]

The Annan Committee on the Future of Broadcasting, which reported in 1977, supported the BBC's perspective; the BBC's views are also shared by the IBA, although members of that body rarely attempt to formulate or justify their position. The Annan Report, which started from the premise that 'Northern Ireland is a special case', ticked off the BBC for 'ignoring both the problems of civil rights and some unsuccessful IRA action in the early sixties,' but then advised the broadcasters to turn a purblind eye to their contemporary equivalents:

> Broadcasters cannot be impartial about activities of illicit organisations. Nevertheless, these organisations are a political force in Northern Ireland; and it would be unrealistic for the broadcasters not to take account of them. This does not mean, however, that the proponents of illicit organisations should be allowed to appear regularly on the screen, in the mid-seventies, still less to appear to argue their case. Terrorism feeds off publicity . . . By killing and destroying, the terrorists are bound to extort publicity – and hence one of their ends – because such news will be reported. But there is no need to abet them by giving additional publicity . . . we think that the decision whether to permit such appearances must remain with the broadcasting organisations, and should not rest on the fiat of a British Government. We would expect these difficult decisions to be taken at the highest levels in the BBC and in the IBA.[44]

In 1980 Richard Francis, by then the BBC's Director, News and Current Affairs, summed up his organisation's policy:

> Nobody involved in the journalistic coverage of terrorism is other than sympathetic to the victims or repelled by the perpetrators of terrorist crimes. We do not deal impartially with those who choose to step outside the bounds of the law and decent social behaviour. Not only do they get very much less coverage than those who pursue their aims legitimately, but the very manner and tone that our reporters adopt makes our moral position quite plain.[45]

He went on to suggest that 'such exposure provides them not with a platform but with a scaffold, in the shape of strengthened public resolve to combat terrorism.'[46]

(3) Journalists

Voices in support of unrestricted interviews with republicans are few and far between. Almost all are journalists who have reported Ireland for television current affairs programmes or 'quality' papers, plus a few television critics. They get little or no support from other journalists or MPs. Speaking at a National Union of Journalists conference on media censorship of the North, Mary Holland, who has reported the conflict from the start for both newspapers and television, pointed out that when journalists had 'got into trouble' over such interviews, there had been very few letters of solidarity in *The Times*, and it had proved 'extremely difficult' to get Members of Parliament – even those affiliated to the NUJ – to speak in their defence. Further, she said, other journalists had very often hindered rather than helped, creating a fuss in the press which had added to the existing problems.[47]

At the most basic level, journalists defend the view that the IRA should be interviewed on the grounds of 'the public's right to know' and 'the journalist's duty to report'. BBC reporter Bernard Falk argued that it was 'in the public interest' both for the security forces to pursue the IRA and for journalists to report on IRA activities: 'if one assumes that this organisation is an enemy of Britain then the public must have a right to know why it is waging war against Britain and what methods it is using.'[48] Not to report the IRA, he wrote, would be a violation of journalistic integrity:

> Responsible broadcasters have no sympathy with IRA methods but to comply with the suggestion of Mr Mason and Mr Neave that we cease to report the activities of the IRA is to ask broadcasters to sacrifice their integrity, to suppress the truth, to distort and to be pliable under the manipulation of politicians.[49]

Guardian reporter Simon Hoggart neatly dismissed the argument that to report 'terrorism' is to assist it. Having expressed scepticism at the idea that the public, seeing a 'terrorist' on television, would be 'dumbly converted to his cause', he asked pertinently, 'but suppose they were? Suppose, faced with David O'Connell or the Derry terrorist, they decided that the Republican cause was just and fair. Should the BBC suppress the case for the convenience of the Government?'[50]

Such arguments implicitly acknowledge that the IRA is a real force in the conflict, on a par with other forces. Andrew Stephen made the point directly: 'the journalist has to accept that the IRA on one side and the UDA and UVF on the other command a widespread support among the Catholic and Protestant communities. For this reason the views of the bombers and gunmen are relevant to what is happening here.'[51] Jonathan Dimbleby, responding to an attack from *Sunday Times* TV critic Peter Dunn, wrote:

> It may be true, as Mr Dunn states, that the absence from the screen of some of the participants in the Northern Ireland crisis is not 'an insurmountable obstacle to the truth,' but by the same token we should be able to shut out the politicians, the soldiers, and the ordinary people of Ulster, and not find truth impaired.[52]

Mary Holland argued strongly that the only criterion for choosing who to interview should be whether they contribute to the story. She protested against the choice of interviewees based on political considerations which do not relate to the topic:

> There is one thing that is most troublesome about this question of interviewing gunmen, terrorists, freedom fighters, men of violence, call them what you will, that one does get into this position of the headcount. How many democratic representatives do you have to put on television even if they don't mean anything and have nothing to say in this case? . . . I once did a programme where we had to insert, at the insistence of the IBA, a representative of the UPNI [Unionist Party of Northern Ireland], a minority group of no backing in the province at all, because that would in some way give balance to the whole thing . . . I think that the criterion for whether people should be interviewed or not is whether they actually add to the story and tell us something about the story. It isn't whether 10 SDLP equals one UDA, five Official Unionists equals one Provisional, one INLA probably equals 20 Official Unionists.[53]

A very few journalists have taken the argument further, explicitly challenging the official line. Jonathan Dimbleby has argued that the key requirement for reporting Ireland properly is to break away completely from the official framework: if Ireland is looked at as a colonial issue, 'that totally recasts the framework of the problem', and allows all the parties to the conflict, and their relationships, to be examined in a more coherent and illuminating way: 'If you can't see that the British army might be perceived by the Catholic population as an army of occupation, then you can't see how the Catholic population reacts to the IRA. If you can't see how the Irish Catholic population reacts to the

IRA, you can't understand the British security problem in dealing with the IRA.'[54]

But any argument that calls for the IRA's rationale to be examined provokes the fury of the right. As Chris Dunkley wrote, 'when you express a desire to understand, you run the risk of being labelled "sympathiser".'[55] The journalist's attitude to the IRA is irrelevant. For on whatever grounds the case is put, it challenges the hegemony of the establishment version by saying that other versions exist which should be considered. Further, to say that the IRA is worth hearing, and is a real force in the conflict, is also to undermine the notion – central to security policy from the mid-seventies onwards – that they are reducible to mere 'murderers and thugs' and represent only a tiny minority.

Bans 1970–71

Numerous programmes concerning republicans have been censored. On 13 August 1971, four days after the start of internment, the BBC's weekly top-level News and Current Affairs meeting was told that *24 Hours* wanted to do an 'in depth' programme about the IRA. The idea was firmly squashed. Minutes of the meeting reveal MDXB – the Managing Director of External Broadcasting, Kenneth Lamb – saying that

> Even if such an interview [of an IRA man] was carried out by someone capable of correcting incorrect statements, he was doubtful about the extent to which the views represented by the interviewer could be expected to be as emotionally as well as intellectually penetrating as those of the interviewee.

And the Chief Assistant to the Director-General, John Crawley, said that 'Such a programme setting out the roots of the IRA would not be acceptable.'[56]

On 1 November 1971, the ITV network was due to show a programme on the IRA made by Granada TV's *World in Action* team. Four days earlier, on 28 October, the Independent Television Authority banned the film without even seeing it. A film on Rhodesia was shown instead. Titled 'South of the Border', the banned programme took as its starting point Provisional Sinn Fein's Ard Fheis – national conference – held in Dublin a few days previously. The film showed speeches made there by Sinn Fein President Ruairi O Bradaigh and IRA Chief of Staff Sean MacStiofain. These speeches, which had already been widely reported, were balanced – half and half in terms of time – by interviews with Southern opposition politicians Garret Fitzgerald and Conor Cruise O'Brien, both of whom strongly criticised the IRA. Southern government representatives refused to participate in the same programme as Sinn Fein and IRA members.

In banning the film, the ITA overrode the views of Granada's staff and entire board, including Chairman Sidney Bernstein. 'You can practically see steam coming out of Sidney's ears,' one executive reportedly said.[57] The ITA also ignored the views of its own permanent staff, whom Granada had consulted and whose preliminary report said, 'It seemed to us that current affairs legitimately used this occasion to give our viewers a better understanding of the ideas and attitudes of the IRA and the way they are regarded in the South.'[58] The ITA's official with permanent responsibility for coverage of the North, Dr Rex Cathcart, viewed the rushes and apparently said it was a documentary which 'ought' to be seen. His opinion, however, was not taken into account for he was looking at the film at the same time as the Authority, at its monthly meeting, was deciding to ban it.

The members of the ITA, a government-appointed body which with the advent of commercial radio became the Independent Broadcasting Authority, were at that time one lord and two baronesses, a merchant banker, the Chairman of Metal Box, a former BBC Northern Ireland executive, two former General Secretaries of trade unions, both knighted, plus a professor of engineering and two other educationalists. Their discussion of the Granada film was apparently clinched when two of the most powerful members, ITA Chairman Lord Aylestone and Henry McMullan, former Head of BBC programmes in the North, came out against it 'on principle'. Lord Aylestone felt it was 'aiding and abetting the enemy'.[59]

An ITA spokesperson said that the ban was because 'the authority was not satisfied that a programme on the subject would be helpful in the current situation,' and also said, 'The programme was about the IRA and the feeling was that as the idea had been presented to them the authority did not think it sounded quite right.'[60]

But Granada staff suspected that pressure from Ulster Television was behind the ban. The day before the ITA's meeting, Granada had told UTV of its plans. According to one of the Granada people, UTV Managing Director Brum Henderson 'did his nut' when he heard about the project.[61] Henderson reportedly

'informed the ITA that the showing of such a programme anywhere in the United Kingdom would be deplorable in that it
would simply give publicity to IRA extremists.'[62]

Another reason for the ban was also canvassed. This view,
shared by a *Spectator* columnist and 'someone in Granada well-
placed to know', held that the offending item was not the republican sequences, but criticisms of the British army made by
Garret Fitzgerald. The *Spectator* quoted from the transcript:

> Commentator: Even pro-British politicians like Garret Fitzgerald
> are critical of the army's conduct.
> Garret Fitzgerald: There is no doubt about it, it is not Republican
> propaganda . . . The army are day by day going around the street,
> shouting obscenities at people, smashing windows and alienating
> people. Now we understand they've been provoked. I'm not blam-
> ing the army for that . . . I'm only saying that by acting in this way
> and by the failure of the officers to control them, the political
> situation in Northern Ireland has deteriorated.[63]

Despite the ITA ban, Granada went ahead and completed
the film. The ITA viewed it in mid-November and confirmed the
ban. They cited a section of the Television Act which deals in
general terms with public taste, public order and impartiality,
but offered Granada no specific reasons for their objection.[64]

It was not just current affairs programmes that came under
the axe. In 1970 the BBC commissioned playwright Jim Allen to
write a contemporary television drama about the North, which
was to be directed by Ken Loach and produced by Tony Garnett.
The play was about the politics of the Official and Provisional
IRAs, and would, Allen says, have been a harsh criticism, arguing
the need for a socialist approach. To research the play, Allen
went to live in Belfast and Derry, making four trips, each lasting
several weeks. He did not ask the permission of BBC Northern
Ireland, nor announce his presence to them. Since they regarded
the North as their patch, there was a row when they found out.
Before the play was finished – Allen had completed about 100
typed pages and needed to do about three months' more work –
the BBC cancelled the project.

Very disappointed, and with their interest in Ireland
stimulated rather than stifled by the experience, Allen, Loach
and Garnett included sequences about the British-Irish war of
1920–21 in their television series, *Days of Hope*,[65] and then
embarked on plans for a feature film about the same period of

Irish history. Titled *The Rising*, it was to be made by Kestrel Films, the company run by Loach and Garnett. 'One of the main points of the film,' Ken Loach explained, 'was to show that the troubles the Irish have had with the British arise from the fact that Ireland has been a British colony. It is now the final stage of our last colonial war.'[66] Again, however, they were to be frustrated. Jim Allen completed the script but, despite the fact that Loach's previous films had been financially successful, Kestrel's efforts to raise money proved fruitless. A Swedish company agreed to pay more than half the budget, provided that some money could be raised in England. Kestrel were led to believe they would be backed by the National Film Finance Corporation – the two other films directed by Loach that they had backed were showing healthy profits. But then, as Ken Loach explained, 'we were told that the NFFC would not support us for even a small fraction of the cost, and this, we were led to understand, was because there was disapproval of the content of the film. In effect, it was a political decision.'[67] Too big for a television production, and lacking the commercial appeal necessary to raise funds in America, the project died.

Bans in the mid-seventies

Bans on republican interviews punctuated the seventies. In November 1974, the Home Office, which controlled cable television, banned the Bristol Channel cable station from interviewing the south-west organiser of Clann na hEireann, Adrian Gallagher. Clann was the British wing of Official Sinn Fein, rivals of the Provisionals, and Gallagher was to have discussed the Birmingham bombings which had occurred a week earlier.[68]

Then in October 1976 the BBC banned an IRA interview from a BBC Scotland programme, *The Scottish Connection*, about the cultural and political links between Scotland and the Six Counties. An interview with a Scottish UDA leader, however, was permitted.[69]

When the Queen visited the North in August 1977 as the last stop in her Jubilee celebrations, Thames TV's *This Week* made a programme titled 'In Friendship and Forgiveness'. The IBA banned it, objecting principally to a speech by Dublin Sinn Feiner Andreas O'Callaghan, who told a Belfast rally:

> While there is a British army of occupation on our streets . . . any Irishman who can get his hands on a weapon . . . has the duty not

to keep that gun in cold storage . . . let them get out and fight the British army themselves.[70]

Claiming that this might contravene the 1973 Broadcasting Act, which prohibits incitement to crime or disorder, the IBA told Thames to seek legal advice. Thames' counsel was equivocal, feeling that in the context of the programme such an effect was unlikely but nevertheless possible. Playing safe, *This Week* dropped O'Callaghan's words and replaced them with commentary:

> Andreas O'Callaghan went on to urge Irishmen to carry on the fight against British soldiers in Northern Ireland using whatever weapons they could lay their hands on. It was an open call to arms.

Thames' counsel felt that the programme was now legally safe. The IBA, however, banned it again. They phoned Thames just two minutes before the scheduled transmission time on 17 August ordering them not to show it. A film shown previously on 'Drinking and Driving' was put out instead.

That the IBA had banned it despite the alteration suggested that their objections lay deeper than the speech in question. Their unease may well have resulted from the fact that this programme had deviated dramatically from other television coverage of the Queen's visit, by showing that it had divided rather than united the province. The film was eventually shown, but two weeks after the visit and not in *This Week*'s normal peak-time slot. Instead it went out in different slots all over the country, ranging from Friday teatime to Sunday lunchtime to nearly midnight on Ulster Television. 'By then,' as the reporter involved, Peter Taylor, wrote, 'the visit was history, the impact and topicality of the film lost.'[71]

The following year the IBA intervened again, banning an LWT *Weekend World* programme assessing the current strength of the Provisional IRA. *Weekend World* editor David Cox told how

> After we started filming, there was a full meeting of the IBA authority itself, and at the end of that afternoon we got a phone call here telling us that the whole programme had got to be scrapped because the authority felt that a programme about the Provisional IRA wasn't appropiate at that time.[72]

The *Weekend World* team went ahead with the programme anyway, hoping that the IBA would change their minds when they saw it. But they dropped film of IRA training sessions and a proposed interview with Republican leader David O'Connell on 'editorial grounds'.[73] But, as David Cox explained,

> we showed the programme to the authority at the next meeting a month later and they banned it again. This time they gave as their reason that because the programme dealt with only the Provisional IRA's present and future it didn't give a sufficiently complete picture of the affairs of Northern Ireland as a whole.[74]

The production team 'decided to carry on arguing' and, said Cox, pointed out to the IBA that 'no individual *Weekend World* about any subject really gives a complete picture of everything to do with that subject'.[75] Eventually IBA Chairman Lady Plowden decided to allow the programme, titled 'The Provisionals – can the violence continue?', onto the air on 21 May 1978, three weeks behind the scheduled date.

The veto tactic

A drama developed in the middle of the recording of a programme on Ireland in David Frost's Yorkshire TV *Global Village* series in May 1979. *Global Village* involved bringing together by satellite contributors from round the world who were then questioned by a studio audience. It normally went out live, but in this instance, because it dealt with the Six Counties, it was recorded and watched by the IBA. Three Unionist politicians, Peter Robinson of Paisley's DUP, recently elected to Westminster, Official Unionist John Taylor and former MP William Craig, walked out of the programme shortly before it was due to start when they heard that Sinn Fein President Ruairi O Bradaigh was to be interviewed from a studio in Hamburg. Two Conservative MPs, John Biggs-Davison and William van Straubenzee, and two Labour MPs, Stanley Orme and Kevin McNamara, took part in the discussion but eventually walked out too. The four, complaining to the press that they had not been told in advance about O Bradaigh and that they had been 'tricked',[76] gave the impression that they, like the Unionists, had walked out as soon as they became aware that O Bradaigh was to appear. But Bernadette McAliskey, who was in the studio audience, gave a different account:

> They sat right through O Bradaigh's remarks. It was only when they found out that the Official Unionist MPs had walked out

> before the programme started that they began to look
> uncomfortable. Finally Biggs-Davison shuffled out and the rest
> followed behind him.[77]

Nor, it seems, was the Unionists' action entirely ingenuous. For, according to a Sinn Fein statement, Ruairi O Bradaigh's invitation to appear had been announced in the Dublin papers four days earlier.[78]

The politicians' protest had the desired effect. During the recording, representatives of the IBA watched the exchanges from London. They discussed the position with Yorkshire television officials and decided jointly that the interview with O Bradaigh should be removed and an explanation given by David Frost when the recorded programme went on the air. O Bradaigh's contribution was excluded, said the IBA, because a number of participants were unaware of it and the understanding on which they had taken part should be respected.[79] The presence of prominent UDA leaders on the programme went unprotested.[80]

1979 also saw the demise of a major *Panorama* project critically assessing the IRA. The programme was in its early stages when politicians, with Margaret Thatcher in the van, and much of Fleet Street created a furore over the 'Carrickmore incident', when *Panorama* filmed an IRA roadblock in a County Tyrone village. Panic ensued in the upper echelons of the BBC, and the project was smothered.[81]

Inhibitions

Broadcasting journalists became, it seems, so intimidated that they did not even try to interview republicans, even for programmes where their absence was patently absurd. At the BBC's top level News and Current Affairs meeting on 22 October 1976, the Head of Talks and Documentaries Radio, George Fischer, reported his planned programme on the IRA. The minutes recorded, 'He emphasized that . . . it was not proposed that there should be any interviews with members of the IRA.'[82]

On 10 April 1980, BBC2's *Newsweek* carried a programme by Keith Kyle analysing the republican tradition. Interviewees included politicians from the North and South of Ireland, among them Conor Cruise O'Brien and John Hume. But there were no republicans. Journalist Eamonn McCann, who was one of those interviewed, wrote,

One of the programme makers explained that to have interviewed somebody from, for example, the Provisional Sinn Fein, would have led to wearying controversy with BBC chiefs and heavy flak from Tory MPs.

It would have taken a fight to have the programme transmitted at all. And, anyway, the Provisionals' points could be covered in questions to other participants.[83]

McCann commented that 'at bottom it was rather like a discussion of feminism with no women or an analysis of racism with only whites interviewed.'[84]

Ian Stuttard, co-producer of Thames TV's major history series on the North, *The Troubles*,[85] explained how it came about that the films contained no footage of the IRA.

In dealing with the modern period it seems to me crucial to give some visual representation to the radical or paramilitary groups which are currently operating and determining the parameters of the conflict. And I didn't want to talk in abstract terms over a bunch of wallpaper of soldiers or housing estates about the Provisional IRA, I wanted to actually film them. But whereas in current affairs because of time you tend to film first then ask questions later, and you usually get it kicked out by the IBA, I thought I'd be civilised about this and approach them first, which I did.[86]

Stuttard wanted to film IRA personnel in training. The IBA turned down the initial request, and in the exchange of letters that followed, refused to alter their decision.

When Ian Stuttard made a film for Thames TV's *TV Eye*, the programme that succeeded *This Week*, about events just before the death of Bobby Sands, he operated on the 'film first, ask afterwards' principle. But again he was thwarted by the IBA. The film, *The Waiting Time*, was transmitted on 30 April 1981, but only after the makers, at the insistence of the IBA, had removed part of a sequence filmed in a West Belfast social club. The sequence showed 500 residents of the area meeting to discuss contingency plans in the event of loyalist attacks. Ian Stuttard explained:

The offending 33-second part of the sequence occurred at the opening of the meeting, when two hooded men mounted the stage. Amid wild applause one of them read the following statement:

'This statement is on behalf of the Provisional IRA. In the serious atmosphere at this time of continuing crisis, the Irish Republican Army wishes to encourage the local people of the

Colin and Beechmount areas to mobilise in the face of ominous threats from certain paramilitaries who are sympathetically regarded by the sectarian RUC, and backed up by the British war machine. Not since 1969 has such a threat been posed to the people of the Nationalist areas of Belfast. They must now organise themselves through local committees and street representatives to set up the civil administration for the two areas – and prepare for possible serious confrontation. If we organise now and nothing happens, that will be a bonus for us all. But if the crunch comes then we will be ready. There will be no more '69s in Belfast.'[87]

Rows about IRA appearances

The few IRA and INLA interviews that have been shown have provoked, as top BBC man Desmond Taylor put it, 'furious objections' and 'instant controversy'.[88] Politicians, the press, the RUC, and military men serving and retired have combined to lambast the television authorities for aiding and abetting the enemy.

'A FORUM FOR THE ENEMY' was how *The Daily Telegraph* greeted Mary Holland's ITV interview with David O'Connell, believed to be the IRA's new Chief of Staff, in January 1973. The editorial held forth that 'A rough parallel to yesterday's exercise would have been a BBC interview on Germany's war aims with Dr Goebbels in 1942.'[89] A group of Tory MPs tried, and failed, to obtain an emergency debate in the Commons. They then tabled a motion of censure on the IBA for allowing O'Connell to appear.[90] One of them, Dame Patricia Hornsby-Smith, said the programme 'was tantamount to British television consorting with the Queen's enemies.'[91] The public at large, however, was apparently undisturbed: a London Weekend Television spokesperson said they had received no complaints about the interview.[92]

Mary Holland interviewed O'Connell again on 17 November 1974 for London Weekend Television's *Weekend World*. The programme made it onto the screen with difficulty. The magazine *Broadcast* reported that 'a ten man team' from the Independent Broadcasting Authority 'was incarcerated at LWT's South Bank headquarters until 4 a.m. on the Sunday morning of transmission. Their arguments and advice obviously vitally affected the nature and form of the final programme.'[93] In the interview, O'Connell referred to the Provisional IRA's bombing campaign in Britain, saying, 'We strike at economic, military, political and judicial targets,' and promising an escalation.[94] The initial response to the interview was almost nil: Ian Paisley expressed outrage in the Commons and his request for an emergency debate was refused.[95]

But just four days after the interview, on 21 November, came the Birmingham pub bombings, when 19 people were killed and well over a hundred injured. During the parliamentary debates that followed, MPs blamed the programme for the bombings and demanded censorship. Gerry Fitt, then SDLP member for West Belfast, said,

> that man's voice as it came out on television indirectly led to the murder of 19 people in Birmingham and every effort should be made by the Home Secretary to prevent such a broadcast again. (Cheers.)[96]

Some politicians went even further. Apparently under the illusion that the IRA are dependent on television to make contact with one another, they claimed that O'Connell had used the interview, in the words of Lord Hailsham, 'to communicate with troops on the ground.' Hailsham asked, 'How can we be sure it was not an executive order broadcast by courtesy of Mary Holland and Thames Television.'[97] Former Northern Ireland Prime Minister Lord Brookeborough put it succinctly: 'O'Connell called his troops to action.' The Lord Chancellor however responded that the government 'had looked into that grim possibility but found no evidence to indicate it was the case.'[98]

As the Prevention of Terrorism Act, described by Home Secretary Roy Jenkins as 'draconian', was rushed through Parliament, Tory MPs tried and failed to add an amendment which would have made it an offence, punishable by a fine or imprisonment, to arrange 'a broadcast, newspaper article, or other publicity knowing that the purpose or consequence might reasonably be suspected to support, sustain or further the activities of a proscribed organisation'.[99]

The government, however, preferred to rely on the well-tried method of obtaining voluntary co-operation from the broadcasting bodies. Roy Jenkins said it would be 'almost a tragedy' if the special powers were to 'permanently damage' the relationship between the Commons and any government with the broadcasting authorities. Pointing out that the new legislation would make the IRA illegal – it had previously been legal in Britain, though not in the Six Counties – Jenkins said, referring to the O'Connell interview, that 'he would personally regard such a broadcast in future as wholly inappropriate.'[100]

The broadcasters proved co-operative. As soon as the Bill was announced, both the BBC and the IBA said they would take the new situation into account when formulating policy.[101] And in the succeeding years neither the BBC nor ITV filmed another interview with an IRA representative.

The second battle of Culloden

It is not just IRA interviews that unleash the establishment's wrath, but also the airing of republican opinions in general, and any visual coverage of the IRA in action – at roadblocks, for example, or in training.

Labour Northern Ireland Secretary Roy Mason, who protested loudly and often about television coverage of the North, took this view to an extreme. Soon after taking office in September 1976, he told local journalists in off-the-record talks that in his opinion the activities and statements of paramilitary groups should not be published or broadcast, and that to achieve this the government should impose a compulsory system of 'D-notices'.[102] Then on 4 November 1976, at a dinner given by the BBC at the luxury Culloden Hotel outside Belfast, he proposed a total three-month blackout on the reporting of 'terrorist' activities. This event was to become known as 'the second battle of Culloden'.

The BBC gave the dinner for 30 people to celebrate the opening of its new studio block in Belfast. Among the BBC top brass present were Chairman of the governors, Sir Michael Swann, his deputy Mark Bonham Carter, six other governors and Northern Ireland Controller Richard Francis. Local dignitaries included the Lord Chief Justice of Northern Ireland, Robert Lowry, the Commander of Land Forces in Northern Ireland, Major-General David Young, and RUC Chief Constable Kenneth Newman.

As liqueurs were being served, Swann invited Mason to say a few words. Mason then stunned the BBC representatives by delivering a 'tirade' – as a BBC memo reportedly described it[103] in which, according to the *Daily Mail*, he said 'the BBC was disloyal, supported the rebels, purveyed their propaganda and refused to accept the advice of the Northern Ireland Office on what news to carry.'[104] One programme that had specially piqued him was a profile of himself done by the local *Spotlight* team. The programme had ended with unflattering remarks about him from *New Statesman* editor Anthony Howard, and Mason was incensed that it had gone ahead after he had refused to take part.[105] Having said that the BBC's coverage of the North was 'quite appalling', Mason observed 'that he was involved in decisions about the BBC's charter and income: and that, he said, was something for those present to ponder.'[106]

After he had proposed a three-month blackout on reporting paramilitaries, a guest asked, 'Does this mean that if the IRA assassinated you tomorrow, we shouldn't report it?' Mason replied, 'That is exactly what I mean.' As he left the dinner he said, 'If any of this ever gets in the papers, I'll have the lot of you.'[107]

According to *The Observer*, Mason's remarks were 'enthusiastically seconded' by General Young, who repeated Mason's allegation that the BBC provided a 'daily platform' for the IRA.[108] Other guests also agreed with Mason. Sir Robert Lowry told the governors that the BBC should remember 'what is good for the country'.[109] Kenneth Newman, however, reportedly disagreed with both Mason and General Young, but 'said he was disturbed by the "ethics" of allowing non-elected trouble-makers to go on the air.'[110]

At around the same time, Mason was also trying to stop the flow of information from another quarter. He wrote to 40 members of quasi-governmental bodies, including the Northern Ireland Tourist Board, warning them that he was 'disturbed by recent disclosures of classified departmental documents to the Press,' and was 'reviewing all possible sources of such disclosures.'[111] And in January 1977 the Official Secrets Act was extended in the North to take in members of public bodies concerned with education, health and housing.[112]

Tonight on the IRA

A major fuss greeted a *Tonight* report on the IRA by reporter Jeremy Paxman that was shown on 15 December 1977. The report traced the splits among republicans: the separation of the Provisionals from the Officials, who later renounced violence, and in turn the emergence of the militant INLA from the ranks of the Officials. Interviewees included Ruairi O Bradaigh and Thomas MacGiolla, Presidents of Provisional and Official Sinn

Fein respectively, and Sean MacStiofain, former Provisional IRA Chief of Staff. Paxman took a very negative view of the Provisionals' fortunes:

> There comes a point in an apparently interminable war, when the guerrilla army, far from being the defenders of the people, come to be seen as their oppressors. There are many who believe the IRA is now at that stage.[113]

A *Times* reporter concluded that 'the overall tone of the programme was far from sympathetic.'[114]

But, as *Financial Times* correspondent Chris Dunkley commented, it was inevitable

> that no matter what attitude the programme took, any serious look at Republican organisations would cause the knee-jerk-reflex group in the Palace of Westminster to start kicking out as usual over the 'irresponsibility' of television.[115]

Northern Ireland Secretary Roy Mason tried to stop the programme going out, writing to BBC Chairman Sir Michael Swann 'expressing profound concern at the Corporation's intention to screen interviews with members of the Republican movement.'[116] The day after transmission, Tory Northern Ireland spokesperson Airey Neave released the text of a letter to BBC Director-General Ian Trethowan. The programme, he said,

> was nothing less than a Party Political Broadcast on behalf of the IRA . . .
>
> I am obliged to ask the question; do the BBC want to prolong the 'armed struggle' in Northern Ireland? . . .
>
> The terrorists are using your Corporation for their own propaganda.[117]

The same day, Mason delivered another broadside:

> I am appalled that the BBC should have deliberatedly provided a platform for the views of men described in the programme as responsible for organising violence in Northern Ireland.[118]

The press added their own gloss: 'TERROR GETS A FREE PLUG' was one *Daily Express* headline,[119] while its Sunday stablemate demanded rhetorically, 'is it not a howling scandal that the BBC . . . should give 35 minutes of free publicity to the skulking killers of the IRA?'[120]

The INLA interview

The BBC's 1979 INLA interview, and the 'Carrickmore affair' a few months later, produced rows of thunderous proportions which had lasting repercussions. In the Carrickmore case, which involved *Panorama*, the uproar occurred while the film was still being made, and it was never completed nor shown.

The INLA interview was shown in the final edition of *Tonight* on 5 July 1979. Northern Ireland Secretary Humphrey Atkins, who had tried to stop the film being transmitted, complained that it was 'ill-timed and unhelpful'.[121] But there was no great outcry from the public at large: Richard Francis, the BBC's Director of News and Current Affairs, noted that

> There was little reaction at the time: 87 telephone calls in all, including 15 to the BBC in Belfast – a remarkably small number given the emotive nature of the subject and compared with previous such occasions. No more calls than we would get for a four-letter word.[122]

And later a BBC Audience Research survey was to show that four-fifths of their 'sizeable sample' thought it had been right to show the interview.[123]

It was not until a week after the programme went out that the uproar began. It was set off by a letter to *The Daily Telegraph* on 11 July from the widow of Airey Neave, who had been killed by an INLA bomb that March. In the interview, she wrote, 'the terrorist was given ample scope to besmirch the memory of my husband . . . the decision to transmit the interview betrayed the traditional standards of British broadcasting.'[124] Next day a *Telegraph* editorial, headed 'FORUM FOR MURDERERS', accused the BBC of committing 'at the very least, an extreme and repulsive error of taste' and of failing to show 'the smallest regard for either the feelings or the interests of the nation.'[125] In Parliament, Prime Minister Margaret Thatcher blasted the BBC: 'I am appalled it was ever transmitted and I believe it reflects gravely on the judgement of the BBC and those responsible.'[126] She announced that the Attorney-General, Sir Michael Havers, would consider whether legal action could be taken against the BBC. Shadow Home Secretary Merlyn Rees backed her up, saying the BBC had made 'a grave error'.[127] Thatcher's statement prompted a spate of denunciatory headlines: 'MAGGIE BLASTS BBC' declaimed the front page of London's *Evening Standard*,[128] 'TERROR QUIZ

AT BBC' cried the *Mirror*, ' "APPALLING" ERROR BY BBC' said the *Mail*, while *The Sun* spelled it out with 'Maggie lashes BBC over "appalling" TV interview with Neave terror chief'.[129]

The interview was transmitted in the week that the INLA was made an illegal organisation in Britain. It was the last such interview.

The Carrickmore affair

In September 1979 *Panorama*, the BBC's weekly current affairs programme, planned a major project on the Provisional IRA, including a historical survey and a critical assessment of its aims and tactics. It was timed to coincide with the tenth anniversary of the founding of the Provisional republican movement. The reporter was again Jeremy Paxman. BBC management approved the project, which was to include interviews with senior republicans such as David O'Connell, Ruairi O Bradaigh and Sean MacStiofain. It was also discussed in advance with the Northern Ireland Office and the army and RUC.[130]

On 17 October, while filming in Ireland, the *Panorama* team received an anonymous telephone call at their Dublin hotel saying that they would find something interesting to film if they went to Carrickmore, a small village in County Tyrone 17 miles north of the border. There, according to later BBC statements, the *Panorama* team saw ten or twelve armed IRA men, and spent about eleven minutes filming them as they sealed off the village and stopped traffic.[131]

The cameraman later said that nothing was happening when they first reached Carrickmore. 'All of a sudden, two men in hoods and carrying guns appeared about 50 yards away and started to walk away from us. I reached for my camera and started filming,' he said. The team followed the men to a crossroads where four or five other men appeared. They stopped five cars, saying, 'This is an IRA road check – can we see your driving licence?'[132]

Within 24 hours, the Northern Ireland Office, the army and the RUC knew about the incident. The army and RUC told *Panorama* that they were withdrawing their co-operation. Senior BBC men had informal talks with the RUC. Northern Ireland Secretary Humphrey Atkins wrote a letter of complaint to William Whitelaw, who, as Home Secretary, had overall responsibility for broadcasting.[133]

Meanwhile a furious internal row brewed inside BBC management. Northern Ireland Controller James Hawthorne had found himself in the embarrassing position of learning about the incident on 25 October, eight days after it happened, from a senior Northern Ireland Office official, Jim Hannigan, at a dinner in London.

Hawthorne had replaced Richard Francis as Northern Ireland Controller a year earlier, having spent eight years as Controller of Broadcasting in Hong Kong. He was originally from the North, and was to say on a radio programme three years later, 'I happen to be a loyalist by the way too, but not necessarily with a capital L.'[134] Now he wrote an angry telex to his top colleagues in London telling how he had reacted to Hannigan's news:

> I first discounted the story, then had to admit that, if true, I knew nothing about it; a reaction which in turn increased the suspicion and disbelief of Mr Hannigan. It then emerged that Mr Hannigan and the NIO had all the details; how could the controller of BBC Northern Ireland not know?[135]

As yet, nothing had been said publicly about the incident. The Northern Ireland Office, army and RUC, it seemed, preferred to keep mum about the affair because of its embarrassing implications. The IRA had carried out the operation under their noses: Carrickmore is 11 miles from the nearest army base and only six miles from a joint RUC/UDR barracks. As journalist Mary Holland wrote later, the incident

> undermines much of the received wisdom about current security arrangements in Northern Ireland – that army surveillance techniques are more efficient than ever, that the border is of crucial importance to the IRA and that their activities get little support from the local community.[136]

All was quite, on the surface at least, until nearly two weeks after the event. Then on 8 November the Dublin magazine *Hibernia* published a major article by Ed Moloney, who later became Northern Editor of *The Irish Times*, describing the Carrickmore incident and calling it 'one of the IRA's most spectacular propaganda coups to date.'[137] Moloney had come across the story by chance. He had gone to Carrickmore to investigate the death of a London man, Peter Grogan. On holiday in the area, Grogan had collapsed and died of a heart attack while being questioned by an army foot patrol. Locals told Moloney about the *Panorama* episode, and that since then the area had been saturated with troops.

With the *Hibernia* story out, events began to move very rapidly. The morning the story appeared, Whitelaw contacted the BBC for an explanation. He then went into a stormy cabinet meeting. Prime Minister Thatcher had, up till then, been told nothing, but that morning her attention had been drawn to a small item, based on information from Ed Moloney, at the bottom of page eight of the *Financial Times*.[138] She then, according to one account, 'went scatty'.[139]

The news that the Carrickmore affair was being raised in the cabinet meeting reached the BBC governors, who were also meeting that morning. As the BBC trade union journal *ABStract* put it, they reacted by 'giving their customary imitation of chickens running around with their heads cut off'.[140] The governors issued a hasty and abject statement: the incident, they said, 'would appear to be a clear breach of standing intructions in relation to filming in Ireland.'[141] BBC men later described this statement as 'incompetent', 'naive' and 'disastrous'.[142] The *Panorama* team pointed out that they had not contravened the rules, which required specific permission to be obtained for *interviews* with IRA members: no interviews had been done at Carrickmore.[143]

That afternoon, the London *Evening Standard* carried a vastly exaggerated version of the *Hibernia* story, apparently supplied by the Press Association's Belfast reporter.[144] Some 140 IRA men, said the *Standard*, had occupied Carrickmore for three hours, and their armaments had included a rocket-propelled grenade launcher. The IRA, the paper said, were thought to have offered to hold the village all night if that would be convenient for the BBC. The *Standard* also suggested that the whole exercise was carried out 'as a stunt for a BBC *Panorama* team.'

A wave of fury

Then, as the *Daily Express* later put it, 'a wave of fury swept the Commons'.[145] Accusing the BBC of setting up the incident with the IRA, Official Unionist leader James Molyneaux said, 'It seems to me to be at least a treasonable activity.' Prime Minister Thatcher declaimed, 'It is not the first time I have had occasion to raise similar matters with the BBC. Both the Home Secretary and I think it is about time they put their house in order.' It was, she said, a matter for the police and the Director of Public Prosecutions. Labour leader James Callaghan joined in, denouncing the BBC for 'stage-managing' the incident and describing the practice of manufacturing news as 'distasteful and reprehensible'. Former Northern Ireland Secretary Roy Mason, using a blunt medieval image, said, 'The *Panorama* team is on the rack. They had better explain themselves.'[146]

Next day the press went to town. 'BLUNDERAMA! BBC's astonishing deal with Provos', cried *The Sun*'s front page. Its centre pages were adorned with a photo of a masked gunman and headlined 'IT'S TREASON, SAYS MP'. 'BBC "TREASON" FURY', yelled the *Daily Express*, remarking in an editorial that 'It is as if, during the Second World War, a BBC crew had gone to film the Nazis occupying the Channel Islands.' 'PANORAMA – DUPES OF THE IRA', announced the *Mail*'s front page.[147] All three papers featured prominently the wilder reports of the previous day. *Sun* reporters David Kemp and Peter Bond wrote:

> WITNESSES said all roads in and out of Carrickmore were blocked off by IRA volunteers in a propaganda exercise.
>
> They brought an arsenal of weapons to display before the cameras.
>
> These included two M60 machine guns, an RPG 7 rocket launcher and Armalite rifles.
>
> Reports said IRA men took up defensive positions in the village while a main body of gunmen drilled in the main street . . .
>
> It was claimed the rebels had control of Carrickmore for more than three hours in broad daylight and only pulled out after the *Panorama* crew said they had enough film.
>
> One report said that up to 140 gunmen took part.[148]

The BBC's denial of such accounts was reported almost as an afterthought.

Ed Moloney, author of the original *Hibernia* report, told *The Guardian*, 'Half the things that are being reported weren't in my piece. I'm a full-time journalist. For the first time I'm really getting an insight into how awful they can be.'[149] The BBC reporter involved, Jeremy Paxman, later said that he had learned very quickly that journalists, 'when it comes to contacts with terrorists', do not have many friends even within their own profession:

> Once the story broke, the people who I had regarded as my colleagues, and who I had had drinks with only a couple of days

beforehand, that evening when I returned to the hotel in Belfast I was staying at, surrounded me in the same way as they would have surrounded any other person they were out to, by whatever means, get an incriminating quote from.[150]

A rare, small voice of reason came from *Guardian* cartoonist Gibbard. He drew a series of sketches of Mrs Thatcher smilingly presenting herself and her policies to a BBC camera. Then the cameraman films the IRA and Thatcher rounds on him: 'I'm furious! How *dare* you stage manage the news.'[151]

Scotland Yard

On 9 November, the day after the Commons debate, Scotland Yard began an inquiry into the affair on instructions from the Director of Public Prosecutions. The investigation, headed by Commander Peter Duffy, head of the Anti-Terrorist Squad, was under the Prevention of Terrorism Act. Section 11, which was added to the Act in 1976, makes it an offence to fail to pass on to the authorities information which might lead to the capture of 'terrorists'. Conviction can bring five years in prison or an unlimited fine, or both. In his 1978 review of the Act, Lord Shackleton recommended that Section 11 be dropped forthwith, commenting that 'It has an unpleasant ring about it in terms of civil liberties.'[152]

The BBC began an internal inquiry into whether *Panorama* had broken the rule that programme-makers must inform the BBC Northern Ireland Controller of any activities in his patch. They set about preparing a report for the Home Secretary and the Board of Governors.[153]

The melodrama reached new heights on 13 November. That morning, Scotland Yard officers arrived at the BBC's Lime Grove studios in London's Shepherds Bush to seize the offending film. Acting under the Prevention of Terrorism Act, they demanded a copy of the 15 minutes of footage shot at Carrickmore. The BBC handed it over, saying later that under the Act they had no option but to co-operate. Neither the BBC nor ITV had ever before surrendered untransmitted footage to the police.[154]

The BBC's top echelons continued to panic. A report by *Spotlight*, BBC Northern Ireland's current affairs programme, into the Carrickmore affair was banned at the last moment.

Spotlight had intended to bring together three journalists and three politicians, believed to have included Austin Currie of the SDLP and Thames TV reporter Peter Taylor, to discuss the implications of the row for press freedom. The official reason given for the banning was apparently the unwillingness of the BBC to provide a spokesperson.[155]

On 15 November the BBC Board of Governors held an emergency meeting to consider the report produced by acting Director-General Gerard Mansell. Next day the governors said they were satisfied there had been no collusion between *Panorama* and the IRA, but that the standing rule that the Northern Ireland Controller should be kept informed of film crews' activities 'was far from fully complied with'. The rules, they said, would be issued afresh with 'a few changes which leave no room for doubt in any direction.'[156]

The same day, Friday 16 November, at a disciplinary hearing conducted by Mansell, Roger Bolton was sacked from his post as Editor of *Panorama*, and John Gau, Head of Current Affairs programmes, was reprimanded. Bolton's 'crime' was that he had not personally informed Northern Ireland Controller James Hawthorne of *Panorama*'s plans: it later emerged, however, that the senior management in BBC Northern Ireland was in fact well aware of *Panorama*'s project.[157]

Angry union meetings were held in Bolton's support, and all the National Union of Journalists' branches in both BBC and ITV went on standby for industrial action. Bolton was then reinstated. Other current affairs editors and senior BBC officials including department heads joined the campaign to keep Bolton in his job: they felt that sacking him would seem a capitulation to government pressure and would undermine the BBC's independence.[158] When the disciplinary hearing resumed the following week, the BBC gave up the idea of sacking Bolton and reprimanded him instead.

The success of the NUJ's defence of Bolton led to 27 senior members of BBC management applying to join the union.[159] But while the journalists had won this battle, they had lost the war. Two months later a BBC spokesperson declared that the *Panorama* film on the IRA was 'definitely dead'[160] and it was never shown. The affair also led to a tightening of the BBC's guidelines for programme-makers working in the Six Counties, and to a new legal threat to journalists.

The Havers judgement

Several months later, a judgement from Attorney-General Sir Michael Havers effectively put a stop to current affairs programmes filming IRA or INLA activities or interviewing their representatives.

A report on the INLA interview and the Carrickmore affair supplied to Havers by the Director of Public Prosecutions made it clear that there was enough evidence to bring a prosecution under Section 11 of the Prevention of Terrorism Act.[161] Havers declined to prosecute because, *The Guardian* reported, 'he clearly decided that a court case would have caused an embarrassing row about press freedom.'[162] Justifying his decision later, Havers said he feared that instituting proceedings, 'particularly if unsuccessful', would add to 'INLA and Provisional IRA propaganda'. He went on to congratulate the BBC for tightening its control over Irish reporting, and said 'There were grounds to believe that the action that the BBC had already taken would prevent a recurrence of the conduct in question.'[163]

But although he decided against prosecuting the BBC, he went on to threaten them with prosecution if similar incidents occurred in the future. Replying to Tory and Unionist MPs who were furious about his decision, he said,

> I saw the chairman of the BBC governors, Sir Michael Swann, to convey to him personally my views on the matter and the strength of my feelings. I also wanted to make certain that he understood that my decision did not imply that I took the view that conduct of the kind which had taken place could not constitute an offence. I followed this with a letter reaffirming the views that I had expressed at our meeting, making it quite clear that if similar incidents took place again I would take a stricter view of what had happened and those who participated would be on warning that, subject to the evidence and circumstances of the case, they risk criminal proceedings under the Prevention of Terrorism (Temporary Provisions) Act. I trust that there will be no repetition, and I welcome the fact that the BBC has taken clear steps to prevent one. But the warning remains.[164]

In his letter to Sir Michael Swann, Havers had said,

> Although I have reached a decision not to institute criminal proceedings in respect of these two incidents I should like to make it clear that I regard conduct of the nature which took place as constituting, in principle, offences under Section 11 as well as

abhorrent, and unworthy of the high standards the public expects from the BBC.[165]

One passage in the letter particularly dismayed the BBC:

Any interview with a person purporting to represent a terrorist organisation is potentially a source of information of the nature referred to in Section 11 of the Act arising not only from the actual contents of the interview *but also from any negotiations leading up to and the actual arrangements for it.*[166] [emphasis added]

Sir Michael Swann replied, in a letter that otherwise went out of its way to reassure Havers that the BBC was 'well aware of its obligations', that

This last phrase *could* be read as meaning that the police should be informed, at every turn, of the letters, phone calls, or meetings with go-betweens which are, I have no doubt, necessary if a journalist is ever to acquire information from known or suspected terrorists. If this is really what the law says, then all reporting of who terrorists are and what they say would, in practice, be halted abruptly.[167]

Swann's response failed to budge Havers. In the Commons, Tory MP Stephen Hastings said,

In their reply, the BBC purport to imply there is some imprecision about section 11 of the Act. It is the absolute duty of any employee of the BBC or of any other media, who have any contact whatsoever with known or suspected terrorists, to report that immediately to the police or the security forces.

Havers affirmed bluntly: 'I regret the manner of the reply by the BBC in not accepting the law which is perfectly clear on this point.'[168] Thereafter, the threat of prosecution was to hang like Damocles' sword over journalists working on Ireland.

8. The reference upwards system

Development of the rules

The Carrickmore affair prompted the BBC into a rapid revision of its guidelines for programme makers working on Ireland. New instructions were issued on 27 November 1979, less than three weeks after the row had broken out.[1]

The BBC's rules were first worked out in 1971, the year which saw the IRA go on the offensive – on 6 February Gunner Robert Curtis became the first British soldier to die at their hands in the current 'troubles', and soon afterwards they began a commercial bombing campaign – and a year which brought, too, escalating troop brutality and, in August, internment and torture.

Television coverage of the North came under a barrage of attack from politicians and the press. Political scientist Jay G. Blumler summed up:

> For supposedly allowing instant interviews after controversial incidents, hectoring official spokesmen, giving a platform to IRA sympathisers, and publicising complaints about the security forces, television (mainly the BBC) is accused of harassing and disheartening the army and giving aid and comfort to the enemy.[2]

In response, the BBC drew up rules which were designed to minimise the number of items which might attract political flak. This was done by giving BBC management an unprecedented degree of control over programming decisions. On virtually every other topic, programme editors, producers and journalists are trusted to make appropriate decisions about what subjects to select and how to present them. They are expected to 'refer up' to their superiors for guidance only in cases of real doubt or difficulty. On Ireland, however, no one was to be trusted. The rules made it compulsory for programme-makers to consult management about all programmes on Ireland, so that the power to decide what would be made and broadcast was centralised in the hands of a few top executives. Desmond Taylor, who, as Editor of News and Current Affairs was a key figure in the control of Irish coverage, justified the growing supervision by saying it 'protected reporters and avoided mistakes of judgement', and commented that, 'I am just acting more like an editor and less like a bureaucrat'.[3] Reporter Jeremy Paxman, looking at the procedure from a different viewpoint, wrote that 'judgements about how to proceed can be made not by the journalists involved, but by their bosses.'[4]

Also in 1971, a similar system evolved in ITV. The Independent Television Authority, forerunner of the IBA, exercised increasingly tight control over programmes on the North made by Independent Television News and the programme companies.[5]

The rules have two basic components. Firstly, programme-makers have to consult top management, including the Northern Ireland Controller, and obtain their approval for all programmes on Ireland. This consultation has to take place at all stages of production, from the ideas stage onwards. All programmes that might be in the least bit controversial have to be viewed and approved by top management before transmission. Secondly, there are special restrictions governing interviews with members of banned organisations.

Worked out and put into operation in 1971, the new regulations were spelled out in the May 1972 edition of the BBC's *News Guide*, a handbook for journalists. The previous edition, produced in 1967, had said nothing about Ireland. The 1972 edition specified:

1. News staff sent to Northern Ireland work through Controller Northern Ireland and News Editor Northern Ireland; they must be consulted.
2. No news agency report from Northern Ireland should be used without checking with Belfast newsroom first.
3. The IRA must not be interviewed without prior authority from ENCA [Editor of News and Current Affairs]. There can be no question of doing the interview first and seeking permission for broadcast afterwards.[6]

The *News Guide* also forbade the use of broadcasts by illegal radios without reference to ENCA, and the reporting of bomb scares concerning BBC buildings: these strictures did not apply only to the North of Ireland.

The role of the Northern Ireland Controller

In the BBC's reference upwards system, the role of the Northern Ireland Controller is crucial. *The Sunday Times* noted at the start of 1972,

> In practice, every item on Ulster has to be cleared in advance with Waldo Maguire, the BBC's regional controller in Belfast. Mr Maguire is a man of extreme caution, prone to a fast veto on 'controversial' topics. Appeals against his decisions can be made to Desmond Taylor, the BBC's Editor of News and Current Affairs, but it requires politicking at a high level.[7]

The power of the Northern Ireland Controller was in part a legacy of the 1930s, when G.L. Marshall, Director of BBC Northern Ireland, had been given the right to be consulted on all matters relating to Ireland.[8] When Waldo Maguire became Northern Ireland Controller in 1966, he inherited this power.

Theoretically Maguire had only the right to be consulted, not the right to make final decisions about programmes: editorial authority resided in London, not Belfast. But the BBC had earlier made a rule that the content of programmes transmitted in Britain and in the North of Ireland should be identical: nothing could be shown in Britain which could not also be shown in the North. So, as Maguire had authority over what was transmitted in the North, he could effectively veto programmes by threatening not to show them in his territory. Further, the Director-General had also told producers not to do anything which would provoke Maguire into such an action. BBC Northern Ireland was allowed to opt out of only one major programme, a *Panorama* report made in 1970 which, according to Anthony Smith, included 'a widow crying for vengeance for her dead husband, shot by terrorists.' It was decided that this might provoke further bloodshed if it were shown in the North.[9]

Ulster Television, by contrast, was at first allowed to opt out of programmes shown on the ITV network provided that the ITA official in Belfast gave permission, and UTV did in fact opt out of six or seven programmes.[10] But during 1971 it became ITA policy not to encourage UTV to opt out. In mid-September that year the ITA said that the withholding of a network transmission of a programme on the North 'was in some sense a public admission of failure'.[11] So the Managing Director of UTV came to exercise a strong influence over programmes on Ireland. But his role was not as powerful nor as formalised as that of the BBC's Northern Ireland Controller. UTV was again to opt out of a networked programme – this time drama rather than current affairs – in August 1978, when the company refused to show the fourth episode in Southern Television's serial *Spearhead*, about a group of British soldiers. Set in the North, the episode was due for transmission on 8 August, the anniversary of internment.

During the Carrickmore affair, BBC Northern Ireland Controller James Hawthorne had, to his embarrassment, learned about *Panorama*'s filming of an IRA roadblock not from within the BBC, but from a Northern Ireland Office official. As a result, shortly afterwards, according to *The Guardian*, BBC staff were instructed to inform Hawthorne personally when they planned to mention the North.[12] Then new guidelines were issued which dealt with the consultation process, and particularly the Northern Ireland Controller's role, in great detail.

The new rules were first released as an appendix to the minutes of the News and Current Affairs meeting held on 27 November 1979. It is at these top level meetings that BBC policy evolves and decisions are taken that become precedents for the future.[13] Then in 1980 the rules were incorporated in the new edition of the BBC's *News and Current Affairs Index*, a slim yellow handbook which is issued to journalistic staff in both television and radio. The 'Standing Instructions and Guidance' on 'Coverage of Matters Affecting Northern Ireland' occupy just over four pages of the *Index*. Under the heading 'Referring to Northern Ireland Staff', the *Index*, using bold type for mandatory instructions, specifies:

> (a) **Controller Northern Ireland must be consulted and his agreement sought to all programme proposals having a bearing on Ireland as a whole and on Northern Ireland in particular.**
> – He does not have a right of veto, but in cases of disagreement the proposal shall be suspended until it has been referred to DNCA and finally, if necessary, to DG for their ruling.
> – CNI will be the first point of contact on network programme proposals other than news and same-day programme items . . .
> – HPNI [Head of Programmes Northern Ireland] will be the principal point of reference for the continuous process of consultation and advice in detail.

(b) **News Editor, Northern Ireland, is the first point of contact in all day-to-day matters of coverage for network radio and television news bulletins and sequences . . .**
(c) **Consultation is a two-way process requiring the fullest possible disclosure of the programme proposal, upon which** CNI **can form an opinion; it is also a continuing process.** After the first consultation at the outset of the proposal, CNI is to be kept informed about its progress and consulted about any significant change, incident or problem which may occur. He also needs to be informed of the transmission date envisaged and of the context in which it is being transmitted.[14]

The scope of the rules

The reference upwards system acts firstly as a filter, removing 'undesirable' programmes or items at an early stage and, in theory, eliminating the need for embarrassing acts of censorship. Secondly, it is an early warning system, so that if a 'sensitive' programme is allowed through, such as Keith Kyle's 1977 *Tonight* film in which Bernard O'Connor alleged he had been tortured, not only can it be checked and double-checked, but also the upper echelons can prepare themselves for the inevitable on-slaught from the right. Justifying the system, which he admitted was a departure from the normal procedure because it transferred responsibility from the individual producer or editor to top management, Richard Francis said, 'Early warning, briefing and consultation is essential if the Controller in Northern Ireland or the Editor of News and Current Affairs in London is not to be caught between last-minute "censorship" or disregard.'[15]

No item on Northern Ireland, however minor, escapes scrutiny. In early 1982, even a ten-minute summary of the North-ern situation made for *See Hear*, a BBC programme for the deaf and the blind, had to be referred up prior to transmission. Nor does the procedure apply just to news and current affairs, but to every area of programming. In a talk on *The TV Play and Northern Ireland*, Richard Hoggart described how drama is affected:

> anything on the troubles is very sensitive and involves reference upward, discussion, sometimes stalling; and so quite a number of plays have been delayed, denied repeats or relegated to late-night slots. Unless a writer has a very strong sense that this is his [sic] topic he is not likely to expose himself to that sort of delay and fine-tooth combing over his work . . . imaginative insights into the complexity of the situation are largely denied us . . . A play which

viewed the struggles from the angle of the terrorists, no matter how full of insight it might be, would probably . . . have a pretty rough ride.[16]

In ITV, programmes on Ireland have to be referred to the management of the television company concerned, and then to the IBA. Paul Fox, Managing Director of Yorkshire Television and previously Controller of BBC1, told in late 1981 how he was agonising over whether a three-part drama serial on Ireland should be made:

It's an extremely difficult decision, and very delicate . . . I'm concerned that when that play is made, and a transmission date happens, and the transmission date coincides with an attack or a bombing attack in London, what do you do? Do you show that play? Or do you pull the play out? . . . It's written by a news-paperman, it's an exceptionally good script, it's been read by people in Northern Ireland who approve it, and yet I have enormous doubts about it.[17]

The play in question was *Harry's Game*, based on Gerald Seymour's best-selling thriller of the same name.[18] In the event, Yorkshire Television went ahead with it and it was transmitted on the network in October 1982.[19] A somewhat unlikely tale of a British agent who operates undercover in West Belfast in pursuit of an IRA killer, the play did not seriously challenge conventional British ideas about the conflict: instead, it was marked by a dearth of politics and an emphasis on IRA cruelty.

Even songs come under the microscope. In 1972 the BBC banned Paul McCartney's song, 'Give Ireland Back to the Irish'. At that time, before the advent of commercial radio, the BBC had a monopoly challenged only by the pirate stations. The chorus of the song went:

Give Ireland back to the Irish,
Don't make them have to take it away.
Give Ireland back to the Irish,
Make Ireland Irish today.[20]

In September 1981 the BBC, apparently following in the footsteps of ITV,[21] banned a video made by the rock group Police to accompany their single, *Invisible Sun*. The video was described by *Times* correspondent Richard Williams as 'A collage of Ulster street scenes, incorporating urchins, graffiti, Saracens and sol-diers.'[22] The BBC's justification for the ban was enigmatic. A spokesperson said, 'The theme of the single is anti-violence, but the presentation film could be said to convey meanings which are not present in the single.'[23] The group refused to change their film, and refused to perform the song live on *Top of the Pops*.[24]

The reference upwards rules even extend to the BBC's internal 'central news traffic' system. Central traffic, located at Broadcasting House in central London, is the means by which sound items are transferred from their place of origin, for example a regional studio, to the programmes for which they are intended. When an item is coming through, it is announced on a tannoy and can be listened to in any news or current affairs office in the main BBC buildings. It is forbidden to send 'sensitive' items on Ireland through central traffic.

Rules on republican interviews

In both the BBC and ITV there are special rules governing interviews with members of banned groups. In practice, these rules almost exclusively affect republicans.

Though the loyalist Ulster Volunteer Force began killing Catholics in 1966, and started bombing in 1969, the BBC's rules drawn up in 1971 referred only to interviews with the IRA. In 1971 the BBC considered totally banning interviews with 'Republican extremists', but instead decided that 'such interviews should only be filmed and transmitted after the most serious consideration, and that the BBC should be seen to be clearly opposed to the indiscriminate methods of the extremists.'[25]

The rule adopted was that permission had to be obtained in advance from the Director-General, then Charles Curran, before the IRA could be interviewed. The rule amounted to a ban: Curran later said that he had only given prior permission for two IRA interviews, one in 1972 and another in 1974.[26] The BBC was apparently not anxious to publicise the restrictions. They did not admit to them openly until late November 1971, after a BBC radio *World at One* journalist had told a meeting of journalists protesting against censorship of news from the North that 'BBC staff were now forbidden to interview any member of the IRA except with the direct permission of the Director-General.'[27] Next day a BBC spokesperson confirmed that, 'In general we do have a ban. There can only be interviews with members of illegal organisations in exceptional circumstances and that would involve consultation at a high editorial level.'[28]

As a result of the regulations, journalists wishing to interview members of republican paramilitary groups faced a daunting rigmarole. Roger Bolton, who was editor of *Tonight* when, in its last edition in July 1979, it showed an interview with an INLA spokesperson, described the procedure that led up to it:

> We argued amongst ourselves so that we were convinced that such an interview was the proper thing to do; I then went through the BBC machinery which leads ultimately to the Director-General first to get authority to research the story, secondly on a separate occasion to get authority to see whether such an interview would be possible and thirdly the authority to do such an interview, and finally the interview was seen before transmission by the Director-General's appointed deputy.[29]

When the BBC's rules were redrafted at the end of 1979, they referred not just to the IRA but to 'terrorist organisations'. In practice this meant illegal groups, so, since the largest loyalist paramilitary organisation, the UDA, remained legal, republicans were still the main target of the rules. The loyalist groups banned in the North – though not in Britain – are the Ulster Volunteer Force, the tiny Red Hand Commandos, and, ironically, the Ulster Freedom Fighters – a cover name used by the UDA.

The BBC's 1980 *Index* instructs journalists to refer up for permission to interview not only 'members of terrorist organisations' but also 'those who are or may be associated with such organisations'. It says,

> In these cases the producer or editor making the proposal will make it first to his Head of Department who will refer to DNCA [Director of News and Current Affairs] and notify the Network Controller and CNI [Controller Northern Ireland]. **Interviews with individuals who are deemed by DNCA to be closely associated with a terrorist organisation may not be sought or transmitted – two separate stages – without the prior permission of the Director-General.**[30]

The restrictions no longer applied solely to members of paramilitary groups, but also to representatives of republican political organisations. In 1981, for example, it was necessary to obtain the Director-General's permission before interviewing Sinn Fein Vice-President Gerry Adams. Richard Francis, then Director of News and Current Affairs, said of the new guidelines, 'The decision about who is or is not associated with a terrorist organisation – the question of classification – now rests with me.'[31]

The IBA's regulations on Irish coverage appear in its *Guide-*

lines handbook under the heading 'Crime, anti-social behaviour, etc.'[32] Somewhat ironically, the section includes the statement that 'Political dissidents from foreign countries who are guilty of offences under the laws of their own countries may be interviewed, subject to the normal requirements of impartiality.' Immediately below this, under the heading 'Interviews with people who use or advocate violence or other criminal measures', the *Guidelines* specify:

> Any plans for a programme item which explores and exposes the views of people who within the British Isles use or advocate violence or other criminal measures for the achievement of political ends must be referred to the Authority before any arrangements for filming or videotaping are made. A producer should therefore not plan to interview members of proscribed organisations, for example members of the Provisional IRA or other para-military organisations, without previous discussion with his [sic] company's top management. The management, if they think the item may be justified, will then consult the Authority.
>
> In exceptional and unforeseen circumstances, it may be impossible for a news reporting team to consult before recording such an item. Consultation with the Authority is still essential to determine whether the item can be transmitted.[33]

The *Guidelines* add a further restriction:

> An interview conducted in Northern Ireland with a hooded person or the contriving by a production team of an incident involving hooded persons could be in breach of the Northern Ireland (Emergency Provisions) (Amendment) Act 1975. It is not an offence to show film or pictures of persons wearing hoods so long as it is clear that the incident was not 'set up' in collusion with those wearing hoods.[34]

Both the BBC and IBA handbooks detail the legal hazards facing journalists working in the North, including the onus on them, under Section 5 of the Criminal Law Act (Northern Ireland) 1967, to supply the police with any information relating to criminal activities. The BBC's *Index*, collated after the Carrickmore affair, also drew attention to the similar section in the Prevention of Terrorism Act.

Balance

Two further requirements circumscribe the way television portrays the nationalist case. Firstly, programmes which include republican views or allegations against the British army or RUC have to be 'internally balanced', with the opposite view put within the same programme. Secondly, all republican interviewees or people making allegations against Britain have to be treated in a hostile manner.

The minutes of the BBC's top-level News and Current Affairs meeting on 13 August 1971, four days after the start of internment, record Waldo Maguire, then Northern Ireland Controller, asking that 'the controversial broadcasting rule (believed to be in force at Suez) – that each item or programme should be self-balancing – should be reintroduced. The meeting couldn't remember such a rule ever being enforced.'[35] Within less than three months, the 'self-balancing' requirement had become policy.

At the ENCA meeting on 10 September 1971, *24 Hours* was criticised for interviewing Jack Lynch, Prime Minister of the South of Ireland, without 'balancing' the interview with someone from the Unionist government in the North.[36] On 17 September, *24 Hours* was again criticised for interviewing Lynch without a 'balancing' Unionist interview. By 22 October, such reproaches were no longer necessary. The meeting that day saw Editor of News and Current Affairs Desmond Taylor congratulating everyone on the BBC's performance and saying he

> had been glad to see that editors and producers had observed the policy of providing immediate balance in all current affairs items when contentious material had been sought out by the BBC, just as Controller, Northern Ireland, had recommended in the previous spate of allegations.[37]

The rule was a retreat from the position of former Director-General Sir Hugh Carleton Greene, who maintained that 'balance' could be spread over a number of items.[38] It also conflicted with normal journalistic practice. Desmond Taylor, who became Editor of News and Current Affairs in 1971, wrote later, 'In our efforts to be fair, and fairness came to replace balance in our minds, we got to the point where each programme had to include both sides, even where normal editorial considerations did not call for it.'[39]

'Fairness' or 'balance' became an excuse for the suppression of nationalist views. Thus BBC film of the 'Alternative Parliament' set up by the Social Democratic and Labour Party was never shown because, according to *The Sunday Times*, 'it was deemed unbalanced'.[40]

As Jonathan Dimbleby, then a *World at One* reporter, pointed out, the 'balance' rule is applied in a strictly one-sided way:

> The damage caused by an absurd rule is compounded when that rule is broken consistently and discriminately. Thus Brian Faulkner and John Taylor (the junior Home Affairs Minister at Stormont), British army spokesmen, members of the British government, and (less easily) their Labour Shadows, can air their opinions in an 'unbalanced' way with impunity. But in the case of members of the SDLP, the government and the Opposition of the Irish Republic, all critics of the British army, the government, or of Stormont policy, the rule is strictly applied.[41]

Hostile interviews

Television and radio reporters interviewing republicans are required to deal with them in a 'tough' or hostile manner. This applies not only to interviews with members of illegal groups, but also to interviews with Sinn Fein representatives. Richard Francis, then Controller of BBC Northern Ireland, was including Sinn Fein in the 'paramilitary' category when he said, 'Such interviews always demand forthright handling by experienced interviewers – invariably, paramilitary interviewees are treated as hostile witnesses.'[42]

This means that the interviewee is questioned aggressively, usually with frequent interruptions. The interviewer repeatedly challenges or even flatly contradicts statements made by the interviewee. It also means, particularly where the interview is part of a film rather than a studio discussion, that the interviewee is presented in a very critical or unsympathetic context.

The reporter introduced *Tonight*'s July 1979 INLA interview, for example, by emphasising what Richard Francis later called 'the seedy perquisites of anonymity'.[43] Reporter David Lomax explained how

> In Dublin a man calling himself Mr Gray gave us telephone instructions to go to a series of different hotels. The trail led eventually to a room which we found had been booked in my name in a hotel on the outskirts of the city. There we met two men wearing wigs, dark glasses and false moustaches. They also wore surgical rubber gloves and had strange bulges in the pockets of their anoraks.[44]

Interestingly, as Richard Francis confirmed two years later, the BBC had first approached the IRA for an interview and had been turned down. 'Mr Dick Francis, BBC director of news and current affairs, said that an approach was made to the INLA after the IRA rejected the opportunity,' reported *The Irish Times* on 17 July 1981. According to Sinn Fein spokesperson Richard McAuley, the IRA refused to do a back-to-camera interview because of the negative impression that would be given. Instead, the Republican Press Centre offered to provide a spokesperson who would answer any questions *Tonight* wanted to ask about the IRA, on condition that it was made clear at the start of the programme that the interviewee was not a member of the IRA.[45]

That *Tonight* approached the IRA first casts some doubt on a BBC spokesperson's claim that the INLA had been interviewed to add to public knowledge about 'a new force in terrorism'.[46] The interview was intended for, and transmitted in, *Tonight*'s last edition, and the BBC team's rejection of the Republican Press Centre's offer suggests that they were less interested in illuminating the thinking behind the violence than in providing their programme with a sensational exit.

In November 1982, BBC's *Panorama* showed a film entitled 'Gerry Adams: the Provos' Politician' which was a classic example of the hostile technique.[47] The film was prompted by the previous month's Assembly election, but reporter Fred Emery showed little interest in exploring why Adams had topped the poll in West Belfast. Instead, his overriding concern was to undermine Adams' new status and to establish that Adams was a member of the IRA. This approach was, except in propaganda terms, fruitless, since the courts had failed to prove the accusation, and since Adams was hardly likely to admit it. A more enlightening approach would have been to ask why a man who was associated – wrongly or rightly – in the public mind with the IRA, had won such widespread support among nationalist electors.

Emery set the scene by painting Adams as a sinister, conspiratorial figure, who 'assumes a spurious legitimacy', was 'the manipulator' of the hunger strike, and now works 'in the guise of community politician'. A succession of interviewees were wheeled out to testify against him, among them hardline Unionist Harold McCusker – 'I think he has been drenched in bloodshed for the best part of 10 or 12 years' – as well as Ian Paisley, former Northern Ireland Secretary Merlyn Rees and even Andy Tyrie of the loyalist paramilitary UDA – 'I am absolutely convinced . . . that Gerry Adams is Chief of Staff of the IRA.'

The interview with Adams lasted no more than 15 of the programme's 50 minutes, and was like a cross between an inquisition and a battle, with Adams fighting to establish his analysis against Emery's completely opposing version of events:

> *Emery (interrupts)*: And it's not on your conscience then that the sort of things you've advocated have helped fill up –
> *Adams (interrupts)*: Well, what have I advocated?
> *Emery*: Well, in advocating the support of the armed struggle, you've helped fill the prisons with young men, you've helped fill the cemeteries with young men –
> *Adams (interrupts)*: I mean the situation very, very simply –
> *Emery (interrupts)*: Young Catholic men.
> *Adams*: The situation very, very simply is that for – there have been hundreds of thousands of young men and young women who have been through prison, right, and the responsibility for that, I mean before my time, lay with the British government. The responsibility for that during my time – I haven't anyone in prison, the British government has people in prison.

The interview in the end elicited little about Adams save his determination to stand his ground, and the programme as a whole threw no light on why nearly 10,000 people had just voted for him; Emery's approach ruled out the possibility of a sympathetic examination of nationalist attitudes.

Emery's treatment of Gerry Adams was very different from his approach to the other interviewees, including UDA leader Andy Tyrie. It was also in sharp contrast to the treatment given by television to another prominent nationalist, Gerry Fitt. In addition to his many other television appearances, Fitt had at the start of 1982 featured on BBC2's *The Light of Experience*, a quasi-religious programme in which the subject speaks directly, and at length, to the camera about his or her experiences.[48] On 17 October the same year Fitt was given a long and gentle interview on BBC1's *Out on a Limb*.

The media's hostility to Gerry Adams and sympathy for Gerry Fitt do not reflect their standing in the nationalist community, but rather attitudes held in London. The disintegration of Fitt's support in Belfast was made plain in May 1981 when, because of his hostility to the hunger strikers, he was humiliatingly defeated by an anti-H Block candidate in the local elections, losing his seat on Belfast City Council which he had held for 23 years. At Westminster, however, he continued to be almost universally admired. That he lost his parliamentary seat to Gerry Adams in June 1983 made little impact on British establishment attitudes towards him. Politicians and media alike eulogised him in his defeat, and his elevation to the peerage meant that he could continue to be treated as a 'spokesperson' on matters Irish even though he had been rejected at the ballot box.[49]

Censorship

The known instances of censorship have occurred at various points in the reference upwards procedure. Some programmes have been quashed while still at the planning stage, some when filming was in progress, and others have been banned, cut or altered at the final stage, when they were viewed by the IBA or top BBC executives.

The programmes or items that have been censored fall basically into two categories. Either they were critical of British policy, especially of the activities of the army or the police, or – and this is the bigger group – they illustrated republican activities or views. Not surprisingly, no item sympathetic to British government policy has ever been banned. Only one programme dealing with unionism has been censored. This was a BBC *24 Hours* film made in 1971. Implicitly challenging British strategy, the film showed the growing opposition inside the Official Unionist Party to 'moderate' Stormont Prime Minister Major James Chichester-Clark and the extent of sympathy with Ian Paisley. The film predicted Chichester-Clark's resignation, and was suppressed because Northern Ireland Controller Waldo Maguire thought it would help the campaign against him.[50] Chichester-Clark resigned soon afterwards, so the film became redundant.

While most of the decisions to censor programmes appear to have been taken autonomously by the broadcasting bodies, some have been made as a direct result of political pressures. Thus *Panorama*'s 1979 project on the IRA met its end largely because of the uproar surrounding the Carrickmore incident. But political influence can also be more subtly exerted.

In 1973, BBC producer Michael Blakstad made a film called *Children in Crossfire*, based on a book by Morris Fraser about the psychological impact of the troubles on the children of the North. Northern Ireland Controller Richard Francis saw it in

December and was said to have been 'content' with it.[51] In January 1974, however, the political situation altered when the power-sharing executive took office, and in February Francis expressed concern about the film to Blakstad. Blakstad had gained the support of the British army's eccentric public relations officer, Colin Wallace, but this did not impress Francis. The army, he told BBC Head of Science Features Phillip Daly in a cable, 'are no judges of political consequences and poor judges of social context.' Francis's cable continued: 'After the inauspicious start to the script, given the concern about this film expressed to me at the highest political level, I need to be satisfied that the final version can be made acceptable.' The 'highest political level' was believed to be Francis Pym, who was briefly Northern Ireland Secretary in January and February 1974. Francis went on to complain that the film made no reference to the 'progress' represented by declining violence in Derry and by job creation, and it contained 'not a single reference to the new executive and the remarkable effects of having Catholic Ministers of Housing, Community Relations, etc.'[52]

The film went out in March with a preface, written by Francis, appended to it. This, according to the magazine *Time Out*, said that 'power sharing was in the process of transforming the Northern Ireland political scene' and implied that the rioting shown in the film was a thing of the past.[53] Two months later, in May, the power-sharing executive collapsed and direct rule was reintroduced.[54]

The manner in which approaches are made to broadcasters by 'the highest political level' was illustrated in a Granada TV programme in their series titled, *The State of the Nation: the bounds of freedom*.[55] In this series, influential people were brought together and asked how they would react to hypothetical situations. The sixth programme dealt with the question of televising interviews with 'terrorists'.

Former Northern Ireland Secretary Merlyn Rees was asked if, in order to try to stop such an interview being shown, he would phone the Managing Director of the broadcasting company. Rees replied that he would tell a member of his staff to 'pop round and have a word with him': 'Tell him that I am concerned but I haven't got the full facts. And then perhaps if he wants to have a word about it, perhaps he'd pop over to the House [of Commons] this evening. We could have a drink, talk about it.'

Richard Francis was asked if he thought it right for a minister to invite him to dinner to convey such a request. Francis replied that he thought it 'would be a very suitable way to do it, because . . . it recognises the proper distinction between the roles which the broadcasters have to play and those of the ministers responsible for the situation.' Agreeing that at the end of the day he would take his own decision, he said, 'the business of having dinner together is precisely designed to make it quite plain that it isn't a ministerial order and it isn't constraining us to take decisions for which we're not taking full responsibility.'[56]

Self-censorship

The ramifications of the system of internal controls go far beyond the known cases of censorship. The introduction of 'reference upwards' in 1971 led rapidly to the most insidious form of censorship: broadcasters began to censor themselves. As the secretary of the Federation of Broadcasting Unions protested to BBC Chairman Lord Hill, they were demoralised by the need to argue at length over programme suggestions, and feared that their careers were suffering because they had 'disagreed with others' over Irish stories.[57] Jonathan Dimbleby wrote at the end of 1971 that, 'They ignore a story here, resist an idea there, look for a safe angle, or seek out events which are not contentious and of marginal significance.'[58]

As the years passed, and Ireland remained the most politically sensitive topic for television, self-censorship continued. 'For every programme that gets banned, there are about twenty that don't get made,' remarked Mary Holland in 1981.[59] Reporters were inhibited by the procedure for obtaining clearance for stories. Editors dreaded what reporter Jeremy Paxman described as 'heavy duty negotiations with senior management', and broadcasters at all levels feared the political fuss that questioning programmes inevitably provoked. They developed an instinct for how far they could safely go. BBC reporter Nick Ross observed, 'I think much more pernicious than any external authority which tells you, you must do this, you mustn't do that, is the sense of you ought to keep your copy book clean and that you shouldn't do anything which is going to rock the boat.'[61]

Unsurprisingly, only a few questioning reporters and filmmakers stayed the course. Some well-known 'crusading' reporters avoided the topic altogether. Some gave up trying after negative experiences. A handful battled on. As Mary Holland, one of the survivors, put it, to resist the pressures that are brought to bear on anyone trying to report against the political consensus 'takes cunning, it takes patience, and more than anything else it takes boundless energy. As you get older, the energy tends to flag, but it's the duty of journalists I think to try and keep it up.'[62]

A BBC radio editor once likened the situation in the BBC to 'dealing with ectoplasm': 'Nobody is entirely to blame, but the end result of all the "balancing" acts and concerned editing is effectively censorship.'[63] The system ensured that censorship was not only hard to pinpoint, but was also almost invisible to the general public. Precisely because of its subtlety, this 'British way of censorship', as Mary Holland dubbed it, has won the admiration of the international fraternity of 'anti-terrorism' experts, who have recommended it as an example worth following.[64]

Radio Telefis Eireann

In the South of Ireland, events had taken a different course. In both Britain and the South, the formal relationship between government and broadcasters is roughly similar. In both countries, the broadcasting companies are supervised by government-appointed bodies – the BBC Board of Governors and the Independent Broadcasting Authority in Britain, and the Radio Telefis Eireann Authority in Ireland – but the government does not exercise direct control. Both the British and Irish governments, however, have the legal power to stop the broadcasters transmitting either specific programmes or any specified class of material.[65]

When the conflict in the North intensified, and demands for censorship were heard on both sides of the Irish Sea, the British government stopped short of using its censorship powers, while the Irish government went ahead. This was partly due to the difference in the status of broadcasting in the two countries. In Britain, the broadcasters' appearance of independence from government had been carefully cherished: this not only maintained their credibility, but also, because of the BBC's international reputation, sustained Britain's image abroad as a 'free society'. The Irish broadcasting service, Radio Telefis Eireann, had no such international significance, and Irish political leaders publicly rejected the notion that it should be free of government supervision.[66]

Over the first year of the conflict, the Irish government's public posture shifted dramatically. In August 1969, as Catholic homes burned and British troops began patrolling the streets of the North, Taoiseach Jack Lynch announced that the Irish army would establish field hospitals on the border. He blamed 'successive Stormont governments' for the situation, and said the Irish government could 'no longer stand by and see innocent people injured and perhaps worse'.[67] He said the employment of British troops was 'unacceptable' and called for a UN peacekeeping force to be brought in.[68] Then in 1970 government ministers were involved in an attempt to run guns to the IRA, in an operation possibly sanctioned by the whole Irish cabinet.[69]

Within a year, however, the Irish government had changed its stance, and Lynch began publicly endorsing British policy. Historian Michael Farrell comments, 'The Southern establishment was evidently more interested in stability and good relations with Britain than in the plight of the Northern minority.'[70] The burgeoning IRA, which challenged the existence of the Southern state and had been ruthlessly dealt with by successive Irish governments since partition, began to be treated as the greater threat.

In mid-1971, the Southern government began trying to stop television interviews with the IRA. Unlike the pro-censorship lobby in Britain, they were, initially at least, less concerned about the reporting of British atrocities. Whereas the British authorities were mainly worried about the growth of pro-withdrawal sentiment in Britain, the Irish government feared an increase in IRA support. There was, and remains, a deep ambivalence towards the IRA in the South: the state, after all, owed its existence to the war against Britain waged by an earlier IRA.[71]

In June 1971 the Irish minister responsible for broadcasting tried without success to stop RTE showing an interview with two leading but unnamed IRA men, done by the station's Northern correspondent, Liam Hourican.[72] Then the current affairs programme *Seven Days* put out interviews with two IRA leaders, and a late night news bulletin carried a statement by Sinn Fein leader Ruairi O Bradaigh before a statement by the Prime Minister.

The government then acted. On 1 October 1971 Gerry Collins, the Minister for Posts and Telegraphs, invoked Section 31 of the Broadcasting Act and issued a directive requiring RTE

> to refrain from broadcasting any matter of the following class,
> i.e. any matter that could be calculated to promote the aims or

activities of any organisation which engages in, promotes, encourages or advocates the attaining of any particular objective by violent means. [73]

The Section 31 directive was, as the RTE Authority protested at the time, 'imprecise'. [74] The Authority told its staff that 'The primary intention of the directive is to prohibit the direct participation in broadcasting of persons who through that participation would succeed in promoting the aims or activities of those organisations described in the direction'. [75] The directive did not, said the Authority, prohibit the reporting or analysis of violent events; nor did it prevent current affairs programmes from discussing the activities and policies of the organisations in question, provided this was done very carefully, so that 'reasonable people' would not regard the programmes as promoting those organisations.

This interpretation, which apparently went unchallenged by the government, allowed journalists some leeway. But in November 1972 their room to manoeuvre was abruptly ended. In the early hours of 19 November, IRA Chief of Staff Sean MacStiofain was arrested as he drove away from the home of RTE news features editor Kevin O'Kelly. O'Kelly had been interviewing MacStiofain for a *This Week* radio programme to be transmitted the same day. The aim was to discover whether Provisional IRA thinking had changed as a result of a policy statement made by British Prime Minister Ted Heath on a visit to the North the previous week. [76] On 24 November, ostensibly because of this interview, the Minister for Posts and Telegraphs sacked all nine members of the RTE authority and appointed a new authority. Reporter Kevin O'Kelly was arrested and on 25 November was sentenced to three months' imprisonment for refusing to identify MacStiofain in court as the man he had interviewed. O'Kelly was given bail and leave to appeal, and the sentence was later commuted to a £250 fine. [77]

Apparently the only explanation the minister gave for sacking the Authority was on 14 December, when he told the Dail that he had a personal responsibility to ensure that opportunity was not given to people of violence to use RTE as a recruiting platform and thereby increase the death toll in Ireland. [78]

The new Authority then issued a set of guidelines giving a rigorous interpretation of the Section 31 directive. Radio and TV interviews and recordings involving representatives of the Provisional IRA and Official IRA were now banned. Proposals to film representatives of Provisional or Official Sinn Fein had to be cleared in advance with the head of news or, for current affairs programmes, the Director-General. The Authority also stressed that 'the strictest care must be taken in these matters' and threatened action against any individual who flouted the guidelines.[79]

Conor Cruise O'Brien

The change of government in March 1973, when a coalition of Fine Gael and the Irish Labour Party ousted Fianna Fail, was to bring an even more repressive approach to broadcasting. Conor Cruise O'Brien, a Labour member of the Dail, became Minister for Posts and Telegraphs. O'Brien had been a prominent liberal and an advocate of British withdrawal.[80] He had strongly condemned the Section 31 directive, calling it 'sinister'. The day before the dismissal of the RTE Authority he said:

> I do not think the Irish public would like to see RTE brought into line and being made the object of what the National Socialists used to call Gleichschaltung, co-ordination, being brought into line with the party, and being made transmission systems for the party's ideology . . . in any modern democracy the autonomy of radio and television is as vital as the freedom of the press and of Parliament.[81]

Once in office, O'Brien began implementing precisely the policy he had so unequivocally denounced. He reportedly 'blew his top'[82] when in 1974 the *Seven Days* programme showed parts of an independently made film, *Behind the Wire*,[83] containing interviews with some of the men who had been subjected to sensory deprivation in 1971. He summoned RTE's Director-General to his office, and on O'Brien's instruction *Seven Days* producer Eoghan Harris was moved from current affairs to the agricultural department.[84]

O'Brien's politics were undergoing a rapid shift to the right. He began to oppose Irish re-unification and outspokenly attacked Irish culture.[85] He soon became, as the *New Statesman* put it, 'the British Government's best friend over the water'.[86]

In October 1976, O'Brien issued a new directive under Section 31, banning interviews with Provisional Sinn Fein. The ban came after the radio programme *This Week* had transmitted an interview with Sinn Fein Publicity Director Sean O Bradaigh which reportedly 'infuriated' leading members of the government.[87] The directive also explicitly banned not only interviews, and reports of interviews, with both IRAs, but also with all organisations banned in the North. Irish journalist Tom McGurk commented that this was 'a unique piece of legislation' in that access to Irish broadcasting for certain organisations 'was now to be decided by the dictates of the British Government.'[88]

In May 1977 O'Brien called for censorship in Britain. A large number of homes in the South can receive British stations, and O'Brien complained – with some exaggeration, given the scarcity of IRA interviews on British television – that 'IRA godfathers' were 'wafted into our living-rooms' courtesy of British broadcasting.[89] His support for censorship extended to Irish newspapers. In one highly controversial incident he revealed that he was keeping a file of letters supporting Irish unity that had been published in *The Irish Press*, and would like to prosecute the editor. The editor, Tim Pat Coogan, duly re-published the letters.[90]

O'Brien's policies led to a drastic decline in his popularity, and in the June 1977 election he lost his Dail seat in a humiliating defeat. A few months later he moved to London to become editor-in-chief of *The Observer*, staying in this job till March 1981, when he became consultant editor.

At *The Observer*, he continued in the same heavy-handed style. He marked his arrival with a lengthy, signed editorial condemning Taoiseach Jack Lynch's call for British withdrawal as 'poisoned rhetoric'.[91] Some months later, without informing the author, he ordered changes in a colour supplement article by Mary Holland about a woman from Derry, Mary Nelis, two of whose sons were in prison for IRA activities.[92] Part of the magazine was already printed, and had to be pulped. He followed this up with an extraordinary letter to Mary Holland, complaining that her article conveyed the impression 'of a good woman, hostile to violence, who and whose family have been and continue to be, victims of the events of the past ten years.' He viewed this picture, he said, 'with a great deal of scepticism':

> Since Irish Republicanism – especially the killing strain of it – has a very high propensity to run in families, and since the mother is most often the carrier, I incline to the view that a mother whose sons behave in this way has had something to do with what they believe and how they behave.[93]

He felt 'personally ashamed' that the piece should be published in *The Observer*, because he was sure it would be 'of considerable assistance' to the H Block campaign. He acknowledged that Mary Holland's motives were 'honourable', then wrote:

> I also think however that it is a serious weakness in your coverage of Irish affairs that you are a very poor judge of Irish Catholics. That gifted and talkative community includes some of the most expert conmen and conwomen in the world and I believe you have been conned.[94]

Mary Holland had worked for *The Observer* almost continuously since 1964, and in 1970 had won the Journalist of the Year award for her coverage of the North. In November 1979 her freelance contract with the paper was terminated.[95]

The effects of Section 31

Successive Irish governments continued to renew the Section 31 restrictions. Their suffocating effects on RTE's reporting were described by journalists who responded to an NUJ questionnaire in 1977. One wrote:

> The ultra-cautious atmosphere which section 31 and the guidelines have fostered in the newsroom and programme sections has meant that enquiries into controversial issues have not been encouraged . . . Issues like allegations of RUC ill treatment of suspects, British Army 'accidental' killings, paramilitary racketeering, internal paramilitary feuds . . . Establishment views (security forces, Government, Church, etc.) are aired at great length, often without analysis or counterpoint . . . there is now a general anxiety about tackling stories which might embarrass the Government on the issue of security.[96]

The restrictions often had ludicrous results. Since 1974 Sinn Fein had been the fourth largest party in local government in the South,[97] yet its councillors could not be interviewed on television or radio, even to discuss such mundane subjects as drainage.[98] On one occasion, in April 1977, an RTE camera crew was instructed to film a Sinn Fein rally without sound. The rally turned into a serious riot. Looking at the silent film, RTE executives concluded that it resembled a Keystone Cops classic, and hastily borrowed sound tapes from the BBC and ITV, who had been filming the scene.[99] Then in 1981 RTE had to be given a special exemption by the government in order to be able to show the last two programmes of Robert Kee's major history series, since these contained republican interviews. The series was a BBC/RTE co-production.[100]

The absurdity of the rules became even more obvious when republican candidates were elected to Westminster and the Dail in 1981, to the Northern Ireland Assembly in 1982, and to Westminster in 1983. None of the candidates, nor people speaking on their behalf, could be interviewed on RTE. Journalists protested to no avail that RTE's election coverage was 'farcical'[101] and was making them 'a laughing stock'.[102]

In February 1982, Sinn Fein put up seven candidates – the number needed to qualify for a party political broadcast – in the Southern general election. Since such broadcasts were not banned under the Section 31 directive, the RTE Authority allocated Sinn Fein two minutes on radio and two minutes on television. Then on 9 February the Minister for Posts and Telegraphs made an order extending the directive to exclude all broadcasts by Sinn Fein.[103] Sinn Fein challenged the ban, and on 16 February a High Court judge ruled that it was unconstitutional.[104] The government immediately appealed to the Supreme Court, which refused to put a stay on the High Court order. There was now less than 24 hours to go before the election, and RTE refused to allow Sinn Fein to broadcast, arguing that it was too late.[105] In March, the Supreme Court reversed the High Court's decision, upholding the ban on Sinn Fein.[106]

The issue flared again in 1983 when Sinn Fein stood candidates in the Westminster general election. The RTE Authority asked the Minister for Transport and Communications, Jim Mitchell, to waive the ban for the duration of the election.[107] At the request of their Belfast colleagues, Dublin RTE journalists who belonged to the NUJ passed a motion saying that RTE NUJ members would boycott all filming of candidates from the close of nominations to the start of polling 'in any constituency where Section 31 of the Broadcasting Act prevents equal treatment for all contestants.'[108] Since Sinn Fein was standing in 14 of the North's 17 constituencies, this threat, if carried out, would have severely affected RTE's coverage. The government refused to lift the ban.[109] Another, larger meeting of RTE NUJ members in Dublin then withdrew the threat of action. The election coverage went ahead minus Sinn Fein, and the absurdity of this was emphasised when Sinn Fein Vice-President Gerry Adams won West Belfast from sitting MP Gerry Fitt.

Although censorship in the South of Ireland is more blatant than censorship in Britain, it has led to less protest from journalists. This apparently paradoxical situation may be partly due to the fact that the restrictions in the South are directly targeted against republican organisations, and may thus deter non-republicans from joining the anti-censorship lobby. It is perhaps significant that the recent stirrings of dissent within RTE have been prompted by Sinn Fein's emergence as a political force on the island. Indeed, it is only recently that Sinn Fein itself has taken a serious interest in challenging the restrictions.

In Britain, television censorship casts its net wider, making it difficult to report anything which appears to challenge Britain's hegemony. While the censorship mechanisms are less immediately obvious than those in the South of Ireland, the fact that they have affected such a wide range of programmes and programme-makers has generated much more disaffection.

9. Reporting nationalist perspectives

Bans

To many in Britain, including the media, the success of Sinn Fein in the 1982 Assembly election, like the victory of Bobby Sands in the Fermanagh-South Tyrone by-election in April 1981, was entirely unexpected. The BBC described Gerry Adams' 'easy victory' in the Assembly election as a 'surprise',[1] while the *Daily Star* summed up the response in a simple headline: 'IRA POLL SHOCK'.[2]

But did the election results really come out of the blue, or was the surprised reaction the result of the media's failure to investigate the feelings of the nationalist community? *The Guardian* admitted that with Bobby Sands' election 'years of myth-making go out of the window . . . And the biggest myth is that the IRA in its violent phase represents only a tiny minority of the population.'[3]

Down the years the media, along with the politicians, had obscured not only the political rationale of the IRA but also its relationship with the nationalist community. The anti-British sentiments of nationalists were as taboo as those of Sinn Fein and the IRA. To air their views and experiences would implicitly provide an understanding of why the IRA existed and acted as it did. It would also throw an uncomfortable light on the workings of the Six Counties regime, and on Britain's role, past and present. In establishment eyes, there is little difference between airing nationalist perspectives and supporting the IRA. A reporter who worked for BBC Northern Ireland in the early eighties said, 'There are some people who regard the IRA as the problem. Others regard the state itself as the problem, and the IRA as a symptom. But if you try to define the problem in those terms, you're immediately branded as an IRA sympathiser.'[4]

It was not just television programmes dealing directly with republicans that were banned or cut. Films sympathetic to the general nationalist outlook, or which gave a voice to ordinary members of the nationalist community, were also censored. Thus in 1972 the BBC refused to show *A Sense of Loss*, by the well-known French film-maker Marcel Ophuls – son of Max Ophuls – on the grounds that it was 'too pro-Irish'.[5] Yet the film was strongly against violence and, though the Official IRA did feature, the Provisional IRA was deliberately excluded.[6] The film's crime in the BBC's eyes was doubtless that it portrayed British politicians, British soldiers and prominent unionists in an unflattering light, and sympathised with the civil rights cause.

Another BBC casualty was 'A Street in Belfast', a film which focussed on the daily lives of three families in the Short Strand, a small Catholic enclave in an overwhelmingly Protestant area east of the River Lagan in Belfast. The BBC commissioned freelance film-maker Erich Durschmied to make the film for the *Man Alive* slot. Durschmied, who had covered the North of Ireland for a considerable time, shot the original footage in 1975, and returned in 1977.[7] The film was never shown.

Attempts to get permission to view the film have provoked mild panic in the BBC. The BBC bought the copyright lock, stock and barrel, leaving the film-maker with no rights in it, apparently with the express intention of ensuring that it was never seen by anyone. The BBC told one researcher that after the film was shelved, all the evidence of its whereabouts was erased.[8]

Creggan

One programme about the experiences of the nationalist community that did reach the screen – though only after long delays and behind-the-scenes manoeuvrings – was *Creggan*, made for Thames Television by Mary Holland and Michael Whyte. It focussed on the lives of people in the nationalist Creggan estate in Derry. They tell of their experience of housing problems and unemployment, and then of the civil rights movement and Bloody Sunday. Eventually the film reveals that some of these very ordinary working class people have children imprisoned for IRA activity.[9]

Originally due to be shown on 9 August 1979 with the title

An Estate of the Nation, the film was first delayed by a strike at ITV and then subjected to further, unexplained delays. It finally went out on 17 June at the late hour of 11 p.m.

Creggan went on to win the prestigious international television prize, the Prix Italia, and was also named the best documentary of 1980 by the British Broadcasting Guild, which is composed of some 70 television critics.[10] Following the Prix Italia win, *Guardian* TV correspondent Peter Fiddick wrote,

> it has always been axiomatic, on BBC and ITV, that winning a Prix Italia is the way to a rapid repeat of the programme, with the laurels included in the billing. Doubtless the network controllers will be finding prime time space for *Creggan* in the next few months, to give those of us who missed a chance to catch up?[11]

But *Creggan* was not repeated.

It is not only the attitude of ordinary nationalists to the 'security forces' that goes largely unexplored, but also the social and economic problems that they face. Despite several Fair Employment Agency reports indicating that Catholics are still heavily disadvantaged, the issue of continuing discrimination has been virtually ignored by the British media. Questions such as unemployment, bad housing and poverty – problem which afflict both nationalists and unionists but hit the former harder – have scarcely been touched on.

Such issues are innocuous subjects for television in the British context, but not when it comes to the Six Counties. When, in March 1983, the BBC's *Panorama* programme finally did a major report on unemployment in the North, the Tories were furious. Right-wing backbencher Sir John Biggs-Davison described the film as 'unbalanced' and 'distorted', and Northern Ireland Secretary James Prior complained to the BBC.[12] Senior BBC executives reprimanded the *Panorama* team.

'Credible witnesses'

The way the media portray the nationalist community is also constrained by the fact that reporters generally only give credence to certain unrepresentative categories of people. Sociologist Frank Burton, who spent several months living in the Ardoyne area of Belfast, noted, 'In Ireland this category of the credible contains, preferably, the non-Irish and/or the professional classes.'[13] Thus, for example, if allegations of British army brutality are to be taken seriously by the media, either the reporter should have personally witnessed the incident in question, or the condemnations should be voiced by an ex-British soldier living in the North, or by a doctor, lawyer or priest. When in 1972 a group of 65 priests accused the army of brutality, including the shooting of civilians by non-uniformed soldiers, *The Guardian* commented, 'Charges like these have been made many times during the past three years. But previous claims have been made by hysterical women, committed Republicans, or politically motivated groups, and it will not be so easy for the military or the Government to dismiss the claims'.[14]

But even 'credible respondents' like members of the clergy are selectively reported. Bishop Daly of Derry has complained that 'when he attacked the IRA for their misdeeds he was widely quoted, but when he has criticised the security forces he was hardly mentioned.'[15] Father Denis Faul, a priest who has campaigned vociferously against army and RUC abuses since the late sixties, was first approached by BBC television six years after the troubles started – and then for a programme on abortion.[16] But during the 1981 hunger strike, when he tried to persuade the hunger strikers to end their fast, he appeared on television many times.

British government propagandists have consciously attempted to exploit the ambivalance of middle-class nationalists. In 1981 the Central Office of Information made a film, *Northern Ireland Chronicle*, which was aimed at damping down support for republicanism in the United States. It was sponsored by the Foreign Office, and two senior Northern Ireland Office public relations men acted as advisers. The draft script for the film included some revealing observations. It said that statements such as 'that the men and women convicted of scheduled offences in the Diplock Courts are imprisoned not for their beliefs but for their criminal actions' would be 'far more cogently made by, say, a Catholic Bishop than . . . by any on-or-off-screen Government spokesman.' The outline also counselled against the use of loyalist politicians, noting:

> these are the people whom the film's target audience . . . would
> be most inclined to reject. That Molyneaux would speak out
> against the IRA is obvious; that, say, John Hume or Bishop Daley
> [sic] would might be a revelation. These are the people who, in
> terms of the film, will carry the most authority and have the most
> 'muscle'.[17]

When the script was leaked in September 1981, Bishop Edward Daly of Derry and John Hume were furious.[18] The completed film, which unsurprisingly presented Britain as the honest broker between warring factions and made much of IRA violence, featured just two nationalists: Gerry Fitt, and the equally anti-republican Cathal Daly, who later became Bishop of Down and Connor, the diocese that includes Belfast.

The peace people

Perhaps the most striking example of how the media encourage particular trends in Northern politics was the coverage given to the peace people, a movement which burgeoned in 1976 and faded away within a year.

The peace movement started after an incident in West Belfast on 10 August 1976. British troops fired at a car, killing the driver, IRA volunteer Danny Lennon. The car then swerved onto the pavement, hitting Mrs Anne Maguire and her three children. The children died.

The next evening an interview with the children's aunt, Mairead Corrigan, was broadcast on BBC news bulletins. This prompted Andersonstown housewife Betty Williams to start a petition for peace, which demanded an end to the IRA's military campaign. She read the petition on local television.[19]

After the children's funeral, Betty Williams asked reporters to mention in their articles that a demonstration would be held next day. Some 10,000 turned out for the protest. It was heavily publicised, but the killing of a child, Majella O'Hare, by a British soldier in South Armagh the same day received only a passing mention in the press.

Northern Ireland Secretary Merlyn Rees lost no time in voicing support for the new movement, saying, 'They have shown the way . . . The terrorists can be beaten only with the support of the entire populace.'[20] Media interest was intense from the start, and soon the two women were keeping an 'appointments register' to keep track of their dates with the press.[21]

In the newspaper reports, the role of the British troops in the deaths of the Maguire children was obliterated. The deaths were almost everywhere ascribed to 'an IRA's gunman's crashing getaway car'.[22] The peace people held a succession of rallies, and the media wildly exaggerated the attendance figures.[23] Sceptical reporters had problems with their editors, and some had their reports rejected because they were not considered effusive enough.[24] The media spared no effort to promote the movement. The women's biographer, reporter Richard Deutsch, records that they travelled to the Derry demonstration 'in a large limousine rented by the BBC, which had devised this ingenious stratagem so as to be able to interview the women without interruption.'[25] On their trip to London, a women's magazine paid for their journey and a commercial television station paid for their hotel.[26]

BBC Northern Ireland Controller James Hawthorne later commented that the peace movement was 'a "good" story which journalists fastened onto and tried to make the most of, but it's also an example of journalism doing its best to give some kind of backing to a special development in Irish affairs, but it wasn't sufficient to ensure success for the peace movement.'[27] The movement was 'good' and 'special' in establishment eyes because it attacked IRA violence and offered no other criticisms of the status quo. It was precisely this blinkered approach that led to the movement's decline. Less than three months from starting, the movement was collapsing in the North, its credibility among nationalists undermined by the leaders' failure to condemn British army violence.[28] The heavy promotion given to Corrigan and Williams began to backfire as their trips abroad, fur coats and new cars compounded nationalist resentment.[29] The movement declined amid splits and recriminations, and by the time Corrigan and Williams met the Queen in August 1977, and won the Nobel peace prize in October that year, they had very little support on their home territory.

The 1981 hunger strike

The 1981 hunger strike, in which ten republican prisoners died, generated far more popular support in Ireland than the peace people had, but the authorities and the British media responded very differently. This time the protests did not complement British strategy but challenged its foundations, for the prisoners were asserting the legitimacy of the republican struggle and refusing to accept the British definition of it as 'criminal'.

Both politicians and the media treated the hunger strike as if it had been concocted out of thin air by the IRA: as if there were no real feeling behind either the prisoners' actions or the support given them by the nationalist community. When Bobby Sands began his fast on 1 March, the government behaved as if nothing were happening. Northern Ireland Secretary Humphrey Atkins did not offer regular statements in the House of Commons, nor did the opposition demand them. Labour spokesperson Don Concannon told the Commons that Parliament should 'in no way assist the IRA in its efforts. We shall not therefore be pushing the Secretary of State of make statements, in fact quite the reverse.'[30]

The media, too, paid only passing attention to Bobby Sands, but when he was elected to Westminster on 9 April the issue could no longer be ignored. As his death neared, the world's press flooded into Belfast. Some 23 nations sent camera crews, and the American TV networks, ABC, CBS and NBC, sent 16 camera crews.[31] There were at least 400 reporters in the North, and 300 photographers covered his funeral.[32]

When Bobby Sands died, on 5 May, the international re-action was spectacularly unflattering to the British government. There were demonstrations across the world, accompanied by widespread condemnation of the government's failure to resolve the issue.[33] At the end of May, *The Sunday Times* published a survey of foreign press reaction, titled 'IS BRITAIN LOSING THE PROPAGANDA WAR?', for which it had canvassed the views of 64 newspapers.[34] The *Sunday Times*' chief European correspon-dent, Keith Richardson, was quoted as saying, 'General European impression ranges from pig-headed Thatcher obstinacy, through scandalous misgovernment, to outright genocide. In other words, it could not be worse.' The article concluded that,

> world opinion has begun to shift away from the British govern-ment and in favour of the IRA. The image of the gunman has actually improved. And the general opinion is emerging that the time has come for Mrs Thatcher to begin negotiations with Dublin leading to eventual union with the South.[35]

In marked contrast, the British media almost unanimously supported the government's stance. As Bobby Sands approached death, they repeatedly invoked 'IRA propaganda' as a means of explaining – or explaining away – the extensive international interest and sympathy. In the week leading to his death, for instance, half of the news reports on the subject broadcast by the London commercial radio station LBC used the phrase 'IRA propaganda war' or variations on it.[36]

'IRA propaganda', indeed, became a catch-all explanation, a means of dismissing all the events of the hunger strike. *Panorama* reporter Philip Tibenham explained to the nation that Bobby Sands' 'impending death has to be seen for what it is: a potentially tragic end to a skilful piece of exploitation and propaganda.'[37] A *Daily Star* leader said on 29 April:

> Since his hunger strike began 59 days ago, Sands and his allies have manipulated the situation as a cynical propaganda exercise.
>
> They duped 30,000 voters in Fermanagh to elect Sands as an MP. They duped thousands of others to stage violent protests on the streets of Ulster and London.
>
> And if and when Sands dies they will dupe many thousands to step up the bloodshed.
>
> That is the real purpose behind the present campaign, and it is one that no British Government can tolerate.

That the British government might have any responsibility for the crisis was not even considered. Bobby Sands' death was widely described as 'suicide' – 'There is only one killer of Sands and that is Sands himself,' said *The Times*[38] – or as an act of IRA violence. In a full-page leader titled 'Propaganda of death', the *Daily Express*, grotesquely distorting the casualty figures, described him as the IRA's 2,095th victim.[39] Bobby Sands was said to have 'had a choice', while the IRA's victims 'had no choice'.[40] The significance of the Fermanagh-South Tyrone by-election was denied: 'Any Catholic candidate would have won,' said *The Times*, adding, 'The myth of Fermanagh must not be allowed to gain credibility.'[41]

The anxiety of BBC chiefs to discredit the hunger strike was revealed in the minutes of a meeting of heads of department the day after Bobby Sands died:

> Sheila Innes [Head of Continuing Education, Television] wondered about the many different ways in which Sands had been named. It was agreed that the combination of *Bobby* Sands and a smiling photograph gave a misleading impression of a convicted felon. Mr Woon [Peter Woon, Editor, Television News] said that Television News had tried very hard to get another photograph of him out of the Northern Ireland Office, but had consistently failed.[42]

The IBA, too, proved mindful of the official view. At the end of May, they postponed a Granada *World in Action* film about the propaganda surrounding the hunger strike after Tory

MP Tom Normanton and Labour spokesperson Don Concannon had attacked it.[43] The IBA finally banned the film after the makers refused to remove a sequence showing dead INLA hunger striker Patsy O'Hara lying in his coffin: this sequence, said the IBA, 'crossed the dividing line between reporting propaganda and adding to it.'[44] Yet the film as a whole echoed the official line, as did the commentary over the offending sequence, which described the scene in the O'Hara house as 'a potent mixture designed to turn a convicted terrorist into a hero.'[45] Ironically, part of this sequence, a ten-second shot of Patsy O'Hara in his coffin, had been shown several times on television prior to the ban as part of a promotional film for the programme.[46]

Although the tone of the television coverage was unsympathetic to the hunger strikers, the sheer quantity of it enraged the establishment. On 14 May, members of the House of Lords lambasted the BBC. Lord Monson said the BBC should ensure that it gave 'at least as much coverage to the victims of IRA atrocities and their families as was recently accorded to the IRA hunger strikers and their families.' He went on to complain 'that on the evening of 5th May BBC1 devoted approximately 16 minutes of its main *Nine o'Clock News* bulletin – or more than half the programme – to the death of a hunger striker and that BBC2's *Newsnight* allocated no fewer than 33 out of 50 minutes to this event'.[47] Among those who backed him up was Lord Paget, a 72-year-old Labour peer, educated at Eton and Cambridge, and formerly a barrister, Labour MP and Master of the Pytchley Hounds. Paget said: 'My Lords, since the whole object of hunger strikes is to attract publicity, why is it that we allow them to have publicity? Why do we not forbid any news of a hunger strike or what is happening to come out of the goal? And, when the strikers die of hunger, why do we not bury them in the gaol?'[48] A week later Prime Minister Thatcher joined in: 'Newspaper and television coverage,' she said, 'can give the convicted criminals on hunger strike the myth of martyrdom they crave, but the true martyrs are the victims of terrorism.'[49]

In an article in *The Times*, BBC Director-General Sir Ian Trethowan tried to defend his organisation, pointing out the 'dilemmas' faced by journalists in trying to fulfil their duty to report while avoiding assisting 'the men of violence'. He stressed the significance of Bobby Sands' election and asked, 'When last did an elected MP starve himself to death?' He went on: 'The irritation of many viewers at being shown so much about Sands was entirely understandable, but however much they disliked it, the Sands affair became a major international event which had to be reported to the British public.'[50]

Trethowan's defence notwithstanding, the pressure from the right produced results. There was a noticeable increase in the coverage of funerals of people killed by the IRA and INLA. BBC Northern Ireland Controller James Hawthorne said at the start of 1982, 'I now rather feel that we are bound, we are locked in to covering every funeral'.[51]

Three days before Bobby Sands died, the *Daily Express* contended that 'Sands will find no victory in the grave. A united Ireland will not be hastened by his death . . . The shadow of Bobby Sands will pass.'[52] This view was shared by most politicians and dominated the media coverage. With hindsight, it is easy to see how wide of the mark it was. Though the hunger strike ended without the strikers' demands being met in full, the British government's victory was a hollow one. The hunger strike led to a succession of election victories for Sinn Fein, and an upsurge in sympathy for their cause round the world. Yet again, the British media had got it wrong, their analysis based not on an examination of actual developments, but rather conditioned by the requirements of goverment policy.

Opinion in Britain

The existence of a large body of opinion in Britain that opposes the British presence in the North has largely been ignored by the media, except where particularly dramatic protests have forced their attention. Since 1971, opinion polls have repeatedly indicated that a majority of people support troop withdrawal, for a variety of reasons, yet this view has scarcely been aired, perhaps because it has had little open support in powerful circles.

The *Daily Mirror* has been the only paper with a consistent editorial policy – often at odds with the tone of its news reports – of support for British withdrawal.[53] Until the arrival of Andrew Neil as editor in October 1983, *The Sunday Times* also spasmodically advocated withdrawal, favouring the 'independent Ulster' scenario.[54] Possibly the first TV programme to ask ordinary people their views on withdrawal was Channel 4's *Friday Alternative*, which ran an item on 12 November 1982 titled 'Should we leave the Irish to it?' Meetings and demonstrations held in Britain have generally received more attention in the Irish media, and sometimes overseas, than in the British media.

It was not until after Ken Livingstone became leader of the Greater London Council in May 1981 that massive publicity was bestowed on an advocate of withdrawal. It came in the form of intense vilification. For years, as an obscure councillor, Livingstone had spoken in support of withdrawal at meetings organised by the Troops Out Movement and other groups. As GLC leader, he continued to speak out. The right-wing press, anxious to undermine the socialist policies he stood for, spotlighted his views on Ireland as part of their campaign to discredit him.

A month after his election, Livingstone spoke at a London demonstration in support of the H Block hunger strikers, and was condemned by Sir Horace Cutler, former Tory GLC leader. Press interest mounted when on 22 July Livingstone welcomed Mrs Alice McElwee, mother of hunger striker Tom McElwee, to County Hall. *The Sun* fulminated, 'In his brief spell on the stage, the insufferable Mr Livingstone has proved himself a menace to stability in public life.'[55] A month later, Livingstone responded to the backlash by meeting the three sons of Mrs Yvonne Dunlop, who had died in the firebomb attack for which Tom McElwee had been convicted. Tory GLC members had helped to organise the trip. The *Daily Mail* headlined the story, 'Victims face IRA's backer'.[56] In the meantime, Livingstone had fuelled the opprobrium by supporting H Block protestors who let off hundreds of black balloons from the steps of County Hall on royal wedding day. At the end of August there was another storm when he gave an interview – which was never broadcast – to the British Forces Broadcasting Service in which he appealed to both the IRA and British soldiers in the North to lay down their arms.[57]

A much more serious uproar occurred shortly after the ending of the hunger strike. On 10 October an IRA nail bomb exploded in Chelsea as a bus full of soldiers was passing. Two civilians were killed, and 22 soldiers and 16 civilians were injured. Two days later Livingstone went to Cambridge to speak at a student meeting of the Tory Reform Group on the question of rates. At the end of the meeting, he was asked a question about the bombing, and the press pounced, distorting his response to make it appear as if he condoned the tragedy. The *Daily Mirror* displayed a picture of bomb victim Mrs Nora Field's body, with the headlines, 'What Ken Livingstone said about the killers who did THIS. "They are not criminals".'[58] *The Sun* proclaimed, 'This damn fool says bombers aren't criminals'.[59] But *The Sun* also carried quotes from Livingstone's remarks which suggested that his views were not so simple:

> 'Nobody supports what happened last Saturday in London – but what about stopping it happening?
>
> 'As long as we are in Ireland people will be letting off bombs in London . . .
>
> 'People in Northern Ireland see themselves as subject peoples. If they were just criminals and psychopaths they could be crushed. But they have a motive force which they think is good.'[60]

The Sun commented, 'Isn't it unbelievable that a man with any scrap of decency could talk in this way?' Clearly, moral indignation was the only permissible response, while to seek the causes of such bombings or to posit political solutions was 'indecent'. Livingstone denied the version of his remarks given in the headlines, saying on the BBC's *Nationwide* programme that 'I at no point said that people who set off a bomb aren't criminals.'[61] He reported *The Sun* to the Press Council, accusing it of 'total distortion'.[62]

Livingstone's views on Ireland did not make headlines again for over a year, but in the meantime the lash briefly fell on his GLC colleague Steve Bundred, when he joined a Troops Out Movement delegation to Belfast in August 1982. 'TRAITOR', 'Leftie police boss boosts the IRA' were *The Sun*'s front page headlines.[63] Next day *The Sun* followed this up with a picture of Bundred among Troops Out demonstrators headlined 'TRAITOR'S MARCH'. The paper blatantly revealed its double standards on the question of violence by running in the same two issues a 'sensational *Sun* series' based on interviews with former members of the SAS, and containing no hint of condemnation of their violence. 'KILLING MEN NEVER BOTHERED ME, BUT I COULDN'T HURT A RABBIT', was the heading of the first piece,[64] while the second told how another ex-SAS man danced in the street 'demonstrating how to remove a bayonet from a Japanese corpse.' 'He was taking a trip down memory lane,' said *The Sun*, 'which in his case is well-stocked with corpses.'[65]

'Red Ken in IRA storm'

The biggest furore yet came in December 1982, when a group of Labour GLC councillors invited Sinn Fein leaders Gerry Adams and Danny Morrison, who had recently been elected to the

Northern Ireland Assembly, to visit London.

The visit was announced quietly enough on a Sunday morning on the commercial radio network, which also carried an interview with Labour's junior Northern Ireland spokesperson, Clive Soley, who indicated in a roundabout way that he was willing to meet the visitors.[66] By evening, however, the protests had begun to flow. The BBC news quoted Richard Brew, leader of the GLC's Tories, as saying the proposed visit was 'horrific and appalling', while Official Unionist James Molyneaux had said it was 'quite monstrous'.[67]

Next morning, Monday 6 December, the press were in full cry. Livingstone was vilified for inviting 'IRA men' to London: a device which obscured the significant fact that the two were elected Sinn Fein representatives, and, given the IRA's image in Britain, allowed the issue to be presented in a highly emotive way. 'FURY OVER RED KEN'S TOP IRA GUESTS', cried *The Sun*.[68] 'Fury over Red Ken's invitation to IRA's two henchmen', said the *Daily Express*, demanding in huge letters, 'KEEP OUT!'[69] ' "IRA MEN'S VISIT AN OUTRAGE" ', said the *Daily Mail*, quoting Tory MP Harvey Proctor. 'RED KEN IN IRA STORM' announced the *Daily Star*, while the *Mirror* headlined a quote from Orange order leader Thomas Passmore: ' "AN INSULT TO THE MEMORY OF IRA VICTIMS" '.[70] The cartoonists soon took up the theme, showing Livingstone shaking hands with hooded figures armed with bombs.[71]

Labour leader Michael Foot rapidly succumbed to the pressure. His public rebuke to Livingstone was recorded by London's evening paper, *The Standard*, in the headline 'FOOT KICKS RED KEN'.[72]

Late that Monday night, an INLA bomb exploded in a pub frequented by British soldiers in Ballykelly, County Derry. Eleven soldiers and five civilians were killed. The papers immediately appropriated the tragedy as part of their campaign against the Sinn Fein visit. That the INLA, not the IRA, had planted the bomb was ignored, and the differences between the two organisations went unacknowledged: as Mary Holland pointed out in the *New Statesman*, the IRA was unlikely to commit such a bombing, with a high risk of civilian casualties, at a time when the republican movement was seeking electoral support from the nationalist community.[73]

'ARMY PUB BOMBED' and 'Stop Red Ken's guests NOW' were Tuesday's front page headlines in the *Daily Express*.[74] The

Mirror had 'SOLDIERS KILLED IN DISCO BLAST' and 'FOOT SLAMS RED KEN'.[75] London's *Standard* explicitly linked the two stories: a picture of the Ballykelly devastation was accompanied by a quote from a surgeon at the scene, ' "Red Ken should see this" '.[76] The upmarket papers were rather more reticent. *The Times* pointed out that Home Secretary Whitelaw had invited Adams to London in 1972 for secret talks, and, in a leader, advised against 'apoplexy' over the visit on the grounds that this was what the GLC councillors wanted.[77]

In Parliament that Tuesday afternoon MPs were, as BBC political editor John Cole put it, 'vying with each other' to proclaim their outrage at both the bombing and the proposed visit.[78] Prime Minister Thatcher said the bombing was the product of 'evil and depraved minds' and that 'it would be intolerable if that invitation were not withdrawn.'[79] Labour Northern Ireland spokesperson Don Concannon said, 'let them come, if they dare, and allow the people of the country to respond and let them know, in a peaceful fashion, what they think of their barbaric acts.'[80]

Next day the fury intensified, and with it came a chorus of demands for the visit to be banned. *The Daily Telegraph* ran a series of headlines one below the other: 'We shall not rest until these merciless killers are brought to justice, MPs are told', 'OUTRAGE AT ARMY DISCO CARNAGE', 'Livingstone refuses to cancel Sinn Fein visit'.[81] The *Daily Star* took its cue from Concannon: 'Today's message to Red Ken's guests – AT YOUR PERIL!' *The Sun* devoted a full page to a leader accompanied by a gruesome cartoon showing a skeleton standing over a pile of corpses. The first few paragraphs excoriated Ballykelly, while the rest denounced Livingstone: 'His friends tell us he is sincere. So were Hitler and Stalin. To come nearer to home, so are the National Front.'[82]

The Sun and the *Mirror* called on Whitelaw to ban the visit, while *The Guardian* said, 'It hardly matters now whether the Home Secretary invokes the Prevention of Terrorism Act . . . to keep Mr Adams and Mr Morrison out. They were unwelcome in the first place'.[83]

That night Whitelaw did invoke the Prevention of Terrorism Act to ban Adams, Morrison, and a third Sinn Fein Assembly member, Martin McGuinness, from entering Britain. 'BANNED', cheered the front pages of Thursday's papers.[84]

The *Daily Mail*'s leader held forth: 'There will be massive public support for the Home Secretary's decision . . . there will not be a wet eye in the country now that he has acted.'[85] But it is doubtful whether public opinion was quite so unanimous. Some of the opposition to the ban came from predictable quarters, such as the *New Statesman* and *Tribune*.[86] But dissension also came from a more unexpected source. *Daily Express* columnist George Gale wrote immediately after the Ballykelly bombing that it would be hypocritical for Whitelaw to ban Adams, since he had met him secretly ten years ago. Gale went on to say, 'Slowly, inexorably, events are pressing us towards a settlement which will inevitably involve an accommodation with Dublin. In such an accommodation the republicans of the north cannot be excluded.'[87]

Another, and rather curious, indication that Livingstone was perhaps not as unpopular as the press made him appear came two weeks later, when BBC radio's *Today* programme revealed that he had come second in their 'Man of the Year' poll, sandwiched between the Pope and the late Colonel 'H' Jones of Falklands fame.[88]

When Livingstone travelled to Belfast the following February, he kept the visit secret. By this means he not only avoided travelling with a media entourage, but also guarded against an advance mobilisation against his visit, which could have made it politically difficult for him to go.

When the media caught up with him, alerted by an airport worker,[89] their response was predictable. 'RED KEN IN SHOCK TRIP TO IRA', cried the *News of the World*, 'Britain's biggest selling newspaper'.[90] 'RED KEN IS GREETED BY IRA'S PALS', announced the *Sunday People*.[91] *The Sunday Times* more soberly said, 'Livingstone meets Sinn Fein'.[92] 'RED KEN IN THE DEN OF HATE', proclaimed the *Daily Star* next day.[93]

As usual, Labour leader Michael Foot soon expressed his disapproval: 'CONDEMNED – Foot and GLC slam Red Ken's IRA visit', said the *Daily Mirror*.[94] But since the visit was a *fait accompli*, there was nothing either Foot or the media could do to stop it, and the coverage petered out very rapidly.

Like the vilification of Livingstone, the exclusion of Adams and Morrison from Britain the previous December had highlighted the desire of many politicians and editors to banish the whole discomfiting issue to the other side of the Irish sea, and to deny any contact, whether through personal meetings or the transmission of ideas, between republicans and people in Britain.

But the exclusion order had also been problematic for the government, since it had demonstrated that people in the North had a different status from those in Britain, that the government was operating a system of internal exile within the UK, and that it was once again paying no heed to the views of nationalists expressed through the ballot box. So when Gerry Adams was elected to Westminster in June 1983, the government preempted hostile publicity by immediately lifting the exclusion order.

The media remained, by and large, impervious to the significance of Sinn Fein's latest election victory, and when Adams visited London at the end of July, *The Sun*'s advice was simple: 'Go home now!' The paper described Livingstone as a 'squalid pest' and said Adams was 'surely the most unwanted visitor to Britain since Hitler's raiders.'[95]

History

For the first decade of the current conflict, history was an area that the broadcasting bodies, like British politicians, preferred not to look at too closely. It threw up too many uncomfortable parallels, and threatened to open up awkward questions about Britain's responsibility for the contemporary mess, and about possible solutions.

Politicians preferred to evade the issue. Tory Northern Ireland Secretary Humphrey Atkins fended off an American questioner on a radio phone-in programme by saying, 'I don't know what happened in 1920, I wasn't actually alive then, I don't know if he [the caller] was. But the thing is we're dealing with 1980, and we've got to seek to do the best we can with what problems we find in 1980'.[96]

The broadcasters began to display their squeamishness early on. In 1971 the BBC commissioned playwrights John Arden and Margaretta D'Arcy to write a radio play. But when D'Arcy and Arden offered the theme of James Connolly, Ireland's best-known socialist and leader of the 1916 rising, the BBC dropped the commission, saying the play could 'inflame passions in Northern Ireland'.[97] The same year, a BBC minute records that the Director-General 'expressed reservations' about a proposal for a documentary history of the Irish Republic to mark its fiftieth anniversary. 'One ought to be prepared for the possibility that a documentary of that kind might have to be postponed, even after being billed,' he was quoted as saying.[98] Then in 1972 publishers Weidenfeld and Nicholson met with a total lack of success when they tried to interest television programmes in discussing Robert Kee's history of Irish nationalism, *The Green Flag*.[99] Eight years later, after repeated protests about the absence of Irish history from television, the book was to form the basis of the BBC's prestigious 13-part series, fronted by Robert Kee, *Ireland — A Television History*.[100]

Michael Collins

Kenneth Griffith's film biography of Michael Collins, who led the IRA during the war against Britain in 1920–21, was banned amid some publicity in February 1973. The film's title, *Hang Up Your Brightest Colours*, was taken from a letter of condolence sent by George Bernard Shaw to Collins' sister after his death: 'Tear up your mourning and hang up your brightest colours in his honour'.

Using a formula which he had employed successfully in earlier films, Griffith appeared throughout the film as the narrator, and interwove Collins' story with the history of the key events in which he was involved: the 1916 Easter rising, the 1918 general election in which Sinn Fein won a landslide victory, the war then unleashed by Britain, and the treaty of 1921, to which Collins was a signatory, which gave qualified independence to 26 of Ireland's 32 counties and led to civil war. The film concluded with Collins' death in 1922 at the hands of anti-treaty forces. The film's director was Anthony Thomas who, ironically, had left South Africa in 1967 because of censorship of his films.[101]

Hang Up Your Brightest Colours offered an uncompromising denunciation, passionately delivered by Griffith, of Britain's imperial adventures in Ireland. He opened the film by pointing out that 'there's no Irish problem, only an English problem,' and went on immediately to describe the destruction of the Collins family home in 1919: 'the English soldiers ordered the Collins family, two women and eight children, out of the cottage before burning it to the ground. The soldiers threw everything onto the flames, household effects, baby's cradle, everything.' It was 'a typically English military operation in Ireland'.

Griffith recalled earlier Irish history by telling how Collins

> learned about the murderous conquest of the English
> Elizabethans, he learned about the murderous progress of the

> English Cromwellians. His grandmother, Joanna O'Brien, told
> him about the human bodies dead from starvation which she had
> seen on the road around Clonakilty. During his own father's
> lifetime, well over one million Irish people died of starvation
> under English patronage.

When it came to the activities of Collins' British contemporaries, Griffith did not mince words. He told how Lloyd George and Winston Churchill 'turned a couple of blind eyes' to the activities of the auxiliaries, a volunteer army of British ex-officers, who 'were comparable to Nazi SS troops' and 'murdered and tortured freely'. He went on to call Churchill 'an imperial bully boy' and to describe Lloyd George's behaviour over partition as 'grossly dishonest to the Irish people.'

The film was viewed by a three-person committee of the IBA in November 1972. After this, as it emerged years later, the IBA encouraged Sir Lew Grade, the head of ATV which had commissioned the film, not to offer the film for transmission. By this device, Grade took the heat for suppressing the film while the IBA avoided blame.[102]

Grade told the press in February 1973 that 'in view of the present delicate political and military situation in Northern Ireland, I have decided that this is not the time for such a film to be shown in the United Kingdom.'[103] Griffith commented later that 'if there were no "delicate military and political situation in Northern Ireland" I would not have committed my energies towards making films about the Irish island.'[104] Significantly, Grade admitted that he had no quarrel with the factual content of the film.[105] Its politics were the problem, and also Griffith's view that his role as a film-maker was to intervene in the debate. Telling how he and Grade had 'argued for two hours', Griffith said, 'He is saying we should not rock the boat at this time. But I say the boat is leaking and sinking, and my film could help in giving the country a new and necessary perspective.'[106]

Following the ban, some Members of Parliament asked if they could see the film. A group of 12 Tories saw it first. Predictably, they were 'not disposed to quarrel with Grade's judgement,' as the *Telegraph* put it.[107] Some days later, 18 Labour MPs saw it. John Grant, Labour spokesperson on broadcasting, summed up the response: 'There were very mixed opinions. I thought it should be shown, but everyone agreed that it was a brilliant production.'[108] In a letter to Griffith, Michael Foot described it as 'a wonderful film.'[109] But Grade remained unmoved by the compliments, and instead reportedly took the fact that MPs' opinions had been mixed as an endorsement of the banning of the film.[110]

At the time of the ban, all copies of the film were locked in Sir Lew Grade's private safe,[111] and ATV said 'that the film would be shown when the Ulster situation improved.'[112] A decade later, it remained locked away and inaccessible.

Curious Journey

Undeterred by his experiences, Kenneth Griffith set about organising another film with the same target as the Collins film: 'to inform the British television viewer about the root historical *cause* of Irish inner rage against Britain.'[113] He managed to obtain backing for the film, titled *Curious Journey*, from the Welsh TV company, Harlech.

This film too was, on the face of it, entirely concerned with events many years in the past. Griffith interviewed nine very old people – two women and seven men – all by now 'shining pillars of respectability', and all of whom had been IRA activists between 1916 and 1921. Because complaints had been made about his highly evocative narration of the Collins film, Griffith decided not to appear in person and instead confined himself to delivering the historical quotations which punctuated the film.

But the quotations were to prove contentious. The Network Committee, the body that decides which programmes will be transmitted by all ITV companies, asked Griffith to cut the film by 15 minutes and stipulated which cuts they wanted: '*All* the cuts are quotes from Irish history, quotes from Wolfe Tone, Emmet, Gladstone, Parnell and Casement,' said Griffith.[114] Griffith agreed to shorten the film, but refused to be told which bits to remove. He again refused when Harlech asked him to remove a comment from nineteenth century British Prime Minister Gladstone on the Act of Union of 1800 which made Ireland part of the United Kingdom: 'There is no blacker or fouler transaction in the history of man! We used the whole civil government of Ireland as an engine of wholesale corruption. We obtained that union . . . by wholesale bribery and unblushing intimidation.'

Harlech refused, as ATV had with the Collins film, to offer *Curious Journey* to the IBA for transmission. One of their lawyers told Griffith that if they did so their franchise, due for renewal the following year, might be threatened.[115] Harlech then sold Griffith the film and all rights to it for the sum of £1, on condition that their name be removed from the credits and that Griffith should never mention their name in connection with the film. Griffith observed these conditions rigorously, though they were somewhat absurd as many people knew whom he had made the film for. Later, in conjunction with Timothy O'Grady, Griffith produced a book, also titled *Curious Journey*, based on the interviews done for the film.[116]

Not long after the banning of *Curious Journey*, Griffith observed that in the 18 or so films he had made, only the Irish dimension had been suppressed. His film on Napoleon had just one line cut from its 90-minute span. The Emperor was saying, 'If I had achieved sufficient power, I would have separated Ireland from England.'[117]

The Green, The Orange and the Red, White and Blue

In the seventies, the only television account of Irish history that was actually transmitted was a BBC series titled *Ireland: Some Episodes From Her Past*, which did not cover events after 1968.[118] Critics of coverage of Ireland, such as Jonathan Dimbleby, repeatedly drew attention to the absence of a historical dimension, as well as to the failure to supply a context when reporting day-to-day events.

In 1977 producer David Elstein and reporter Peter Taylor, both of Thames TV's *This Week* programme, began work on an outline for a major historical series. In three 90-minute parts, it was to combine documentary film with dramatic reconstruction of key events. Aiming to illuminate the historical roots of the conflict, it was to draw parallels between events of past and present, such as between Bloody Sunday in 1920 and Bloody Sunday in 1972, and between fundamentalist preacher Rev. Hugh 'Roaring' Hanna in the nineteenth century and Ian Paisley today. The series would show that the main forces involved were still the same: *The Green, The Orange and the Red, White and Blue*, as the programme titles put it.

Jeremy Isaacs, who was then Thames TV's Programme Controller, was enthusiastic about the treatment supplied by Elstein and Taylor. He passed it up to Thames' new Managing Director, Bryan Cowgill, who had recently transferred from the

BBC. Cowgill blocked the project, apparently without giving any explanation.[119]

Because of the drama sequences, the project would have been expensive. But it was widely suspected that the series was stopped not on grounds of cost, but because of the people involved. 'Thames management,' wrote Peter Lennon in *The Sunday Times*, 'felt that the IBA would be alarmed by such a series coming from two current affairs reporters who had already produced some controversial material on Ulster.'[120]

This problem was not unexpected. Fearing trouble ahead, Elstein had taken the precaution of telling Ian Stuttard, who had directed the controversial films, that if the project was approved he would not be working on it.[121] Stuttard's open sympathy for republicanism would, it was felt, cause difficulties. Indeed, some three months after the blocking of the project, two Special Branch officers visited Jeremy Isaacs at Thames to enquire about Stuttard.[122] Ironically, Stuttard was to be co-producer on the Thames history series that did reach the screen, *The Troubles*.

Two major series

After the years of neglect, not one, but two major television histories of Ireland were to hit the screen at the same time, the turn of the year 1980–81. In late 1978 Thames producer Richard Broad put forward a list of four possible 'tele-history' projects that could follow his much acclaimed series, *Palestine*. They were for series on India, Africa, Vietnam and Ireland. For a number of reasons Broad favoured Ireland. Managing Director Bryan Cowgill accepted the idea, saying this was because of his high regard for Broad and his team. It was, it seems, primarily the reputation of *Palestine* – which, while indicting British policy, had treated a 'sensitive' area with great care – that allowed Broad to succeed where Elstein and Taylor had failed.[123]

Also in 1978, Jeremy Isaacs left his job as Programme Controller at Thames and went freelance. The first project he set up was a 13-part series for the BBC on the history of Ireland. Called *Ireland: A Television History*, it was fronted by Robert Kee and loosely based on his trilogy, *The Green Flag*.[124]

The two series were markedly different in approach. Kee took a long look at Irish history, taking seven programmes to reach the 1916 Easter rising, with the aim, in his words, of 'ungarbling the past': 'The past and garbled accounts of it,' he said in the first programme, 'are the root cause of the troubles in Northern Ireland.' *The Troubles*, in contrast, ran rapidly through the years before partition to concentrate on the development of the Northern state, and aimed primarily at making the present conflict comprehensible. For Broad, the problem lay not in mythology but in reality:

> To many people, the troubles in Northern Ireland seem bizarre; crazy people doing crazy things. In our programmes we are not trying to make moral judgements on one side or the other but simply to say: 'These are logical events; given the way things were moving, people were rationally quite likely to behave in this way.'
> We are saying that there is a sort of order, a logic behind those fragments of mayhem you see in *News at Ten*.[125]

Accordingly, *The Troubles* attempted to trace the development of social forces, while Kee focussed on individuals and dramatic events: as some critics observed, he presented history as 'one damn thing after another'.[126]

While in *The Troubles* violence was seen as a rational response to the failure of politics, and as a symptom of the problem rather than the cause, in Kee's version violence – and specifically republican violence – was portrayed as the obstacle preventing a solution, and as essentially irrational. 'The whole point' of the last programme in the series, said Kee, 'was to say that violence was totally senseless.'[127] In the end, however, *The Troubles* refused to follow through its own logic, and, instead of offering concrete proposals for a solution, put forward a rather obscurely worded recommendation that it was necessary 'slowly to shift . . . political alignments'.

A limited backlash

Both programmes came under some attack, mainly from loyalists. Kee was attacked by Ian Paisley for favouring republicans, and by Enoch Powell for making the assumption that Ireland could be governed as one nation.[128] *The Troubles* came under heavier fire. Before transmission began, Ulster TV refused to provide facilities for the films to be shown to the press in Belfast. Producer Ian Stuttard guessed this was because UTV thought the series too delicate politically.[129] The third episode, 'Legacy', which dealt with the period between 1920 and 1970, particularly angered Unionists. James Kilfedder MP protested that, 'The programme distorted the truth. It deliberately set out to give the scandalous impression that the Protestants of Ulster, collectively and individually, persecuted and harmed their Roman Catholic neighbours. That is utterly false.'[130]

But the two series provoked no backlash from mainstream British politicians and reached the screen virtually unhindered by the broadcasting bodies. Their smooth passage was probably due in part to their distanced handling of the subject: they had none of the fire or commitment of Kenneth Griffith's work. Commenting on the differences between the two series and his own films, Griffith said, 'I could no more be factual and detached about Ireland than I could about Auschwitz or Buchenwald.'[131]

The series were also probably helped on their way by the changed political climate. Roy Mason's regime, under which any talk of Irish unity was regarded as tantamount to treason, was over. Southern Ireland's new Prime Minister, Charles Haughey, who verbally at least espoused the cause of reunification, met British Prime Minister Thatcher in May 1980 and again in December. Though the content of their exchanges remained mysterious, the 'Irish dimension' to the conflict was now officially acknowledged, and was therefore no longer forbidden territory for broadcasters.[132]

When the two series appeared, Chris Dunkley, a longstanding critic of television's Irish coverage, wrote that 'television people keep asking me questions of the "Well, are you happy now?" variety'. This, he said, made him very uneasy: 'it indicates a misunderstanding of what I (and others) wanted' and 'it carries the implicit suggestion that with these two series television will have done its duty after which it can get back to normal.'[133] Valuable though the series were, they could not compensate for the lack of thorough and regular coverage, putting daily events in context and not merely focussing on violence but also offering political analysis and debate. As Dunkley observed, 'A broadcasting system which really believed in free speech would not have to wait for "history" before allowing in the intellectual arguments.'[134]

The Crime of Captain Colthurst

The arrival of the two series did not mean that history had stopped being a sensitive area for broadcasters. At the end of April 1981, as Bobby Sands lay dying, there was a flurry of behind-the-scenes activity over a BBC play about an incident in 1916: the murder of pacifist prisoner Francis Sheehy-Skeffington by a British officer, Captain J.C. Bowen-Colthurst, who was subsequently court-martialled and found guilty but insane. Made for BBC2's *Chronicle* slot, *The Crime of Captain Colthurst* was based on the court martial records.

The play went out as scheduled on Monday 27 April, but only after BBC chiefs had spent a panicky few days. The intensity of the heart-searching was revealed in the minutes of two top-level meetings that followed transmission of the play.

Northern Ireland Controller, James Hawthorne, who had not seen the play because he had been 'unwell' when a showing was arranged for him, had wanted transmission stopped because of 'the prevailing security conditions'.[135] The argument against transmission, explained Bill Cotton, Deputy Managing Director of Television, had been that 'if there was violence the Army would go out, and there was a strong feeling in some quarters that the programme could have rekindled hostile feelings about the Army.'[136]

Over the weekend, Managing Director of Television Alasdair Milne had come under pressure to stop the play from, among others, Tory MP and Scottish minister Alex Fletcher, who telephoned Milne and said he 'had been approached by one of his constituents, a relative of Captain Colthurst, who had information which he believed should have gone into the programme.'[137] Fletcher was quoted in *The Daily Telegraph* as saying he had asked the BBC to postpone the film because it was not objective and was 'inflammatory' against the British army operating in the North.[138] Forceful representations against transmission had also come from Lady Faulkner, the BBC's National Governor for Northern Ireland and widow of Brian Faulkner, former Stormont Prime Minister and head of the power-sharing executive.[139]

Alasdair Milne had, nevertheless, decided the programme should go ahead. His decision was, it seems, influenced by the fact that the play had already been publicised. He said later that 'he slightly regretted that the programme had been scheduled and billed in "Radio Times" at a time when the programme planners could have counted the days of Robert Sands's fast.'[140] Richard Francis, Director of News and Current Affairs, who had also seen the play in advance, 'heartily endorsed' Milne's decision, saying 'The reaction would have been sharper in Northern Ireland if the BBC *had* pulled the programme.' He went on to reveal that, 'Had Bobby Sands died that day before the scheduled transmission time, it would have been pulled in any case.'[141]

At the meeting of heads of departments two days after the play was screened, Cecil Taylor, Head of Programmes for Northern Ireland, supported the decision to show the play and said BBC Belfast had had only three complaints about it compared to 127 complaints in three days over the weekend about coverage of Bobby Sands. The play, he said, 'would not have been of great significance to the people of Northern Ireland in relation to the weight of the coverage about Sands. The story about one man who killed people sixty years ago would have caused hardly a ripple. The anxiety felt in London seemed rather unreal.'

But some of the London-based executives still had reservations. Peter Woon, the Editor of Television News, said he had thought it 'an extremely good programme' but 'his one reservation was that if Sands had died that night, the British public could have thought that the BBC was showing something critical of the Army at a time when the Army was going into action.' Malcolm Walker, Head of Television Presentation, the department that handles the links between programmes, 'drew attention to the trailing difficulties which could have arisen. If Sands had died on the Monday night, Presentation could have been in the position of handing over directly from the news of his death to the programme.'[142]

Two weeks later, the BBC management came in for a battering from the Board of Governors, who are government-appointed and have an advisory role. Chairman George Howard – ex-Eton and Balliol, stately home owner, former president of the Country Landowners Association and one-time officer in the Green Howards, the family regiment – opened the meeting by saying he 'did not understand why "The Crime of Captain Colthurst" had found its way into *Chronicle* or why the story had to be told at this moment'. Another governor, Mrs Clarke, said she 'had been appalled at the programme's timing. From the point of view of people who hourly expected violence on the streets, the programme had been mistimed.' Lady Faulkner delivered an emotive diatribe:

> Had there been trouble in Belfast that night, and had anyone been able to point a finger at the BBC as an instigator of the trouble, the BBC would have been in a very serious situation indeed. Her strong feelings in advance of transmission had been expressed against a background of her awareness in another capacity of refugee

problems in Northern Ireland . . . She did not accept the Chairman's suggestion that M.D. Tel.'s [Managing Director of Television] judgement had been vindicated by events. The BBC had been lucky. Besides, there were hidden factors. What of the person who, hitherto uninvolved, saw the programme, was embittered and picked up the telephone to give the IRA information leading to a terrorist attack?[143]

The only board member to express a dissenting view was the National Governor for Wales, Professor H. Morris-Jones, who said that 'In his opinion it would have been an overtly political act – and a counter-productive one at that – to pull the programme from the schedules.'[144]

Anti-Irish racism

The trepidation about confronting unpalatable historical facts has, along with other features of the coverage – the unwillingness to explain why the IRA exists and acts as it does, the eagerness to paint the IRA as the fount of all evil, the presentation of acts of violence devoid of context – helped to sustain a view of the conflict in which British altruism opposes Irish irrationality.

'It is difficult for the peace-loving English,' opined the *Leicester Mercury* in August 1969, 'to understand the forces that drive an aroused Irishman to the point of self-destruction. But that is what is happening. But now the killing has begun it is impossible to foresee its bloody end.'[145] Fourteen years later, *The Sunday Times* held forth that 'Since 1969 (to look no further back) the main note of British policy in Northern Ireland has been altruism.' The paper went on to comment that to equate British 'military heavy-handedness' with 'the systematic murderousness of the IRA' was 'to turn morality upside down.'[146]

This view of Britain nobly trying to resolve a problem not of its own making is the contemporary incarnation of Kipling's notion of 'the white man's burden':

Take up the White Man's burden –
Send forth the best ye breed –
Go bind your sons to exile
To serve your captives' need;
To wait in heavy harness
On fluttered folk and wild –
Your new-caught sullen peoples,
Half devil and half child.

Take up the White Man's burden –
The savage wars of peace –
Fill full the mouth of Famine
And bid the sickness cease;
And when your goal is nearest
The end for others sought,
Watch sloth and heathen Folly
Bring all your hope to nought.[147]

In less liberal hands than those of *The Sunday Times*, the racism latent in the notion of 'British altruism' comes blatantly to the surface. Just before Bobby Sands' death in May 1981, when Britain was exposed to considerable international criticism over the handling of the hunger strike, Peregrine Worsthorne, invoking the nineteenth century concept of a hierarchy of human races, wrote in *The Sunday Telegraph*:

> The English have every reason to feel proud of their country's recent record in Northern Ireland, since it sets the whole world a uniquely impressive example of altruistic service in the cause of peace. Nothing done by any other country in modern times so richly deserves the Nobel prize . . .
>
> The British do not have their heart in Northern Ireland. The spur is duty, not love or affection or even interest . . . in terms of true feelings Northern Ireland is profoundly alien.
>
> Yet the responsibility remains, and is seen to remain, perhaps all the stronger for being so patently lacking in emotional commitment. This, I think, is where the IRA makes its greatest mistake: in underestimating the maturity of the British people, their unique capacity to carry on without the kind of sentimental uplift which less adult breeds find so essential for sustained resolve and sacrifice.[148]

This view of the relative positions of British and Irish people is embodied in defamatory stereotypes of the Irish, who are depicted as stupid, drunken and backward. Defending Conor Cruise O'Brien against Irish politicians who had attacked his disparaging attitude towards Irish unity, *Times* columnist Bernard Levin wrote: 'There they go still, the Irish "patriots" [sic], with minds locked and barred, mouths gaping wide to extrude the very last morsel of folly, and consumed with a wild terror at the prospect that sense may one day prevail.'[149] In 1982, after Gerry Adams, Danny Morrison and Martin McGuinness were banned from entering Britain, Levin wrote an imaginary account of a meeting between them and Labour members of the Greater

London Council. Titled 'The secret's out: what Red Ken told the boys in green, hic!', the piece portrayed Livingstone and his colleagues as jargon-spouting leftists, while the three republicans were depicted as ignorant drunks: 'Look, friend, me and me pal have got throats on us like the inside of a Japanese wrestler's jockstrap – would ye have a ball o' malt on the premises, for Christ's sake?'[150]

A long tradition

Such chauvinist attitudes to the Irish are deeply embedded in British culture. American historian Ned Lebow has traced how British historians from as early as the twelfth century denigrated the Irish, justifying colonisation in the process.[151] Giraldus Cambrensis (Gerald de Barry), an archdeacon who accompanied Prince John to Ireland in 1185, was the earliest of these historians and exerted an influence on British perceptions that was to span almost seven centuries.

The Irish, like the Normans, were Christians, and indeed Irish missionaries had converted the British. Further, as Lebow puts it, 'Irish civilisation was one of the few bright lights that penetrated the cultural darkness of medieval Europe.'[152] Cambrensis painted a very different picture. Comparing the Irish to the English, he wrote,

> No realme, no nation, no state, nor commonwealth through all Europa, can yeeled more no so manie profitable laws, directions, rules, examples and discourses . . . than doe the histories of this little Isle of Britanne or England. I would to God I might or were able to saie the like or halfe like of Ireland, a countrie, the more barren of good things, the more replenished with actions of bloud, murther, and louthsome outrages; which to anie good reader are greevous and irksome to be read and considered.[153]

The Tudor and Cromwellian conquests brought destitution and rebellion to Ireland, thus lending apparent substance to the defamatory stereotypes. British commentators attributed Irish poverty and violence not to the colonial system, but to the Irish character: a view which served to justify not only continued British rule, but also the use of methods which would be unacceptable if used in Britain. Though in the late eighteenth century some British historians began to reinterpret Irish history, locating the conditions imposed by Britain as the root of the problem, the dominant view remained that expressed in *The*

Times in 1846: 'The great obstacle to tranquillity in Ireland is the national character . . . When Ireland acts according to the principles of civilised man, then she can be ruled by the laws of civilised man.'[154]

The nineteenth century saw the development of theories of evolution and an intense debate about the ancestry of humans and their possible relationship with animals. Race supplanted 'national character' as an explanation for the supposed inferiority of the Irish and other colonised peoples. Humourists seized on the notion. In 1862, for example, when the radical Fenian movement was growing and when large numbers of Irish people, driven by famine, were arriving in Britain, a *Punch* satirist described the Irish immigrant as 'a creature manifestly between the gorilla and the negro' which sometimes 'sallies forth in states of excitement, and attacks civilised human beings that have provoked its fury.'[155]

Cartoonists had for many years represented the Irish, along with rebels and radicals of all nationalities, as brutish figures. Now they drew the Irish as apes, while their British adversaries were shown as fine-featured and handsome. Bestial images of the Irish were explicitly used to justify Britain's colonial role. As historian Lewis P. Curtis explains, famous illustrators like Tenniel 'leaned heavily on the theme of Beauty (Hibernia or Erin) being rescued from the clutches of the Beast (Fenianism) by a handsome Prince or St. George (Law and Order).'[156]

Cartoons and jokes

The contemporary conflict brought with it an upsurge in cartoons which echoed their nineteenth century predecessors. Cartoonist Michael Cummings of the *Express*, claiming cartoonist's licence for giving expression to the biased British view of the Irish, told *The Irish Times* in 1982 that the British saw the Irish as 'extremely violent, bloody-minded, always fighting, drinking enormous amounts, getting roaring drunk.' IRA violence, he said, tended to 'make them look rather like apes – though that's rather hard luck on the apes.'[157]

Following the dictates of their trade, cartoonists have reflected and exaggerated, often in virulent terms, the dominant themes of media coverage of the conflict. Researcher John Kirkaldy has observed that between October 1968 and August 1969, cartoonists shared the general distaste for the regime in the

North and disapproved of Protestant politicians. But after the intervention of the British army, they rapidly returned to traditional English stereotypes of the Irish.[158]

On occasion particular cartoons have provoked protests, especially from Irish people, or people of Irish descent, living in Britain. In October 1971, 351,000 copies of the *Scottish Daily Express* were lost when workers at the paper's Glasgow headquarters refused to handle a Cummings cartoon which linked the Soviet Union, the Catholic Church and republicanism. This showed 'Father O'Brezhnev, missionary to Ulster' alighting in priestly costume from an aircraft marked 'Irish Republican Airlines' which was disgorging a line of tanks with labels on them such as '250 samovars for Falls Road'.[159]

In 1982 protests from London's Irish community against a cartoon by Jak persuaded the Greater London Council to stop advertising in *The Standard*, the capital's evening paper. Parodying a cinema poster, the cartoon showed a graveyard occupied by hideous creatures whose armaments included a drill and a saw. The words on the poster read: 'SHOWING NOW: EMERALD ISLE SNUFF MOVIES PRESENT – THE ULTIMATE IN PSYCHOPATHIC HORROR – THE IRISH – FEATURING THE IRA, INLA, UDF, PFF, UDA, etc. etc.'[160] *The Standard* remained unrepentant, claiming that the situation in 'Ulster' 'does make the average American horror movie look positively anodyne.'[161] Attempts to persuade the Attorney-General, the Commission for Racial Equality and the Press Council to take action proved equally fruitless.[162]

The escalation of conflict in the seventies also brought a plague of anti-Irish jokes. Hinging on the notion of Irish stupidity, such jokes were already in circulation by the eighteenth century. The *Joe Miller Irish Miscellany*, published in 1749, contained jokes which had probably even then been around a long time. For instance: the Englishman asks how far it is from Waterford to Cork, and Paddy answers, after thinking for a while, 'Be Chreesht! I cannot tell dee how many miles it is from Waterford to Cork – but it is about ayteen milesh from Cork to Waterford.'[163]

In the seventies, such jokes became a staple feature of television comedy shows such as Granada's *The Comedians*, BBC1's *The Two Ronnies*[164] and Jim Davidson's show on Thames TV. They provoked consistent protests from Irish people in Britain, often expressed through the letters column of *The Irish Post*.

Books of anti-Irish jokes achieved astonishing sales. Between 1977 and 1979 the publishing house Futura sold 485,000 copies of three 'Official Irish Joke' books.[165] A subsidiary trade developed in 'Irish' novelties, such as mugs with their handles inside.

Anthropologist Edmund Leach examined several of the joke books and concluded that 'the prototype of the stage Irishmen' who emerged

> is not so much a figure of fun as an object of contempt merging into deep hostility. He is a drink-addicted moron, reared in the bog, who wears his rubber boots at all times, cannot read or write, and constantly reverses the logic of ordinary common sense. His female counterpart shares the same qualities, except that she is sexually promiscuous, rather than perpetually drunk.[166]

Such jokes are also told in other contexts – by Americans against Polish immigrants, by Australians against 'Poms', by Glaswegians against 'teuchters' – country bumpkins – and by Irish people against the countryfolk of Kerry. Revolving round the simple notion that the target group is 'thick', the jokes affirm the superiority of the tellers. They are quite different from the kind of jokes told by members of a community about themselves. Leach contrasted anti-Irish jokes with Jewish humour:

> Jokes about Jews are told by Jews to other Jews. They are an expression of international Jewish cultural solidarity, and they are often very clever. 'Irish' jokes are, in every respect, just the reverse. The sheer stupidity of both the joke and the characters described flatters the reader into a belief that there are others, who are not like me, who may be intellectually even more limited than myself. The ethnic element in 'Irish' jokes is thus latently racist.[167]

The notion of the Irish as buffoons also influences the way journalists approach routine news stories about Ireland. 'Why is it,' an *Irish Times* writer asked, 'that when British television crews come to Dublin they think they have to be funny, whether funny Irish or funny ha-ha?'[168] In January 1982, for example, the Irish government fell primarily because of a budget proposal to subject clothing and footwear to Value Added Tax, but in Britain the government's fall was widely reported as due to a proposal to increase the price of drink. In August 1983, the presenter of Channel 4's 'in depth' evening news programme rounded off an account of an oil find off the Irish coast with the words, 'I hope their oil doesn't turn out to have a white head on it.'[169]

Irish journalists also regularly remark on 'the tedious English habit of claiming any notable Irish achievements as British', as an *Irish Times* writer put it.[170] Thus when Irishman Sean Kelly raced in the 1983 Tour de France, his rating appeared in *The Times* as a 'British placing',[171] and the same year poet Seamus Heaney was so annoyed at finding himself included in the *Penguin Book of Contemporary British Verse* – he had thought the volume would be titled *Opened Ground* – that he wrote a 33-stanza 'open letter' to emphasise that he is an Irish, not a British poet.[172] It seems that the British concept of the Irish as a distinct nationality extends only to their supposed failings, not their successes.

The product of centuries of colonial domination, the consistent and often unthinking denigration of the Irish is fuelled by the inadequacies of media coverage, by the absence of Ireland from educational curricula and by the desire of politicians and commentators to present Britain's role in North in a favourable light. It is deeply offensive to Irish people, and is thought to have a negative effect on the self-image of Irish children growing up in Britain.[173] In British people it fosters a complacent ignorance and acceptance of the status quo which can only hinder the pursuit of a long-term political solution.

10. Propaganda machines

British army propaganda

The British army brought with it to the North the experience of what its *Land Operations* manual describes as 53 'operations of the counter revolutionary type'. In these operations, the army confronted 'a technique of revolutionary warfare which relies mainly on popular support for its success,' and a principal military objective was therefore to isolate the enemy 'physically and psychologically from their civilian support.' One means of doing this was to mount 'psychological operations' or 'psyops'.[1]

The manual defines psyops as 'the planned use of propaganda or other means, in support of our military action or presence, designed to influence to our advantage the opinions, emotions, attitudes and behaviour of enemy, neutral and friendly groups.'[2] Psyops involve exploiting every possible difference in the enemy camp:

> The political attack as well as the military must be pressed with vigour and should be aimed at the basic weaknesses of an insurgent movement, many of whose members may be selfish, ambitious or misfits who are maladjusted to normal society. Frequently their leaders will have ambitions. The movement may contain mutually suspicious ethnic groups and it may be possible to persuade the weaker ones that their interests are not being considered by their leaders. There may also be ideological differences between extremists and moderates. Finally there are the weaknesses inherent in a situation in which as well as the constant danger of betrayal there are difficulties brought about by bad living conditions and relatively poor military equipment and facilities. All these factors can be successfully exploited by military psychological operations in co-ordination with political action.[3]

The manual identifies two kinds of psyops resources: military and civilian. In the Malayan war, for instance, military psyops included the use of aircraft to drop leaflets or broadcast messages into enemy-held territory. On occasions, former guerrillas were prevailed on to record or write such messages in attempts to persuade their erstwhile comrades to surrender.[4]

Civilian psyops resources include radio 'and TV if it exists'. These, says the manual, 'are ideal for psyops, in that they can reach more people more quickly from one source than any other media. Radio propaganda can be put over in speeches by leading personalities, news commentaries, interviews and even in such things as drama, musical and religious programmes.'[5] Other resources include newspapers, visits by officials to towns and villages, and 'rumours', which 'can be spread by local agents' to confuse or demoralise the enemy but should be 'introduced with caution' because they can have unforeseen results.

The handbook also recommended that military psyops should be co-ordinated with army intelligence and public relations, with the civil authorities and with the police Special Branch and interrogation units. But the manual warns that 'care must be taken to avoid any overt connection between psyops and PR so that the credibility of PR is not compromised.'[6]

In the wars in the third world, psyops had played a minor part, but in the North it was to receive a greater emphasis. Writing just before he became the British army's Belfast commander in 1970, counter-insurgency expert Frank Kitson wrote that in the type of insurrection taking place in the North, and which could occur in Britain, the operational emphasis would 'swing away from the process of destroying relatively large groups of armed insurgents towards the business of divorcing extremist elements from the population which they are trying to subvert.' This meant

> that persuasion will become more important in comparison with armed offensive action . . . In terms of preparation, the effect of this is to enhance the priority which should now be given to teaching officers the methods of carrying out large scale persuasion, and to providing the Psychological Operations specialists and units which will be required.[7]

He emphasised, 'It is only necessary to stress once again that wars of subversion and counter subversion are fought, in the last resort, in the minds of the people, for the importance of a good psychological operations organization to become apparent.'[8]

The Irish experience also added a new dimension to psy-ops: the British and international media became much more important. Coverage of the wars in the third world had been patchy, partly because of the distances and difficult terrain involved. Ireland was different. 'Right from the beginning,' wrote Marine officer Alan Hooper in his book *The Military and The Media*, 'the Army's actions in Ulster were subjected to incessant news coverage and every soldier from the General Officer Commanding Northern Ireland (GOCNI) downwards, had to adjust to this new factor.'[9]

'Information Policy'

Finding itself in the spotlight after August 1969, the army began to pay more attention to the media, setting up a network of press officers at headquarters and unit level and briefing officers and soldiers on how to handle journalists.

According to former major-general Richard Clutterbuck, the army's public relations department consisted of a mixture of former journalists, civilian PR staff, officers temporarily seconded from combat units and specialist army PR staff.[10]

One press officer who began work at the army's Lisburn headquarters in 1969 was Colin Wallace, a civilian who had up to then worked as a public relations man with the Royal Irish Rangers in his home town, Ballymena in County Antrim. His role there had not been controversial, but when the troops arrived in force in 1969 he reportedly took on a new importance and the army 'relied greatly on his local knowledge.'[11]

Wallace was the author of a briefing document issued to officers coming to serve in the North.[12] A foretaste of things to come, it included a lurid item purporting to be the oath taken by members of Sinn Fein. This began:

> I swear by Almighty God, by all in heaven and upon earth, by the Holy and Blessed Prayer Book of our Church, by the Blessed Virgin Mary and Mother of God, by her Sorrowings and Sufferings at the foot of the Cross, by her tears and wailings, by St Patrick, by the Blessed and Admirable Host, by the Blessed Rosary and Holy Beads, by the Blessed Church in all ages and by our Holy National Martyrs, to fight until we die wading in the fields of Red Gore of the Saxon Tyrants and murderers of the glorious Cause of Nationality . . .[13]

And so it went on. George Gale quoted the 'oath' in an article in the *Spectator* in 1971, saying it demonstrated 'the attitude of Sinn Fein and of the IRA'.[14] Tim Pat Coogan, editor of *The Irish Press* and author of a book on the IRA,[15] wrote to the *Spectator* pointing out that the oath was a forgery of a type which had previously surfaced in loyalist papers, and that Sinn Fein in fact had no oath at all. Gale apologised: 'I regret accepting the "Sinn Fein oath" which I gullibly took from an Army document.'[16]

In September 1971, soon after the start of internment, the army reorganised its information services in the North, setting up an 'Information Policy' department. This was initially headed by paratroop Colonel Maurice Tugwell,[17] whose title was Colonel General Staff (Information Policy). Tugwell had previously been an intelligence officer in Palestine, and had also served in Malaya, Cyprus, Arabia and Kenya. He stayed at Lisburn till March 1973, when he transferred to Iran as an instructor at the Imperial Iranian Armed Forces College. He was awarded the CBE the same year. In 1975 he went to Nottingham, and in 1976 he took up a defence fellowship at King's College, London, where he wrote a thesis on 'the problems of dealing with revolutionary propaganda'.[18]

At Lisburn, all aspects of army propaganda were closely co-ordinated. David McKittrick of *The Irish Times* recorded that in 1974 and 1975 the same corridor housed the army's press office, an office labelled 'Psyops', the office of *Visor*, the magazine for soldiers serving in the North, and the office of Colin Wallace, who by then held a senior post in both army public relations and intelligence.[19]

Tugwell's job as 'Information Policy' chief was, as described by Clutterbuck, 'not merely to react to the media – or to events – but to take a positive initiative in presenting the news to the best advantage for the security forces.'[20] In the wake of internment, reported Robert Fisk in *The Times*, Tugwell and other officers at Lisburn

> made it their business to chat to journalists confidentially and to point out that the IRA's command structure had been severely fractured by the information gained during the 'deep' interrogation. The interrogation methods themselves they would say, were harmless.[21]

Tugwell repeated these contentions, which as Fisk pointed out were untrue, in an article published in Canada in early 1973 titled

'Revolutionary propaganda and the role of the information services in counter-insurgency operations':

> Interrogation methods used by the security forces in 1971 brought in a mass of valuable intelligence. These methods, combined with the internment of known terrorists, threatened to destroy the IRA's capability and to destroy it quickly . . . None of those interrogated by these methods suffered any injury or ill-effects.[22]

Tugwell and Colin Wallace specialised in giving journalists non-attributable information of this kind, which is often introduced in newspaper articles by phrases such as 'army sources believe' or 'senior officers in HQ allege'.[23] Lower-ranking press officers dealt with routine enquiries, and journalists could also contact local battalion public relations officers.

Adjusting to the North

The army began training officers in how to be interviewed on television, and by the end of 1971 more than 200 officers had been through courses at the Army School of Instructional Technology at Beaconsfield.[24] Here they were taught basic lore, such as always to look at the interviewer to give the impression of sincerity, and told how to answer 'typical' TV questions. Thus the model answer to the question 'What is your religion?' was: 'I do not think my religion comes into the Northern Ireland situation, but I consider myself a Christian. I hope that Christians will be able to live together in peace.'[25]

From 1977 courses were also run specifically for officers who had been selected to act as press officers for their units, and by 1982 the school was putting some 90 press officers and 300 other officers through courses each year.[26]

In November 1971 a new chapter was added to the *Land Operations* manual, giving detailed advice on public relations. It identified three main aims:

> a. The requirement to provide information for national and world-wide publication, to convince national and world opinion that the cause to which the army is committed is a good one.
> b. The importance of fostering good relations with the local community.
> c. The need to preserve and improve the image of the army.[27]

On the advice of the Information Policy staff, in late 1971 the army relaxed restrictions on soldiers answering questions from reporters. Clutterbuck praised this decision, writing, 'Corporals in charge of patrols, in particular, came through on television into the living room far better than generals or colonels.' Having 'someone like the boy next door' on the screen, he wrote, helped to counter 'the "jackboot" image which hostile journalists will try to project about the army or police'.[28]

The army also altered its tactics on the ground in order to improve its media image. Colonel Robin Evelegh, who served in the North in 1972 and 1973, has explained how the army developed a policy of 'retrospective arrest' partly to avoid television pictures of 'some poor little fellow arrested being dragged away by four or five huge squaddies.' The new strategy was adopted in 1973. Instead of arresting people – often the wrong ones – on the spot, rioters were now held back by rubber bullets while 'specially-detailed identifiers' photographed the crowd, gathering evidence for later arrests and court cases.[29]

In 1970 the army's psyops resources were, in Kitson's view, too limited. There were 18 psyops full-timers, including a 12-man operational team which was probably in Oman, since Kitson described it as 'subsidized by the government of the territory in which it is deployed.'[30] The Joint Warfare Establishment at Old Sarum in Wiltshire had been running psyops courses since at least 1967,[31] and these were now boosted and extended to civilians. By October 1972, some 262 civilian agents, including policemen, and 1,858 army officers had reportedly completed the two-week course.[32] In the mid-seventies, a Ministry of Defence official went to the office of *The Irish Times*' then London editor, Conor O'Clery, and produced documentation showing that 'dozens of civil servants were being trained in psyops', including representatives of the Ministry of Defence and the Home Office.[33] Officers also received psyops training at Fort Bragg in the United States: among them was Lieutenant-Colonel Jeremy Railton, who subsequently became Information Policy chief at Lisburn, working there in 1974 and 1975.[34]

Propaganda on the ground

In the early years, a stream of propaganda was directed at the nationalist community through local army units. This increased after Operation Motorman breached the no-go areas in July 1972. A Belfast correspondent writing in *Time Out* that year described how army posts were covered in anti-IRA slogans, and army vehicles carried large posters reminding people of the 'Bloody Friday' explosions: 'July 21st was a lovely summer's day. For nine people it was their last. The IRA murdered them. Reject the IRA.' Also, leaflets were pushed through doors in the early hours of the morning which urged people 'to give information about IRA men, their supporters and arms dumps.' In some areas, soldiers had stuck leaflets on people's windows which read, 'You Can't Beat Us – You Can Join Us'.[35]

The glossier material, such as the 'Bloody Friday' poster, was apparently produced by the Stormont government and, after the introduction of direct rule in March 1972, by the Northern Ireland Office. In 1972, some 250,000 copies of a brochure titled *The Terror and the Tears* were issued: this consisted of newspaper photographs of the effects of IRA violence and entirely ignored violence from other sources.[36]

The army also produced its own posters and leaflets. A 1974 poster showed republican leader David O'Connell holding a pair of scales, one of which held a picture of the Birmingham bombings and the other a coffin in Belfast. It was captioned, 'YOUR LIVES IN THE BALANCE – PROVO SCALES OF JUSTICE'.[37] Some of the leaflets were crudely produced, possibly because, as *Time Out* put it, these were 'more in line with the type of leaflets ghetto dwellers are used to'.[38]

More underhand methods were also used. The army forged Sinn Fein posters in Newry and Belfast.[39] The most famous forgery was a response to a rather over-optimistic Provisional poster which showed the silhouette of an armed IRA man with the slogan 'Freedom '74'. The army version added, 'but not through the barrel of a gun'.[40]

As the army lowered its profile in the mid-seventies in line with the Ulsterisation policy, these methods died out. Letterbox deliveries ended, and leaflets were handed out by policemen and soldiers at checkpoints, and delivered to shops. The government line was increasingly sold through sophisticated advertising campaigns.[41]

'Black' propaganda

In 1980 Colin Wallace, who had by then left his army job, admitted to David McKittrick of *The Irish Times* that much of the information he had given journalists in the North 'was what he called black propaganda and misinformation aimed at discrediting the various individuals or groups.'[42] McKittrick told how he had 'visited Wallace many times throughout 1974 and 1975 for off-the-record briefings' and recalled:

> It was clear that he had access to the highest levels of intelligence data. He had an encyclopaedic memory, which he occasionally refreshed with calls made on his personal scrambler telephone to the headquarters intelligence section a few floors above his office.
> He was astonishingly frank. He would freely give the names, addresses, phone numbers and names of mistresses of paramilitary figures, both Republican and Loyalist. He was also ready to admit mistakes made by the British army and to acknowledge that the Provisionals or any other group were doing well.[43]

Wallace, 'a mild-mannered, soft-spoken man', confided to McKittrick in 1980 that,

> 'If you are in the Int world – especially army intelligence, you are in a totally unreal world. You are always at war, even in peace-time. You don't exist, you have no legal standing. You see conspiracies everywhere. Ordinary rules don't apply. You feel it is unfair when you're asked to abide by the normal code of society.'[44]

Some of the 'black' propaganda stories supplied by Wallace and his colleagues were true, some were partly true and others were entirely fabricated. One of the army's most successful leaks surfaced in a story in *The Sunday Times* in April 1973 under the by-line of reporters Paul Eddy and Chris Ryder.[45] Their front page article, headed 'IRA Provo chiefs milk £150,000 from funds', concerned a document that the British army claimed to have intercepted as it was being smuggled out of Long Kesh on its way to the IRA's Belfast commander, Seamus Twomey. Said to have been written by a senior IRA detainee, the document alleged that seven named Belfast Provisionals had embezzled funds acquired by the IRA through armed robberies. 'From extensive enquiries we have made in Andersonstown,' wrote Eddy and Ryder, 'we are convinced that the document is genuine.' *Guardian* reporters Derek Brown and Christopher Sweeney later suggested that the information given by the army to *The Sunday Times* was 'doctored', and described the affair as 'one of the most serious dirty tricks' reported to them. But they added that *The Sunday Times* had 'carried a detailed, cautious and accurate account' of the embezzlement, 'having checked all the information with other sources.'[46]

One of the sources quoted by Eddy and Ryder was a man

they described as the former intelligence officer of E Company of the IRA's First Battalion, who confirmed the embezzlement story in a tape-recorded interview. He was, as Eddy and Ryder later revealed,[47] 19-year-old Louis Hammond, and he was badly injured by the IRA three weeks after the *Sunday Times* article appeared. The IRA said he was a British agent: Eddy and Ryder agreed he had worked for British army intelligence, but said he was an IRA double agent.[48] After this affair Ryder was apparently threatened by the Provisionals and left Belfast.[49]

Whatever the provenance of the document, the military were delighted with their leak. Counter-insurgency expert Major-General Anthony Deane-Drummond cited the *Sunday Times* story as an example of how 'true stories can be put about on the methods or motives of the terrorists which can help to destroy their morale and lead to disintegration,' and claimed that it had 'directly led to the virtual disbandment of the IRA unit.' It was, he said, 'a benign use of the psychological weapon'.[50]

Other information handed out by the army to certain journalists included dossiers on American and Irish business-men, which were described by Robert Fisk in *The Times* in 1975. The dossier on American businessmen and their contacts ran to six pages, and some of the material had evidently been gathered in the United States. It included names, addresses and home telephone numbers, and one passage referred to an American suspect's 'alleged 40 adulteries during a three month period'. The dossier on Irish businessmen suggested their involvement in IRA activities, but occasionally added that there was no evidence to substantiate the allegations. Attached to the back of the document was a photocopy of a letter apparently sent by a Belfast businessman to a New York supporter of Sinn Fein, asking for funds which could be deposited in a branch of the Allied Irish Bank in Belfast.[51]

Tara

On several occasions in 1973 and 1974 the army tried to spread compromising rumours about loyalists, but the media treated these far more circumspectly than they did unflattering stories about the IRA.

One of the most spectacular smears, which appears to have gone unreported at the time, turned out some years later to be partially true. In August 1973 Colin Wallace approached Kevin

Dowling, then working for the *Sunday Mirror*, and gave him details of a shadowy loyalist paramilitary group called Tara, which he called 'a bizarre homosexual army'. Wallace named several officers in Tara, including William McGrath, who he said was a known homosexual. Dowling wrote a memorandum to his editor recommending that an article be written on Tara, but his suggestion was not taken up.[52]

Then in 1975 Wallace gave similar information to David McKittrick of *The Irish Times*. He said McGrath was the head of Tara, and supplied his address and phone number. He also named other leading members of Tara, two of whom later became prominent in the Official Unionist Party and another in Paisley's Democratic Unionist Party.[53] Later that year Wallace gave McKittrick a document about Tara which described the group's militant anti-Catholicism and repeated the allegations about McGrath. It added an unlikely flourish: 'He is also thought to owe more allegiance to the Red Flag than to either the Union Jack or the Tricolour.' It also gave the names of three other leading members of Tara. McKittrick did not publish any of this at the time because, he wrote later, 'I could not be certain it was not simply a smear.'[54] *The Sunday Times*, too, was briefed by the army about Tara, but David Blundy dismissed the information about McGrath as 'startlingly inaccurate'.[55]

In the context of the Six Counties, the allegations concerning homosexuality were potentially explosive. The 1967 Act, which legalised homosexuality in Britain, had not been extended to the North because of widespread opposition, and loyalists, particularly Ian Paisley who in 1978 launched the 'Save Ulster From Sodomy' campaign, were the most vocal opponents of change.

The significance of the British army document on Tara did not become apparent until December 1981, when William McGrath was jailed for sexual offences against boys at the Kincora Boys Home, a hostel for teenage boys in loyalist east Belfast where he had been a housefather since 1971. The warden and deputy warden – against whom allegations had been made as far back as 1961 – were also jailed, as were officials from other homes.[56] Then in January 1982 *The Irish Times* revealed that in 1976 the Northern authorities had blocked an RUC enquiry into an alleged homosexual prostitution ring, said to have involved numerous people in public positions, centred on Kincora and other boys' homes.[57] Further, social workers had repeatedly raised the issue with the welfare authorities after complaints from boys, but nothing had been done. It then emerged that Ian Paisley had received complaints about McGrath's activities in 1974, but had allegedly failed to act on them.[58]

When McGrath was convicted, Irish journalists recalled the information supplied by Wallace and concluded that while army intelligence was aware of McGrath's activities, they had seemingly failed to alert the police.[59] Soon speculation began 'that British military intelligence might have been aware of events at the Kincora home and might have been using that knowledge to its advantage.'[60] Then in December 1982 both *The Sunday Times* and *The Irish Times* claimed, in reports based on information supplied by the RUC, that army intelligence had been using homosexual loyalist politicians to gather information about loyalist paramilitary groups. In *The Sunday Times*, Chris Ryder wrote that McGrath was 'one politician used in this way'.[61]

The Niedermayer smear

Another major smear reportedly originated by Wallace[62] later proved, unlike the Tara case, to be completely without foundation. On 27 December 1973 Thomas Niedermayer, the West German honorary consul in Belfast and managing director of the Grundig company in Dunmurry, was kidnapped from his home at Suffolk, near Belfast. His body was not found until March 1980, and it eventually emerged that the IRA had been responsible for abducting him.[63]

In October 1974 a British army intelligence officer, a major attached to the 39th Brigade at Lisburn, approached journalists working for *The Irish Times*, *The Times* and *The Guardian*. He made spurious allegations that prominent unionist politician William Craig was behind the kidnapping.[64] Neither the Irish nor British journalists took the story up, but the German paper *Bild* did. In November 1975 Craig and his wife won a libel action against *Bild*, 'which had alleged that Mrs Craig was having a love affair with Mr Thomas Niedermayer' and 'suggested that in consequence Mr Craig may have been in some way concerned with Mr Niedermayer's disappearance'.[65] *Bild* had carried the story under the headline, 'Did the consul die because of a romance?'[66] *Bild* unreservedly withdrew the allegations and apologised to the Craigs, who received some £8,000 in damages.[67]

The reason why army intelligence initiated the smear can

only be guessed at. Craig was then a leading opponent of British government moves towards power-sharing and links with the South of Ireland, and had been a vocal supporter of the loyalist stoppage of May 1974 which sabotaged the government's plans. The smear may, therefore, have been a crude attempt to undermine hardline loyalism.

Also in 1974, a series of leaflets purporting to come from a left-wing loyalist organisation, the 'Ulster Citizens' Army', arrived in Belfast newspaper offices over a period of months. The 'Ulster Citizens' Army' claimed to oppose the strong-arm methods of other loyalist paramilitaries, and the leaflets gave the names of senior UDA and UVF officers, accusing them of corruption and involvement in sectarian assassinations. *The Guardian* later reported that the handouts 'were traced back to a press officer who has since left army service.'[68] *The Sunday Times* obtained a leaflet purporting to come from a Protestant group called 'The Covenanters', which likewise attacked the UDA and UVF. A source in the Northern Ireland Office told *The Sunday Times* that this was definitely a forgery: he had been shown it by a member of the army's Information Policy unit, who had said it was their own work.[69]

The affair of the 'Ulster Citizens' Army' leaflets had a curious sequel: they were used in what may have been an attempt to get a man killed for personal reasons. On 29 October 1974, a UDA officer contacted David McKittrick of *The Irish Times* and said he had discovered who the author of the leaflets was. The UDA officer supplied the name and address of the person accused, a music teacher, and said he had been given the name by a reporter from a newspaper in the south of England, whom he had previously helped with a story about UDA gun-running.

The same night, McKittrick and another *Irish Times* reporter interviewed the music teacher, who denied any interest in or involvement with the UDA or the Ulster Citizens' Army. Next day McKittrick visited Colin Wallace at army headquarters: 'After some moments Wallace said he seemed to recall serving with the alleged author in the British Army . . . Wallace said the whole affair seemed "very fishy" and asked that he be told before anything was printed about the affair.'[70]

The next day McKittrick telephoned the English journalist, who said he had no knowledge of the affair. He added that his only contact with the UDA had been over a gun-running story some months previously, and also said 'very emphatically' that his only visits to Northern Ireland had been two British army promotional trips. Several days later, McKittrick received a leaflet headed 'Ulster Citizens' Army', which said in part, 'unless you cease activities immediately, your neutral position as a journalist will be regarded as invalid and direct action taken against you.'[71]

The mystery has never been fully unravelled, but other facts later came to light. David McKittrick wrote in 1981 that he had learned 'that the English journalist had, in fact, served for a year as a civilian Press Officer with the British Army, working with Colin Wallace at army headquarters. He and Wallace had been close friends, and Wallace had attended the journalist's wedding.'[72]

The Northern Ireland Office committee

The Information Policy unit also used 'black' propaganda against their paymasters, the British government. There was considerable resentment among army officers when Merlyn Rees, who became Northern Ireland Secretary in February 1974, began releasing internees and then arranged a ceasefire with the IRA. Lisburn officers frequently gave journalists off-the-record briefings complaining that their 'war' effort was hindered by 'low profiles' and government orders to suspend arbitrary screening procedures.[73]

In July 1974, reporters were given a briefing at Lisburn at which the army blamed a recent upsurge in violence directly on the release of 65 internees. An army spokesperson said that intelligence reports suggested that well over half of all released internees became re-involved in violence within a couple of months. As Colin Wallace later admitted to David McKittrick, army intelligence had falsified the figures in an attempt to change Rees's policy of phasing out internment. The true figure, according to *The Sunday Times*, was less than 20 per cent.[74]

Later in 1974 Wallace told an English reporter that Merlyn Rees was lying when he told the House of Commons that there was no contact between his administration and the Provisionals. Wallace said there was a go-between, who was a Quaker. With help from David McKittrick, the identity of the go-between, an official of the Rowntree Trust charity, was discovered. McKittrick commented that Wallace's disclosure 'was clearly aimed at exposing and ending the contact with the Provisionals.'[75]

In late 1974, according to *Sunday Times* reporter David Blundy, a committee consisting of representatives of the Northern Ireland Office, army and RUC 'met at Stormont Castle and discussed, among other things, ways of discrediting politicians judged hostile to Government policy.'[76] The Northern Ireland Office said this version was 'cobblers', and that the committee was formed merely to co-ordinate information policy.[77]

The committee, wrote Blundy, was chaired by Michael Cudlipp of the Northern Ireland Office, and other members included the army's Chief Information Officer, David McDine, and psyops-trained Lieutenant-Colonel Jeremy Railton, then Head of the army's Information Policy unit. After a series of meetings which lasted into early 1975, the committee produced a report which went to army, police and Northern Ireland Office officials. Neither the Ministry of Defence, nor the Northern Ireland Office, nor the Home Office either confirmed or convincingly denied the existence of the report.[78]

It is possible that the Northern Ireland Office's main motive for setting up the new committee was to bring the army under control. At the end of March 1975, Robert Fisk reported that the government had effectively stopped the flow of 'black' propaganda stories from the army 'by taking over control of the department that decides the army and police information policy in the province.'[79] A major shake-up of the army's information services is believed to have taken place, which led, among other things, to the departure of Colin Wallace.[80]

If the Northern Ireland Office's intention was to hold the army in check, it only partially succeeded. While scandals on the scale of the Niedermayer smear were not repeated, the military continued to use various means to try to undermine government policy.

In April 1975 General Sir Frank King, then General Officer Commanding in the North, said that the IRA would have been beaten in a matter of months but for political interference from Whitehall. He chose an odd location for his remarks – a meeting of the St John's Ambulance Brigade in Nottingham, the town in which former Information Policy chief Maurice Tugwell was then stationed. King's remarks, wrote Robert Fisk, reached the press 'with extraordinary speed'.[81]

That summer, a military classified document headed 'Intsum No. 16 for week ending June 15, 1975', which had been typed out by an intelligence officer in 40 Commando Royal

Marines, was handed to Ian Paisley via a soldier in the UDR who was also a reserve policeman. The report said IRA leader Seamus Twomey was 'no longer a wanted man' and had been seen in his Belfast home. Clearly intended to embarrass the government, the report had been leaked directly from the army's headquarters at Thiepval Barracks in Lisburn.[82] By now, the Northern Ireland Office had reportedly become obsessed by security leaks and was spending 'hundreds of man hours' trying to trace them.[83]

Colin Wallace left the North in 1975, going first to Preston in Lancashire, and then apparently to London. In 1980 David McKittrick traced him to Littlehampton in Sussex, where he was working as Chief Information Officer for Arun District Council. In September that year Wallace was charged with murdering 29-year-old Brighton antique dealer Jonathan Lewis, with whose wife, Jane, he had been having an affair. The Duke of Norfolk, for whom Wallace's wife Eileen worked as a secretary and who had been an army intelligence chief at the Ministry of Defence in the mid-sixties, appeared in court to offer bail for him. In March 1981, Wallace was sentenced to ten years imprisonment for manslaughter. The press dubbed the trial the 'It's a knockout' case, because Wallace and Jane Lewis, who worked as his assistant, had become friendly while organising a heat for the BBC television competition.[84]

Surveillance

While using the press as a channel for 'black' propaganda stories, army intelligence was also involved in surveillance of journalists. Robert Fisk revealed in March 1975 that the army 'have had at their disposal extensive classified files on British and Irish reporters working in Belfast.'[85] The files contained information, 'some of it almost certainly gathered from tapped telephone calls', on Kevin Myers, former Belfast correspondent of *The Observer*, Vincent Browne of the Dublin-based *Sunday Independent*, a reporter on *The Daily Telegraph*, and Fisk himself, who was working for *The Times*.

The file on Fisk included a report submitted to the army's Special Investigation Branch by a former member of the SAS, who, while second in command of the 3rd Battalion of the Parachute Regiment in Belfast, had invited Fisk to dinner and questioned him about the sources for several of the stories he had written. Suspicious of the officer's motives, Fisk invented several names and fictitious contacts, all of which appeared in the army file.[86]

Fisk also knew that his phone was tapped. 'On one occasion,' he wrote, 'an appointment I made with a reporter on a local Belfast newspaper, to talk about alleged police corruption in Belfast, was discussed at a military conference in Lisburn within 12 hours.'[87]

In December 1977, Anne McHardy, then reporting from Belfast for *The Guardian*, received 'a very unpleasant shock' when she discovered that her phone was being tapped and that the Northern Ireland Office had access to the tapes.[88] She learned this when a Northern Ireland Office official repeated to her part of a private conversation she had had with her husband. 'I was at a dinner party given by the NIO for journalists,' she told *The Irish Times* later, 'and an information officer got very very drunk and started revealing details of a private conversation he'd heard a tape of. I asked how he knew and he said he'd been listening to the tapes.'[89]

At around the same time, a senior Irish journalist discovered that conversations he had had with a captain and a colonel were being reported in full to various army departments. The captain invited him several times to Palace Barracks in Holywood, and assured him their conversations were off the record. The journalist learned that this was not in fact the case when the captain returned him some documents and accidentally enclosed with them two sheets of paper containing an account of one of their conversations, with a list of departments to which copies were being sent.[90]

Fake press cards

The calculating opportunism with which army intelligence approaches journalists was illustrated by the episodes of the fake press cards.

In February 1976, *The Times* published a picture of a press card forged by the army, which had borne the name and photograph of a soldier. In the accompanying article, Robert Fisk wrote that there was evidence that 'soldiers in plainclothes and carrying press cards have been operating south of the border.'[91] A soldier was said to have visited Dublin in December 1975 posing as a journalist. The army denied this, but admitted that press cards had been forged, saying this had happened more than 18 months ago.[92]

The cards were printed, wrote Robert Fisk, 'at a building next to the tennis courts at Thiepval Barracks, Lisburn, Antrim, after real press cards had been photographed on a Polaroid camera.'[93] *The Sunday Times* later explained that the army routinely photographed journalists' identification cards when reporters handed them in during visits to the Lisburn head-quarters. The main reason for taking the photographs was so that they could be filed together with background notes on the reporters.[94]

The card reproduced in *The Times* was headed 'PRESS' in a typeface similar to that used on cards issued by the National Union of Journalists. The bearer was described as 'the accredited representative of Inter Press Features, 142 Fleet Street, London, EC4, England, in Northern Ireland.' The agency, Fisk dis-covered, had left its office two years before. He visited the owner, a semi-retired journalist and part-time *Sunday Express* sub-editor named Jack Aitken, at his home in Kent. Aitken, who said his agency specialised in the production of film stars' ghosted life stories, said the card was a complete fake and he had never issued one like it.[95]

There were angry protests from journalists' unions and some Labour MPs, pointing out that the army's conduct could put journalists' lives at risk.[96] Roy Mason, then Defence Secretary, responded to the furore by saying that he had instructed the army not to forge any more bogus press cards. He wrote to the National Union of Journalists saying, 'I entirely accept that this action could have jeopardised the personal safety of reporters and called into doubt the validity of real Press cards.' He added that the practice had been 'discontinued some years ago as soon as it came to the notice of higher authorities at Headquarters, North-ern Ireland.'[97]

Eighteen months later, however, *The Sunday Times* pub-lished two further forged cards, which had been given to them by a senior army officer serving in the North.[98] The cards identified the holder as a member of the NUJ. From the lettering, it was clear that both cards were based on genuine NUJ cards issued in 1976 or 1977. One of the fakes bore the name of an army captain who had served in the Six Counties, plus a photograph and signature. The other was blank, and, wrote David Blundy, was 'one of a batch of identical forgeries that was held, at least until recently, at an army centre at Ashford in Kent, where intelligence officers are trained for service in Ulster.'[99]

The officer who had supplied the cards, and an NCO who had served at the Lisburn headquarters, told *The Sunday Times* that forged NUJ cards had been used 'within the past two years by soldiers posing as photographers when visiting both Loyalist and Republican strongholds.'[100] The Ministry of Defence and the Northern Ireland Office denied any knowledge of the forgeries. 'Officials now suggest,' wrote Blundy, 'that someone may be trying to discredit the army by producing fake fakes.'

Routine PR

The backstairs intrigues of the intelligence men and psyops specialists probably had less impact on British media coverage in the long run than the army's routine public relations activities. From 1971 the army's information service in the North was run by a Ministry of Defence official and a colonel – the colonel was replaced by a major in 1982.[101] Until 1975, Colin Wallace worked under them as a civilian press liaison officer, but his post disappeared with his departure.[102] Beneath this trio were the army officers – majors and captains – who staffed the press desk at the Lisburn headquarters. Additionally, each unit on the ground has a designated press officer, who usually has other duties as well. In 1973 *Guardian* reporter Simon Hoggart described the Lisburn desk:

> Here seven men and a coordinator, working on a rota system, read out a log of the day's activities to any journalist who cares to ring and ask. Mostly this is a rather skeletal description of day-to-day incidents – a bombing, a riot, a few shots fired, a death. If an IRA rocket narrowly misses a school or hospital, this will usually be tacked on, since it is a fair bet for the first paragraph of a radio bulletin or newspaper report.[103]

For the first few years of the conflict, the army and police were the sole source of information on day-to-day violence. Assisted by the fact that British editors expected reporters to give the authorities' line but not to seek out opposing versions, the army was able to get across its version of incidents virtually unchallenged. Simon Hoggart wrote in 1973 that

> the army has the immense advantage of getting in the first word, and it is left up to the integrity of the journalist to check that word

one. Some do, some don't. Most only check when there is time or the incident looks like becoming controversial, and a few hardly bother at all. When the British press prints an account of an incident as if it were established fact, and it is clear that the reporter himself was not on the spot, it is a 99 per cent certainty that it is the army's version which is being given.[104]

Their position was, however, eroded somewhat in the mid-seventies, as the republicans improved their own publicity operation and began to use their telex systematically.

Each army press officer, reported Andrew Stephen in 1976, is given a buff-coloured restricted document titled *Manual of Public Relations*. One paragraph in this is headed 'Establishing Rapport', and says that reporters and photographers 'should always be treated as guests of officer status' and 'hospitality should be offered to them on suitable occasions.'[105] Journalists are wined and dined at the officers' mess as Lisburn, a ritual that apparently impresses British reporters more than Irish ones.[106]

While hospitality is the carrot, the stick is denial of information. Simon Hoggart recorded that after he and his *Guardian* colleague Simon Winchester had produced three anti-army stories in one week, for about a fortnight Lisburn gave them ' "minimal cooperation" – curt, unwilling accounts of violence, and no background or extra information at all.'[107] Like the Northern Ireland Office and the police, the army has sometimes made approaches to journalists' employers. When *Times* reporter Robert Fisk refused to accept the army's interpretation of a confidential document he had obtained, the civilian head of army PR, Peter Broderick, sent a message to the *Times* office describing Fisk as 'a hostile reporter'.[108]

One of the army's most successful publicity techniques has been the running of all-expenses-paid 'facilities trips' for reporters. 'They jet you out from wherever you happen to live in England,' explained a journalist who used to work for a Yorkshire paper, 'and then you live in barracks with the boys for three days or so. Then you go home with lots of pictures of local lads from your own area and a nice little piece about our brave boys going out there and braving the bullets, etcetera.'[109]

These facilities trips have resulted in a steady flow of 'satisfied soldier' stories in British provincial papers. The former Yorkshire reporter felt that the trips have an additional significance:

Journalists think that they know about the situation because they've been on an army trip. Not only do they get journalists writing stuff in the paper about our brave boys out there, but also the journalists who come back to England feel that they've made this heroic trip into the unknown, and that now they understand, and that they're qualified to pontificate in bars and pubs and newsrooms, and as they go up the ladder that they know about Ireland.[110]

Journalists visiting Lisburn are given a folder full of information sheets, sometimes accompanied by glossy pictures of soldiers on patrol and a copy of the local army magazine, *Visor*, which in 1982 attracted protests from the Equal Opportunities Commission in the North because of its regular use of photographs of naked women.[111]

The folder supplied in January 1981 included a 'press officer contact list', a 'press facts sheet' listing events in the North from August 1969, and lists of statistics on deaths, injuries, arms finds, shootings and explosions and the numbers of people charged with 'terrorist offences'. It also contained a pamphlet titled *Northern Ireland: Points At Issue*. This was set out in short chapters, each headed by a question such as 'Is Ireland a "colonial" problem?' Each answer consisted of a few paragraphs ending with a single sentence in large type, such as: 'All representative shades of opinion in Ireland agree that the problem today is not a "colonial" one.' Among the pamphlet's other conclusions were that 'Partition was caused by an irreconcilable clash between Irishmen,' and 'The present-day Provisional IRA is a small group of violent terrorists without popular support and with no claim to be a genuine liberation movement.'

Also included in the folder was a photocopy of a letter published in *An Phoblacht/Republican News* on 20 September 1980, in which the writer recommended that republicans set about building 'a movement for radical social transformation', and rejected the possibility of achieving social emancipation through existing parliamentary and trade union structures. An American journalist who was given this folder said that the press officer invited him to use the material without crediting it to the army.[112]

Much of the work of unit press officers, in particular, involves contacting the media and suggesting stories to them. 'They might tell you, "We've just helicoptered a cow out of a marsh in Fermanagh", or "We've adopted a dog",' said an Irish journalist scathingly.[113] Some such stories exploit an existing 'angle', while others are specially staged. The army's PR efforts of this type are not, of course, confined to Ireland. In 1982, for instance, BBC TV's *World About Us* series made a film about the thriving wildlife in the military training area at Sennelager in West Germany after the idea had been put to them by the army's Public Information Office in the district.[114]

The success or failure of the authorities' PR probably depends less, in the end, on their methods than on the sympathies or allegiances of journalists and their employers. Most Irish reporters, and a few British ones, are very sceptical. A top Irish reporter peppered his comments on army press officers with words such as 'asses', 'idiots' and 'numbskulls'. In stark contrast is the attitude of Alan Protheroe, one of the most influential figures in the BBC, and, incidentally, an officer in the territorial army. In June 1982, by which time he was Assistant Director of News and Current Affairs, Protheroe expressed regret that the army's information service had not been utilised during the South Atlantic war, but instead had been 'shunted into a siding by the mandarins.' The army's public information branch, he wrote,

> knows about the technical and logistic requirements of contemporary journalism. More importantly, it is *trusted* by journalists. They speak our shorthand, understand our pressures. It is a machine that works exceptionally well, is honed and exercised for just such an eventuality as the Falklands crisis.[115]

It was, he wrote, 'largely because of Northern Ireland and the involvement of soldiers in so many parts of the world' that the army was more experienced than the other services in dealing with the media.[116]

The divergent attitudes of journalists were graphically illustrated by a contretemps over banners at the annual conference of the National Union of Journalists in April 1980. The meeting was held, despite objections, in the Unionist-dominated seaside town of Portrush in the Six Counties. Among the banners hung round the hall was one which said 'Smash the H Blocks', and another which read, 'End Political Murder. Support Law and Order'. Near the start of the conference, the first banner was removed. After a protest from radical freelance photographer Larry Herman, it was eventually reinstated. Then the 'law and order' banner disappeared. This provoked protests from Bob

Rodwell, a Belfast-based reporter who contributes to *The Guardian*, among other papers. It transpired that Oxford NUJ member Peter McIntyre had destroyed the banner, an act which he later justified by saying, 'there was a difference in character between the two banners in question because one was supporting the oppressor and the other supported the oppressed.' The upshot was that the conference passed a motion saying that only official NUJ banners should be displayed.[117]

Use of the law

Legal or police action has occasionally been taken against journalists reporting the North. In May 1971, BBC reporter Bernard Falk spent four days in prison in Belfast after being sentenced for contempt of court. A man called Leo Martin had been charged with IRA membership, and Falk had refused to identify him in court as the man he had interviewed for a *24 Hours* programme. Martin was acquitted in June, after Falk had for a second time refused to identify him.[118]

Ron McKay, a reporter working for the London magazine *Time Out*, was arrested and charged under the Prevention of Terrorism Act in March 1979. He was held at Glasgow airport as he returned from Belfast where he had been interviewing IRA leaders. He was held for more than 20 hours and was fingerprinted and photographed by the police. The Special Branch confiscated an article he was carrying about the British army's highly sophisticated intelligence computer in the North, which by then held details on up to half the population. They held the article to check whether it contravened the Official Secrets Act. McKay was charged under sections 6 and 8 of the PTA with failing to complete a landing card – these cards are issued to some passengers travelling to and from the North – and with failing to supply adequate information to an examining officer. The charges were later dropped and *Time Out* printed the article about the army computer unhindered.[119]

In September 1979, Pierre Salinger, former Press Secretary to US President John F. Kennedy and a distinguished author and journalist, was arrested in West Belfast and held for 12 hours in Castlereagh interrogation centre. As Paris correspondent for ABC television, one of the three big US networks, Salinger had been sent to Belfast in the wake of the killing of Lord Mountbatten to make a two-part programme on Ireland and the IRA. He was interviewing Sinn Fein representatives in the Ballymurphy community centre when the army and RUC raided the building. Along with Salinger, they arrested an American producer for ABC and two French crew members – a cameraman and sound recordist – as well as three senior Sinn Fein members, Danny Morrison, Richard McAuley and Joe Austin. The RUC confiscated the videotape which the ABC crew had been working on and watched it on their own playback machinery to see what had been taped. 'We had no choice,' said Salinger. 'They had the tape. I was in no position to object.' Salinger condemned the RUC's action and said he found it 'bizarre' not that he personally was arrested, but that newsmen were arrested in the execution of their duties.[120]

But these individual instances of harassment had no general intimidatory effect on journalists covering the North. Much more significant was the general threat contained in the Prevention of Terrorism Act. Preferring not to test the Act, television companies have refrained from stepping into potentially risky territory. From the end of 1974, when the Act was passed, there were no more television interviews with IRA representatives. From mid-1979, when the INLA was added to the list of proscribed organisations, no more of their spokespeople appeared on television. The judgement by Attorney-General Havers that followed the last INLA interview and the Carrickmore affair made the threat tangible and also extended it. The journalists could, he said, have been prosecuted in both instances. From then on, it was not just interviews with the IRA or INLA that put journalists in danger of prosecution, but also filming their activities and indeed any kind of contact with them at all.[121]

Harassment

Harassment on the streets is directed at photographers and film-makers rather than reporters. Photographic equipment is conspicuous, and pictures are more powerful than words. Photographer Chris Steele-Perkins told how when he was taking pictures in West Belfast for a book, he was several times stopped by soldiers and told, 'Don't take pictures or we'll take the film.' He commented, 'I don't know what the legal situation is about that but in terms of what is actually going to happen, it's not really important what the legal situation is.'[122] Colin Jones, who took photographs in Derry's Creggan estate for *The Observer* in 1978, said he found the authorities much harder to deal with than the local people. He went on:

> The army are definitely opposed to photographing, you can't take pictures in the street, you'd be picked up. There was a time when you could photograph body searching, but now they bring you in as well; they harass you unless you introduce yourself to them.
> The army would rather I left, the less publicity the better.[123]

Obtaining the army's permission to film does not guarantee an easy ride, and unsurprisingly the army does not permit the rougher end of its operations to be filmed. Television director Ian Stuttard, discussing the making of Thames TV's history series, *The Troubles*, said:

> They allowed me to film soldiers running around Ardoyne and places, and they allowed me to film in a base, from an observation point, and soldiers getting ready to go out . . . But things I wanted, I really wanted, like strong personal searches and house searches and so on, they wouldn't allow that . . .

The RUC, UDR and British army were, said Stuttard, 'fairly obstructive on the street':

> The procedure is that you inform them that you're going to be filming in the Lower Falls or Ballymurphy or wherever it may be, so that they know you're going to be in the area. But that doesn't seem to be good enough, because you get – I wouldn't say harassed – but they keep stopping you, going through your gear, checking you . . . You know, you go round one corner and get stopped, you go 300 yards, run into another bunch and get the same routine.[124]

In 1981, two photographers were injured by plastic bullets.[125] One of them was *Daily Mirror* photographer Cyril Cain, whose right leg was fractured in several places. A year later he was still on crutches, and would never be able to work as a news photographer again. While this may have been an accident, Cain expressed doubts. Two days before he was shot, the *Mirror* had printed one of his pictures on the front page, showing a soldier apparently engulfed in petrol bomb flames. Next day the *Mirror* carried a picture of the same soldier back on patrol, evidently unharmed. Derry freelance Trevor McBride, who took the second picture, said in fact the soldier 'hadn't been hurt at all – they put out the flames straight away.'[126] Cain told the NUJ paper, the *Journalist*,

There is a big question to be asked. Why, if the Army says the plastic bullet was brought in to replace the rubber bullet because it is so accurate, was a *Daily Mirror* photographer shot? . . .

The Army was very angry about the pictures. They thought they weren't the kind of publicity they wanted. Several TV journalists told me Army PRs had been asking after me that day.

It makes you wonder: where are we safe to work? The Press Card says we are approved by the police and security forces, but we are doing our job and get shot. It's bloody well not on.[127]

The RUC press office

As Ulsterisation progressed, the main responsibility for handling the press was transferred to the RUC. In February 1976, the army had had more than 40 press officers operating in the North.[128] By January 1981 there were 14 press officers for units on the ground, including the UDR, and six officers and a Defence Ministry official at the Lisburn press office.[129] In 1982 the status of the Lisburn office was formally downgraded when the lieutenant-colonel then in charge was replaced by a major.[130]

In around 1978, the army stopped providing a 24-hour service, reducing it first to 18 hours a day, and then to 12 hours, closing down at 6 p.m. At the same time, the RUC press office expanded, and began to work round the clock. Journalists who phoned the army requesting information about day-to-day incidents were now increasingly referred to the RUC.

Both agencies adopted a distinctly reticent approach towards supplying information. In December 1980, Thames TV producer Peter Gill wrote to *The Times* drawing attention to 'new, and quite unpublicized, restrictions' introduced earlier in the year by the army and RUC which meant that 'only the barest information on incidents is released'. 'There is in current force,' he wrote, 'an over-riding policy that Press attention on the Army's role in Northern Ireland should be kept to an absolute minimum.'[131]

Journalists generally regard the RUC's press office more highly than the army's. Situated in RUC headquarters at Knock in East Belfast, it was headed from around 1970 by a former journalist, Bill McGookin. One long-serving Belfast-based reporter with no love for the authorities said, 'The RUC has always been in my judgement far more reliable, far more accessible and far more agreeable about giving accurate information.'[132] Another praised McGookin and his colleagues for being 'very, very straight' and 'really excellent on factual details', but added that 'it was very difficult to tease sensitive stuff out of them'.[133] Like the army, however, the RUC gets into difficulties when it comes to accounting for their own violence. From 1976 to 1979, for example, the RUC consistently denied that suspects were being ill-treated during interrogation, and accounts given by the RUC of killings of republicans at the end of 1982 were widely queried.[134]

By 1982 there were 18 people in the RUC press office, of whom Bill McGookin and three others had journalistic experience. The office was next door to the RUC's central control room, so the staff had easy access to up-to-date information.[135]

At the end of 1982, the system was reorganized. The press office was integrated into the control room. Civilian press officers – though not Bill McGookin – were phased out, and uniformed officers now answered journalists' queries. Reporters phoning in now asked not for the press office, but for 'Force Control'.

Irish Times reporter Peter Murtagh described the control room:

> On one wall of a huge room with a high ceiling, there is a map of Northern Ireland about 20 feet high. Beside it are two maps of the North's motorways and the wall also has two large charts indicating precisely how many RUC reservists are available at any one time and where.
>
> There are eight console desks with phones, computer terminals and the room also has computer visual display units. The air is filled with the humming of electronic machinery at work.
>
> Operations are co-ordinated from a central console desk. This includes the confidential telephone line which is tape-recorded and never answered direct by staff. The desk also has a radio receiver which allows control to listen to every single radio transmission made by police anywhere in the North.
>
> Every RUC station has a message switching system, a means of communication similar to a telex. Information also arrives via radio and computer. A number of senior officers, the Chief Constable and some sections at headquarters have special visual display units into which selected important information is put, thus allowing them to follow events minute by minute.
>
> The entire system means that the RUC knows what is happening anywhere in the North before anyone else, save those directly involved.[136]

In theory, putting journalists in direct contact with control room staff should have allowed them to obtain information more quickly. But reporters were soon complaining that the reverse was happening. The uniformed officers, said one journalist, did not like the press, and it seemed, too, that there was now a tighter control over the release of information. It could take days or weeks for the RUC to confirm that incidents, which journalists had heard about from local sources, had taken place. In one case, it took three weeks for the RUC to confirm that a large booby-trap bomb had been found in County Tyrone.[137]

The Northern Ireland Office press office

Like the army and the RUC, the Northern Ireland Office has its own separate public relations organisation. Working closely with the Foreign Office, the Northern Ireland Office is concerned with projecting a favourable image abroad as well as in Britain and the Six Counties.

The Northern Ireland Office's press office comes under the control of the political affairs division, which until September 1982 was headed by an official seconded from the Foreign Office. Then Anthony Merrifield, from the Department of Health and Social Security, replaced Foreign Office man David Wyatt as political affairs chief. Merrifield's deputy, however, remained a Foreign Office official.[138]

Journalists rarely come into contact with the political officer, though political correspondents might occasionally take him out to lunch. The press deal mainly with the two principal press officers – one in London, running a small office, and the other in Belfast in charge of a much larger department – and their subordinates.

In the first years of the troubles, the Belfast press office was headed by Tommy Roberts, who had been Stormont Prime Minister Terence O'Neill's press officer. Roberts became press officer for the short-lived power-sharing executive, and died in the late seventies. Some Northern Ireland Secretaries brought their own press officers with them, a practice which stopped in the mid-seventies when David Gilliland became principal press officer. Gilliland, who was born in Derry, had worked as a journalist and, like Roberts, had served in the Stormont press office.

Below Gilliland are ten or so press officers, several of whom, including his deputy Bob Templeton, have also been in the press office a long time. Their job is mainly to supply journalists with routine information. A reporter explained, 'They'd ring you up and say, "Humphrey Atkins is on a walkabout in Belfast city centre, and there's a photo opportunity – send a photographer if you like." '[139] Statements are telexed out, then typed up on headed paper and delivered to newspaper offices in the city. The press office has a big support staff of secretaries, typists and photocopyists.

There is also a social secretary, whose job includes fixing up lunches and dinners for visiting reporters, at which they meet Northern Ireland Office press officers, local journalists, and others. Some reporters apparently ask the Northern Ireland Office to arrange the whole of their itineraries.

Any discussion on policy matters is handled by the principal press officer. A journalist explained that political correspondents and representatives of British papers phone David Gilliland every so often, and perhaps every couple of months take him out to lunch. He added:

> Occasionally you'd have a chat with the Secretary of State, and Gilliland would almost always be in on that. Humphrey Atkins gave us dinner a couple of times. He would pick out about six or eight journalists at a time, you'd have dinner, and he would come along and bring one of his ministers, and Gilliland would come with his deputy and some other civil servants. The general format is that there would be six reporters and six civil servants and ministers, and you would sit alternately round the dinner table and talk. And then perhaps at the end of the evening Humphrey would say a few words, and we'd ask him some questions.[140]

The principal press officer deals with journalists who are regarded as important. Those who are considered very important have no difficulty obtaining access to the Northern Ireland Secretary or his deputy. Most attention is paid to British and foreign 'quality' papers, and to British television companies. The Irish papers are not easily influenced, while the British 'pop' reporters 'write unbribed', as an Irish journalist put it.

One journalist described Gilliland as an 'old fox', who knew all the reporters from way back and understood how to handle them all, from the sophisticated sceptics to the drunks. Another reporter said,

> David Gilliland is extremely shrewd in his handling of the press in their relationship to the Secretary of State, and I think he does an excellent job for the government in making sure that Secretaries of

State are not allowed to get into dangerous hands journalistically, by making sure that what few press conferences they have are carefully controlled. Tape machines are very often excluded, so that any slip of the tongue is not going to be quite as easily recorded.[141]

Saying that he had experienced great difficulty in getting access to the Northern Ireland Secretary, the reporter went on:

I think they do a very good job from the government's standpoint of making sure that the Secretary of State has access to the television and radio reporters in a very carefully calculated way, so that there are individual interviews and very often by sympathetic reporters. That way he never runs into any real danger of being caught out or being given hard questioning.[142]

When reporters have been considered particularly hostile, the Northern Ireland Office has, as Anne McHardy put it, 'indulged in whispering campaigns' against them: 'Fleet Street editors have been offered lunch and warnings that Belfast reporters were becoming too partial to the wrong side.'[143] One victim was Andrew Stephen. When he moved from *The Observer* to *The Sunday Telegraph*, one of his new editors was invited to lunch by a senior Northern Ireland Office official who said Stephen was 'irresponsible', 'unhelpful' and 'misguided', and perhaps should be put on other stories. The official's approach was rejected, but could well have sown doubts in the editor's mind.[144]

Methods

The Northern Ireland Office has run extensive TV and press advertising campaigns aimed at persuading the public in the Six Counties to renounce 'terrorism'. In the early seventies, the huge and long-running 'Confidential telephone' campaign was launched, urging the public to inform on 'terrorists'. By 1974 the Northern Ireland Office was spending around £48,000 per year on this campaign, out of an advertising budget of roughly £80,000. '7 years is enough' was the theme of 1976, to which the republican riposte was '700 years is too much'. In 1978 the 'Check on your Children' campaign began, inviting parents to keep their children from the clutches of gunmen. By now, the spending had reached some £150,000 per year on advertising, while recruitment publicity was costing £160,000 per year for the police in press advertising alone, and £120,000 for the prison service.[145] A local advertising agency was used to design the material.

The Northern Ireland Office has also produced a variety of publications. For several years it published a monthly magazine called *Ulster Commentary*, which dated from Stormont days. Edited by a member of the press office staff, this promoted an optimistic view of life in the North and advertised achievements in industry. It was closed down at the start of the eighties.

In early 1979, apparently in response to hostile publicity in the States, the Northern Ireland Office published the first of several glossy booklets illustrating the supposed benefits of the prison system in the North. Large quantities of these were distributed free to the media and politicians at home and abroad. In 1981, trying to combat international criticism of the government's handling of the hunger strike, the Northern Ireland Office produced a booklet of quotations sympathetic to the government's line from British and foreign newspapers. In August and September that year, it distributed 'fact files' on the men then on hunger strike. Consisting of reproductions of newspaper articles on the hunger strikers' 'crimes and convictions', the 'fact files' were probably aimed at counteracting the media's use of sympathetic profiles that had been carried by *An Phoblacht/Republican News*.

At the same time, the Northern Ireland Office proved extremely reluctant to allow journalists into the H Blocks to assess the situation for themselves. The first republican prisoner went 'on the blanket', refusing to wear prison clothes or do prison work, in September 1976, and prisoners began refusing to wash or slop out in March 1978. But it was not until March 1979, after pressure from the American press, that journalists were allowed in. Even then, only a small group was let in, and they were not permitted to speak to the protesting prisoners.[146]

During 1980 and 1981, journalists wishing to interview the hunger strikers were met with blank refusal. In 1980, just one television interview with a hunger striker, done by Granada TV's *World in Action*, was permitted.[147] The interview, with hunger striker Ray McCartney, consisted of a single question and a single answer: no more were allowed. It was transmitted despite considerable opposition from Unionists, who tried to persuade both Prime Minister Thatcher and the IBA to ban it.[148]

In 1981, the Northern Ireland Office refused journalists

any access to the prisoners. At its annual conference that April, the National Union of Journalists pledged to ensure that during the Fermanagh-South Tyrone election campaign Bobby Sands would be 'accorded the same coverage and access to the media as the other candidate, Mr Harry West.'[149] The resolution proved fruitless, since the Northern Ireland Office refused to allow journalists to interview Bobby Sands, who therefore nominated four people to speak on his behalf. Sinn Fein was advised by lawyers that it had no legal remedy, even though the Representation of the People Act stipulates that broadcasters must observe strict impartiality between candidates.

Some journalists went to visit Bobby Sands and other prisoners on ordinary visitors' passes. But if their identity as journalists was discovered, they were required to sign a form saying that they would not publish anything about the visit. Bobby Sands' diary for 3 March[150] records a visit from David Beresford of *The Guardian* and Brendan O'Cathaoir of *The Irish Times*. Entering the prison as ordinary visitors, both were stopped and required to sign the form. Both nevertheless wrote articles, but whereas *The Irish Times* went ahead and published, *The Guardian* did not. One reporter who was made to sign the form complained that the practice meant journalists were discriminated against and accorded lesser privileges than the ordinary citizen: 'anybody else could have gone in, done an article and published it.'[151]

The Northern Ireland Office and the Foreign Office have also used more devious propaganda methods. In the early seventies, the Foreign Office's Information Research Department published an 80-page booklet, ostensibly anonymously produced, titled *The IRA and Northern Ireland – Aims Policy Tactics*. This was distributed to selected journalists and academics. According to the London magazine *Time Out*, which obtained a copy, it included 'derogatory biographies, complete with gossip, on leading Sinn Fein figures'.[152]

Interventions overseas

The government makes strenuous efforts to ensure that its case is heard overseas. The USA is the principal target, since it is the republicans' main foreign source of material and moral support.

In 1980 the Central Office of Information – a government organisation based in south London that employs over 1,100 people to produce publicity material[153] – began work on a propaganda film titled *Northern Ireland Chronicle*. The film was directed primarily at the USA,[154] and a Foreign Office spokesperson said it 'was commissioned in response to a number of requests from Foreign Office posts.'[155] The Foreign Office supplied the guidelines, while David Gilliland and Bob Templeton of the Northern Ireland Office press office advised the filmmakers.[156] At the start of 1981, it was reported that the film's budget was around £100,000: this was large by Central Office of Information standards, but small in comparison with the government's overall publicity expenditure, which totalled almost £100 million in 1980.[157]

The government's most powerful propaganda resource for influencing American opinion is the British Information Services agency, which is able to feed stories directly into radio networks across the United States. A BIS official in Britain's New York consulate explained in 1982:

> We have a satellite link with the Central Office of Information in London, and when a government minister makes an important statement of policy, and we think that it's newsworthy for our customers, we can feed it, if necessary live, as we did on many, many occasions during the hunger strike, and this July during the London bombings, direct through special lines into 10 radio networks. These 10 networks in turn service no less than 6,000 of the 9,000 radio stations in the country. And this means that we can put our policies right at the top of the news.[158]

The BIS spokesperson cited a tape which was used by 500 radio stations in the States after the London bombings in July 1982. This began with the announcer saying that 'nine people' had been killed – somewhat disingenuous, since all the dead were soldiers – and went on to reproduce Prime Minister Thatcher's condemnation of the 'callous and cowardly crimes'. The spokesperson said he had been happy with the item 'because the Prime Minister's views were right at the top of the news and her absolute condemnation received great prominence here.'[159]

Patrick Nixon, head of BIS in New York, said that Northern Ireland was the biggest single item of British policy that he was called on to explain. He said:

> We keep in very close touch with the editorial writers and foreign editors of all the leading papers. Our job is to know the opinion-formers, and brief them on British policy. There's a whole variety

of activities we engage in. We have our own printing press so that we can mail material to all the leading newspapers around the country.[160]

In 1981, Northern Ireland Office anxiety over hostile publicity following Bobby Sands' death was such that in late June its two most senior press officers, David Gilliland and Bob Templeton, went to the States themselves, 'with a brief to counter H-Blocks propaganda among diplomats in New York and Washington.'[161]

The Foreign Office also exerts its influence to try to stop the dissemination of material critical of British policy. In 1978, for example, a painting by Conrad Atkinson titled *Silver Liberties*, which linked torture in the Six Counties with police brutality in South Africa and in Britain, was shown in a Paris exhibition. British ambassador Nicholas Henderson complained to the British Council that it should not have supported such a work. Two years later Henderson, by now ambassador in Washington, complained again when the same work was exhibited in the States.[162]

The Patriot Game, a pro-republican film by American socialist Arthur MacCaig, considerably upset the British government. Launched in 1979, it was acclaimed at several European film festivals before being shown in London that June.[163] Then on 7 March 1980 it was shown on Belgian television. On 11 March the Belgian Minister of Foreign Affairs, Mr Simonet, went to London for talks with British Foreign Secretary Lord Carrington. Simonet subsequently wrote to the Belgian Minister for the Dutch Community saying that in the course of the discussion:

> Lord Carrington complained about the fact that Belgian television had shown a programme which constitutes an apology for Irish terrorism without leaving any room for the moderate tendency in Northern Ireland. The British minister for foreign affairs . . . was of the opinion that this programme should be considered not as objective information but as one-sided propaganda to the benefit of the IRA . . .
>
> For my part, I must of course express regret for any one-sided report which is harmful to the international relations of our country. In fact, I have often had occasion to observe how sensitive those countries who have had to deal with terrorism are to any manifestation abroad, which could be considered as a justification or apology for terrorism.[164]

The Minister for the Dutch Community then sent a copy of this letter to the Director-General of the Belgian television service, accompanied by a memo saying, 'I would like to ask you to give this complaint your careful consideration and to send me a full report on the broadcasting of this film.'[165] What transpired after this has not been revealed, but it seems likely that in future Belgian television would be more cautious about transmitting similar material.

The Belgian television broadcast also prompted Peter Baldwin of the Foreign Office's Overseas Information Department to send a circular to information officers in British embassies round the world warning them against *The Patriot Game*. In the view of the information officer in Brussels, wrote Baldwin, the film 'gave a quite unashamedly one-sided presentation which is tantamount to pure PIRA propaganda'. Implicitly suggesting that the information officers should exert their influence to try to stop the film winning awards, Baldwin wrote: 'While the film itself may have technical merit which deserves recognition, any awards would undoubtedly enhance a production which is damaging and highly critical of HMG.'[166] When the film was shown the following year on French television, ambassador Sir Reginald Hibbert was 'reportedly furious that it was allowed.'[167]

Such protests are not confined to independent films bought in by television companies. In June 1980, *The Sun* reported that the government was considering protesting to the major American television company, ABC, over a film called *To Die for Ireland*. In the film, complained *The Sun*, 'British troops in Ulster were depicted as oppressors who had no right to be there.'[168]

Republican publicity

In the years before 1981, journalists very occasionally gave their readers glimpses of republican publicists, usually in articles describing the public relations efforts of all sides. Thus in 1980, implying that reporters are subjected to equal pressure from all quarters, *The Guardian*'s Anne McHardy wrote, 'Spokesmen from all sides offer chatty company and hospitality and expect sympathetic reporting in return. The Provisionals and the UDA offer tea and buns, the NIO and the Army gin and tonic and dinner.' She added that the Provisionals were better publicists than other paramilitaries, since they 'have the advantage of a romantic history and a fund of well-known traditional songs to soften people up.'[169]

During the 1981 hunger strike, however, as Bobby Sands neared death, the British authorities and media invested the republican publicists with extraordinary powers, crediting them with having concocted almost from nothing the enormous local and international sympathy for the hunger strikers. The notion of the 'Provisionals' propaganda machine – indefatigable, never resting', as *The Observer* described it,[170] was itself a propaganda device, designed to reassure the world that the British government was in the right, but helpless against the duplicity and superhuman efficiency of the 'enemy'. Concrete descriptions of the 'machine', which would have spoilt the impression by revealing the mundane reality, were eschewed.

Development of the press centre

The republican movement has its headquarters in Dublin, but Belfast republicans inevitably became the more important source of information on day-to-day developments. They were in the thick of things and, unlike their colleagues in other parts of the North, were close to the offices of the main media organisations. Their publicity work, however, developed in an ad hoc manner and was not treated as a priority.

The Belfast Republican Press Centre and the paper *Republican News* were started in 1970 by a handful of people centred around veteran republican Jimmy Steele.[171] Steele died in August the same year. The Press Centre was a very loose arrangement, with no fixed headquarters nor formal meetings. It put out statements to the media which were delivered by hand to the various offices in the city.[172] Reporters relied for information mainly on informal contacts with leading republicans such as Sinn Fein Vice-President Maire Drumm, who was assassinated by loyalists in 1976, and in the mid-seventies with Belfast organiser Seamus Loughran, who fell from grace within the movement when radicals gained the ascendancy in Belfast.[173] There were occasional IRA press conferences, clandestine affairs which were, according to *Guardian* reporter Simon Hoggart, 'usually marked by considerable confusion'.[174] Hoggart described one such press conference in 1972, when the Provisionals invited the Irish press and two British papers to meet Seamus Twomey, then the officer commanding the Belfast Brigade:

> This was a great cloak and dagger operation, with people arriving at staggered times, and ostensibly going to see a homeless family's

relief centre. Unfortunately for the IRA, the word got out, and so the hall was besieged with reporters, making it quite obvious to any passing army patrol what was going on. Mr Twomey arrived very late, and seemed not quite aware of what he was supposed to do.[175]

After Operation Motorman in July 1972, when the British army moved in strength into the nationalist districts and destroyed the no-go areas, press conferences were generally restricted to Dublin.

The first issue of *Republican News*, then a monthly bulletin with eight A4-sized pages, appeared in June 1970.[176] The main 'Provisional' republican paper was the Dublin-based *An Phoblacht*, which started after the movement split at the end of 1969. The 'Officials' retained the original paper, *United Irishman*.

Republican News was started to cater for Belfast republican circles. As its first editorial pointed out, it followed a long tradition of Belfast republican journals, most of which were eventually banned under Special Powers legislation.[177] The editorial, written by Jimmy Steele, promised:

> We shall preach the Gospel of Tone in seeking to unite all our people, Protestant, Catholic and Dissenter in the common cause of our Nation's unity and independence. We shall condemn and denounce from whatever quarter it may seek to raise its ugly head, the monster of religious bigotry and intolerance.
>
> The socialism of James Connolly, the idealism of Patrick Pearse and the unrepentant Republicanism of Tom Clarke, we shall try to inculcate into our people – pointing out to them the rugged freedom road which they travelled in that service.[178]

The paper was produced and printed secretly. Production and distribution difficulties increased after the internment swoops of August 1971, in which some members of the paper's editorial board were arrested.[179] Nonetheless, the two remaining board members started producing the paper weekly from the end of September 1971.

By August 1972 the paper was extending its appeal beyond Belfast, calling itself the 'voice of Republican Ulster'.[180] In April 1974 it changed to newspaper format, with eight large pages.[181]

The years 1974 and 1975 brought developments that had a significant impact on republican publicity. In the early years, the nationalist community had been relatively monolithic, with members of the middle class making militant gestures – the SDLP, for example, initiated the rent-and-rates strike against intern-ment – and taking an ambivalent attitude towards the IRA except when its operations had particularly horrendous results. The SDLP's participation in the power-sharing executive meant the end of nationalist homogeneity. Papers such as *The Irish News* followed the SDLP line, and some republicans felt it necessary to mount a more effective challenge to them.[182]

At the end of the summer of 1974, Belfast republicans took over the first and second floors of a dilapidated building in the Falls Road, number 170. This was to become their main Belfast office, and remained so until the Northern Ireland Housing Executive, which owned the building, evicted them and they moved across the road to an equally ramshackle building in June 1980. In the autumn of 1974 a telex machine was installed in number 170, which became known as the Republican Press Centre, and by mid-1975 was the official address for *Republican News*.

The truce between the British army and the IRA, which began on 11 February 1975 and petered out at the end of the year, brought more changes. During 1974 detainees, politicised by their experiences, had begun to be released from the intern-ment camps. With the truce, a few of the radicals who might otherwise have centred their activities on the IRA, became in-volved in agitational work.[183] At the same time, the Press Centre, along with other republican offices in the North, acquired a new status when it became the main Belfast 'incident centre' for monitoring truce violations, equipped with a direct telephone line to British officials.

The office, run at the time by Tom Hartley, began to be a focus for the press and for foreign support groups, supplanting the previous informal network. The telex machine was put to increasing use, and became a crucial tool, allowing republicans to convey their version of incidents immediately to the press, and for the first time enabling them to compete seriously with the various British public relations operations.

Republican News also underwent changes. These were in part the result of the developing polarisation of the 'Provisionals' into left-wing and right-wing camps. The dispute focussed on the right's support for federalism, a policy which advocated that the government of Ireland should be based on four regional parli-aments, one in each of the historic provinces. This arrangement would leave loyalists with considerable power in Ulster – an idea which pleased the right and alarmed the left. There were clashes over the content of *Republican News* between the Belfast republican leadership and its editor, Sean Caughey. On one occasion, apparently, a whole edition of the paper was burned on IRA orders because Caughey had printed a claim from an anonymous Catholic paramilitary group that they would bomb Protestant schoolchildren. The printing plates were then altered and the paper was reprinted without the offending piece.[184] In mid-1975 Sean Caughey lost his job and Danny Morrison, who had been among the internees released in 1974, took over as editor.

Raids on *Republican News*

In December 1977 the British authorities, by now intent on presenting republicans as 'criminals', launched the first in a series of raids on *Republican News*. At around 2.30 a.m. on Thursday 15 December, some 400 RUC men raided several Sinn Fein advice centres in Belfast, the press in Lurgan where *Republican News* was printed, and the homes of 36 republicans. Fifteen people were arrested, including printer Gary Kennedy – a member of the SDLP – and several senior Sinn Fein personnel. Danny Morrison and Tom Hartley, the editor and business manager of *Republican News*, were 'not at home' and escaped arrest.

RUC men, accompanied by British soldiers, stripped the Press Centre, removing all the office equipment, posters, and the paper's photo-library. The telex machine – which, fortunately for the republicans, was hired from the post office – was thrown out of an upstairs window into an army truck. At the printshop in Lurgan, the RUC seized that week's edition of *Republican News*, along with the following week's edition, which had been prepared early for Christmas, and 12,000 1978 republican calendars.

Labour Northern Ireland Secretary Roy Mason had repeatedly attacked the media that year for allegedly assisting the republicans, and in the same week as the raids he lambasted a BBC *Tonight* report on the IRA.[185] David McKittrick, then Northern editor of *The Irish Times*, wrote in a report on the raids that 'according to reliable sources in Belfast' the British authorities were hopeful of bringing charges against some of those arrested and also hoped that *Republican News* could be closed down. 'Mr Mason,' noted McKittrick, 'appears to take exception to the existence of a fairly well-produced Provisional Republican weekly newspaper.'[186]

But the paper re-emerged the same week with a defiant one-page edition.[187] The next week, a replacement for the confiscated Christmas edition was on the streets.[188] All those arrested were released after three days without charge. There were two further raids in the next fortnight, in which Danny Morrison and Tom Hartley were among those arrested. Both were released after being held for some days in Castlereagh interrogation centre.

There was another major raid in the early hours of 27 April 1978 – again a Thursday, the day the paper came off the presses. Again the targets were republican personnel, Sinn Fein offices, including the press centre, and the press in Lurgan. Fifteen people were arrested, of whom 12 were charged with either or both IRA membership and conspiracy to pervert the course of justice – a reference to plans to set up a system of community courts. Those charged included the entire officer board of Belfast Sinn Fein, *Republican News* workers, printer and SDLP member Gary Kennedy, and a French photographer, Alain Frilet. The RUC confiscated 30,000 copies of a four-page *Republican News* supplement on the H Blocks from the printshop.

Again, *Republican News* reappeared immediately with an emergency edition,[189] and by the end of April was again coming out weekly. It was now being produced 'on the run', from the houses of sympathisers. Gary Kennedy's printing business was now in jeopardy – advertising from unionist sources had stopped[190] – and the printing of *Republican News* was shifted to the South. Those arrested were eventually released on bail, and in February 1979 the charges against them were dropped for lack of evidence.[191]

As *Republican News* developed it had come into increasing competition with the official paper of the movement, *An Phoblacht*. The latter was far less militant, and the existence of the two papers emphasised the division between the Northern radicals and the more conservative Southerners. By the end of 1977, the Belfast team were pushing for a merger, but the raids and arrests delayed the negotiations. The two finally merged in January 1979, with the Northerners taking over the editorial direction of the new paper. In effect, *Republican News* swallowed up *An Phoblacht*.[192]

The setting up of the Falls Road centre also stimulated the production of other publicity material, especially posters. During the hunger strikes of 1980 and 1981, output increased. At the end of 1980, republicans produced their first video, an hour-long exposition of the background to the prison protest. This was shown in republican clubs and at meetings north and south of the border. This increase in the production of posters, badges and pamphlets in 1981 led to the formation of a new department, Republican Publications, to handle distribution. Staffed by two or three volunteers, Republican Publications is housed in a bunker-like shop in Turf Lodge. The material is produced almost entirely for local use, and most is not subsidised. As with *An Phoblacht/Republican News*, costs are expected to be met through sales.

Veracity

There have been far fewer specific complaints by journalists about the accuracy of republican statements than about the accuracy of statements from the British army press office in its heyday. Nor is there any evidence that republicans have engaged in 'black propaganda' operations.

Republicans freely admit that until the mid-seventies the IRA issued exaggerated claims about the numbers of soldiers they had killed or injured in particular incidents. These, they consider, were partly due to over-optimistic assessments by the IRA personnel involved, compounded by the confusion that surrounds such incidents. Eventually *Republican News* began refusing to publish such claims unless the number of victims was confirmed by other sources.[193]

However from the early days republicans appear to have adopted a policy of admitting to violent actions that had 'gone wrong', despite the negative propaganda effects. A senior republican said, 'The IRA realised very early on that telling the truth was the best policy because it gave them credibility. The IRA claimed actions that went wrong, so people believed them when they said they had not done something.'[194]

That this policy existed in the early seventies is supported by a front-page editorial in *Republican News* following the Abercorn restaurant bombing in March 1972. The authorities blamed the IRA for the bombing, in which two people were killed and some 130 injured, but both the 'Official' and 'Provisional' IRA denied it. *Republican News* printed an impassioned article condemning the 'horrible crime'. It supported the IRA's denial by listing several actions which the 'Provisional' and 'Official' IRAs had admitted though the actions 'were liable to be misunderstood by their own supporters and . . . were bound to be misrepresented by their enemies.'[195] These included a 'Provisional' shooting of a member of a wedding party and the bombing by the 'Officials' of a barracks at Aldershot in which seven civilians were killed. *Republican News* went on to contrast this 'record of truth' with a series of lies told by the British army and RUC. Inside, it reproduced a page from a bulletin issued by the loyalist UDA, in which the Abercorn was mentioned as one of many 'rebel establishments' in which the national anthem was not played and which loyalists were asked to boycott.[196]

The same month, the 'Provisionals' admitted responsibility for the widely condemned Donegall Street bombing and in July said they were responsible for the 'Bloody Friday' bombings which again resulted in civilian deaths and many injuries. In both cases the IRA said that warnings had been given. Down the years, the IRA continued to admit to such tragedies – though the circumstances of the 1974 Birmingham bombings remain unclarified – despite the fact that they alienated its supporters and provided ammunition for the British propagandists: the Central Office of Information film, *Northern Ireland Chronicle*, for example, is punctuated by gruesome footage of the aftermath of bombings such as those of Bloody Friday and the incineration of the La Mon restaurant in February 1978. Following La Mon, the IRA said in a statement that 'our supporters . . . have rightly and severely criticised us.'[197]

There were exceptions, however. These appear to have been mostly in the early seventies, and mainly concerned killings of alleged informers and, during the spate of sectarian killings in 1975, those of Protestants.[198] The IRA did not deny such killings, but simply refrained from claiming them. In later years there were far fewer incidents in which Protestants were killed solely on sectarian grounds, and the IRA began more often to claim killings of alleged informers. A departure from this was the killing of Peter Valente in November 1980. Valente was killed during the first H Block hunger strike, and had a brother 'on the blanket' in the H Blocks. Apparently in order not to cause demoralisation among anti-H Block campaigners, the IRA said nothing at the time, and did not contradict the general belief that he was a victim of loyalists.[199] Soon after the start of the 1981 hunger strike, Chris Ryder revealed in a *Sunday Times* piece, evidently based on information from the RUC, that Valente had been an informer.[200] Ten months later the IRA – then offering an amnesty to informers – finally admitted they had killed Valente, 'an IRA volunteer . . . who was a central RUC informer for a number of years'.[201]

Republican publicists working from the Belfast press centre appear to have a reasonably good reputation for veracity among journalists, though qualified by the acceptance that any organisation is bound to attempt to present its affairs in a favourable light. A journalist who reported for some years from Belfast for a British paper said that while he rarely spoke to the British army, neither the RUC nor the republicans had ever to his knowledge given him a 'bum steer'. An Irish journalist said, 'Sometimes they won't tell you things, but what they tell you is almost always true.' But one said bluntly, 'There's nobody in Northern Ireland who's going to tell you the truth – they'll all tell you from the point of view of their agency,' while another Irish reporter complained that the republicans, like the Northern Ireland Office, had given him misleading information during the 1981 hunger strike.[202]

Such complaints, heard during both the 1980[203] and 1981 hunger strikes, centred on republicans glossing over their difficulties and, in particular, saying that the 1981 hunger strike was not coming to an end at a time when in fact it was. Questioned about this, a republican spokesperson responded with some amusement:

> I see nothing wrong with that. I mean you have to have an expedient position if you're trying to hold a line. You have the position where every year, absolutely every year, reporters come to you after the closed session of the ard fheis [annual conference] and say, 'Was there a statement from the IRA read out?' And everybody categorically denies it. It's routine. Now that's stating that without prejudice to the fact whether or not a statement is actually read out! There you have a perfect paradox!
>
> You have to operate like that. It's like the Official Unionists saying there's no split inside the Official Unionists – when Harold McCusker is challenging Molyneaux for the leadership.
>
> It's obviously for defensive reasons that one gets into ambivalence. Where it's more important to hold the organisation together, you may have to brazen your way through something – expediently, but in the overall interests of the struggle or of a particular section of the movement.[204]

Relations with journalists

In his book *The Media and Political Violence*,[205] former British army major-general Richard Clutterbuck asserts: 'the investigative reporter can probe the army or police with no risk more serious than forfeiting their co-operation, but if he attempted a similar probe into a terrorist organisation he would forfeit his life.'

In fact no journalists have been killed in the North by 'terrorists', and there are no recorded instances of any being injured by the Provisional IRA. Indeed, the British army has arguably proved more dangerous to journalists, by using undercover operatives equipped with phoney press cards and by shooting photographers with plastic bullets.

When, in an isolated case, a reporter was beaten up in Belfast in March 1983, the violence came from another source. Alan Rusbridger reported in *The Guardian*,

> John Hicks of the *Daily Mirror* was attacked by three men as he was drinking in a bar and severely knocked about. It is thought this was in retaliation for an article he had written about Mr Eamon 'Hatchet' Kerr, a Worker's Party member who was shot dead in his bed at the end of last week. Mr Hicks had not been too respectful towards Mr Kerr, a renowned hit man in his day.
>
> NUJ officials are extremely disturbed at the attack, for, although many journalists working in the province have been given verbal threats, it has been very rare for any kind of physical violence or intimidation to have been used.[206]

One journalist who was threatened by the Provisionals was Chris Ryder of *The Sunday Times*. His colleague David Blundy, testifying in his defence in a libel suit taken by the Andersonstown Co-operative, said that in late 1976 or early 1977 Seamus Loughran had told him 'that Mr Ryder's presence would not be welcome and said if he came into the area he would get his head blown off.' Blundy explained, reported *The Irish Times*, that 'The Provos had been unhappy about articles written by Mr Ryder about IRA extortion.'[207]

Since then, with the centralisation of press relations in the Falls Road centre, it seems there has been no repetition of such incidents. Republicans stress that they will assist any journalist, even those who are flagrantly pro-British, but with the reservation that they would not help a reporter whom they believed to be a 'Brit agent'.

Improvements

Ironically for the British, the raids in 1977 and 1978 inadvertently contributed to improving the republicans' public relations work. Before the raids, people who worked in the press centre had kept their identities secret from outsiders, refusing to give their real names to journalists or to be photographed. Now, however, their names were in the newspapers. Danny Morrison explained:

> Up until then, for the sake of one's family, for the sake of one's personal security, we had been operating with aliases. So the Brits actually forced our hand . . and of course once it was done, we saw the advantages of it, in terms of increasing our credibility, increasing our profile, especially in the media, because they would now come and talk to a named, known person . . . It was a centre of gravity for them, and they could relate to that.[208]

The prospect of being in the spotlight did not make liaising with the press a popular area of work. Richard McAuley, who took over from Joe Austin as the movement's Belfast press officer in 1980, said:

> Most people don't want to do PR work because it's very dangerous. It's dangerous in two senses. It heightens your public profile and could lead you to getting stiffed by loyalists or put out of the road by the Brits. It's also dangerous in that if you say the wrong thing – and I have made some cracking boobs over the years – you can embarrass yourself and embarrass the movement.[209]

From mid-1980, the press centre was located in a small, spartan room in number 51–53 Falls Road, a shabby building with minimal facilities. It shared the upper floor with the Belfast Sinn Fein office and the prisoners' welfare department, while the ground floor was used as a waiting room for prisoners' relatives and friends awaiting transport to the prisons. The press centre's equipment was limited to a desk, a phone – the bills apparently paid by *Republican News* as the centre has no funds allocated to it[210] – and a telex machine in a tiny room nearby. It had one volunteer staffing it full-time, though other senior Sinn Fein personnel could be called on to do interviews, and other workers in the building assisted in answering the phone. Richard McAuley was scarcely exaggerating when, during the 1981 hunger strike, he said to American journalist Neil Hickey, 'Do you know the sum total of the famous Republican propaganda machine that everybody talks about? . . . I'm it.'[211]

The movement's press officer works in the same way as any other public relations person, answering queries from reporters, giving interviews, and arranging for journalists to meet other people or visit different areas.

One difference, however, from the usual public relations pattern, is that neither the press officer nor leading republicans will accept invitations from journalists for meals. Although some journalists have expressed resentment of this, evidently feeling snubbed by such refusals, republicans say that to accept such invitations would not only put them under an obligation to the journalist concerned, but would compromise them in the eyes of the movement if the reporter subsequently produced a hostile story or damaging 'leak'.

With the 1981 hunger strike, republican public relations began to become less reliant on the Falls Road centre. Journalists for the first time travelled regularly to districts other than Belfast and Derry. The process of decentralisation was accelerated by the 1982 Assembly elections, when Sinn Fein offices mushroomed throughout the North, particularly in those areas where Sinn Fein candidates had been elected. Offices outside Belfast now increasingly handled press queries about their areas themselves, with the Falls Road centre acting as a conduit when required.

Republicans have never prioritised press relations. The improvements they have made – except for the acquisition of the telex machine – have been largely a by-product of other developments. Such publicity as they have won has come less through the publicists' efforts than through the impetus of events: the 1981 hunger strike went virtually disregarded until Bobby Sands' election to Westminster. Once the media became interested, the existence of the press office doubtless helped, but it was not a determining factor. 'I've always felt the Provos are really bad at propaganda,' said a journalist working from Belfast for a British paper. 'I thought it was one of their great failures of the hunger strike that they didn't exploit it in the way they should have.' He went on to quote examples of events which the republicans could have drawn to the attention of the press, but did not.[212]

Republicans cannot, in any case, hope to match the facilities and finance available to the Northern Ireland Office, RUC and army press offices. Even if they could, it is doubtful whether this would win them a good press in Britain: the ties between the media and the authorities are too strong. In Ireland, as elsewhere, the anti-colonial cause is unlikely to win the British media's respect until it is on the verge of victory.

Conclusion

The record of British media coverage of Ireland has been far from heroic. Those in positions of power, both in government and in the media, have proved most reluctant to provide a full picture of events in the North or their context, and have made considerable efforts to prevent journalists, dramatists and film-makers from exploring the situation from any angle other than that favoured by the British establishment. While the authorities have not promoted the triumphalism of a full-blown war – as in the South Atlantic campaign – they have also not shown the openness to investigation that might be expected if they were genuinely engaged in a peace-keeping operation. Instead, Britain's activities in the North have been handled like guilty secrets.

Indeed, since the mid-seventies, the whole situation there has been kept in the shadows. With the Ulsterisation of security policy came the Ulsterisation of information. News and political analysis has been contained within the borders of the Six Counties, spilling over into Britain only rarely: when the authorities or media have wanted to promote a particular trend, as with the 1976 'peace people', or when nationalist disaffection has forced the pace, as with the hunger strikes of 1980 and 1981, with shootings and bombings, especially in Britain, and with the election of republicans to Parliament. Even when such events hijack the headlines, they are reported in an inadequate and partial way: explanation and context are omitted, and the 'human angle' is explored only in so far as it affects British people – or their dogs and horses. The British public is generally allowed to see only the worst of the 'enemy's' side and the best of their own. As a result, cause and effect become topsy-turvy – IRA violence comes to appear the alpha and omega of the problem, and Britain's historical and contemporary responsibility is obscured.

The resulting mixture of ignorance and prejudice makes it difficult for British people – who after all hold the purse strings and sanction government policy with their votes – to participate in rational discussion about how to resolve the situation. It helps, too, to preserve the gulf between how the British see themselves and how they are seen by many people abroad.

Even the ways in which information is controlled are known to, and discussed by, only a minority of the population, mainly journalists and people campaigning on Ireland. For over a decade, Ireland has been the most closely controlled issue on British television. The special rules and restrictions that have been adopted could well be extended in future to the coverage of other 'sensitive' topics. Since these controls – which affect all areas, from news to drama – are exercised within the labyrinths of the broadcasting organisations, they remain invisible to the public at large. The few decide what the majority will see and hear of the most profound conflict affecting their nation, and the majority remain unaware even that such decisions are being taken.

That said, from time to time discomfiting questions about Britain's role in Ireland have been raised on television and in the press. That this is so, has been almost entirely due to a few determined souls who have been willing to brave the establishment's wrath – and, in some cases, risk their careers – in the belief that their duty, as journalists, required them to portray the situation as they saw it and not to act simply as the mouthpieces of the powerful. Such journalists and film-makers, assisted by a few television critics and other media professionals, generated persistent criticism which helped, among other things, to bring the two major history series to the screen in 1980–81. The widespread awareness, in progressive media circles at least, of the failings of the Irish coverage also prompted the new Channel 4 to give some space to Ireland, albeit usually in off-peak times. Ominously, however, it was rumoured in late 1983 that Channel 4 commissioning editors were being told to 'lay off Ireland'.

The 'system' is not – yet – monolithic and protest can produce results. Though the broadcasting chiefs respond more readily to pressure from the establishment – which hands out the cash, orchestrates the sound and fury of the headlines, and generally shares a similar world view – they are not impervious to criticism from their employees or the public. Their credibility, after all, is at stake. So it is worth phoning the broadcasting companies to complain about – or praise – programmes, and writing to editors, journalists and producers suggesting topics they ought to cover. Unless the public intrudes itself on them, broadcasters listen only to their colleagues.

It is worth, too, protesting to the 'quality' papers about the slimness and superficiality of their coverage, about the way some of their reporters periodically become vehicles for British propaganda, and about the narrow perceptions of their leader writers, who, it seems, derive their views largely from tête-à-têtes with secretaries of state and certain leading 'moderate' Irish politicians.

The 'pop' papers are a lost cause. Along with *The Daily Telegraph*, the tabloids have been in the forefront of the campaign to stifle television coverage of the North. Their articles on Ireland, as on other issues, have more in common with works of fiction – such as thrillers and romances – than with reporting actuality. Their leader writers are unlikely to be converted from their splenetic jingoism until the establishment as a whole decides it has come to the end of the line in Ireland. The *Daily Mirror* is a partial exception. Its editorials have consistently advocated disengagement from Ireland, but its day-to-day reporting is little different from *The Sun*'s, and in any case it saves most of its Irish news for its Irish edition.

The record of the media unions is undistinguished. The film and television technicians' union, the ACTT, has sporadically taken action when its members have been directly threatened over films on Ireland. But hampered by its unionist members in the Six Counties, and by the lack of awareness among its British membership, the ACTT has failed to mount a consistent challenge to the censorship and controls exercised by the broadcasting companies. The National Union of Journalists has done better, passing resolutions at successive conferences condemning censorship and calling for improvements in the coverage. But the members who so enthusiastically back the resolutions are not, it seems, the people who actually write or edit the copy on the North. So NUJ policy has had no discernible effect on the reportage, though it has helped to raise awareness of the problem within media circles.

Protests from the public can pay off, and indeed have done so. But given the way television coverage hangs on the coat-tails of the establishment, substantial change can only be expected when British policy towards the North shifts radically, or when there is a major split in the political arena over what policy should be pursued.

The issue of Ireland is too important to be left to the vagaries of professional politicians and the media. It is essential that people take it on themselves to find out what is going on. This is not impossible. Irish papers, as well as 'alternative' publications and films, are available in Britain. Efforts can be made to build up such sources of information and analysis and circulate them more widely. Teachers and students can press for Ireland to be studied in schools and colleges. People can also join, or organise, fact-finding trips to Ireland, North and South.

To become informed is the first step towards taking an active part in trying to resolve a conflict whose history goes back hundreds of years and which continues to generate incalculable hardship and suffering. British people must, in the end, carry the responsibility for the policy their government pursues: they pay the piper and could, if they wished, call an end to the tune. Whatever the shortcomings of the coverage and the secretiveness of the authorities, it is possible for people to take the initiative and seek out the information for themselves. Ireland is, after all, only next door.

Appendix: Television programmes on the North of Ireland banned, censored or delayed

Note: Entries marked ******* describe events which were important but did not involve censorship of particular programmes, and occurred after the completion of the main text of this book.

1959 — BBC — *See It Now (Ed Murrow talk show)*
Lord Brookeborough, then Prime Minister of Northern Ireland, personally intervened to secure the dropping of the second of two interviews with actress Siobhán McKenna, because she had, in the first, described IRA internees in the Republic as 'young idealists'.

1959 — BBC — *Tonight*
Seven 10-minute reports by Alan Whicker about the Six Counties were dropped after Lord Brookeborough personally intervened. Eight reports were planned, but only the first was transmitted: its subject was betting shops, but passing references to the political situation led to a major row and the banning of the succeeding reports.

July 1966 — ITV — *This Week*
A programme which depicted Ian Paisley as a tub-thumping bible basher was not allowed to be shown in the North of Ireland.

June 1968 — BBC
The BBC refused to do a feature programme about Austin Currie's protest occupation of a Dungannon council house which had been allocated to an unmarried Unionist. This became a *cause celebre* within the BBC.

1970 — BBC
The BBC commissioned Jim Allen to write a contemporary play about the North of Ireland, to be directed by Ken Loach and produced by Tony Garnett. It was about the politics of the Officials and the Provisionals, and the BBC stopped it when the script was partially written. Allen went on the write a film script, *The Rising*, for Kestrel Films about the 1919-21 war against Britain. A Swedish company agreed to put up more than half the money providing some money could be raised in England, but no English company would finance it.

July 1970 — BBC — *Panorama*
This programme included interviews with relatives of six people killed in Belfast. BBC Northern Ireland 'opted out' on the grounds that the programme was inflammatory. This was the first such 'opting out': BBC policy was that programmes should be identical in Britain and the North of Ireland.

February 1971 — BBC — *24 Hours*
A film which showed widespread disenchantment among Unionists with Northern Ireland Prime Minister Major Chichester Clark was delayed by BBC NI Controller Waldo Maguire. When the predicted resignation took place, the film became superfluous and was never shown.

August 1971 — BBC — *24 Hours*
Senior BBC executives prevented 24 Hours from doing an in-depth programme about the IRA. (*Private Eye*, 15.11.71.)

October 1971 — BBC
The BBC filmed the proceedings of the Assembly of the Northern Irish People, set up by the SDLP and the Nationalist Party as an alternative to the Stormont Parliament. The footage was never shown, possibly because it was deemed 'unbalanced'. (*The Sunday Times*, 2.1.72)

November 1971 — Granada — *World in Action: 'South of the Border'*
Granada wanted to do a programme showing how the 'troubles' in the North were building up pressures in the South of Ireland. The film included Seán Mac Stiofáin (Provisional IRA Chief of Staff) and Ruairí Ó Brádaigh (Provisional Sinn Fein President), and also Dublin politicians who were hostile to the IRA. The Independent Television Authority banned the programme before it was completed. Granada went ahead and completed the programme, but, on viewing it, the ITA confirmed the ban.

1971 — ITN
ITN suppressed a film about an army post surrounding a lone policeman on the Creggan estate in Derry.

November 1971 — BBC — *24 Hours*
The BBC filmed a number of statements by ex-internees about their treatment by the British army during detention. Despite the mounting evidence of torture carried in the press, the BBC delayed screening the films until after the publication of the Compton Report. The films were balanced by a discussion between Tory MP Anthony Buck and former Labour Defence Minister, Roy Hattersley.

February 1972 — Thames — *This Week: 'Aftermath of Bloody Sunday' (also titled 'Bloody Sunday — Two Sides of the Story')*
Thames was preparing a story piecing together, through interviews with witnesses and soldiers, the story of Bloody Sunday in Derry. When the Widgery inquiry was announced, 10 Downing Street sought a blanket ban on media coverage. Thames compromised by showing a complete unedited roll of an interview with a Welsh ex-warrant officer, who lived in the area, balanced by a complete roll of accounts by Scottish paratroopers (one of whom, a lieutenant, later admitted to the Widgery Tribunal that his statement in the film that he had seen a gunman was a lie). Twenty rolls of film, including interviews with Catholic Bogsiders, were never used: these contained more damaging material.

August 1972 — BBC — *Panorama: 'Operation Motorman'*
A Panorama team, with reporter Alan Hart and producer William Cran, went into Creggan Heights in Derry on 31 July alongside the Coldstream Guards, as the British army stormed the 'no-go' areas. They later interviewed local people about their reactions. The film was suppressed by a senior executive.

2 October 1972 — BBC — *Play for Today: 'Carson Country'*
This play by Dominic Behan about 'the origin of the Stormont state' was postponed from May, and finally transmitted on 23 October, 'to avoid provoking possible trouble during the marching season'. (*Evening Standard*, 11.5.72) David Attenborough, Controller of TV programmes, and NI Controller Waldo Maguire made the decision.

November 1972 — Thames — *Armchair Theatre: 'The Folk Singer'*
The IBA asked to view this play by Dominic Behan, about a Liverpool folk singer who visits Belfast, before its transmission date on 7 November. The IBA gave permission, but Thames showed it at 10.30 p.m., instead of at 9 p.m. as usual.

November 1972 — BBC — *A Sense of Loss*
The BBC refused to screen this powerful documentary by Marcel Ophuls on the grounds that it was 'too pro-Irish'. (*The Sunday Times*, 5.11.72) The BBC had a financial involvement in the film, following their screening of Ophuls' acclaimed *The Sorrow and the Pity*.

February 1973 — ATV — *Hang up your brightest colours: The life and death of Michael Collins*
Following the success of Kenneth Griffith's BBC film on Cecil Rhodes, ATV commissioned him to make a historical documentary in the same vivid story-telling style. Griffith chose as his subject Michael Collins, IRA leader in the war against Britain in 1920 and a signatory of the treaty which led to civil war. The film is deeply committed and condemns Britain's role. Sir Lew Grade, ATV's managing director, banned the film, and for many years even Kenneth Griffith did not have access to it. It was first shown by BBC Wales on 3 March 1993, and later nationally.

March 1974 — BBC — *Children in Crossfire*
The Tory Northern Ireland Secretary tried to get this film stopped. BBC NI Controller Dick Francis ordered major changes in the film. Not satisfied with the changes made, he had its transmission stopped twice. It finally went out on 12 March with a one-minute announcement appended at the start implying that the government's Sunningdale policy had eased the tensions, depicted in the film, between the British army and people in the republican areas of the North. It was repeated in January 1982, with a follow-up film, *A Bright Brand New Day...?*.

November 1974 — Bristol Channel (Cable) — *Newspeak*
On 29 November, when this local news programme had started, a ban came through from the Home Office on an interview with Adrian Gallagher, South-West organiser of Clann na hEireann (the equivalent of Official Sinn Fein). He was to discuss the Birmingham bombings. The Home Office regulated this and four other cable television experiments, and programme schedules had to be submitted to them at least two weeks in advance.

May 1975 — Thames — *This Week: 'Hands across the sea'*
The IBA postponed his report on fund-raising for the IRA in America for a week. It was originally timed for the day of the elections for the Northern Ireland Convention, to go out half-an-hour after the polls had closed.

8 January 1976 — BBC — *Nationwide*
Nationwide showed a film on the SAS training, which had been on the shelf. Both negative and print were apparently later destroyed on 'advice' from the Ministry of Defence.

March 1976 — BBC — *Article 5*
The BBC commissioned this play from Brian Phelan about three mercenaries/torturers, who are commissioned by an Englishman to protect his interests in an unspecified country. The play's message is against governments' use of torture. It was recorded in January 1975 and banned by the BBC. It has since been staged as a fringe theatre production.

October 1976 — BBC Scotland — *The Scottish Connection*
The BBC NI Controller insisted that an interview with a Provisional IRA man be dropped from this film about the links between Scotland and the North of Ireland. Director-General Charles Curran confirmed the cut. The producers intended to insert a statement saying that they could not show an interview with a Provisional IRA spokesman because it was against BBC policy, but that interviews with the legal Ulster Defence Association were permitted. This statement was omitted when the film was shown in Scotland on 23 October 1976 and on the network on 5 January 1977.

February 1977 — London Weekend — *Eighteen Months to Balcombe Street*
Shane Connaughton, the writer, asked for his name to be withdrawn from this reconstruction of the Balcombe Street siege because it had not been produced as he intended. 'I wanted to explain why the bombers were there,' he said. (*The Irish Post*, 26.2.77)

March 1977 — BBC — *Tonight: Interview with Bernard O'Connor*
Keith Kyle's interview with Bernard O'Connor, a Catholic schoolteacher who alleged he had been ill-treated by the RUC at Castlereagh holding centre, was transmitted a week later than scheduled. The BBC governors thoroughly investigated the film before allowing transmission. In July 1980, O'Connor won £5,000 in compensation as exemplary damages for maltreatment. Both Roy Mason, then Northern Ireland Secretary, and Tory spokesperson Airey Neave, condemned the BBC for showing the programme, and some newspapers blamed it for the killing of an RUC man by the IRA a few days later.

1977 — BBC — *Man Alive: 'A street in Belfast' (also known as 'Short Strand')*
The BBC commissioned this film from Eric Durschmied, a freelance film-maker, then refused to show it. An illuminating glimpse of the lives of three women in an embattled nationalist enclave, the film has never been shown, though a copy is held by the BBC.

August 1977 — Thames — *This Week: 'In Friendship and Forgiveness'*
Peter Taylor, the reporter, described this film as 'an alternative diary' of the Queen's Jubilee visit to the North of Ireland. It challenged the media picture of a pacified province by showing that the visit had heightened the political divisions. The IBA banned it two weeks before transmission on 17 August. It was eventually shown, with small alterations, two weeks after the visit, when its topicality was lost, at various times in the various ITV regions.

October 1977 — Thames — *This Week: 'Inhuman and degrading treatment'*
This Week investigated 10 cases of alleged ill-treatment of people held by the RUC for interrogation. The IBA insisted that the RUC be represented, but the RUC refused to co-operate or to be interviewed. The day before transmission, the Chief Constable offered a five-minute RUC statement to camera. *This Week* agreed, because otherwise the IBA would not have allowed the programme to go out.

February 1978 — Thames — *The Green, the Orange and the Red, White and Blue*
David Elstein and Peter Taylor, producer and reporter with *This Week*, offered Thames a historical project on the North of Ireland mixing documentary and dramatised reconstruction. Thames refused it, probably because the two had previously been involved in controversy. The BBC also turned it down.

May 1978 — London Weekend — *Weekend World*
Soon after work started on this film assessing the current strength of the Provisional IRA, the IBA ordered *Weekend World* to scrap it. They went ahead, though dropping film of IRA training sessions and a mooted interview with IRA leader David O'Connell. The IBA banned the newly completed film, but finally allowed it to be shown on 21 May, three weeks after its planned date.

May 1978 — BBC — *The City on the Border* and *The Irish Way: 'A Bridge of Sorts'*
The City on the Border, about Derry and directed by Colin Thomas, was intended as a preface to the seven-part series, *The Irish Way*. Two sections were cut: one showed a tombstone which read 'Murdered by British Paratroopers on Bloody Sunday'. One of the two films Thomas had directed in the *Irish Way* series, 'A Bridge of Sorts', was referred to BBC Northern Ireland, who demanded substantial changes. Thomas refused to comply, and resigned. The altered film was shown with a new title, 'A Rock in the Road'.

June 1978 — Thames — *This Week: 'The Amnesty Report'*
Thames planned to transmit on 8 June a programme about the Amnesty Report on the ill-treatment of suspects by the RUC, which had already been widely leaked. The IBA banned the programme. The local ACTT union shop prevented the screening of a subsequent programme, and TV screens remained blank. Extracts were later shown on the BBC's *Nationwide*.

August 1978 — Southern — *Spearhead: 'Jackal'*
UTV refused to screen the fourth of seven episodes of this drama series about an army battalion. Like the first episode, which UTV had screened, the fourth was set in the North of Ireland. The network transmission date, 8 August, coincided with the anniversary of the introduction of internment. This was the first time a drama programme, as opposed to current affairs, had been dropped by UTV.

August 1978— BBC — *Play for Today: 'The Legion Hall Bombing'*
This play, showing the operation of the Diplock Court system and based on the transcripts of the trial of Willie Gallagher, was scheduled for transmission on 23 February and was repeatedly postponed. The BBC insisted on commentary changes and that the epilogue be dropped. A discussion was meant to follow the play, but this too was dropped. The play was shown on 22 August at 10.25 p.m., an hour later than usual. The director, Roland Joffé, and writer Caryl Churchill requested that their names be removed from the credits.

1979 — Granada — *World in Action*
An interview with republican spokesperson Danny Morrison was dropped from a film on the North after Northern Ireland Secretary Humphrey Atkins said he would refuse to appear unless the interview was excluded.

May 1979 — Yorkshire TV — *Global Village*
IBA and Yorkshire TV officials forced the removal of an interview with Sinn Fein President Ruairí Ó Brádaigh from David Frost's *Global Village* programme on the North of Ireland. The cut was made because several Westminster MPs had walked out when they heard that Ó Brádaigh was due to appear. The programme normally went out live, but this one was recorded and previewed by the IBA because it dealt with the North.

August 1979 — BBC — *The Vanishing Army*

A repeat of this play by Robert Holles, about an army sergeant who had become disillusioned after being wounded in the North, was cancelled because of the Mountbatten and Warrenpoint killings. It was eventually repeated on 3 April 1980.

November 1979 — BBC — *Panorama*

As part of a film assessing the Provisional Republican movement on its tenth anniversary, *Panorama* filmed an IRA roadblock in Carrickmore, Co. Tyrone. This led to an outcry in Parliament and in the press. The film was seized by Scotland Yard under the Prevention of Terrorism Act. The BBC fired *Panorama* editor Roger Bolton, reinstating him after union pressure. The film was never completed.

November 1979 — BBC Northern Ireland — *Spotlight*

Spotlight planned a programme about the implications of the *Panorama* 'Carrickmore' affair. The BBC banned it at the last minute. Ironically, the official reason for the banning was the BBC's refusal to provide a spokesperson.

March 1980 — Harlech — *Curious Journey*

Harlech TV banned Kenneth Griffith's documentary centring on interviews with Irish veterans of 1916 and 1918. Harlech wanted Griffith to cut several quotations from historical figures: one such was from the British Prime Minister William Gladstone, roundly condemning the 1800 Act of Union between Britain and Ireland. Griffith refused, and Harlech eventually sold him the film rights for £1. (See Kenneth Griffith and Timothy O'Grady, *Curious Journey*, 1982)

9 March 1980 — BBC — *Gone for a Soldier*

Philip Donnellan's film, about the history of the British army seen through the eyes of ordinary soldiers, provoked a row in the House of Commons which led to the BBC banning repeats and foreign sales.

June 1980 — Thames — *Creggan*

Transmission of this film about Derry, by Mary Holland and Michael Whyte, was delayed nearly a year. It was finally shown on 17 June with two cuts and a commentary alteration. It won the prestigious Prix Italia, and was named best documentary of 1980 by the British Broadcasting Guild, but was not repeated until September 1989.

30 April 1981 — Thames — *TV Eye: 'The waiting time'*

This film was about events immediately preceding the death of Bobby Sands MP. The IBA forced the producers to cut a 33-second sequence showing IRA members making a statement in a West Belfast social club and receiving rapturous applause.

June 1981 — Granada — *World in Action: 'The propaganda war'*

Granada withdrew this film rather than comply with the IBA's command to excise a 27-second sequence showing hunger striker Patsy O'Hara lying in his coffin surrounded by an INLA guard of honour. The IBA apparently felt that the pictures might have invested those shown with a status they did not merit and would have given the 'wrong impression' to a British audience. Ironically, part of the offending sequence was transmitted several times in an advance promotion for the programme. The film was finally transmitted on 23 April 1991 with other cuts (see below).

September 1981 — BBC — *Top of the Pops*

The BBC banned a video made by the rock group Police for their single *Invisible*

Sun and due to be shown on *Top of the Pops* on 24 September. *The Times* wrote: 'A collage of Ulster street scenes incorporating urchins, graffiti, Saracens and soldiers... it seem good-hearted and utterly uncontentious'. (16.12.81) ATV showed a short clip of the video on *Tiswas*, omitting all references to Belfast.

January 1982 — BBC — *Open Door*
Senior BBC executives banned the Campaign for Free Speech on Ireland from making a programme for the BBC access slot, *Open Door*. The *Open Door* selection committee had approved the Campaign's application in November 1979. The project was 'referred up' to senior executives, including the Managing Director of BBC TV, the Controller of BBC2, the Director of News and Current Affairs and Controller Northern Ireland. Three independent observers on the *Open Door* selection committee complained about the ban.

March 1983 — Yorkshire Television — *First Tuesday*
Yorkshire Television management ordered an end to work on a *First Tuesday* documentary on plastic bullets. Several months research had already been done and filming was due to start the following week. The ban came after the RUC and the IBA had put pressure on Yorkshire TV, after the Belfast *Irish News* mentioned the programme.

3 October 1983 — Channel 4 — *Eleventh Hour: 'The Cause of Ireland'*
Made by Chris Reeves and largely funded by Channel 4, a main theme was that Catholic and Protestant workers in the North could not be united prior to the reunification of Ireland. Jeremy Isaacs, head of Channel 4, approved the completed film, but members of the IBA asked to see it and then demanded that six minutes be cut. One statement cut was: 'While the firepower of republicanism is usually aimed at the security forces or public representatives of the British state, loyalist violence has been directed indiscriminately at the Catholic community.'

1983 — Thames — *TV Eye*
According to the Dublin *Sunday Tribune* (29.4.84), *TV Eye* had compiled a programme in 1983 on cross-border activities by the British army and RUC, including alleged murders and attempted kidnappings. It was suspected that the programme had been blocked because of political pressure from Prime Minister Margaret Thatcher's office, though Thames denied this.

December 1983 — Channel 4 — *Right to Reply*
Several programmes were cut after the IRA's bombing of Harrods in London on 17 December 1983, including a confrontation planned by *Right to Reply* between Sinn Fein MP Gerry Adams and John Ware of Granada's *World in Action*. Adams would have criticised a film made about himself by Ware, titled 'The Honourable Member for West Belfast', shown on 19 December. (*New Statesman*, 6.1.84)

December 1983 — Channel 4 — *Comedy Classics* and *England*
Following the Harrods bombing, Channel 4 cut several comedy sequences. Two cuts were made to the *Comedy Classics* slot on 27 December. One, from a 1961 edition of *Saturday Night at the London Palladium*, featured a running gag in which Norman Wisdom made repeated attempts to sing 'When Irish eyes are smiling'. Part of *Beat the Clock* was also cut, as were two references to Harrods in gags on Paul Hogan's *England* on 30 December. (*New Statesman*, 6.1.84)

January 1984 — Channel 4 — *Green Flutes*
Nancy Schiesari's documentary about a republican flute band from Glasgow was

due to be shown on 16 January in the *Eleventh Hour* slot. After Harrods, Channel 4 executives decided to withdraw it. It was finally shown on 5 March. It had previously been delayed twice.

January 1984 — Yorkshire TV — *Jimmy Young Show*
The producers arranged for Gerry Adams MP to appear as a guest on the programme for 15 January. *The Sunday Times* reported that day: 'although Adams's contribution was going to be carefully balanced with other political views, Young refused to do the interview on the grounds that Sinn Fein should not be allowed airtime on British TV.' Adams instead appeared on David Frost's breakfast programme on TV AM — an invitation which was angrily attacked by Tory MPs.

September 1984 — London Weekend — *Weekend World: 'From the Shadow of a Gun'*
The fourth part of this documentary presented by Mary Holland was shown on 16 December 1984. The plan was that former diplomat Nicholas Henderson would act as honest broker and interview members of the various political parties in the North. But he refused to sit down with Sinn Fein, so LWT offered them a separate interview, done by Mary Holland. Sinn Fein refused to appear on this basis.

February 1985 — Channel 4/RTE — *The Price*
In this six-part thriller about a woman being kidnapped by republican 'terrorists', actor Mark Holland played an RUC Special Branch detective who was scripted to take part in a shoot-out south of the border in the last episode. Holland revealed that his part was dropped from that episode on RUC instructions, because they did not want even a fictional RUC officer to be seen operating south of the border. (*Sunday Press*, 17.2.85)

May 1985 — BBC — *Panorama*
A programme investigating allegations of an RUC 'shoot-to-kill' policy in South Armagh was delayed for more than a year. *The Irish News* reported (12.8.85) that the BBC had 'torpedoed' the programme on legal advice. It was finally shown on 12 June 1986.

July 1985 — BBC — *Real Lives: 'At the Edge of the Union'*
One of the biggest rows of the 1980s was over this programme, produced by Paul Hamann, about the lives of two Derry politicians, republican Martin McGuinness and loyalist Gregory Campbell. It was scheduled for 7 August 1985. On 28 July *The Sunday Times* carried a report headed, 'Thatcher slams IRA film', and alleged that McGuinness was the IRA's Chief of Staff. The BBC had vetted the film internally, and executives defended the decision to show it. Next day, 29 July, Home Secretary Leon Brittan wrote to the BBC saying the film — which he hadn't seen — was 'contrary to the national interest' and likely to give 'succour to terrorist organisations'. On 30 July, the BBC's governors held a special day-long meeting, viewed the programme, and decided to ban it, thus violating their usual relationship with the board of management.

This capitulation to political pressure and flagrant abandonment of the BBC's much-vaunted independence from government caused a major public outcry. The NUJ called a 24-hour protest stoppage on 7 August, winning almost total support from broadcasters. No national news was broadcast in Britain that day, and the BBC World Service broadcast music all day. The film was finally shown on 16 October with minor amendments, including the addition of a 20-second colour film sequence, showing bodies being carried away after the IRA's 'Bloody Friday' bombings in Belfast in 1972.

July 1985 — BBC — *Open Space: 'On the Word of a Supergrass'*
During the *Real Lives* controversy, the BBC postponed this independently made programme from 14 August to 19 September. *(Guardian, 31.7.85)*

July 1985 — BBC Scotland — *Open to Question*
On 31 July, during the *Real Lives* row, Sinn Fein publicised the fact that Gerry Adams had accepted an invitation from a BBC Scotland researcher to appear on *Open to Question*, a discussion slot on which teenagers questioned public figures. The programme was not made. *(Daily Telegraph, Star, 1.8.85)*

August 1985 — BBC Radio Manchester — *Irish Line*
The BBC cut sections, including an interview about strip-searching, from this weekly programme made voluntarily by the Irish in Britain Representation Group.

November 1985 — UTV — *Witness*
On 25 November, UTV refused to screen a five-minute religious broadcast by David Bleakley, General Secretary of the Irish Council of Churches. David Bleakley said he was 'dumbfounded' and was trying to provide a 'vision of reassurance and reconciliation'. *(The Irish Times, 30.11.85)*

December 1985 — ITV — *Christmas Eve Mass*
Christmas Eve Mass, celebrated by Bishop Cathal Daly, was due to be broadcast from the Mater Hospital, Belfast. Shortly before transmission time, it was announced that another programme, recorded previously, would be screened instead. No reason was given.

December 1985 — BBC — *Songs of Praise*
Protestants apparently angry about the Anglo-Irish Agreement signed on 15 November forced the BBC to scrap plans for a cross-community edition of *Songs of Praise* from Dungannon, Co. Tyrone. *(Irish News, 31.12.85)*

January 1986 — BBC — *Question Time*
The BBC scrapped plans for *Question Time* to be broadcast from Belfast on 30 January 1986, shortly after the by-elections prompted by Unionist MPs resigning over the Anglo-Irish agreement. Those invited had included NI Secretary Tom King and Peter Barry, Southern foreign affairs minister. *The Irish News* reported (18.1.86): 'It is thought that unionist politicians, currently refusing to speak to Mr King, would have been reluctant to take part in the broadcast, leaving the programme-makers with problems over balancing content.'

December 1986 — Channel 4 — *Eleventh Hour: 'They Shoot to Kill Children'*
On 8 December the IBA, with the agreement of Channel 4's management, banned a 14-minute video by young people about the use of plastic bullets. Part of a compilation by the Birmingham Film and Video Workshop, it included an interview with Paul Corr, hit in the face by a plastic bullet when aged 12, and a song mentioning 14 of those killed.

March 1987 — BBC — *Crossfire*
This five-part thriller was referred back to the BBC in London for changes by James Hawthorne, the BBC's NI Controller. He is believed to have asked for the series' two final parts to be reshot. He said he had not previously been consulted by the programme-makers and, having viewed it, found it portrayed the IRA too sympathetically and the 'security forces' too unfavourably. Due to be screened

from 6 March 1987, it went out from 15 March 1988. Actor Tony Doyle, who played the IRA Chief of Staff, revealed that he had had to redub certain lines on the RUC's insistence: 'In one line I said "The organisation has safe houses in Belfast." I had to change that to "The organisation has bridgeheads in Belfast." They are of the opinion that there are no safe houses in Belfast.' (*Sunday Press*, 10.4.88)

December 1987 — Channel 4 — *Court Report: 'The Birmingham Six'*
On 3 December, the Court of Appeal granted the Attorney-General an injunction preventing Channel 4 from broadcasting that night a dramatised version of the Birmingham Six's appeal hearing. The Court of Appeal was also the court hearing the Six's appeal. The three judges finally lifted the injunction on 29 January 1988, after they had rejected the appeal. Channel 4 cleared the schedules to show the two-hour programme that evening.

January 1988 — Channel 4 — *Acceptable Levels*
Channel 4 chief Michael Grade removed *Acceptable Levels* — a feature film about media self-censorship when a child is killed by a soldier's plastic bullet — from the schedules on 28 January because he felt it would be 'inappropriate' to screen it on the day of the Birmingham Six appeal verdict. It had been shown before on Channel 4 on 30 April 1984. *Right to Reply* discussed its suppression, and it was shown on 18 February.

*** The Casement Park trials
On 6 March 1988 the SAS killed three IRA members in Gibraltar. At their funerals in Belfast on 16 March, loyalist Michael Stone launched a gun and grenade attack, killing three, including IRA member Caoimhín Mac Brádaigh. Three days later, a car drove at high speed into Mac Brádaigh's funeral cortege. In the car were two armed men in civilian clothes. Fearing another loyalist attack, the crowd dragged them out, beat them up, then handed them over to the IRA, who killed them. They turned out to be British soldiers. Two days later, RUC Chief Constable Sir John Hermon asked the TV companies to hand over their untransmitted film: they refused unless faced with court orders. Mrs Thatcher then backed up the request, and on 23 March RUC detectives, citing the Prevention of Terrorism Act and the Emergency Provisions Act, went to the BBC and ITN who handed film over. Mrs Thatcher then said that broadcasters had a duty to 'give witness' in court. When the trials relating to the killings began in April 1989, some 27 media personnel gave evidence, some openly and others from behind screens. Two journalists were threatened by the IRA and left Belfast. The seized film was shown in court, along with British army 'heli-telly' footage. (See chapters by Ed Moloney and Bill Rolston in ed. Bill Rolston, *The Media and Northern Ireland*, 1991.)

*** The *Death on the Rock* controversy
A major storm blew up in April and May 1988 over Thames TV's *This Week* programme, 'Death on the Rock', which cast doubt on the government's version of the SAS's killing of three IRA members in Gibraltar in March that year. On 28 April Foreign Secretary Geoffrey Howe asked Lord Thompson, IBA chair, to postpone the programme until after the inquest in Gibraltar. The IBA refused, and the programme went out on 5 May. Prime Minister Thatcher, Northern Ireland Secretary Tom King, and much of the press, then accused Thames TV of 'trial by television'. Thames initiated an independent inquiry into the programme under Lord Windlesham: this concluded that the making of the programme was appropriate. In October 1991, in a move widely seen as retribution, the Independent Television Commission (replacement of the IBA) refused to renew Thames TV's franchise. (See *The Windlesham/Rampton Report on Death on the Rock*, 1989; Roger Bolton,

Death on the Rock and Other Stories, 1990; David Miller, 'The Media on the Rock', in ed. Bill Rolston, *The Media and Northern Ireland*, 1991.)

April 1988 — London Weekend — *ABC of British Music*
A scene from a video, accompanying a Pogues song, showing the killing of a British soldier was removed from the *ABC of British Music*, directed by Ken Russell.

April 1988 — Channel 4 — *Friday Night Live: The Pogues*
The Pogues were performing their song 'Streets of Sorrow/Birmingham Six' live when they were cut off two-thirds of the way through by a commercial break. They accused Channel 4 of censorship, which the Channel denied. (*Irish Post*, 7.5.88)

June 1988 — Channel 4 — *Network 7*
This live magazine programme planned a discussion on 'Should the troops remain in Ireland?' The IBA demanded that it be pre-recorded to allow them to vet the tapes. The programme had commissioned a poll on 'troops out' that revealed 57 per cent for and 43 per cent against. A planned live phone-in poll — standard practice on *Network 7* — was dropped after pressure from the IBA, who claimed it would be 'open to abuse by unrepresentative opinion'.

August 1988 — BBC — *Elephant, Monkeys* and *Nightwatch*
After the IRA's Ballygawley bus bombing, when eight British soldiers were killed, the BBC announced on 23 August that it was postponing three plays made by BBC Northern Ireland. They dealt, respectively, with killings in the North, intelligence services and mercenaries elsewhere, and failed car manufacturer John de Lorean. They were shown from 25 January 1989.

September 1988 — Channel 4 — *After Dark*
Professor Paul Wilkinson of Aberdeen University publicised and protested against the fact that Gerry Adams MP was to appear on this live late-night show on 10 September. Tory MPs angrily attacked Channel 4. Liz Forgan, Channel 4's Director of Programmes, decided that it should be abandoned. She thus avoided a confrontation with the IBA, which said that if necessary it would have used Section 4 of the Broadcasting Act to stop Adams appearing. (*Guardian*, 19.9.88)

October 1988 — BBC — *Panorama*
A programme on the SAS in the North of Ireland, scheduled for 3 October, was postponed after BBC Director-General Michael Checkland and his deputy John Birt had viewed it. (*Guardian*, 3.10.88) It was shown on 17 October after changes. Part of an SAS training video showing an exercise in the regiment's 'killing house' was removed on advice from Admiral William Higgins, Secretary to the D-notice committee. It showed the SAS rescuing a hostage from the IRA.

October 1988 — The broadcasting ban
After a succession of IRA bombings in 1988, Prime Minister Margaret Thatcher wanted to bring back internment. Ministers thought this would be counterproductive, and suggested a package of less severe measures, including the ending of the right to silence in court, and the broadcasting ban. Home Secretary Douglas Hurd, who introduced the ban, wrote in his diary, 'I'm not proud of it. Did it to help Tom King.' (*Sunday Times*, 20.9.98)

Douglas Hurd issued 'notices' to the BBC and IBA under, respectively, clause 14(4) of the BBC's Licence and Agreement, and section 29(3) of the Broadcasting Act 1981. Designed for wartime use, and similar to the South of Ireland's Section

31, this legislation empowers the Home Secretary to ban the broadcasting of any matter he/she specifies. This power was later included in the 1990 Broadcasting Act, which covers cable and satellite services as well as commercial television.

The ban prevented the broadcasting of words spoken by representatives of 11 Irish organisations, and of words spoken in support of those organisations. When the ban was introduced, three of the affected organisations were legal — Sinn Fein, Republican Sinn Fein, and the Ulster Defence Association — but the UDA was subsequently outlawed. The ban also covered all organisations banned under the Emergency Provisions Act or the Prevention of Terrorism Act. These were the IRA, INLA, Cumann na mBan, Fianna Éireann, the Red Hand Commandos, Saor Éire (long since defunct), the Ulster Freedom Fighters, and Ulster Volunteer Force. The ban did not affect proceedings in parliament, where parliamentary privilege guarantees freedom of speech, nor in election periods, when coverage of candidates and their supporters is safeguarded by the Representation of the People Act.

Broadcasters immediately began altering plans for interviews and programmes. They interpreted the ban very broadly, applying it to people who were not members of the listed groups, nor advocating support for them. Any opposition to government policy on Ireland became suspect. Radio was immediately and heavily affected, partly because organisations challenging British policy — like other pressure groups — had until then had easier access to radio than TV. Those silenced included Errol Smalley, uncle of Paul Hill of the Guildford Four; Bernadette McAliskey; Richard Stanton, a Brighton Labour councillor and Troops Out Movement member; and US author Margie Bernard, author of *Daughter of Derry*, along with the subject of her book, Brigid Shiels Makowski.

Also silenced were three pop groups. The Pogues' song about the Birmingham Six' was banned by the IBA (see below, November 1988); Dingle Spike's rendering of 'The Bold Fenian Men' was reportedly banned by Radio Tay in Dundee; and That Petrol Emotion were told that their song 'Cellophane' could not be played on radio or TV.

Television news coverage was severely affected. The Glasgow University Media Group studied the ban's effects on British national TV news. (*Speak No Evil*, 1990) They compared the year before and the year after the ban, and found that after it Sinn Fein appearances dropped by more than 63 per cent, to 34.

Broadcasting chiefs issued a succession of guidelines on how staff should interpret the ban. On 24 October 1988, responding to a BBC query, the Home Office issued a detailed clarification. This stated that voiceover accounts of the words of affected people were permissible, as were reconstructions of actual events using actors. Further, the ban would not apply to members of listed organisations where they were speaking in a personal capacity, or purely as a member of an organisation not covered by the ban, such as an elected council.

After the ban, most interviews with Sinn Fein representatives were broadcast with the person's voice removed, and replaced either with a reporter's voiceover, or with subtitles, or with an actor's voice. Determined programme-makers creatively interpreted the Home Office ruling both in order to get information across and to mock the ban. Some went to great lengths to ensure that the actor's voice was accurately dubbed. Others, however, applied the ban way beyond its scope, for example subtitling Bernadette McAliskey (see below, September 1992). There were few censored interviews with loyalist paramilitary representatives.

In contrast to their strong stand in the *Real Lives* affair, the media unions failed to effectively challenge the ban. A planned day of industrial action was called off by the NUJ General Secretary after he had received promises from the broadcasting chiefs of vigorous opposition to the ban — promises which did not materialise. The ban survived for six years, and it was political developments, particularly the IRA ceasefire of 1994, which prompted its end.

Three legal challenges were made to the ban. One was made by a group of NUJ members. Another was made by Derry Sinn Fein councillor Mitchel McLaughlin. A third was made by Bernadette McAliskey. The cases taken by the NUJ members and by Mitchel McLaughlin were rejected by the British courts and were then taken to Europe. But the European Commission of Human Rights ruled that both cases were inadmissible, as it had earlier done with a case against Section 31. Bernadette McAliskey's judicial review was still pending when the broadcasting ban was revoked in 1994, so the matter was then deemed academic and did not go any further. (On the ban see Ed Moloney in ed. Bill Rolston, *The Media and Northern Ireland*, 1991.)

October 1988 — Channel 4 — *Mother Ireland*

Made by Derry Film & Video and funded by Channel 4, *Mother Ireland* explores the personification of Ireland as a woman in Irish culture and nationalism. For months before the ban, Channel 4 had been requesting alterations. They wanted the removal of film of Emma Groves immediately after a British soldier shot her in the face with a plastic bullet, blinding her; of Christy Moore's song 'Unfinished Revolution'; of a montage of Irish women in resistance roles; and of an interview with Gibraltar victim Mairead Farrell.

On 2 November, Channel 4 issued a statement saying that the ban 'made further discussion on such a version academic, for it was clear that under any legal interpretation, the ban would rule out many other sections of the programme, including contributions from elderly participants in the 1920s Civil War.' This was in line with advice given by Don Christopher of Channel 4's legal services on 24 October: 'The ban is not limited to material produced or recorded after 19th October. It would cover any such material recorded at any time in the past — for example newsreel footage shot before the creation of the Republic of Ireland.'

Mother Ireland went on to be shown in many countries. The footage of Emma Groves was shown on BBC2 in May 1989 in a film made by Ken Loach for the *Split Screen* slot.

30 October 1988 — Channel 4 — *The Media Show*

A report on the ban included an interview with Derry Sinn Fein councillor Dodie McGuinness, whose voice was replaced with another voice repeating exactly what she had said: that the ban meant she could not publicise the council's campaign against the closure of a local maternity unit. A voiceover introduction said that Channel 4's senior management thought the interview 'borderline but acceptable' but were overruled by the IBA. By contrast the local BBC station Radio Foyle broadcast an interview with Cllr McGuinness on 16 November with sound intact.

November 1988 — Commercial TV and radio — *The Pogues: 'Streets of Sorrow/Birmingham Six'*

The Observer (20.11.88) revealed that the IBA had issued a circular to all commercial radio stations saying that this song should not be played. It supported the pleas of innocence by the Birmingham Six and Guildford Four, then still imprisoned. The IBA said: 'The song alleges some convicted terrorists are not guilty and goes on to suggest that Irish people are at a disadvantage in British courts of law. That allegation might support or solicit or invite support for an organisation proscribed by the Home Secretary's directive, in that they indicate a general disagreement with the way in which the British government responds to, and the courts deal with, the terrorist threat in the UK.'

On 20 December 1988, reporting the NUJ's court case against the ban, ITN's 5.45 news bulletin showed the Pogues in freeze-frame with a caption and voiceover giving the song's words: 'There were six men in Birmingham/ In Guildford there's four/ That were picked up and tortured/ And framed by the law/ And the filth got promotion/ But they're still doing time/ For being Irish in the wrong place/ And at the wrong time.'

The IBA was subsequently replaced by two bodies, the Radio Authority and the Independent Television Commission. In 1991, after the freeing of the Birmingham Six, the Radio Authority lifted the ban on the song. The ITC, unlike the IBA, is not the legal broadcaster. It is now up to the licensees — the companies holding the franchises — to decide what to broadcast. The ITC said: 'The ITC now only intervenes after the event if it feels there has been a breach... it would be highly unlikely that the ITC would seek to intervene if the song were broadcast today.' (letter to David Miller, 17.3.93)

December 1988 — BBC — *40 Minutes: 'Greenfinches'*
After consulting the Ministry of Defence, the BBC cut part of this documentary about three women members of the Ulster Defence Regiment. One section cut was reportedly a suggestion by one of the women 'that some UDR members join purely to get firearms training to fight a civil war against the Catholics, should the army be withdrawn.' (*Independent*, 24.11.88; *Irish News*, 25.11.88)

1989 — Channel 4 — *The Silent Scream* (originally *Sixteen Dead*)
Channel Four commissioned this documentary about the use of plastic bullets from Belfast Independent Video (now Northern Visions) then refused to show it.

1989 — all channels — *Death of a Terrorist*
William Cran, a former BBC producer, made this documentary about Gibraltar victim Mairead Farrell for the Boston station WGBH, which is part of the Public Broadcasting Service network of more than 200 US TV stations. It was shown on the PBS network on 13 June 1989, and then in Japan and in some European countries. Executives from the BBC, Channel 4 and Thames TV asked to see it: all said they liked it, but that it was unbroadcastable under the present rules. (*The Listener*, 3.8.89)

5 March 1989 — BBC — *Here is the News*
The BBC ordered cuts in this thriller by G.F. Newman, including a fragment of conversation between the Attorney-General and a journalist, suggesting that the prime minister knew the truth about the Gibraltar killings. (*Guardian*, 3.3.89)

8 May 1989 — Channel 4 — *Eleventh Hour: 'Trouble the Calm'*
This film by Faction Films looked at political attitudes in the South of Ireland. Channel 4 insisted that about two minutes be cut from an interview with a prisoner's wife. The film-makers persuaded Channel 4 to replace the cut section with a caption: 'Under government broadcasting restrictions... this woman cannot explain her husband's beliefs and motivations which led to his imprisonment in Portlaoise jail.'

28 June 1989 — Channel 4 — *Dispatches: 'A State of Decay'*
This assessment marking 20 years since the deployment of British troops included a voiced-over interview with Gerry Adams MP. It was repeated on 21 September.

August-September 1989 — Thames — *The Troubles*
From 17 August, Thames repeated its acclaimed history series, *The Troubles*, first shown in 1981. Six pieces of sound were now excised and replaced with subtitles.

These included interviews with Joe Cahill and Gerry Adams, both of Sinn Fein; prisoners' voices from 1979 film of the 'blanket' and 'no wash' protests; and blanket men calling out, 'We're political prisoners. We want political status.' The voice of hunger-striker Raymond McCartney, interviewed by Granada's *World in Action* in November 1980 and declaring that the prisoners were 'a product of the political troubles' was replaced by a caption.

13 August 1989 — BBC — *Forever Divided*
This 90-minute programme by Jonathan Dimbleby marked the twentieth anniversary of troop deployment. A comment by Gerry Adams MP on the IRA bombing of Brighton's Grand Hotel was subtitled. (*Independent*, 14.8.89)

22 August 1989 — Channel 4 — *Creggan*
Channel 4 repeated this film by Michael Whyte and Mary Holland, about people on a Derry housing estate, in a series of prize-winning Thames films. (See above, June 1980) Sections of interviews with two women were replaced with subtitles, including: 'I don't agree with everything that the Provos done, I think very few people do. But at the same time I could understand how they felt.'

23 August 1989 — *Visnews*
Public Eye, a Australian current affairs programme on Channel 10, criticised the British ban, and showed how Maxine Mawhinney of the Belfast office of Visnews, the world's largest TV news agency, now routinely made two versions of stories involving Sinn Fein representatives: one, using their voices, for sale internationally; the other, without their voices, for sale to Sky News for transmission to the UK.

September 1989 — BBC — *Bentham*, retitled *1996*
G.F. Newman wrote a three-part series titled *Bentham*, based on his book *The Testing Ground*, loosely based on the Kincora boys' home scandal and the Stalker 'shoot-to-kill' investigation. The BBC insisted that he change the setting from Ireland in the past to Wales in the future. The new version, a single play titled *1996*, was shown on 17 September.

September 1989 — ITV — *Saracen*
After the IRA bombed a Marine barracks in Kent, killing 10 bandsmen, ITV postponed the episode of the thriller *Saracen* due to be shown next night, about an SAS man who took up with an Irish woman not realising he had killed one of her relations. It was shown a fortnight later on 7 October.

September 1989 — BBC — *The Squad*
This programme, about the West Midlands Serious Crimes Squad, was withdrawn from the schedule for 28 September when the Police Federation won an injunction from the High Court preventing its screening for seven days. The squad had been involved with the Birmingham Six case. The BBC applied successfully to the Court of Appeal, and it was shown on 26 October.

October 1989 — BBC — *Late Show*
This month saw the first anniversary of the broadcasting ban, and was marked by widespread protests. A *Late Show* item on 9 October about the ban carried an interview with Sinn Fein councillor Mitchel McLaughlin voiced over in sync by actor Harry Towb, to strange effect.

15 October 1989 — Channel 4 — *Media Show*
Mitchel McLaughlin was silenced and subtitled in a report on the ban.

19 October 1989 — Channel 4 — *Hard News*
In an item on media coverage of Ireland, Sinn Fein's Director of Publicity, Danny Morrison, was silenced and subtitled.

19 October 1989 — BBC Northern Ireland — *Spotlight*
The voice of UDA leader Tommy Lyttle was replaced by a reporter reading his words.

*** Green activist Jonathan Porritt and Paul Boateng MP recited the lyrics of the Pogues' song on the Birmingham Six on the BBC's *Question Time* on 19 October, to highlight the absurdity of the IBA's ban. The BBC had no such ban.

October 1989 — Channel 4 — *After Dark*
A programme on censorship planned for 21 October was scrapped when the IBA said it could not include members of organisations covered by the ban. The producers had aimed to include Danny Morrison, silencing his words and having a stand-in repeat them.

28 October 1989 — Channel 4 — *Right to Reply*
Two contributors from Derry were voiced over: Tony Doherty complaining about the ban in the video box, and Sinn Fein member Mary Nelis discussing the BBC series *Families at War*.

18 January 1990 — UTV — *Counterpoint*
An interview with Sinn Fein councillor Máirtín Ó Muilleoir about the planned concert hall for Belfast was carried without his voice. (*Irish News*, 22.1.90)

18 February 1990 — BBC — *On the Record*
Three Sinn Fein members — president Gerry Adams, councillor Máirtín Ó Muilleoir, and spokesperson Richard McAuley — were voiced over by actors.

March 1990 — BBC NI — *Murder of Samuel Marshall*
On 7 March Samuel Marshall was shot dead by loyalists as he walked away from a Lurgan police station where he reported as a condition of bail. Sinn Fein held a press conference next day addressed by two witnesses to the killing, neither a member of Sinn Fein. UTV News carried comments by one of the men, but the local BBC news did not carry either man's comments.

9 April 1990 — UTV — *The Struggle for Democracy*
UTV removed this documentary made by Central Television from the schedule after four UDR men were killed by a landmine. It was shown elsewhere on the network. It included references to the IRA's 'Bloody Friday' and Enniskillen bombings.

11 April 1990 — Channel 4 — *Dispatches: 'Terms for Peace'*
This documentary by Mary Holland included a 16-minute interview with West Belfast MP Gerry Adams meticulously dubbed in lip-sync by actor Stephen Rea. Martin McGuinness was also dubbed in lip-sync. *The Guardian* (12.4.90) said it was 'the ultimate demonstration of the total stupidity of the ban.'

June 1990 — UTV — *Shoot to Kill*
This four-hour drama-documentary by Yorkshire television, reconstructing the RUC's County Armagh killings of 1982, was due to be screened on the network on 3 and 4 June. UTV refused to screen it, citing legal advice. The Committee on the Administration of Justice organised a Belfast screening.

July 1990 — ITV — *Dear Sarah*

This drama by journalist Tom McGurk was based on the love story of Sarah Conlon and her husband Giuseppe, who was one of the 'Maguire Seven', a group of innocent people imprisoned on explosives offences. Giuseppe died of tuberculosis in 1980 while still in prison. McGurk first wrote the script as a one-hour BBC drama in 1986, but the BBC rejected it. David Elstein of Thames TV recommissioned it as a 90-minute film, with Frank Cvitanovich as director. Thames's board first rejected, then approved, then rejected it. By now Thames had set up a co-production deal with RTE. After Thames's withdrawal, RTE tried unsuccessfully to interest UTV and Channel 4, and finally took over the entire production, financing it by preselling it to the ITV network. It was shown on 2 July 1990.

3 July 1990 — Yorkshire — *First Tuesday: 'Joyriders'*

Alex Maskey of Sinn Fein was dubbed over by an actor.

*** On 20 July 1990 the satellite channel Sky TV breached the ban by transmitting an interview with Sinn Fein spokesperson Richard McAuley, done by the US programme *NBC Nightly News,* which Sky regularly transmitted live. The Cable Authority said it would raise the matter with Sky. (*Broadcast*, 27 July 1990)

1 October 1990 — BBC and ITN — *News*

On 30 September, joyriders Martin Peake and Karen Reilly were shot dead by British soldiers in West Belfast. Next day, Gerry Adams, MP for the area, asked questions about the killings and was interviewed by various stations. On Radio 4's 1 p.m. news, his words were spoken by a reporter. But BBC TV's 6 p.m. and 9 p.m. news carried his voice. (*Daily Mail*, 2.10.90) ITN used a reporter to paraphrase his words. The BBC said they had legal advice that the interview did not contravene the ban, because 'Mr Adams was speaking as MP for the constituency where one of the victims lived.' (*Irish News*, 2.10.90)

3 October 1990 — BBC — *The Mary Whitehouse Experience*

The BBC reportedly banned a comedy sketch of Terry Wogan 'dressed as an IRA terrorist'. (*The Sun*, 3.10.90)

October 1990 — BBC — *Star Trek*

The BBC reportedly planned to suppress an episode of *Star Trek* from a new series, bought as a package from the US. The controversial episode mentioned 'British forces quitting Ulster after an IRA victory' because they couldn't win. (*Daily Mail,* 17.10.90)

October 1990 — Channel 4 — *Terror: 'The Decay of Democracy'*

In the last part of this three-part documentary, Sinn Fein's spokesman Jim Gibney's voice was replaced by an actor's.

8 November 1990 — BBC — *Question Time*

The BBC transferred *Question Time* from Belfast City Hall to Bradford because of the Unionist-dominated city council's policy, in protest against the Anglo-Irish agreement, of not allowing British government ministers onto the premises.

20 November 1990 — BBC — *Inside Story: 'The Maze — Enemies Within'*

This documentary showed the daily lives of republican and loyalist prisoners. Where they were speaking in a personal capacity, their own voices were heard, but where they were representing the IRA, they were dubbed over by actors. The

'IRA spokesman on food' was dubbed, saying: 'Well, the thing about the sausage rolls... they're getting smaller... The quality is still all right.'

February 1991 — BBC — *Children of the North*
The BBC postponed this four-part thriller set in the North of Ireland because it decided that 'it was inappropriate to air a programme whose theme was violence when British troops were fighting in the Gulf.' (*Observer*'s words 27.10.71) It was eventually shown from 30 October.

April 1991 — Channel 4 — *Banned season*
Channel 4 ran a three-week season featuring controversial TV programmes. Those about Ireland were: *Mother Ireland, World in Action: The Propaganda War, This Week: Death on the Rock,* and *Dispatches: Terms for Peace.* Ironically, all were altered because of the ban.

Some of the cuts to *Mother Ireland* were those demanded before the ban (see above, October 1988): footage of plastic bullet victim Mrs Emma Groves, Christy's Moore's song 'Unfinished Revolution', and footage of IRA women. Additionally, an interview with Mairead Farrell was voiced-over by an actor. Complaints about this censorship were aired on Channel 4's *Right to Reply* on 13 April, which showed two banned sequences — Mrs Groves, and the IRA women — and repeated the dubbed interview with Mairead Farrell.

In *Death on the Rock* (see above, 1988), a sound recording of Mairead Farrell was replaced with subtitles. In *World in Action: The Propaganda War* (see above, June 1981) the sequence showing Patsy O'Hara in his coffin was reinstated, but Sinn Fein spokesman Joe Austin was dubbed over in lip-sync by an actor, as was an H Block blanket protester. The H Block sequence had been shown intact in 1981. *Dispatches: Terms for Peace* was shown as in April 1990.

June 1991 — BBC NI — *Spotlight: 'The Official IRA'*
This programme featured claims that the Official IRA (in theory disbanded) had carried out racketeering, fraud and armed robberies, and that some of those convicted for such crimes belonged to the Workers Party (formerly Official Sinn Fein). The IRSP alleged that the programme had been scheduled for May, then for 13 June, then stopped again. It was shown on 27 June. The BBC denied the allegations. (*Irish News*, 14, 20.6.91)

*** A Channel Four *Dispatches* programme on 2 October 1991, alleging high-level RUC involvement in a loyalist committee which planned the murder of Catholics, led to a long-running battle between the RUC and Channel 4. The RUC investigated, and the Metropolitan Police Special Branch obtained orders under the Prevention of Terrorism Act requiring Channel 4 and the production company, Box Productions, to hand over files and other material. Both companies refused to comply, because they had promised a source that they would protect his identity. Instead, they destroyed or sent abroad material that could have compromised him. Channel 4 and Box Productions were then charged with contempt of court, and fined £75,000 on 31 July 1992. On 29 September the programme's researcher, Ben Hamilton, was arrested at his London home. He was held for questioning, then charged with perjury, but the charges were dropped two months later.

November 1991 — BBC — *Omnibus: 'Ulster says Ho Ho Ho'*
Ninety seconds of a comedian's Ian Paisley routine were cut from this programme about humour in the North of Ireland, and most of his expletives were bleeped. (*Independent*, 19.11.91)

January 1992 — Channel 4 — *Free For All: '20 Years After Bloody Sunday'*
An interview with Raymond McCartney, captioned 'Officer Commanding Republican Prisoners, Maze Prison', was re-voiced.

*** During the spring 1992 general election campaign, Unionist politicians found they could deny Sinn Fein air time by themselves refusing to appear, because under electoral law all candidates or none have to be interviewed. (*Independent*, 21.3.92, *Irish News*, 27.3.92)

March 1992 — BBC Radio 4 — *Afternoon Story*
The BBC banned the broadcasting of a short story, 'We've got tonite', by Sinn Fein publicity director Danny Morrison, then in prison. An innocuous tale of suburban love and adultery, with no mention of Ireland, the story was recorded in February 1992 for transmission on 12 March. (See *Guardian*, 14.10.92)

1 September 1992 — BBC — *Nation: 'Killing for a Cause'*
The BBC extensively subtitled the contribution of Bernadette McAliskey to a pre-recorded discussion. Others subtitled included 77-year-old Brent trade unionist Tom Durkin. None of those subtitled were associated with groups covered by the ban. The gist of Bernadette McAliskey's contribution was that while she did not support violence, she understood the reasons for it: 'No sane human being supports violence. We are often inevitably cornered into it by powerlessness, by lack of democracy, by lack of willingness of people to listen to our problems. We don't choose political violence, the powerful force it on us.'

Why the subtitling took place remains a matter of dispute and speculation. Bernadette learned about it indirectly the night before transmission, and, through solicitor Gareth Peirce, tried in vain to get the BBC to remove either the subtitles or her contribution. Trade unionist Tom Durkin also tried to get his contribution deleted, but was repeatedly fobbed off by BBC information officers. Many protested, including Tory MP Peter Bottomley, who had appeared on the programme with Bernadette.

On 7 September the BBC's Controller of Editorial Policy, John Wilson, returned from holiday and apparently said that the BBC should apologise to Bernadette and transmit the programme without subtitles. This angered the BBC's lawyers, and the Director-General brought in an outside lawyer, David Pannick, to adjudicate. Pannick concluded that it was right to subtitle Bernadette's main remarks, but not her shorter closing remarks.

Bernadette applied for a judicial review. This was refused by Mr Justice McPherson but then, in July 1993, allowed by the Court of Appeal. The review was still pending when the broadcasting ban was revoked in 1994: the matter was then deemed academic and did not proceed. (See Liz Curtis and Mike Jempson, *Interference on the Airwaves*, 1993, for a longer account.)

17 September 1992 — *BBC — Biteback:*
A report on the *Nation* incident showed subtitled sections of the programme. Bernadette declined to be interviewed, fearing she might be subtitled again. *Biteback* also repeated part of *Inside Story: Enemies Within* (see above, November 1990) featuring the subtitled remarks of the 'IRA spokesman on food'.

October 1992 — BBC — *Eastenders*
Scriptwriter David Yallop lost his job on this series in November 1989 after he proposed killing off several characters in an IRA bombing. He sued the BBC for breach of contract, and on 17 October 1992 won £68,195 High Court damages plus inter-

est, representing money owed to him. The BBC's legal bill was unofficially estimated at £250,000. Yallop accused BBC drama of failing to reflect issues such as
job losses, homelessness and bombings. (*Independent*, 17.10.92)

October 1992 — BBC West — *Here Across the Water*
This documentary looked at the lives of four Irishwomen living in Bristol. First
scheduled for October 1992 during the Bristol Irish festival, it was postponed to
18 March 1993, then withdrawn to make way for a story on local job losses. After
pressure from the local Irish community, it was shown on 29 April.

*** Sinn Fein breached the ban on its fourth anniversary by running a pirate radio
station, Radio Free Sinn Fein, from a stage in West Belfast on 17 October.

20 October 1992 — BBC Northern Ireland and UTV
Sinn Fein president Gerry Adams complained that neither BBC nor UTV carried
any response from Sinn Fein to their evening news reports, which had carried
strong criticisms of Adams from the Church of Ireland Primate, Dr Eames. The
BBC said the Sinn Fein statement had been 'lost'. (*Irish News*, 10.11.92)

23 January 1993 — BBC — *'Timewatch: The sparks that lit the bonfire'*
This looked at the early days of the 'troubles' and the Irish government's possible
role in forming the Provisional IRA. Two interviewees each spoke with two voices,
their own and an actor's. Seán Mac Stiofáin was voiced over in an early recording,
made when he was an IRA leader, saying, 'Concessions be damned — we want
freedom', but an interview done for the programme used his own voice. The real
voice of Joe Cahill, former Belfast commander of the IRA, was used when he was
talking about the split between the Official and Provisional IRA, but he was voiced
over when talking about the Provisionals' military campaign. A short clip of a
speech by Gerry Adams was also voiced over.

March 1993 — Channel 4 — *Hidden Agenda*
Ken Loach's feature film about British undercover operations had been screened
on Sky TV on 29 June 1992. Channel 4 planned to show it on 21 March 1993, but
cancelled it after the IRA's Warrington bombing the day before, which killed a
child. Many people protested to Channel 4. It was shown on 16 April.

March 1993 — Channel 4 — *Angel*
Already shown on Channel 4 on 15 November 1984, this thriller by Neil Jordan was
to be repeated on 23 March 1993, but was cancelled after Warrington, probably
because *Hidden Agenda* was being withdrawn, to avoid accusations of double
standards. It was shown on 8 June.

*** During the May 1993 local election campaign, while their rights were protected under the Representation of the People Act, Sinn Fein broadcast pirate radio
programmes in Belfast on 'SFFM'.

4 June 1993 — BBC Scotland — *Axiom*
Sinn Fein councillor Máirtín Ó Muilleoir's voice was dubbed over in this
pre-recorded discussion about the significance of the North of Ireland for
Scotland. He later received a substantial sum in an out-of-court settlement from
the *Sunday Express*, over an article complaining about an 'IRA councillor' being
brought to Scotland at BBC expense. (*Irish News*, 29.7.93)

3 July 1993 — Channel 4 — *Frontline*
Sinn Fein spokesperson Richard McAuley was voiced over in this film by Malachi O'Doherty about the failings of the Northern Ireland inquest system.

Note: Censored items have not been compiled after this date.

The lifting of the bans

The end of both the South of Ireland's Section 31 restrictions and the British broadcasting ban came as a result of political developments. In the late 1980s, republican leaders — now with a solid electoral base in the North but shunned elsewhere because of IRA violence — began behind-the-scenes moves towards peace based on compromise. They talked to the SDLP and also, between 1991 and 1993, held secret meetings with British government representatives. In April 1993, SDLP leader John Hume and Sinn Fein President Gerry Adams announced a peace initiative, though the details remained unspecified. On 15 December, British Prime Minister John Major and Irish Taoiseach Albert Reynolds launched the Downing Street Declaration, promising new structures and dialogue with parties committed to peaceful methods.

In this context, on 11 January 1994 the South's broadcasting minister Michael D. Higgins announced that the Section 31 restrictions, in force since 1971, would be allowed to lapse. The RTE Authority issued new guidelines to staff, similar to the 'reference upwards' rules of British broadcasters: members of illegal organisations could only be interviewed with the permission of the Director-General, and all Sinn Fein interviews must be referred to the divisional head, and might need to be prerecorded.

In April 1994 the IRA announced a three-day 'suspension of military operations' as an gesture of good intent. Then on 31 August they announced 'a complete cessation'. (This broke down in early 1996, but by mid-1998 appeared secure again.) On 6 September came the symbolic tripartite handshake between Albert Reynolds, John Hume and Gerry Adams. The British government was still refusing to talk to Sinn Fein about a settlement, but on 16 September they announced two gestures: the lifting of the broadcasting ban and the re-opening of 10 of the blocked border roads. The ban's demise was widely welcomed. As Channel 4 Chief Executive Michael Grade said, 'The lifting of the ban ends Britain's most embarrassing attempt to censor coverage of the most important domestic political story of post-war years.' (*The Irish Times*, 17.9.94)

Soon afterwards, the goverment lifted the exclusion order, made under the Prevention of Terrorism Act, that had prevented Gerry Adams visiting Britain. He arrived in London on 17 November to be inundated with requests for interviews. The time-honoured transformation of 'terrorist' into 'statesman' had begun.

Note: This list is partly based on Paul Madden's chronology in ed. Campaign for Free Speech on Ireland, *The British Media and Ireland: Truth the First Casualty*, 1979. Versions of the list have appeared elsewhere. For help with later entries, thanks to Helen Dady, Sarah Grimes and David Miller.

Recent books useful for students include: David Miller, *Don't Mention the War*, 1994; ed. David Miller, *Rethinking Northern Ireland*, 1998; eds. Bill Rolston and David Miller, *War and Words: The Northern Ireland Media Reader*, 1996. A collection of newspaper cuttings used to prepare *Ireland: The Propaganda War* is held by the Linen Hall Library's Political Collection in Belfast.

References and notes

All quotations in the text have been taken verbatim from the sources, and retain the editorial conventions of the originals.

1. 1971: Year of crisis

1. Derek Marks, 'The Monster in the Box', *Sunday Express*, 21 November 1971. Authors who contest this view of Vietnam coverage include Noam Chomsky, 'The US media and the Tet offensive', *Race and Class*, vol. xx, no. 1, Summer 1978; also Phillip Knightley, *The First Casualty*, London: Quartet 1978; see also Philip Schlesinger, Graham Murdock, Philip Elliott, *Televising 'Terrorism'*, London: Comedia 1983.
2. *The Daily Telegraph*, 24 August 1971.
3. *The Daily Telegraph*, 20 August 1971.
4. *The Guardian*, 20 August 1971.
5. *The Observer*, 21 November 1971.
6. Anthony Smith, 'Television Coverage of Northern Ireland', *Index on Censorship*, vol. 1, no. 2, 1972.
7. *New Statesman*, 31 December 1971; *Private Eye*, 15 November 1971.
8. *Private Eye*, 15 November 1971.
9. *Ibid*.
10. Paul Madden, 'Banned, Censored and Delayed', in ed. Campaign for Free Speech on Ireland, *The British Media and Ireland: Truth the First Casualty*, London: Information on Ireland 1979, p. 17. This booklet is available from Information on Ireland, Box 189, 32 Ivor Place, London NW1 6DA.
11. Unsigned article by Jonathan Dimbleby, *New Statesman*, 31 December 1971.
12. *The Sunday Times*, 7 November 1971; see also Paul Madden, *op. cit.*
13. See Peregrine Worsthorne, 'BBC belongs to yesterday', *The Sunday Telegraph*, 2 January 1972.
14. Quoted in Milton Schulman, 'The half-truth machine', *Evening Standard*, 9 February 1972.
15. *The Irish Times*, 5 March 1977.
16. *The Daily Telegraph*, 10 November 1971.
17. *Daily Express*, 11 November 1971, quoted in Steve Chibnall, *Law-and-Order News*, London: Tavistock 1977.

18. *Evening Standard*, 19 November 1971; *The Guardian*, 20 November 1971.
19. For Robin Day's complaint, see *Daily Express*, 23 November 1971.
20. *Financial Times*, 16 November 1971.
21. *The Times*, 16 November 1971.
22. *Financial Times*, 17 November 1971.
23. *The Sunday Times, The Observer, The Sunday Telegraph*, 21 November 1971.
24. *The Times*, 24 November 1971.
25. *Bristol Evening Post*, 7 January 1972.
26. *The Observer*, 21 November 1971.
27. *The Times*, 18 November 1971.
28. *Ibid*.
29. *The Sunday Telegraph*, 2 January 1972.
30. 'Our Proper Concern', a speech given by Charles Curran at a meeting of the Radio and Television News Directors' Association, Boston, USA, 1 October 1971, London: BBC.
31. *The Times*, 24 November 1971.
32. *Land Operations Volume III – Counter Revolutionary Operations*, Ministry of Defence, 29 August 1969, amended 1971 and 1973, chapter 3, para. 160; see also Alan Hooper, *The Military and The Media*, Aldershot: Gower 1982.
33. *Ibid*.
34. Robin Evelegh, *Peace-keeping in a Democratic Society: The Lessons of Northern Ireland*, London: C. Hurst & Co. 1978, p. 45.
35. See below, chapter 10.
36. Desmond Taylor, 'Editorial Responsibilities', *BBC Lunchtime Lectures*, Series 10, no. 2, 13 November 1975.
37. *The Times*, 3 February 1972.
38. *New Statesman*, 31 December 1971, pp. 911–12.
39. *The Irish Times*, 24 November 1971.
40. *What do you think of it so far?*, chaired by David Frost, BBC2, 28 August 1976, quoted in ed. Campaign for Free Speech on Ireland, *The British Media and Ireland: Truth the First Casualty*, London: Information on Ireland 1979, pp. 6–7.
41. See Liz Curtis, 'The Falklands and Ireland: a pattern repeated?', 'Back View', *City Limits*, 21–27 May 1982.
42. *New Society*, 23 December 1971.
43. *The Daily Telegraph*, 24 November 1971.
44. *The Daily Telegraph*, 24 December 1971.
45. *TV Mail*, 31 December 1971.
46. Lord Hill quoted in Philip Schlesinger, *Putting 'Reality' Together: BBC News*, London: Constable 1978.
47. *The Daily Telegraph*, 5 January 1972.
48. See Colin R. Munro, *Television, Censorship and the Law*, Farnborough: Saxon House 1979, p. 14.
49. *The Guardian*, 5 January 1972.
50. *Financial Times*, 6 January 1972.
51. *Daily Express*, 13 January 1972.
52. *Birmingham Mail* and other papers, 6 January 1972.
53. Chris Dunkley writing in the *Financial Times*, 6 January 1972.
54. *The Times*, 7 January 1972.

55. *The Guardian*, 7 January 1972; for a summary of the controversy see Paul Madden in *The British Media and Ireland: Truth the First Casualty*, *op. cit.*, pp. 17–18.

2. From silence to civil rights

1. Quoted in Philip Schlesinger, *Putting 'Reality' Together: BBC News*, London: Constable 1978, p. 207.
2. Anthony Smith, 'Television Coverage of Northern Ireland', *Index on Censorship*, vol. 1, no. 2, 1972, pp. 15–32.
3. Quoted in Richard Francis, 'Broadcasting to a community in conflict – The experience in Northern Ireland', lecture given at the Royal Institute of International Affairs, Chatham House, London, 22 February 1977, London: BBC.
4. Anthony Smith, *op. cit.*, p. 18.
5. Anthony Smith, *op. cit.*, pp. 18–19.
6. Richard Francis, *op. cit.*
7. Colin R. Munro, *Television, Censorship and the Law*, Farnborough: Saxon House 1979, pp. 146–47.
8. Alan Whicker, *Within Whicker's World*, London: Elm Tree Books/Hamish Hamilton 1982, p. 113.
9. *Ibid.*
10. *Ibid.*, p. 114.
11. Anthony Smith, *op. cit.*
12. Quoted by Robert Carvel in *Pandora's Box*, BBC Radio 4, 6 October 1982.
13. Anthony Smith, *op. cit.*
14. Ed. Taylor Downing, *The Troubles*, London: Thames/MacDonald Futura 1980, pp. 128, 131.
15. Geoff Dudgeon, quoted in *The Irish Times*, 14 June 1980.
16. Annan Report into the future of broadcasting, pub. 24 March 1977.
17. Anthony Smith, *op. cit.*
18. *Ibid.*
19. Information given by a later *This Week* producer, David Elstein, in a TV discussion following the showing of *Before Hindsight*, BBC2, 11 February 1978. This remark was cut from the transcript published in *The Listener*: see *The Leveller*, April 1978.
20. Keith Kyle interviewed in *Northern Ireland: Are we told the truth?*, a videotape made by students at the Cardiff Centre for Journalism Studies, 1981.
21. Meeting of the EBU Television Programme Committee, London, 14–17 April 1978.
22. *The Sunday Times* Insight Team, *Ulster*, London: Penguin 1972, p. 8; ed. Taylor Downing, *op. cit.*, p. 128.
23. Eamonn McCann, *The British Press and Northern Ireland*, Northern Ireland Socialist Research Centre, 1971.
24. *Punch*, 15 January 1969; thanks to John Kirkaldy for drawing attention to this cartoon.
25. *Daily Express*, 19 April 1969.
26. *Daily Mirror*, 19 April 1969.
27. *The Times*, 23 April 1969.

28. *The Times*, 16 August 1969; for this and the next quotation, my thanks are due to Brian Hamilton-Tweedale.
29. *Daily Mail*, 16 August 1969.
30. Simon Winchester, *In Holy Terror*, London: Faber 1974, p. 124.
31. *The Guardian*, 16 August 1969; thanks to Brian Hamilton-Tweedale for this quotation.
32. *Daily Mail*, 11 September 1969, quoted in Eamonn McCann, *op. cit.*
33. *Daily Sketch*, 29 June 1970, quoted in Eamonn McCann, *op. cit.*
34. *Evening Standard*, 4 August 1970, quoted in Eamonn McCann, *op. cit.*
35. Eamonn McCann, *op. cit.*
36. *The Times Review of the Year*, 31 December 1970, quoted in Eamonn McCann, *op. cit.*
37. Simon Winchester, 1974, *op. cit.*
38. *Ibid.*, p. 122.
39. Quoted in Eamonn McCann, *op. cit.*, p. 19.
40. *Sunday Press*, 4 March 1979.
40. *Ibid.*; Kevin Dowling's novel about a reporter's experiences in the North of Ireland, *Interface: Ireland*, was published in London by Barrie and Jenkins in 1979.
42. Jay G. Blumler, 'Ulster on the small screen', *New Society*, 23 December 1971.
43. *The Sunday Times* Insight Team, 1972, *op. cit.*, p. 280.
44. *The Irish Press*, 5 February 1972, quoted in ed. Campaign for Free Speech on Ireland, *The British Media and Ireland: Truth the First Casualty*, London: Information on Ireland 1979, p. 34.

3. Reporting British violence

1. Frank Kitson, *Low Intensity Operations*, London: Faber 1971, p. 87.
2. Quoted in *The Sunday Times* Insight Team, *Ulster*, London: Penguin 1972, revised edition, p. 290.
3. *Ibid.*, p. 280.
4. John McGuffin, *Internment*, Ireland: Anvil 1973, chapter 15; for a full account, see John McGuffin, *The Guineapigs*, London: Penguin 1974.
5. *The Sunday Times*, 17 October 1971.
6. *Ibid.*
7. *The Observer*, 29 August 1976.
8. Interview by the author, March 1982.
9. ENCA minutes, 17 September 1971, reported in *Private Eye*, 15 November 1971.
10. Unsigned article by Jonathan Dimbleby, 'The BBC and Northern Ireland', *New Statesman*, 31 December 1971.
11. *The Daily Telegraph*, 20 November 1971.
12. *The Sunday Times*, 24 October 1971.
13. *Daily Express*, 23 October 1971.
14. *The Sunday Times*, 24 October 1971; *Private Eye*, 15 November 1971.
15. See Peter Taylor, *Beating the Terrorists?*, Penguin 1980, p. 22.
16. *The Guardian*, 17 November 1971, quoted in 'Struggles of a liberal conscience', Belfast Workers Research Unit, *Belfast Bulletin*, no. 6, Spring 1979.

17. See William Ristow and Dr Tim Shallice, 'Taking the lid off British torture', *New Scientist*, 5 August 1976; also Joe Joyce and Niall Kiely, 'Strasbourg', *Hibernia*, 20 January 1978.
18. *The Guardian*, 5 May 1976.
19. *Ibid*.
20. *Financial Times*, 15 June 1977.
21. *The Leveller*, June 1978.
22. Geoffrey Bell, 'Are we being honest?', *Journalist*, October 1976.
23. *Daily Mail*, *The Times*, *The Guardian*, 3 September 1976.
24. William Ristow and Dr Tim Shallice, *op. cit.*
25. *New Scientist*, 17 February 1977.
26. *The Times*, 3 September 1976.
27. *The Daily Telegraph*, 3 September 1976.
28. John Shirley, 'Judgement at Strasbourg', *New Statesman*, 10 September 1976.
29. *The Times*, 19 April 1977.
30. *The Sunday Telegraph*, 24 April 1977, quoted in unpublished article by Geoff Bell.
31. *Daily Express*, 21 April 1977.
32. *The Irish Times*, 23 April 1977.
33. *Daily Express*, 21 April 1977.
34. *The Times*, *The Guardian*, *The Daily Telegraph*, *Daily Express*, 19 January 1978, summarised in 'British press gloats in the wake of Strasbourg finding', *The Irish Times*, 20 January 1978.
35. *Evening Standard*, 20 January 1978.
36. *The Sun*, 20 January 1978.
37. *The Guardian*, 31 January 1972.
38. *The Times*, 31 January 1972, 1 February 1972.
39. *The Times*, 1 February 1972.
40. *Financial Times*, 31 January 1972, quoted in *Daily Mirror*, 1 February 1972.
41. BBCTV 9.50 p.m. news, 31 January 1972, quoted in *The Times*, 1 February 1972. The interview with General Ford was preceded by an interview with Father Daly, who said emphatically that the paras had not been fired at first.
42. *The Times*, 31 January 1972.
43. *The Times*, 1 February 1972.
44. *The Times* and other papers, 1 February 1972.
45. *Financial Times*, 31 January 1972, quoted in *Daily Mirror*, 1 February 1972.
46. *The Guardian*, 31 January 1972.
47. Eamonn McCann, *What Happened in Derry*, London: Socialist Worker pamphlet, undated.
48. *The Times*, 31 January 1972.
49. *The Guardian*, 31 January 1972.
50. *The Daily Telegraph*, 31 January 1972.
51. *The Times*, 31 January 1972.
52. *The Guardian*, 31 January 1972.
53. *The Guardian*, 1 February 1972.
54. Letter from Brian Joyce, *The Guardian*, 2 February 1972.
55. *The Daily Telegraph*, 31 January 1972.
56. *Daily Express*, 31 January 1972.
57. *Daily Mail*, 31 January 1972.
58. *Daily Mirror*, 1 February 1972.

59. *Ibid.*
60. *Daily Mirror*, 3 February 1972.
61. *Daily Mirror*, 1 February 1972.
62. *Daily Mirror*, 2 February 1972.
63. *Daily Mirror*, 5 February 1972.
64. *Ibid.*
65. Paul Madden in ed. Campaign for Free Speech on Ireland, *The British Media and Ireland: Truth the First Casualty*, London: Information on Ireland 1979, p. 18.
66. Interview with a barrister by the author.
67. *Irish Citizen*, vol. II, no. 2, 1972.
68. *The Sunday Times*, 6 February 1972.
69. *The Observer*, 6 February 1972.
70. Paul Madden, *op. cit.*; *The Guardian*, 8 March 1972.
71. Simon Winchester, *In Holy Terror*, London: Faber 1974, pp. 209–10.
72. For digests of the Widgery report, see *The Guardian* and *The Times*, 20 April 1972; for a brief critique of this and other judicial inquiries in the Six Counties see Kevin Boyle, Tom Hadden and Paddy Hillyard, *Law and State: The Case of Northern Ireland*, London: Martin Robertson 1975.
73. Simon Winchester, 1974, *op. cit*, p. 210.
74. *The Daily Telegraph*, 19 April 1972.
75. *Daily Mirror*, 19 April 1972.
76. *Daily Express*, 19 April 1972.
77. Simon Winchester, 1974, *op. cit.*, pp. 210–11.
78. *The Times*, *The Guardian*, 20 April 1972.
79. *Daily Mirror*, 20 April 1972.
80. *The Daily Telegraph*, 20 April 1972.
81. *Daily Mail*, 20 April 1972.
82. *The Sunday Times*, 30 January 1977.
83. *The Guardian*, 27 December 1979.
84. *The Irish Times*, 15 September 1976.
85. *The Listener*, 31 August 1978.
86. Colin Thomas, 'Taking up the gauntlet', *Film and TV Technician*, November 1978; 'Two images of Ireland', in *The British Media and Ireland: Truth the First Casualty*, *op. cit.*, pp. 28–29. A slightly fuller version of this analysis of Bloody Sunday coverage appeared in Liz Curtis, 'How the British media reported Bloody Sunday', *IRIS*, no. 5, March 1983, pp. 18–25.
87. For a full account of the interrogation system from 1976 to 1979, see Peter Taylor, *Beating the Terrorists?*, Penguin 1980.
88. Keith Kyle, 'Bernard O'Connor's story', *The Listener*, 10 March 1977.
89. Mary Holland, 'Mr Mason plays it rough', *New Statesman*, 11 March 1977.
90. *Ibid.*; Keith Kyle, *op. cit.*
91. Keith Kyle, letter to *The Guardian*, 31 March 1977.
92. *The Irish Press*, 18 March 1977.
93. *Look Here*, London Weekend Television, 8 July 1978.
94. ' "Tonight" on Northern Ireland – Sir Charles Curran replies', *The Listener*, 17 March 1977.
95. Richard Francis speaking on *Look Here*, *op. cit.*
96. *Small Screen = Smokescreen: A response to the Annan report*, London: Campaign for Free Speech on Ireland, 1977.
97. *Belfast News Letter*, 3 March 1977.

98. *Belfast Telegraph*, 3 March 1977.
99. *The Guardian*, 4 March 1977.
100. *The Irish Times*, 4 March 1977.
101. *The Daily Telegraph*, 4 March 1977.
102. *The Irish Times*, 11 March 1977.
103. *The Irish Times*, 10 March 1977.
104. *The Sunday Times*, 13 March 1977.
105. *The Guardian*, 14 March 1977.
106. *The Sunday Times*, 13 March 1977.
107. Eamonn McCann, 'Torture claims the media have ignored', *Hibernia*, 18 March 1977.
108. *The Guardian*, *Daily Mirror*, *Daily Express*, 15 March 1977.
109. Keith Kyle, letter to *The Guardian*, 31 March 1977.
110. *The Times*, 22 March 1977.
111. *The Times*, *The Guardian*, 23 March 1977.
112. *Ibid*.
113. *The Guardian*, 28 July 1977.
114. *The Guardian*, 1 July 1980.
115. *The Guardian*, 13 November 1982.
116. *The Observer*, 5 June 1977; see *The Observer*, 19 June 1977 for Peter Taylor's reply.
117. Peter Taylor, 'Reporting Northern Ireland', *Index on Censorship*, vol. 7, no. 6, London 1978, reprinted in ed. Campaign for Free Speech on Ireland, *The British Media and Ireland: Truth the First Casualty*, London: Information on Ireland 1979, pp. 21–25.
118. See Peter Taylor, *ibid.*, for a full account.
119. *Ibid*.
120. *Ibid*.
121. See *Broadcast*, 7 November 1977.
122. *The Irish Times*, *The Guardian*, *The Irish News*, 28 October 1977.
123. *Daily Express*, 28 October 1977.
124. *Yorkshire Post*, 28 October 1977.
125. *The Daily Telegraph*, 29 October 1977.
126. For a full account of the contents of the programme, see *The Irish Times*, 28 October 1977.
127. *Belfast Telegraph*, 28 October 1977.
128. Quoted in *The Guardian*, 29 October 1977.
129. *The Daily Telegraph*, 29 October 1977; *The Sunday Telegraph*, 30 October 1977.
130. *The Times*, 26 November 1977.
131. Peter Taylor, *op. cit.*; *The Guardian*, 3 November 1977.
132. *The Daily Telegraph*, 3 November 1977.
133. *The Guardian*, 29 October 1977.
134. *The Irish Times*, 8 November 1977.
135. John Howkins, 'Censorship 1977–78: a background paper', Edinburgh International Television Festival 1978, official programme, London: Broadcast 1978.
136. *The Daily Telegraph*, 31 October 1977.
137. *Ibid*.
138. See *Cormac Strikes Back: resistance cartoons from the North of Ireland*, London: Information on Ireland 1982, p. 23.

139. *The Daily Telegraph*, 31 October 1977.
140. *The Sun*, 1 November 1977.
141. *The Daily Telegraph*, 3 November 1977.
142. *The Observer*, 18 December 1977.
143. *The Times*, 20 December 1977.
144. *Daily Express*, 24 December 1977.
145. Quoted in *Socialist Challenge*, 15 June 1978.
146. *The Listener*, 15 June 1978.
147. IBA News Release, 8 June 1978.
148. *The Guardian*, 9 June 1978.
149. *The Irish Times*, 9 June 1978.
150. *The Guardian*, 9 June 1978.
151. *The Sunday Times*, 11 June 1978.
152. *The Economist*, 17 June 1978.
153. *The Sunday Telegraph*, 11 June 1978, quoted in Peter Taylor, *op. cit.*
154. Sir Brian Young, letter to *The Sunday Times*, 18 June 1978.
155. Peter Taylor, *op. cit.*
156. *The Times*, 9 June 1978.
157. *Ibid.*
158. *The Guardian*, 14 March 1979.
159. *The Irish Times*, 13 March 1979.
160. Preview of the programme in *The Guardian*, 10 March 1979.
161. *The Irish Times*, 13 March 1979.
162. *The Guardian*, 12 March 1979.
163. *The Guardian*, 13 March 1979.
164. *Ibid.*
165. *Daily Mirror*, 13 March 1979.
166. *The Daily Telegraph*, 13 March 1979.
167. *The Irish Times*, 13 March 1979.
168. *The Guardian*, 14 March 1979, 15 March 1979.
169. *The Irish Times*, 17 March 1979.
170. Ed Moloney, 'RUC clears itself of Irwin smears', *Hibernia*, 7 February 1980.
171. Press Association release, 16 March 1979, reported in *The Daily Telegraph*, 17 March 1979.
172. *The Daily Telegraph*, 16 March 1979.
173. *The Daily Telegraph*, 16 March 1979, 17 March 1979.
174. *The Daily Telegraph*, 17 March 1979.
175. *Daily Mail*, 20 March 1979.
176. *The Irish Times*, 17 March 1979.
177. Keith Kyle, letter to *The Guardian*, 27 March 1979.

4. Reporting the British army

1. *The Irish Times*, 31 July 1982.
2. Philip Elliott, 'Reporting Northern Ireland: A study of news in Britain, Ulster and the Irish Republic', Centre for Mass Communication Research, University of Leicester, 1966; later published in *Ethnicity and the Media*, UNESCO 1978.
3. Philip Schlesinger, *Putting 'Reality' Together: BBC News*, London: Constable 1978, p. 225.

4. Martin Dillon and Denis Lehane, *Political Murder in Northern Ireland*, Penguin 1973, pp. 293–96.
5. *The Times*, 18 April 1973.
6. *The Irish Press*, 22 June 1976; *The Sun*, 22 October 1976; *The Guardian*, 30 December 1978.
7. Fr Brian J. Brady, Fr Denis Faul, Fr Raymond Murray, *A British Army Murder*, pub. Fr Denis Faul, St Patrick's Academy, Dungannon, 1975, p. 20.
8. *Irish News-sheet: Chronology Nov '76 – June '77*, London: Troops Out 1977, p. 10.
9. *The Irish Press*, 16 August 1976.
10. *The Sunday Times*, 15 August 1976.
11. *Sunday Express*, 15 August 1976.
12. *The Observer*, 15 August 1976.
13. *The Sunday Times*, 26 September 1976.
14. *Irish News-sheet, op. cit.*, p. 11; the trial ended on 2 May 1977.
15. *The Irish Press*, 16 August 1976; Mallon's accusations were also mentioned the same day in *The Guardian* and the *Daily Mirror*.
16. *The Guardian*, *Daily Mirror*, *The Sun*, 16 August 1976.
17. *The Irish Times*, 7 October 1976.
18. *Daily Mail*, 5 October 1976.
19. *The Daily Telegraph*, 5 October 1976.
20. *Belfast Telegraph*, 5 October 1976.
21. Press release put out by the Northern Ireland Army Press Office on 5 October 1976.
22. *The Guardian*, *The Irish Times*, 14 October 1976.
23. Fr Brian J. Brady, Fr Denis Faul, Fr Raymond Murray, *British Army Terror – West Belfast September October 1976*.
24. *The Guardian*, 14 October 1976.
25. *The Guardian*, *The Irish Times*, 14 October 1976; *The Irish Times*, 15 October 1976.
26. *Irish News-sheet, op. cit.*, p. 11; the trial ended on 4 May 1977.
27. Minutes for NCA meeting, 13 August 1971, quoted in *Private Eye*, 15 November 1971.
28. Richard Francis, 'Broadcasting to a community in conflict – the experience in Northern Ireland', lecture given at the Royal Institute of International Affairs, Chatham House, 22 February 1977, London: BBC.
29. *The Guardian*, 26 February 1977.
30. *Ibid*.
31. Interview with a BBC journalist by the author.
32. *Land Operations Volume III – Counter Revolutionary Operations*, Ministry of Defence, 29 August 1969, as amended November 1971, Section 39, para. 533.
33. For the conclusion of the McCartan trial see *The Irish Times*, *The Guardian*, 20 June 1981.
34. See Ed Moloney, 'Mason's secret war', *Hibernia*, 8 February 1979.
35. Quoted in Richard Clutterbuck, *The Media and Political Violence*, London: Macmillan 1981, pp. 100–101.
36. *The Times*, 12 July 1978.
37. *Ibid*.
38. *Ibid*.

39. *The Guardian, The Irish Times*, 5 July 1979.
40. *New Statesman*, 10 September 1982.
41. *The Guardian, The Irish Times*, 25 November 1982, 26 November 1982.
42. *The Irish Times*, 22 December 1982, 24 December 1982; see also *New Statesman*, 7 January 1983.
43. *The Irish Times*, 13 November 1982.
44. *Ibid*.
45. *Ibid*.
46. BBC1, *Nine o'Clock News*, 24 November 1982.
47. *The Irish Times*, 2 September 1983.
48. *Radio Times*, 29 March – 4 April 1980.
49. *The Guardian*, 12 March 1980.
50. *The Guardian*, 19 March 1980.
51. *The Guardian*, 24 March 1980.
52. *The Times*, 31 March 1980.
53. *The Guardian*, 16 February 1981.
54. *Daily Mail*, 23 June 1975, quoted in John Hill, 'Ireland, Ideology and the British Cinema', unpublished paper, New University of Ulster.
55. *The Guardian*, 27 November 1981.
56. *The Guardian*, 26 June 1982; *The Irish Times*, 25 June 1982 and 26 June 1982. Other papers monitored were the *Financial Times, The Daily Telegraph, Morning Star, Daily Mirror, The Sun, Daily Mail, Daily Express*, all for 26 June 1982. *The Times* was on strike.
57. Simon Winchester, *In Holy Terror*, London: Faber 1974, p. 88.
58. For information about rubber and plastic bullets, see *They Shoot Children: the use of rubber and plastic bullets in the north of Ireland*, London: Information on Ireland 1982.
59. *The Guardian, The Daily Telegraph, Daily Mail, The Sun, Daily Mirror, The Times*, 20 April 1982.
60. ITN, *News at Ten*, 13 May 1982.
61. *Land Operations Volume III, op. cit.*, chapter 11, 'Public relations', para. 532.
62. *The Sunday Press*, 4 March 1979.
63. Kevin Dowling, *Interface: Ireland*, London: Barrie and Jenkins 1979, pp. 129–30.
64. Reproduced in David Barzilay and Michael Murray, *Four Months in Winter*, pub. The 2nd Battalion Royal Regiment of Fusiliers 1972.
65. Philip Elliott, 'Reporting Northern Ireland', *op. cit.*
66. *South London Press*, 14 November 1978.
67. Letter dated 14 November 1978.
68. *Sunday Mirror*, 1 April 1979.
69. *Daily Mirror*, 28 January 1976.
70. David Barzilay, *The British Army in Ulster*, vol. 4, Belfast: Century Books 1981, p. 111.
71. Max Halstock, *Rats: The Story of a Dog Soldier*, London: Gollancz 1981.
72. *Nationwide*, BBC1, October 1979; this sequence was reproduced on a videotape titled *No Sense of Ireland*, shown at the ICA, London, 9 February 1980.
73. *Daily Express*, 20 November 1979.
74. Max Halstock, *op. cit.*
75. *Daily Record*, 4 September 1980.
76. Max Halstock, *op. cit.*

77. *Daily Mirror*, 8 October 1981.
78. ITN, *News at Ten*, 25 May 1983.
79. David Young, *Four Five: The story of 45 Commando Royal Marines 1943–1971*, London: Leo Cooper 1972.
80. *Daily Mirror*, 8 August 1967, quoted in David Young, *op. cit.*
81. David Young, *op. cit.*

5. Reporting loyalist violence

1. Statistics supplied by Fr Raymond Murray, Association for Legal Justice.
2. For a history of the UVF, see David Boulton, *The UVF 1966–73: An anatomy of loyalist rebellion*, Dublin: Torc Books/Gill and Macmillan 1973.
3. Quoted in David Boulton, *op. cit.*, p. 85.
4. Michael Farrell, *Northern Ireland: the Orange State*, London: Pluto Press 1976, p. 263.
5. *The Guardian*, 11 November 1972, quoted in Belfast Workers Research Unit, *Belfast Bulletin*, no. 6, Spring 1979.
6. *The Guardian*, 19 November 1972, quoted in *Belfast Bulletin*, no. 6, *op. cit.*
7. *The Times*, 6 December 1971.
8. For more detailed accounts of the media coverage of the McGurk's bar bombing, see unsigned articles by Liz Curtis in *Belfast Bulletin*, no. 3, Belfast Workers Research Unit 1979, and in ed. Campaign for Free Speech on Ireland, *The British Media and Ireland: Truth the First Casualty*, London: Information on Ireland 1979.
9. Quoted in David Boulton, *op. cit.*, p. 152.
10. Quoted in Michael Farrell, *op. cit.*, p. 296.
11. Martin Dillon and Denis Lehane, *Political Murder in Northern Ireland*, Penguin 1973.
12. Dillon and Lehane estimated that of 198 civilian assassination victims between 1966 and mid-1973, less than one in five were killed by the IRA: Dillon and Lehane, *op. cit.*, p. 245.
13. Dillon and Lehane, *op. cit.*
14. Quoted in Dillon and Lehane, *op. cit.*, p. 218.
15. Dillon and Lehane, *op. cit.*, pp. 217–18.
16. Dillon and Lehane, *op. cit.*, pp. 81–83.
17. *Evening News*, 3 October 1972.
18. Philip Elliott, 'Misreporting Ulster: news as a field-dressing', *New Society*, 25 November 1976.
19. Philip Elliott, 'Reporting Northern Ireland: A study of news in Britain, Ulster and the Irish Republic', Centre for Mass Communication Research, University of Leicester, 1976, later published in *Ethnicity and the Media*, UNESCO 1978.
20. Philip Elliott, 'Misreporting Ulster', *op. cit.*
21. Philip Elliott, 'Reporting Northern Ireland', *op. cit.*; see also article by Andrew Stephen in *The Observer*, 29 February 1976.
22. *The Guardian*, 26 August 1983. UDA member Stanley Millar Smith was convicted of her murder in December 1983.
23. *The Sun*, 2 February 1978.
24. *The Sun*, 3 February 1978.
25. *The Observer*, 17 May 1981.
26. *News of the World*, 17 May 1981.

27. *The Sunday Times*, 17 May 1981.
28. *The Guardian*, 18 May 1981.
29. *The Guardian*, 25 May 1981.
30. *The Irish Times*, 7 January 1977, *The Leveller*, June 1978.
31. Richard Francis, 'Broadcasting to a community in conflict – The experience in Northern Ireland', lecture given at the Royal Institute of International Affairs, Chatham House, 22 February 1977; also see interview with Sir Charles Curran, *The Listener*, 18 November 1976.
32. *The Irish Times*, 10 January 1977.
33. Philip Elliott, 'Reporting Northern Ireland', *op. cit.*
34. *Ibid.*
35. *Ibid.*
36. *Daily Mirror*, 29 October 1976.
37. *Socialist Worker*, 7 June 1980.
38. *The Sunday Times*, 31 October 1976.
39. Frank Webster, *The New Photography: Responsibility in Visual Communication*, London: Platform Books/Calder 1980; Webster's chapter 8 includes a discussion of Maire Drumm's funeral as covered in *The Sun*, the *Daily Mirror* and the *Daily Mail* for 2 November 1976.
40. *News of the World*, 15 November 1981.
41. *The Irish Times*, 21 November 1981.
42. *The Guardian*, 17 January 1981.
43. *The Irish Times*, 17 January 1981.
44. *Daily Mail*, 17 January 1981.
45. *Daily Mirror*, 17 January 1981.
46. *Daily Mail*, 17 January 1981.
47. *The Irish Times, The Guardian, Daily Mirror, Daily Express, Daily Mail*, 17 January 1981. The analysis given here is based on an unpublished survey done by Linda Luckhaus of British and Irish press coverage of the attack on the McAliskeys.
48. *The Irish Times*, 22 January 1982.
49. See article by Mary Holland in the *New Statesman*, 23 January 1981.
50. BBC1, *Nine O'Clock News*, 21 January 1982; see also Liz Curtis, 'Back View', *City Limits*, 29 January – 4 February 1982.
51. *The Irish Times*, 30 May 1981, quoting an interview given by Andy Tyrie to the *Washington Star*.
52. *The Sunday Times*, 25 October 1981.
53. *Time Out*, 22–28 October 1976; *Daily Express*, 7 February 1977; *Morning Star*, 7 February 1977; Paul Madden in *The British Media and Ireland: Truth the First Casualty*, *op. cit*. The film was transmitted on BBC Scotland, 23 October 1976, and on BBC2's *Network*, 5 February 1977.
54. *Nationwide* sequence reproduced in *No Sense of Ireland*, videotape shown at the ICA, London, 9 February 1980.
55. Robert Fisk, *The Point of No Return*, London: André Deutsch 1975.
56. *Ibid.*, p. 135.

6. Reporting republican violence

1. Philip Elliott, 'Misreporting Ulster: news as a field-dressing', *New Society*, 25 November 1976.

2. *Ibid*. Elliott deliberately chose two three-week periods which each contained a major election in the Six Counties because he wanted to 'maximise the level of political reporting'.

3. Jay G. Blumler, 'Ulster on the small screen', *New Society*, 23 December 1971.

4. Philip Elliott, 'Misreporting Ulster', *op. cit.*

5. Philip Elliott, 'Reporting Northern Ireland: a study of news in Britain, Ulster and the Irish Republic', Centre for Mass Communication Research, University of Leicester 1976; later published in *Ethnicity and the Media*, UNESCO 1978.

6. *Daily Express*, 6 May 1981.

7. *The Times*, 8 May 1981.

8. In November 1983 the New Ireland Forum released a report on the 'costs of violence' in the North. This included statistics which showed that 2,304 people had been killed in the North between 1 January 1969 and 30 June 1983: republican paramilitaries were responsible for 1,264 of these deaths, loyalist paramilitaries for 613, and the 'security forces' for 264, while 163 were 'non classified'. Other statistics showed that of the 1,297 civilian victims, 773 were Catholics, 495 were Protestants, and 29 were not natives of the North. The report was printed in full in *The Irish Times*, 4 November 1983.

9. *The Irish Post*, 23 May 1981.

10. *The Irish Post*, 20 February 1982. In August 1982 the Press Council upheld similar complaints against the *Daily Star* and the *Daily Express*: see *The Irish Times*, 16 August 1983. See also *The Daily Telegraph*'s leader attacking the Press Council, 17 August 1983.

11. From statistics supplied by Fr Raymond Murray of the Association for Legal Justice.

12. *The Sunday Times*, 26 June 1977.

13. *The Sunday Times*, 1 January 1978.

14. Philip Elliott, 'Reporting Northern Ireland', *op. cit.*

15. *The Daily Telegraph*, 24 February 1979.

16. *The Guardian*, 26 February 1979.

17. *The Sun*, 12 January 1982.

18. *The Guardian*, 12 January 1982.

19. *Daily Express*, 4 March 1977.

20. Interview by the author, April 1982.

21. Philip Elliott, 'Misreporting Ulster', *op. cit.*

22. Philip Elliott, 'Reporting Northern Ireland', *op. cit.*

23. *Ibid*.

24. *Ibid*.

25. Chris Mullin, 'The Birmingham bombings: Did the police get the right culprits?', *Tribune*, 14 October 1977; Gavin Esler, 'Aunt Annie's bomb kitchen', *New Statesman*, 21 March 1980; Chris Mullin, 'Caught for life by cruel chance', *New Statesman*, 1 January 1982.

26. Harris and Spark, *Practical Newspaper Reporting*, quoted in Tim Gopsill, 'Anatomy of a hack', *The Leveller*, January 1978.

27. BBC *News Guide*, 1979.

28. *Tonight* report on the IRA, transmitted 15 February 1977, quoted in ed. Campaign for Free Speech on Ireland, *The British Media and Ireland: Truth the First Casualty*, London: Information on Ireland 1979, p. 29.

29. Philip Elliott, Graham Murdock, Philip Schlesinger, 'The State and "Terrorism" on British Television', published in English in *L'imaggine dell'Uomo*, vol. 1, no. 2, Florence, and in Italian in *Dati per la Verifica dei Programmi Transnessi*, RAI, Rome, 1982.
30. Philip Elliott, 'Reporting Northern Ireland', *op. cit.*
31. *The Guardian*, 28 August 1979.
32. *Daily Mirror*, 28 August 1979.
33. *Daily Mirror*, 6 September 1979.
34. *Daily Mirror*, 28 August 1979.
35. Philip Schlesinger, ' "Terrorism", the media and the liberal-democratic state: a critique of the orthodoxy', *Social Research*, Spring 1981, vol. 48, no. 1.
36. *Daily Express*, 28 August 1979.
37. Geoff Bell, 'Out of the gutter – the press and Mountbatten', *Socialist Challenge*, 20 September 1979.
38. *Daily Mirror*, 28 August 1979.
39. *The Guardian*, 28 August 1979.
40. *The Observer*, 2 September 1979.
41. *Daily Mail*, 17 May 1977.
42. *Daily Mirror*, 17 May 1977; see also *Evening Standard*, 16 May 1977.
43. W. Stephen Gilbert, unpublished article.
44. ITN, 16 May 1977, quoted in W. Stephen Gilbert, *op. cit.*
45. *Daily Mail*, 17 May 1977, quoted in Frank Webster, *The New Photography: Responsibility in Visual Communication*, London: Platform Books/Calder 1980.
46. Frank Webster, *op. cit.*, p. 243.
47. *Ibid.*
48. Max Halstock, *Rats: The Story of a Dog Soldier*, London: Gollancz 1981.
49. *The Sunday Times*, 25 July 1982.
50. *Daily Mail*, 21 July 1982.
51. *The Sun*, 21 July 1982.
52. *The Daily Mirror*, 24 July 1982.
53. *The Sunday Times*, 25 July 1982.
54. Albert Hunt, *The Language of Television*, London: Eyre Methuen 1981, p. 23.
55. In 1983 Souvenir Press released a book about Sefton, *The Story of a Cavalry Horse*, by J.N.P. Watson: the blurb described Sefton as 'the equine hero whose bravery and character captured the hearts of millions'. The same year Quiller Press published *Sefton: 'The horse for any year'*, edited by Brigadier-General Landy, proceeds to the Army Benevolent Fund.
56. Letter from L.J. Millar, *The Guardian*, 23 July 1982.
57. *The Sun*, 8 February 1971, quoted in Eamonn McCann, *The British Press and Northern Ireland*, Northern Ireland Socialist Research Centre 1971.
58. Eamonn McCann, *op. cit.*
59. John McGuffin, *Internment*, Ireland: Anvil 1973, p. 189; *Time Out*, 13–19 October 1972.
60. John McGuffin, *op. cit.*, p. 189.
61. *Time Out*, 13–19 October 1972.
62. *The Sunday Times*, 13 March 1977.
63. *Daily Mirror*, 23 October 1971; see also *Private Eye*, 15 November 1971.
64. *Sunday News*, 24 October 1972, quoted in John McGuffin, *op. cit.*, p. 150.

65. *Private Eye*, 15 November 1971.
66. See *The Sun*, 18 June 1979.
67. *The Mail on Sunday*, 25 September 1983, quoted in *New Statesman*, 28 October 1983.
68. *New Statesman*, 28 October 1983.
69. *Daily Mirror* article reproduced in *Big Flame*, October 1977.
70. *Daily Mirror*, 2 September 1977.
71. *Daily Express*, 28 October 1976; *The Irish Post*, 26 February 1977, 20 August 1977; *The Irish Times*, 18 February 1977; see also *The British Media and Ireland: Truth the First Casualty*, *op. cit.*, p. 44.
72. Steve Chibnall, *Law-and-Order News*, London: Tavistock 1977, pp. 42–43.
73. Quoted in the press on 5 September 1975.
74. *Daily Mail*, *Daily Mirror*, *The Daily Telegraph*, *The Sun*, *Daily Express*, *The Times*, *The Guardian*, 5 September 1975.
75. *The Guardian*, 9 September 1975.
76. Quoted in unsigned article by Liz Curtis, 'The case of Margaret McKearney', in *The British Media and Ireland: Truth the First Casualty*, *op. cit.*, p. 38.
77. See Steve Chibnall, *op. cit.*, p. 189.
78. *The Guardian*, 9 September 1975.
79. *Daily Mail*, 19 December 1978.
80. *The Guardian*, 21 December 1978.
81. *Republican News*, 6 January 1979.
82. *Evening Standard*, 20 December 1978.
83. *The Guardian*, 21 December 1978.
84. *The Irish Times*, 19 January 1979.
85. *The Guardian*, 8 February 1979; *Daily Mirror*, 19 May 1979.
.86. For accounts of the 'Bald Eagle' saga, see Belfast Workers Research Unit, *Belfast Bulletin*, no. 6, Spring 1979; *Republican News*, 6 January 1979; cartoon by Christine Roche in *The British Media and Ireland: Truth the First Casualty*, *op. cit.*, p. 39.
87. Alan Rusbridger, *The Guardian* diary, 31 May 1983.
88. *Daily Mirror*, 27 May 1983.
89. *The Sun*, *Daily Mail*, *Daily Star*, 27 May 1983.
90. BBC1, 5.40 p.m., 27 May 1983.
91. *Daily Mirror*, 28 May 1983.
92. *News of the World*, 29 May 1983.
93. *The Irish Times*, 30 May 1983; see also *Daily Mirror* and *The Guardian*, 30 May 1983, and Mary Holland, *What the Papers Say*, Channel 4, 3 June 1983.
94. IRN News, 30 May 1983; ITN, 5.05 p.m. (*sic*: it was a bank holiday), 30 May 1983.
95. *The Guardian*, 31 May 1983.
96. See Eamonn McCann, *The British Press and Northern Ireland*, *op. cit.*
97. *The Sunday Times*, 22 August 1976.
98. *The Sunday Times*, 3 August 1975.
99. *The Sunday Times*, 22 August 1976.
100. *The Irish Times*, 4 October 1979, 9 October 1979, 10 October 1979, 25 October 1979; *The Guardian*, 25 October 1979.
101. *The Sunday Times*, 27 March 1977.
102. Belfast Workers Research Unit, *Belfast Bulletin*, no. 8, Spring 1980.
103. *The Sunday Times*, 18 October 1981.
104. *The Daily Telegraph*, 22 February 1977.

105. *The Sunday Telegraph*, 27 February 1977.
106. *The Irish Post*, 26 February 1977.
107. Letter from Shane Connaughton to Jonathan Hammond, 8 September 1977.
108. Quoted in *Irish Political Prisoners in English Jails*, London: Prisoners Aid Committee, 1980, p. 14.
109. *The Listener*, 28 February 1980.
110. See, for example, Thames TV's 'The Glory Hole', shown in ITV's *Playhouse* slot, 10 August 1982.
111. 'Northern Ireland: Future Terrorist Trends', Ministry of Defence, dated 2 November 1978, published in full in Sean Cronin, *Irish Nationalism*, Dublin: The Academy Press 1980; London: Pluto Press 1983, pp. 339–57, and in facsimile in Roger Faligot, *The Kitson Experiment*, London: Zed Press 1983.
112. *Ibid*. For a discussion of fictional representations of the IRA, see Philip Schlesinger, Graham Murdock, Philip Elliott, *Televising 'Terrorism'*, London: Comedia 1983, chapter 3.
113. Peter Taylor speaking at a conference on 'Representations in the mass media', National Film Theatre, London, 5 April 1983.
114. *Sunday Times Magazine*, 28 March 1982, p. 25.
115. See Richard Francis, 'Broadcasting to a community in conflict – the experience in Northern Ireland', lecture given at the Royal Institute of International Affairs, Chatham House, London, 22 February 1977.
116. *Hibernia*, 9 March 1978.
117. Quoted in Philip Schlesinger, ' "Terrorism", the media and the liberal-democratic state: a critique of the orthodoxy', *Social Research*, Spring 1981, vol. 48, no. 1, p. 80.
118. Quoted in Philip Schlesinger, *Putting 'Reality' Together: BBC News*, London: Constable 1978, pp. 229–30.
119. *BBC News Guide*, 1979.
120. Quoted in Philip Schlesinger, 1981, *op. cit.*
121. Interview given by Mrs Thatcher to *The Oregonian*, USA, 2 July 1980, quoted in *The Irish Post*, 26 July 1980.
122. *Desire*, pilot issue, 1981.
123. Article in *The Listener*, quoted in *The Guardian*, 12 November 1981.

7. Televising republicans

1. *Daily Mail*, 6 January 1977, *The Observer*, 23 January 1977.
2. *Financial Times*, 6 April 1977.
3. *The Observer*, 21 November 1971.
4. *The Listener*, 20 June 1974; a transcript of the June 1974 interview with David O'Connell, done by Tom Mangold, appeared in *The Listener*, 13 June 1974.
5. Richard Francis, 'Broadcasting to a community in conflict – the experience in Northern Ireland', lecture given at the Royal Institute of International Affairs, Chatham House, London, 22 February 1977, London: BBC.
6. *Ibid*.
7. Thames TV, *This Week* 'special', 'Five Long Years', transmitted on ITV on 12 August 1974.

8. TV Co-op, *Ireland: The Silent Voices*, transmitted on Channel 4 on 7 March 1983.
9. *The Mail on Sunday*, 6 March 1983.
10. *The Guardian*, 14 June 1974.
11. *Ibid*.
12. *The Daily Telegraph*, 22 January 1973.
13. *The Times*, 19 November 1974.
14. *The Daily Telegraph*, 29 November 1974.
15. See Colin R. Munro, *Television, Censorship and the Law*, Farnborough: Saxon House 1979, for a straightforward account of the legal constraints on television.
16. *The Times*, 23 January 1973.
17. *The Times*, 11 December 1974; also see article by Robert Fisk, *The Times*, 3 December 1974.
18. *Daily Mail*, 6 January 1977.
19. *The Irish Press*, 16 December 1977.
20. *The Sunday Times*, 13 March 1977.
21. Conservative Central Office News Release, 16 December 1977.
22. *The Irish Times*, 22 December 1977.
23. *The Guardian*, 17 July 1979.
24. *The Irish Times*, 4 June 1980.
25. *New Statesman*, 11 March 1977.
26. See, for example, books by Richard Clutterbuck, and by Christopher Dobson and Ronald Payne.
27. 'Terrorism and the News Media', an international conference organised by the Centre for Contemporary Studies and the University of Aberdeen, at the Royal Society of Arts, London, 5–6 May 1982.
28. Quoted in Maurice Tugwell, 'Politics and Propaganda of the Provisional IRA', in ed. Paul Wilkinson, *British Perspectives on Terrorism*, London: George Allen & Unwin 1981. For a critique of Jenkins et al. see Philip Schlesinger, Graham Murdock, Philip Elliott, *Televising 'Terrorism'*, London: Comedia 1983.
29. Quoted in Philip Schlesinger, ' "Terrorism", the media and the liberal-democratic state: a critique of the orthodoxy', *Social Research*, vol. 48, no. 1, Spring 1981.
30. Frank Burton, *The Politics of Legitimacy: Struggles in a Belfast Community*, London: Routledge and Kegan Paul, 1978, pp. 118–19.
31. Quoted in Desmond Taylor, *Editorial Responsibilities*, London: BBC 13 November 1975.
32. *The Listener*, 20 June 1974, p. 784.
33. *Broadcast*, 2 December 1974.
34. Letter to *The Daily Telegraph*, 14 July 1979.
35. Richard Francis, *op. cit.*
36. *Ibid*.
37. Extract from BBC Northern Ireland's *Scene Around Six*, *The Listener*, 18 November 1976.
38. Richard Francis, *op. cit.*
39. Speech to the Broadcasting Press Guild, 12 July 1979, quoted in *The Listener*, 19 July 1979.
40. *The Daily Telegraph*, 14 July 1979.
41. *The Irish Times*, 28 January 1981.

42. Richard Francis, *op. cit.*
43. *The Listener*, 19 July 1979.
44. Report of the Committee on the Future of Broadcasting, chaired by Lord Annan, published 24 March 1977.
45. *The Listener*, 27 March 1980.
46. *Ibid.*
47. National Union of Journalists/Association of Cinematograph and Television Technicians Conference on Media Censorship of Northern Ireland, Birmingham, 28 February 1981.
48. Letter from Bernard Falk to *The Sunday Times*, 19 February 1978.
49. *Ibid.*
50. *The Guardian*, 14 March 1977.
51. *The Observer*, 29 February 1976.
52. *The Sunday Times*, 12 September 1976.
53. NUJ/ACTT conference, 28 February 1981, *op. cit.*
54. *You the Jury*, BBC Radio 4, transmitted on 8 March 1978.
55. *Financial Times*, 6 April 1977.
56. *Private Eye*, 15 November 1971.
57. *The Sunday Times*, 7 November 1971.
58. *Ibid.*
59. *Ibid.*
60. *The Guardian*, 2 November 1971.
61. *The Sunday Times*, 7 November 1971.
62. Anthony Smith, 'Television Coverage of Northern Ireland', *Index on Censorship*, vol. 1, no. 2, 1972.
63. Quoted in the *Spectator*, 27 November 1971.
64. *The Guardian*, 20 November 1971.
65. Four plays transmitted on BBC1, 11 September – 2 October 1975.
66. Letter to the author.
67. *Ibid.*
68. Paul Madden in ed. Campaign for Free Speech on Ireland, *The British Media and Ireland: Truth the First Casualty*, London: Information on Ireland 1979.
69. See above, chapter 5.
70. Quoted in Peter Taylor, 'Reporting Northern Ireland', *Index on Censorship*, vol. 7, no. 6, 1978, and reprinted in ed. Campaign for Free Speech on Ireland, *The British Media and Ireland: Truth the First Casualty*, *op. cit.* See also John Howkins, 'Censorship 1977–78: a background paper', Edinburgh International Television Festival 1978 official programme, London: Broadcast 1978.
71. Peter Taylor, *op. cit.*
72. Speaking on LWT's *Look Here*, 8 July 1978; see *Film and TV Technician*, August/September 1978 for extracts.
73. Paul Madden, *op. cit.*
74. *Look Here*, 8 July 1978, *op. cit.*
75. *Ibid.*
76. *The Sun*, 17 May 1979.
77. *Socialist Challenge*, 24 May 1979.
78. *The Irish Times*, 17 May 1979.
79. *Ibid.*
80. The programme was transmitted on 15 May 1979.

81. See above pp. 165ff, 'The Carrickmore affair'.
82. *The Leveller*, January 1978.
83. *Socialist Worker*, 17 May 1980.
84. *Ibid.*
85. Transmitted over five weeks from 5 January 1981.
86. *Desire*, pilot issue, 1981. Records of the production of *The Troubles* are deposited with the Imperial War Museum.
87. Ian Stuttard, article for *The Sunday Tribune*, 15 July 1981.
88. Desmond Taylor, 'Editorial Responsibilities', BBC Lunch-time Lectures, series 10, no. 2, 13 November 1975.
89. *The Daily Telegraph*, 22 January 1973.
90. *The Daily Telegraph*, *The Times*, *The Guardian*, 23 January 1973.
91. *The Daily Telegraph*, 23 January 1973.
92. *Ibid.*
93. *Broadcast*, 2 December 1974.
94. Richard Deutsch and Vivien Magowan, *Northern Ireland 1968–74: A chronology of events*, vol. 3, Belfast: Blackstaff Press 1975, p. 165a.
95. *The Times*, 19 November 1974.
96. *The Times*, 26 November 1974.
97. *The Times*, 29 November 1974.
98. *Ibid.*
99. *Ibid.*
100. *Ibid.*
101. *The Daily Telegraph*, 26 November 1974.
102. *The Irish Times*, 7 January 1977; *The Observer*, 23 January 1977.
103. *Daily Mail*, 6 January 1977.
104. *Ibid.*
105. *The Observer*, 23 January 1977.
106. *Ibid.*
107. *Daily Mail*, 6 January 1977.
108. *The Observer*, 23 January 1977.
109. *Ibid.*
110. *Ibid.*
111. *Ibid.*
112. *The Guardian*, 17 January 1977.
113. Quoted in *The Times*, 16 December 1977; see also Jeremy Paxman, 'The path of the IRA', *The Listener*, 15 December 1977, pp. 778–79.
114. *The Times*, 16 December 1977.
115. *Financial Times*, 21 December 1977.
116. *The Irish Press*, 16 December 1977.
117. Conservative Central Office News Release, 16 December 1977.
118. *The Daily Telegraph*, 17 December 1977.
119. *Daily Express*, 16 December 1977.
120. *Sunday Express*, 18 December 1977.
121. *The Guardian*, 7 July 1979.
122. *The Listener*, 19 July 1979.
123. Richard Francis, 'Television reporting beyond the pale', *The Listener*, 27 March 1980.
124. *The Daily Telegraph*, 11 July 1979, quoted in *Evening News*, 11 July 1979.
125. *The Daily Telegraph*, 12 July 1979.
126. *Evening Standard*, 12 July 1979; other papers 13 July 1979.

127. *Morning Star*, 13 July 1979.
128. *Evening Standard*, 12 July 1979.
129. *Daily Mirror*, *Daily Mail*, *The Sun*, 13 July 1979.
130. Tony Banks, 'The Carrickmore affair', *ABStract*, January 1980.
131. *The Irish Times*, 8 November 1979, 9 November 1979.
132. *The Guardian*, 16 November 1979.
133. *The Guardian*, 10 November 1979.
134. *Pandora's Box*, BBC Radio 4, 6 October 1982.
135. *The Observer*, 11 November 1979.
136. *New Statesman*, 16 November 1979.
137. *Hibernia*, 8 November 1979.
138. *The Observer*, 11 November 1979.
139. Vincent Hanna speaking at the NUJ ADM, April 1980, minutes, p. 73.
140. Tony Banks, *op. cit.*
141. *The Guardian*, 9 November 1979.
142. *Ibid*.
143. *Ibid*. See also *The Observer*, 11 November 1979.
144. *The Guardian*, editorial, 10 November 1979.
145. *Daily Express*, 9 November 1979.
146. *The Guardian*, *The Sun*, *Daily Express*, 9 November 1979.
147. *The Sun*, *Daily Express*, *Daily Mail*, 9 November 1979.
148. *The Sun*, 9 November 1979.
149. *The Guardian*, 10 November 1979.
150. NUJ/ACTT conference on the media and Ireland, 28 February 1981, *op. cit.*
151. *The Guardian*, 9 November 1979.
152. See Catherine Scorer and Patricia Hewitt, *The Prevention of Terrorism Act: the case for repeal*, London: NCCL 1981. The Prevention of Terrorism Bill, drafted to replace the existing Act, was at the committee stage in late 1983. The Bill retained the Section 11 powers.
153. *Evening News*, 9 November 1979; letter from Vincent Hanna to *The Guardian*, 12 November 1979.
154. *The Guardian*, 14 November 1979.
155. *Hibernia*, 15 November 1979.
156. *The Guardian*, 17 November 1979.
157. *The Times*, 19 November 1979; *The Guardian*, 19 November 1979.
158. *The Guardian*, 21 November 1979.
159. Report of Proceedings of NUJ Annual Delegate Meeting, 18–21 April 1980, p. 73; see also Vincent Hanna, 'Carrickmore Carry-on', *Taking Liberties*, London: NUJ 1982.
160. *Hibernia*, 17 January 1980.
161. *The Guardian*, 12 July 1980.
162. *Ibid*.
163. *Hansard*, 1 August 1980, col. 2011.
164. *Hansard*, 1 August 1980, col. 2012.
165. *The Times*, 2 August 1980.
166. *Ibid*.
167. *Ibid*.
168. *The Times*, 5 August 1980.

8. The reference upwards system

1. Appendix to the NCA minutes of 27 November 1979.
2. Jay G. Blumler, 'Ulster on the small screen', *New Society*, 23 December 1971.
3. Quoted in Anthony Smith, 'Television Coverage of Northern Ireland', *Index on Censorship*, vol. 1, no. 2, 1972.
4. Jeremy Paxman, 'Reporting Failure in Ulster', *The Listener*, 5 October 1978.
5. See Anthony Smith, *op. cit.*
6. *News Guide*, 1972, quoted in Philip Schlesinger, *Putting 'Reality' Together: BBC News*, London: Constable 1978, p. 214.
7. *The Sunday Times*, 2 January 1972.
8. Anthony Smith, *op. cit.*
9. *Ibid.*
10. *Ibid.*
11. *Ibid.*
12. *The Guardian*, 20 November 1979.
13. See Philip Schlesinger, 1978, *op. cit.*, chapter 6.
14. *News and Current Affairs Index*, BBC, October 1980.
15. Richard Francis, 'Broadcasting to a community in conflict – the experience in Northern Ireland', lecture given at the Royal Institute of International Affairs, Chatham House, London, 22 February 1977, London: BBC.
16. *The Listener*, 28 February 1980.
17. Interview with Paul Fox, BBC Radio 3, 18 November 1981.
18. Glasgow: Fontana 1975.
19. Transmitted on 25, 26, 27 October 1982.
20. See ed. Campaign for Free Speech on Ireland, *The British Media and Ireland: Truth the First Casualty*, London: Information on Ireland 1979, p. 34.
21. *The Irish Post*, 26 September 1981.
22. *The Times*, 16 December 1981.
23. *Daily Mirror*, 23 September 1981.
24. *Ibid.*
25. *Principles and Practice in News and Current Affairs*, BBC 1971, quoted in Philip Schlesinger, 1978, *op. cit.*
26. *The Listener*, 20 June 1974.
27. *The Guardian*, 23 November 1971.
28. *Financial Times*, 24 November 1971.
29. *Pandora's Box*, BBC Radio 4, 6 October 1982; see also ed. Brian Lapping, *The State of the Nation: the bounds of freedom*, London: Constable in association with Granada Television 1980, chapter 6.
30. *News and Current Affairs Index*, BBC, October 1980. The position of Director of News and Current Affairs was abolished with Richard Francis's departure to Managing Director of Radio; DNCA's main functions passed to the Assistant Director-General.
31. *Broadcast*, 25 August 1980.
32. *Television Programme Guidelines*, IBA, revised edition, June 1979.
33. *Ibid.*, p. 11.
34. *Ibid.*
35. Quoted in *Private Eye*, 15 November 1971.
36. *Ibid.*

37. *Ibid.*
38. *The Sunday Times*, 2 January 1972.
39. Desmond Taylor, 'Editorial Responsibilities', BBC Lunch-time Lectures, series 10, 13 November 1975.
40. *The Sunday Times*, 2 January 1972.
41. Unsigned article, *New Statesman*, 31 December 1971.
42. Richard Francis, 'Broadcasting to a community in conflict', *op. cit.*
43. *The Listener*, 27 March 1980.
44. *Tonight*, BBC1, 5 July 1979; for further discussion of the INLA interview, see Philip Schlesinger, Graham Murdock, Philip Elliott, *Televising 'Terrorism'*, London: Comedia 1983, pp. 50–52.
45. Interview with Richard McAuley by the author.
46. *The Sun*, 7 July 1979.
47. BBC1, 22 November 1982.
48. BBC2, 16 January 1982.
49. The *Panorama* programme on Gerry Adams was discussed by Liz Curtis in *City Limits*, 10–16 December 1982, p. 65, and in Philip Schlesinger et al., 1983, *op. cit.*, pp. 55–56.
50. *The Observer*, 21 November 1971; see also Paul Madden in *The British Media and Ireland: Truth the First Casualty*, *op. cit.*
51. *Time Out*, 26 July – 1 August 1974.
52. *Ibid.*; see also *The Leveller*, 22 January – 4 February 1982.
53. *Time Out*, 26 July – 1 August 1974.
54. *Children in Crossfire* was repeated on BBC1 on 3 January 1982, and a follow-up film, *A Bright Brand New Day . . . ?*, produced by Jonathan Crane, was shown the next evening, 4 January 1982.
55. Transmitted on ITV on six consecutive Sundays from 17 June to 22 July 1979.
56. Granada TV, *The State of the Nation: The bounds of freedom*, programme 6, 'Terrorism', transmitted on ITV on 22 July 1979; see also the book of the same title, ed. Brian Lapping, London: Constable in association with Granada Television, 1980.
57. *The Times*, 3 February 1972.
58. Unsigned article in *New Statesman*, 31 December 1971.
59. Speaking at NUJ/ACTT Conference on Media Censorship of Northern Ireland, Birmingham, 28 February 1981.
60. *Ibid.*
61. London Weekend Television, *Look Here*, transmitted on ITV on 8 July 1978; see also *Film and Television Technician*, August/September 1978.
62. NUJ/ACTT conference, 28 February 1981, *op. cit.*
63. *The Sunday Times*, 2 January 1972.
64. See Philip Schlesinger et al., 1983, *op. cit.*
65. BBC Licence and Agreement of July 1969, Clause 13(4); Independent Broadcasting Authority Act 1973, Section 22(3); Broadcasting Authority Act 1960, Section 31. A useful outline of the legal constraints on British broadcasting is found in Colin R. Munro, *Television, Censorship and the Law*, Farnborough: Saxon House, 1979.
66. See, for example, the speech by Irish Taoiseach Sean Lemass to the Dail in October 1966, quoted in Paul O'Higgins, 'The Irish TV sackings', *Index on Censorship*, 1/1973.
67. Quoted in Michael Farrell, *Northern Ireland: The Orange State*, London: Pluto Press 1976, p. 261.

68. Quoted in *Ireland: the story in pictures of the North's distress*, Government of Ireland Information Bureau, 1969.
69. See Michael Farrell, *op. cit.*, p. 269.
70. *Ibid.*, p. 274.
71. For an assessment of attitudes in the South, see the survey published in October 1979 by the Dublin-based Economic and Social Research Institute, which found that 21 per cent of people in the South supported the IRA's activities and 41 per cent sympathised with their motives.
72. *The Times*, 3 December 1974.
73. Quoted in Paul O'Higgins, *op. cit.*
74. *Ibid.*
75. *Ibid.*
76. Statement by dismissed RTE Authority Chairman Donal O Morain, quoted in Paul O'Higgins, 1973, *op. cit.*
77. Richard Deutsch and Vivien Magowan, *Northern Ireland 1968–73: A Chronology of Events*, vol. 2, pp. 242a, 244ab, 245a, 327b.
78. Paul O'Higgins, *op. cit.*
79. National Union of Journalists, *Report on Censorship in RTE*, unpublished, 1977.
80. See *The Observer*, 6 February 1972.
81. Speech in the Dail, 23 November 1972, quoted in the *Journalist*, April 1974.
82. *The Sunday Tribune*, 11 January 1981.
83. Berwick Street Film Collective, London; distributed by The Other Cinema, 79 Wardour Street, London W1; tel. 01-734 8508/9.
84. *The Sunday Tribune*, 11 January 1981.
85. See Workers Research Unit, *Belfast Bulletin*, no. 9, Spring 1981, for an account of Conor Cruise O'Brien's career.
86. *New Statesman*, 13 January 1978.
87. *The Times*, 19 October 1976.
88. *The Sunday Tribune*, 11 January 1981.
89. *The Irish Press*, 24 May 1977.
90. See *Troops Out*, February 1978.
91. *The Observer*, 15 January 1978.
92. 'Mary of Derry and ten years of troubles', *The Observer* colour supplement, 1 October 1978.
93. Facsimile of letter dated 30 September 1978 in *Belfast Bulletin*, no. 9, *op. cit.*
94. *Belfast Bulletin*, no. 9, *op. cit.*
95. *The Guardian*, 27 November 1979; *The Irish Times*, 29 November 1979; *Hibernia*, 6 December 1979.
96. NUJ, *Report on Censorship in RTE*, unpublished, 1977.
97. *Hibernia*, 17 January 1980.
98. See *The Irish Times*, 14 July 1979.
99. NUJ, *Report on Censorship in RTE*, *op. cit.*
100. *The Irish Times*, 18 February 1981.
101. *The Irish Times*, 20 February 1982.
102. *The Irish Times*, 26 August 1981.
103. *The Irish Times*, 10 February 1982.
104. *The Irish Times*, 17 February 1982.
105. *The Irish Times*, 18 February 1982.
106. *The Irish Times*, 29 July 1982.
107. *The Irish Times*, 20 May 1983.

108. *The Irish Times*, 24 May 1983.
109. *The Irish Times*, 25 May 1983.
110. *The Irish Times*, 28 May 1983.

9. Reporting nationalist perspectives

1. BBC1, 5.40 p.m. news, 21 October 1982.
2. *Daily Star*, 22 October 1982.
3. Editorial in *The Guardian*, 11 April 1981.
4. Interview by the author, 1982.
5. *The Sunday Times*, 5 November 1972. *A Sense of Loss* is distributed by Contemporary Films, 55 Greek Street, London W1.
6. *The Guardian*, 23 January 1976.
7. Paul Madden in ed. Campaign for Free Speech on Ireland, *The British Media and Ireland: Truth the First Casualty*, London: Information on Ireland 1979. See also John Howkins, 'Censorship 1977–78: a background paper', Edinburgh International Television Festival 1978, official programme, London: Broadcast 1978.
8. Interview by the author.
9. See reviews by Carl Gardner in *Socialist Challenge*, 12 June 1980, and *Time Out*, 13–19 June 1980 and 20–26 June 1980.
10. *The Irish Times*, 22 September 1980, 16 March 1981.
11. *The Guardian*, 22 September 1980.
12. *The Guardian*, 24 March 1983; *Panorama*, 'Britain's Wasteland', reporter Peter Taylor, BBC1, 14 March 1983.
13. Frank Burton, *The Politics of Legitimacy: Struggles in a Belfast Community*, London: Routledge and Kegan Paul, 1978, p. 137.
14. *The Guardian*, 21 November 1972, quoted in Frank Burton, op. cit.
15. *Catholic Herald*, 15 October 1976.
16. Fr Raymond Murray in *The British Media and Ireland: Truth the First Casualty*, *op. cit.*, p. 26.
17. *Northern Ireland Chronicle*, draft script, copy in author's possession.
18. *The Sunday Press*, 6 September 1981.
19. Richard Deutsch, *Mairead Corrigan and Betty Williams*, New York: Barron's 1977.
20. 13 August 1976, quoted in Richard Deutsch, *op. cit.*, p. 9.
21. *The Observer*, 22 August 1976.
22. *The Guardian*, 16 August 1976; see also, for example, *The News of the World*, 15 August 1976; *Daily Mirror*, 16 September 1976; *The Observer*, 22 August 1976.
23. See unsigned article by Liz Curtis and David Brazil, 'The Press and the Peace People', *The British Media and Ireland: Truth the First Casualty*, *op. cit.*, pp. 40–41.
24. Sarah Nelson, 'Reporting Ulster in the British press: the example of the peace movement', *Fortnight*, August 1977.
25. Richard Deutsch, *op. cit.*, p. 102.
26. *Ibid.*, pp. 114–15.
27. BBC Radio 1, *Studio B15*, 14 February 1982.
28. See *The Guardian*, 12 October 1976, 14 October 1976.

29. See *The Observer*, 2 January 1977; *Belfast Telegraph*, 1 August 1977; *Hibernia*, 31 January 1980.
30. *The Irish Times*, 4 March 1981.
31. Neil Hickey, 'The battle for Northern Ireland: How TV tips the balance', *TV Guide*, 26 September 1981, USA.
32. *The Sunday Times*, 31 May 1981.
33. See *The Guardian*, 6 May 1981, 7 May 1981.
34. *The Sunday Times*, 31 May 1981.
35. *Ibid*.
36. Survey of LBC news bulletins from 27 April to 2 May 1981; see Liz Curtis in ed. Local Radio Workshop, *Nothing Local About It*, London: Comedia 1983, pp. 172–76.
37. *Panorama*, 23 April 1981.
38. *The Times*, 6 May 1981.
39. *Daily Express*, 6 May 1981.
40. See, for example, quotation from Gerry Fitt and cartoon by Cummings in *Daily Express*, 6 May 1981.
41. *The Times*, 6 May 1981.
42. BBC News and Current Affairs minutes for 6 May 1981, quoted in *The Irish Times*, 10 October 1981. For a comparison of television treatment of Bobby Sands's funeral with that of the funeral of a black striker in South Africa, see Philip Schlesinger, Graham Murdock, Philip Elliott, *Televising 'Terrorism'*, London: Comedia 1983, pp. 59–61.
43. *The Daily Telegraph*, *The Guardian*, 2 June 1981.
44. *The Guardian*, 6 June 1981.
45. Quoted in *The Daily Telegraph*, 6 June 1981.
46. *The Guardian*, 6 June 1981.
47. *Hansard*, 14 May 1981, col. 623.
48. *Ibid.*, col. 623–24.
49. *The Guardian*, 21 May 1981.
50. *The Times*, 4 June 1981.
51. BBC Radio 1, *Studio B15*, 14 February 1982.
52. *Daily Express*, 2 May 1981.
53. See, for example, *Daily Mirror* editorials on 3 February 1972, 14 August 1978, 3 July 1981, 1 November 1982, 15 August 1983.
54. See, for example, *Sunday Times* editorials on 16 and 23 August 1981. New editor Andrew Neil told *The Irish Times* (22 October 1983) that the paper from now on would support direct rule.
55. *The Sun*, 23 July 1981.
56. *Daily Mail*, 22 August 1981.
57. See Peter Gerard Pearse and Nigel Matheson, *Ken Livingstone*, London: Proteus Books 1982.
58. *Daily Mirror*, 13 October 1981.
59. *The Sun*, 13 October 1981.
60. *Ibid*.
61. Quoted in Pearse and Matheson, *op. cit.*
62. *Ibid*.
63. *The Sun*, 9 August 1982.
64. *Ibid*.
65. *The Sun*, 10 August 1982.
66. LBC Radio, Sunday 5 December 1982.

67. BBC1, 5 December 1982.
68. *The Sun*, 6 December 1982.
69. *Daily Express*, 6 December 1982.
70. *Daily Mail, Daily Star, Daily Mirror*, 6 December 1982.
71. *Daily Mail*, 7 December 1982; *Daily Express*, 8 December 1982.
72. *The Standard*, 6 December 1982.
73. *New Statesman*, 17/24 December 1982.
74. *Daily Express*, 7 December 1982.
75. *Daily Mirror*, 7 December 1982.
76. *The Standard*, 7 December 1982.
77. *The Times*, 7 December 1982.
78. BBC TV news, 7 December 1982.
79. *The Guardian*, 8 December 1982.
80. *Ibid*.
81. *The Daily Telegraph*, 8 December 1982.
82. *The Sun*, 8 December 1982.
83. *The Guardian*, 8 December 1982.
84. *Daily Express, Daily Mail, Daily Mirror, Daily Star, The Sun*, 9 December 1982.
85. *Daily Mail*, 9 December 1982.
86. *New Statesman*, 10 December 1982; *Tribune*, 17/24 December 1982.
87. *Daily Express*, 8 December 1982; see also articles by George Gale in the *Daily Express*, 21 May 1981, 29 November 1982, 10 December 1982.
88. *The Irish Times*, 25/27/28 December 1982; the top two 'Women of the Year' were Margaret Thatcher and Princess Anne.
89. *The Sunday Times*, 27 February 1983.
90. *News of the World*, 27 February 1983.
91. *Sunday People*, 27 February 1983.
92. *The Sunday Times*, 27 February 1983.
93. *Daily Star*, 28 February 1983.
94. *Daily Mirror*, 28 February 1983.
95. *The Sun*, 27 July 1983.
96. LBC Radio, 3 December 1980.
97. John Arden and Margaretta D'Arcy in *The British Media and Ireland: Truth the First Casualty*, *op. cit.*, p. 48.
98. BBC minute, 'News from London – 116'.
99. *The Sunday Times*, 7 May 1972.
100. First transmitted on BBC2, starting on 2 December 1980.
101. *The Observer*, 4 February 1973.
102. See *The Observer*, 4 February 1973; *The Guardian*, 5 February 1973; Kenneth Griffith in *The British Media and Ireland: Truth the First Casualty*, *op. cit.*, p. 9; Kenneth Griffith and Timothy E. O'Grady, *Curious Journey*, London: Hutchinson 1982.
103 *The Sunday Times*, 4 February 1973.
104. Griffith and O'Grady, *op. cit.*
105. *The Observer*, 4 February 1973.
106. *The Sunday Times*, 4 February 1973.
107. *The Daily Telegraph*, 23 February 1973.
108. *Financial Times*, 28 February 1973.
109. Griffith and O'Grady, *op. cit.*
110. *The Times*, 28 February 1973.

111. *Ibid.*
112. *The Times*, 5 February 1973.
113. *Stills*, vol. 1, no. 3, Autumn 1981.
114. Kenneth Griffith in *The British Media and Ireland: Truth the First Casualty*, *op. cit.*, p. 9.
115. Griffith and O'Grady, *op. cit.*
116. *Ibid.*
117. *The Guardian*, 22 November 1980.
118. Shown on BBC2 in 1973 and repeated on BBC1 in 1974; in 1974 the BBC published a book under the same title by Howard Smith.
119. *Time Out*, 3–9 March 1978.
120. *The Sunday Times*, 16 November 1980.
121. *Time Out*, 3–9 March 1978.
122. *Time Out*, 9–15 June 1978; *Desire*, pilot issue, 1981.
123. Manuel Alvarado and Bob Ferguson, unpublished paper.
124. London: Quartet 1976.
125. *TV Times*, 3–9 January 1981.
126. Robert Johnstone, *Fortnight*, no. 180, March/April 1981; Geoff Bell and Carl Gardner, *Time Out*, 16–22 January 1981.
127. *Did You See . . . ?*, BBC2, 8 March 1981.
128. *Ibid.*
129. *The Irish Times*, 30 December 1980.
130. *The Irish Times*, 22 January 1981.
131. *The Sunday Tribune*, 15 February 1981.
132. See comment by Mary Holland in *Broadcast*, 13 April 1981.
133. *Financial Times*, 21 January 1981.
134. *Ibid.*
135. Minutes of Board of Governors meeting, 13 May 1981.
136. Minutes of meeting of Heads of Department, 29 April 1981.
137. *Ibid.*
138. *The Daily Telegraph*, 27 April 1981.
139. In an interesting parallel, the IBA's Member for Northern Ireland from January 1980 was Mrs Jill McIvor, a barrister and wife of Basil McIvor, an Official Unionist who had been a Stormont MP and had served with Brian Faulkner on the power-sharing executive.
140. Minutes of Board of Governors meeting, 13 May 1981.
141. *Ibid.*
142. Minutes of meeting of Heads of Department, 29 April 1981.
143. Minutes of Board of Governors meeting, 13 May 1981.
144. *Ibid.*
145. *Leicester Mercury*, editorial, 13 August 1969.
146. *The Sunday Times*, 28 August 1983.
147. Rudyard Kipling, 1899, Definitive Edition, pp. 323–24.
148. *The Sunday Telegraph*, 3 May 1981.
149. *The Times*, 23 September 1977.
150. *The Times*, 10 December 1982. Levin's piece provoked numerous protests, as *Times* editor Charles Douglas Home admitted in a letter, dated 17 December 1982, to a complainant, Frances Mary Blake.
151. Ned Lebow, 'British Historians and Irish History', *Eire–Ireland*, vol. VIII, no. 4, Winter 1973, St. Paul, Minnesota, USA.
152. *Ibid.*

153. Translation from the Latin published in 1577, quoted in Ned Lebow, *op. cit.*
154. *The Times*, 18 March 1886.
155. *Punch*, 18 March 1862.
156. Lewis P. Curtis Jr., *Apes and Angels: The Irishman in Victorian Caricature*, Newton Abbott: David and Charles, 1971, p. 37.
157. *The Irish Times*, 29 May 1982.
158. John Kirkaldy, 'English Cartoonists: Ulster Realities', *Eire–Ireland*, vol. XVI, no. 3, Fall 1981, St. Paul, Minnesota, USA.
159. *Daily Express*, 18 October 1971; the controversy was described in *The Sunday Times*, 24 October 1971.
160. *The Standard*, 29 October 1982.
161. *The Standard*, 24 November 1982.
162. *The Irish Post*, 25 December 1982, 26 February 1983. The Press Council not only refused to uphold complaints against *The Standard*, but upheld a complaint from *The Standard* against the GLC, and contended that the GLC's ban on advertising 'was a blatant attempt by a local authority to use the power of its purse to influence the contents of a newspaper and coerce the editor.' (*The Guardian*, 8 April 1983.)
163. Quoted in Mary Campbell, 'Paddiana – or gored by an Irish Bull: an analysis of anti-Irish "jokes" ', *The Irish Democrat*, July 1977.
164. See Russell Davies in *The Sunday Times*, 14 December 1980.
165. Sales figures quoted in Edmund Leach, 'The official Irish jokesters', *New Society*, 20/27 December 1979.
166. *Ibid.*
167. *Ibid.*
168. *The Irish Times*, 19 February 1982.
169. Channel 4, 7 p.m. news, 31 August 1983.
170. *The Irish Times*, 10 September 1983.
171. *The Times*, 19 July 1983, quoted in *The Irish Times*, 20 August 1983.
172. *The Irish Times*, 10 September 1983.
173. Joan Inglis, 'The Irish in Britain – A Question of Identity', *Irish Studies in Britain*, Spring/Summer 1982, no. 3.

10. Propaganda machines

1. *Land Operations Volume III – Counter Revolutionary Operations*, Ministry of Defence, 29 August 1969, preface paras 1 and 2; para 172.
2. *Ibid.*, para 447.
3. *Ibid.*, para 173.
4. Frank Kitson, *Bunch of Five*, London: Faber 1977, p. 147.
5. *Land Operations Volume III*, *op. cit.*, para 457a.
6. *Ibid.*, para 460.
7. Frank Kitson, *Low Intensity Operations*, London: Faber 1971, p. 199.
8. *Ibid.*
9. Alan Hooper, *The Military and the Media*, Aldershot: Gower 1982, p. 183.
10. Richard Clutterbuck, *The Media and Political Violence*, London: Macmillan 1981, p. 96.
11. *The Irish Times*, 21 March 1981.
12. *Ibid.*
13. *Spectator*, 15 May 1971.

14. *Ibid.*
15. Tim Pat Coogan, *The IRA*, Pall Mall 1970, Fontana 1971.
16. *Spectator*, 29 May 1971; similar 'oaths' have been quoted in Paisley's *Protestant Telegraph*, April 1967, and the UDA paper, *Ulster*, January 1982.
17. Richard Clutterbuck, 1981, *op. cit.*, p. 96.
18. Ibid., pp. 171–72. My thanks are due to Pete Jordan for the details of Maurice Tugwell's career. Tugwell later appeared at the University of New Brunswick in Canada: see article by Tugwell in ed. Paul Wilkinson, *British Perspectives on Terrorism*, London: George Allen and Unwin 1981, pp. 13–40.
19. *The Irish Times*, 21 March 1981.
20. Clutterbuck, 1981, *op. cit.*, p. 96.
21. *The Times*, 26 June 1974.
22. Quoted in *The Times*, 26 June 1974.
23. Simon Hoggart, 'The army PR men of Northern Ireland', *New Society*, 11 October 1973.
24. *Sunday People*, 19 December 1971.
25. *Ibid.*
26. Alan Hooper, *op. cit.*, pp. 193, 200–201.
27. *Land Operations Volume III*, *op. cit.*, para 522.
28. Clutterbuck, 1981, *op. cit.*, p. 98.
29. Colonel Robin Evelegh interviewed by Max Hastings, *The New Standard*, 1 May 1981.
30. Frank Kitson, 1971, *op. cit.*, p. 188.
31. *Time Out*, 14–20 October 1977.
32. *The Leveller*, June 1978.
33. *Ibid.*; *The Irish Times*, 5 February 1983.
34. *The Sunday Times*, 13 March 1977; see also article by Robert Fisk in *Hibernia*, 3 October 1975.
35. *Time Out*, 13–19 October 1972.
36. Belinda Loftus, 'Images for sale: government and security advertising in Northern Ireland 1968–1978', *The Oxford Art Journal*, vol. 3, no. 2, October 1980.
37. Reproduced in *The Times*, 26 November 1974.
38. *Time Out*, 13–19 October 1972.
39. *Hibernia*, 3 October 1975.
40. Carol Ackroyd, Karen Margolis, Jonathan Rosenhead, Tim Shallice, *The Technology of Political Control*, Penguin 1977, Pluto Press 1980, p. 104.
41. Belinda Loftus, *op. cit.*
42. *The Irish Times*, 21 March 1981.
43. *Ibid.*
44. *Ibid.*
45. *The Sunday Times*, 8 April 1973.
46. *The Guardian*, 14 March 1977.
47. *The Sunday Times*, 13 May 1973.
48. *Ibid.*
49. Interview with a journalist by the author; see also *The Irish Times*, 10 October 1979.
50. Major-General Anthony Deane Drummond, *Riot Control*, Royal United Services Institute 1975, pp. 106–107, quoted in *Belfast Bulletin*, no. 6, Spring 1979. See above, chapter 6, for other examples of anti-IRA stories.

51. *The Times*, 25 March 1975.
52. *The Irish Times*, 12 March 1982.
53. *The Irish Times*, 17 December 1981.
54. *Ibid.*
55. *The Sunday Times*, 13 March 1977.
56. See *The Irish Times*, 17 December 1981.
57. *The Irish Times*, 12 January 1982.
58. *The Irish Times*, 30 January 1982.
59. *The Irish Times*, 17 December 1981.
60. *The Irish Times*, 12 March 1982.
61. *The Sunday Times*, 5 December 1982; *The Irish Times*, 6 December 1982.
62. *The Irish Times*, 21 March 1981.
63. *The Irish Times*, 19 October 1981.
64. *The Irish Times*, 12 November 1975; see also *The Times*, 24 February 1976, and *The Sunday Times*, 13 May 1977.
65. *The Irish Times*, 12 November 1975.
66. *Andersonstown News*, 15 November 1975.
67. *Ibid.*; *The Sunday Times*, 13 March 1977.
68. *The Guardian*, 14 March 1977; see also *The Irish Times*, 21 March 1981. David Blundy reported the appearance of a similar leaflet in *The Sunday Times*, 27 October 1974.
69. *The Sunday Times*, 13 March 1977.
70. *The Irish Times*, 21 March 1981.
71. *Ibid.*; see also *The Irish Times*, 16 November 1974, for an article saying the UDA had accused a man of authoring the leaflets.
72. *The Irish Times*, 21 March 1981.
73. Article by Robert Fisk in *Hibernia*, 3 October 1975.
74. *The Irish Times*, 21 March 1981; *The Sunday Times*, 13 March 1977.
75. *The Irish Times*, 21 March 1981.
76. *The Sunday Times*, 13 March 1977.
77. *The Guardian*, 14 March 1977.
78. *The Sunday Times*, 13 March 1977.
79. *The Times*, 25 March 1975.
80. *The Irish Times*, 21 March 1981.
81. *Hibernia*, 3 October 1975.
82. *Ibid.*
83. *Ibid.*
84. *The Irish Times*, 29 September 1980, 6 March 1981, 21 March 1981, 22 November 1982. In 1982 RUC detectives visited Colin Wallace in Wormwood Scrubs prison during their 'Kincora' enquiries: see *The Irish Times*, 3 March 1982; *News of the World*, 21 March 1982.
85. *The Times*, 25 March 1975.
86. *Ibid.*
87. *Ibid.*
88. *The Irish Times*, 2 February 1980; *The Guardian*, 11 July 1978.
89. *The Irish Times*, 2 February 1980.
90. Interview by the author, 1982.
91. *The Times*, 16 February 1976; *The Irish Times*, 16 February 1976.
92. *The Times*, 16 February 1976.
93. *The Times*, 17 February 1976.
94. *The Sunday Times*, 31 July 1977.

95. *The Times*, 16 February 1976; *The Irish Times*, 16 February 1976.
96. *The Times*, 17 February 1976; see also *The Times*, 18 February 1976, 20 February 1976, 24 February 1976.
97. Quoted in *The Sunday Times*, 31 July 1977.
98. *The Sunday Times*, 31 July 1977.
99. *Ibid.*
100. *Ibid.*; see also *The Guardian*, 1 August 1977.
101. *News Letter*, 11 May 1982.
102. *The Irish Times*, 29 September 1980, 21 March 1981.
103. *New Society*, 11 October 1973.
104. *Ibid.*
105. *The Observer*, 29 February 1976.
106. Interviews with Irish journalists by the author, 1982.
107. *New Society*, 11 October 1973.
108. *Ibid.*
109. Interview by the author, 1982.
110. *Ibid.*
111. *The Irish Times*, 20 February 1982.
112. Interview by the author, 1981.
113. Interview by the author, 1982.
114. *Soldier*, 23 August – 5 September 1982.
115. *The Listener*, 3 June 1982.
116. *Ibid.*
117. NUJ, Report of Proceedings of Annual Delegate Meeting, 18–21 April 1980.
118. Richard Deutsch and Vivien Magowan, *Northern Ireland 1968–73: A chronology of events*, vol. 1, Belfast: Blackstaff Press 1973, pp. 103a, 103b, 104b, 108b.
119. See *The Guardian*, 3 April 1979, 5 April 1979; *Time Out*, 6–12 April 1979, 13–19 April 1979.
120. *The Guardian*, 5 September 1979; *The Irish Times*, 5 September 1979.
121. For a fictional treatment of an imaginary trial of a journalist under the Prevention of Terrorism Act, see Granada TV's *Crown Court*, 'Talking to the Enemy', by Janey Preger, networked on ITV on 23, 24, 25 March 1982.
122. *Camerawork*, no. 14, *Reporting on Northern Ireland*, London: Half Moon Photography Workshop, August 1979.
123. *Ibid.*
124. Interview with Ian Stuttard in *Desire*, pilot issue, 1981.
125. See *They Shoot Children: the use of rubber and plastic bullets in the north of Ireland*, London: Information on Ireland 1982.
126. *Journalist*, April 1982.
127. *Ibid.* Cyril Cain was injured in April 1981.
128. Report by Andrew Stephen in *The Observer*, 29 February 1976.
129. Headquarters Northern Ireland, Press Officer Contact List, as at 1 January 1981.
130. *News Letter*, 11 May 1982.
131. *The Times*, 19 December 1980.
132. Interview by the author, 1982.
133. *Ibid.*
134. See above, chapter 4.
135. *The Irish Times*, 4 August 1982.
136. *Ibid.*

137. Interview with a journalist by the author, 1983.
138. *The Irish Times*, 11 September 1982, 7 May 1983.
139. Interview by the author, 1982.
140. *Ibid*.
141. *Ibid*.
142. *Ibid*.
143. *The Guardian*, 23 February 1980.
144. *The Leveller*, June 1978.
145. Belinda Loftus, 'Images for sale: government and security advertising in Northern Ireland 1968–1978', *The Oxford Art Journal*, vol. 3, no. 2, October 1980.
146. *The Guardian*, 16 March 1979.
147. Shown on the ITV network on 24 November 1980; see *The Guardian*, 25 November 1980.
148. *The Irish Press*, 25 November 1980.
149. *The Irish Times*, 3 April 1981.
150. *The Diary of Bobby Sands*, Dublin: Sinn Fein 1981.
151. Interview by the author, 1982.
152. *Time Out*, 14–20 October 1977; *The Guardian*, 27 January 1978. The Information Research Department was a psychological warfare body, mainly engaged in 'cold war' activities, which ran a secret worldwide propaganda network till 1976, after which it was replaced by the Overseas Information Department: see *The Guardian*, 27 January 1978, 18 December 1981.
153. *Time Out*, 17–23 February 1978.
154. *Northern Ireland Chronicle*, draft script, 1981.
155. *The Irish Times*, 3 September 1981.
156. *Northern Ireland Chronicle*, draft script, 1981.
157. *Time Out*, 9–15 January 1981.
158. BBC Radio 4, *File on Four*, 23 November 1982; also see article by Stuart Simon in *The Listener*, 2 December 1982.
159. *Ibid*.
160. *Ibid*.
161. *The Irish Times*, 22 June 1981.
162. Conrad Atkinson, *Picturing the System*, London: Pluto Press/ICA, 1981, pp. 22–24.
163. The film was launched in London at the Royal Court Theatre on 24 June 1979: the event was organised by The Other Cinema and the United Troops Out Movement.
164. Letter dated 26 March 1980.
165. Undated memo from Mr P. Vandenbussche, Minister for the Dutch Community, to the Director-General of BRT. *The Patriot Game* was also shown on television in Algeria and France; it is distributed in Britain by The Other Cinema, 79 Wardour Street, London W1, tel. 01-734 8508/9.
166. Foreign and Commonwealth Office circular from C.P.P. Baldwin, Overseas Information Department, dated March 1980.
167. *Daily Mail*, 8 September 1981.
168. *The Sun*, 17 June 1980. The film's unflattering portrayal of the troops was due as much to the army itself as to the film-makers: made without commentary, around half the film was taken up with interviews with officers and soldiers, and film of them going about their business.
169. *The Guardian*, 23 February 1980; see also Andrew Stephen in *The Observer*, 29 February 1976.

170. *The Observer*, 3 May 1981.
171. *Republican News*, vol. 4, no. 24, 15 June 1974.
172. Interview with former Press Centre member by the author.
173. See *The Observer*, 29 February 1976.
174. *The Guardian*, 14 June 1974.
175. *Ibid.*
176. An almost complete collection of issues of *Republican News* is held in the Linenhall Library, Belfast.
177. *Republican News*, vol. 1, no. 1, June 1970.
178. *Ibid.*; also quoted in vol. 4, no. 24, 15 June 1974.
179. *Republican News*, vol. 4, no. 24, 15 June 1974.
180. *Republican News*, vol. 2, no. 48, 18 August 1972.
181. *Republican News*, vol. 4, no. 14, 16 April 1974.
182. Interview with a republican spokesperson by the author.
183. *Ibid.*
184. *Ibid.*
185. Shown on 15 December 1977; see above, chapter 7.
186. *The Irish Times*, 17 December 1977.
187. *Republican News*, undated, appeared on Saturday 17 December 1977.
188. *Republican News*, vol. 7, no. 49, Christmas 1977.
189. *Republican News*, vol. 8, no. 17, 29 April 1978.
190. *Hibernia*, 11 May 1978.
191. For an account of the raids on *Republican News*, see Danny Morrison, 'Censorship at source', in ed. Campaign for Free Speech on Ireland, *The British Media and Ireland: Truth the First Casualty*, London: Information on Ireland 1979, pp. 45–46.
192. The first edition of *An Phoblacht/Republican News*, vol. 1, no. 1, came out on 27 January 1979.
193. Interview with a *Republican News* journalist, by the author.
194. Interview by the author.
195. *Republican News*, 12 March 1972.
196. Facsimile of *UDA No. 17* reproduced in *Republican News*, 12 March 1972.
197. *Republican News*, 25 February 1978.
198. See Jack Holland, *Too Long a Sacrifice*, New York: Dodd, Mead and Company 1981, p. 138.
199. See *An Phoblacht/Republican News*, 22 November 1980.
200. *The Sunday Times*, 22 March 1981.
201. *An Phoblacht/Republican News*, 28 January 1982.
202. Interviews by the author, 1982.
203. Alan Murray of *The Irish Press* speaking at the NUJ/ACTT conference on media censorship of Northern Ireland, 28 February 1981.
204. Interview by the author, 1982.
205. London: Macmillan 1981, p. 107.
206. *The Guardian*, 18 March 1983.
207. *The Irish Times*, 10 October 1979.
208. Interview by the author, 1982.
209. *Ibid.*
210. *Ibid.*
211. Neil Hickey, 'The Battle for Northern Ireland: How TV tips the balance', *TV Guide*, 26 September 1981, USA.
212. Interview by the author, 1982.

Index

Note: This index covers the main text only (pages 5 to 278) and does not include the appendix or the references.